CHILDREN OF DIVORCE

CHILDREN OF DIVORCE

Adjustment, Parental Conflict, Custody, Remarriage, and Recommendations for Clinicians

James A. Twaite, Ph.D., Ed.D.
Daniel Silitsky, Ph.D.
Anya K. Luchow, Ph.D.

JASON ARONSON INC.
Northvale, New Jersey
London

Production Editor: Elaine Lindenblatt

This book was set in 11 pt. Goudy Old Style and printed and bound by Book-mart Press, Inc. of North Bergen, New Jersey.

Copyright © 1998 by Jason Aronson Inc.

10 9 8 7 6 5 4 3 2 1

All rights reserved. No part of this book may be used or reproduced in any manner whatsoever without written permission from Jason Aronson Inc. except in the case of brief quotations in reviews for inclusion in a magazine, newspaper, or broadcast.

Library of Congress Cataloging-in-Publication Data

Twaite, James A., 1946-
    Children of divorce : adjustment, parental conflict, custody, remarriage, and recommendations for clinicians / James A. Twaite, Daniel Silitsky, Anya K. Luchow.
      p. cm.
    Includes bibliographical references and index.
    ISBN 0-7657-0113-8 (alk. paper)
    1. Children of divorced parents—Psychology. I. Silitsky, Daniel. II. Luchow, Anya K. III. Title.
HQ777.5.T93 1998
155.44—DC21   97-21488

Printed in the United States of America on acid-free paper. For information and catalog write to Jason Aronson Inc., 230 Livingston Street, Northvale, New Jersey 07647-1726. Or visit our website: http://www.aronson.com

*This work is dedicated to
Jamie Theresa Twaite,
my daughter and the light of my life*

J.A.T.

*To my wife and sons
Bobbie, Jason, and David
who have assisted me in learning about
love, marriage, and resilience*

D.S.

*This book is dedicated to my children
Tami, Ali, Jason, Megan, and Jessica
and their fathers Jed and Donald,
and a special thanks to my partner Jim*

A.K.L.

CONTENTS

Preface								xiii

1. Psychosocial Adjustment of Children of Divorce		1
   Divorce as a Family Disaster					2
   Divorce as a Challenge					10
   Positive Outcomes of Divorce					14
   Correlates of Postdivorce Adjustment				15

2. Parental Conflict						21
   Parental Conflict and Children's Adjustment in General	21
   Parental Conflict among Divorced Couples			23
   Why Does Parental Conflict Predict Negative Outcomes
     for Children?						35
     Stressful Home Environment					35
     Amount and Quality of Contact with Noncustodial
       Parent							35
     Parenting Behavior						36

3. Custodial Arrangements					40
   Historical Background of Custodial Arrangements		40
   Research on Custodial Fathers				42
   Comparisons of Children in Mother-Custody and
     Father-Custody Homes					43
   Joint Custody Arrangements					49

4. Psychosocial Adjustment of the Custodial Parent — 52
Psychological Adjustment of Custodial Mothers — 53
Studies Involving Custodial Mothers and Custodial Fathers — 59
Psychological Adjustment of Custodial Fathers — 62
Parental Adjustment, Effective Parenting Behavior, and Children's Adjustment — 64

5. Remarriage of the Custodial Parent — 70
Empirical Studies of the Impact of the Custodial Mother's Remarriage — 73
Effect of Remarriage of the Custodial Parent on Family System Functioning — 77
Correlates of Children's Satisfactory Adjustment to Remarriage of Their Custodial Mother — 86
Summary — 89

6. Role of the Noncustodial Parent — 91
Father-Absence Hypothesis — 91
Mediating Effect of Parental Conflict — 94
Studies Suggesting the Irrelevance or Possible Negative Impact of Frequent Visitation by the Noncustodial Parent — 98
Child's Relationship with the Noncustodial Parent — 102

7. Child's Age at the Time of the Divorce — 108
Relationship between Child's Age at the Time of Parental Divorce and the Short- and Long-Term Psychosocial Adjustment of Child — 109
Preschool Children — 110
Latency-Aged Children — 112
Adolescents — 115
Divorces that Occur Relatively Early in the Life of the Child Have Better Outcomes — 117
Divorces Occurring Later in the Child's Lifespan Have Better Outcomes — 121
Effects of Parental Divorce Are Qualitatively Different for Boys and Girls of Different Ages — 134
Impact of Divorce When the Child Is a Young Adult — 142

8. The Child's Gender	**145**
Divorce Is Worse for Boys	146
Divorce Is Worse for Girls	148
No Gender Differences in the Child's Adjustment to Divorce	154
Effects of Divorce Are Qualitatively Different for Boys and Girls	157
Zaslow's Review of the Literature on Gender-Related Differences in Children's Response to Divorce	166
Methodological Rigor	167
Custody and Remarriage	169
Populations Sampled	171
Criteria Chosen to Represent Psychosocial Adjustment	173
Timing of Adjustment Reactions	175
Sources of Data	176
9. Stressful Life Changes	**178**
Economic Distress Model	179
Multiple Life Stresses Model	185
10. Social Support	**200**
Decrements in Available Social Supports Following Divorce	201
Among Children	201
Among Parents	203
Social Support and Psychological Adjustment	206
Among Children	206
Among Parents	213
11. Family Systems	**219**
Family-Systems Theories	220
Family-Systems Functioning and Psychosocial Adjustment	232
12. Model for Predicting Children's Adjustment to Divorce	**250**
Parental Conflict	251
Custodial Arrangement	253
Psychosocial Adjustment of the Custodial Parent	254
Remarriage of the Custodial Parent	255

Child's Relationship with Noncustodial Parent	256
Child's Age at Time of Divorce	257
Child's Gender	259
Stressful Life Changes	260
Social Support	262
Family-Systems Functioning	262
Comprehensive Model for Predicting Children's Postdivorce Psychosocial Adjustment	264
Methodological Recommendations for Research on Children's Psychosocial Adjustment Following Divorce	265
Additional Predictors for Future Studies of Children's Postdivorce Adjustment	267
Predictors Included in the Original Model that Require Further Elaboration	268
13. Research Study I	**269**
Methods	270
Subjects	270
Procedure	271
Instruments	272
Results: Original Analysis	277
Description of Sample	278
Predictors of Adolescent Adjustment in Divorced Families	282
Psychosocial Adjustment among Adolescents from Divorced and Intact Families	290
Predictors of Adjustment among Adolescents from Divorced and Intact Families	290
Conclusions Regarding Predictors of Postdivorce Adjustment Based on the Original Analysis	292
Results Obtained When Subgroups within Divorced Sample Are Analyzed Separately	293
Depression of Custodial Mother	294
Substance Abuse of Custodial Parent	296
Parental Anger	298
Parental Insults	300
Parental Physical Abuse	302
Frequency and Regularity of Contact with Noncustodial Parent	304

Adequacy of Family Finances	307
Remarriage of Custodial Parent	309
Divorce-Related Stressful Life Events	311
Social Support	313
Family Adaptability and Cohesion	314
Conclusions Based on Separate Analyses of Subsamples of Adolescents from Divorced Families	317

14. Research Study II

	319
Methods	319
Subjects	319
Procedures	320
Instruments	321
Results	322
Comparison of Groups on Predictors	322
Comparison of Groups on Psychosocial Adjustment Measures	324
Correlates of Psychosocial Adjustment among Adolescents from Divorced and Intact Families	325
Conclusions	330

15. Summary and Conclusions

	332
Between- and Within-Group Differences in Psychosocial Adjustment	332
Conflict between Parents	332
Custody Arrangements	333
Psychological Adjustment of Custodial Parent	334
Remarriage of Custodial Parent	335
Contact with Noncustodial Parent	336
Age of Child at Time of Divorce	337
Gender	337
Finances and Stressful Life Changes	338
Social Support	338
Family System	339

16. Recommendations for Clinicians Involved in the Assessment and Treatment of Divorcing Families

	341
Assessment	341
Parental Conflict	341

Psychological Adjustment of Custodial and
    Noncustodial Parents and Stepparent(s)   345
Parenting Styles and Capacities of Custodial and
    Noncustodial Parents and Stepparent(s)   347
Stressful Life Events   348
Supports Available to Help Families Cope with
    Stresses Associated with Divorce   349
Nature of Adjustment Difficulties Experienced by
    Children   350
Interventions   352
Parental Conflict   352
Psychological Adjustment of Custodial and
    Noncustodial Parents and Stepparent(s)   354
Parenting Styles and Capacities of Custodial and
    Noncustodial Parents and Stepparent(s)   354
Stressful Life Changes Associated with Divorce   355
Supports Available to Help Families Cope with
    Stresses Associated with Divorce   356
Nature of Adjustment Difficulties Experienced by
    Children   357

References   359

Index   385

PREFACE

THE WORK PRESENTED here began with two empirical studies designed to identify the factors that best predicted the psychosocial adjustment of children from divorced families. In developing the sets of predictor variables to be employed in these studies, we reviewed the literature in this area. Initially, the review was very focused in nature. We proceeded through the various theoretical and empirical studies of the outcomes of divorce as a shopper proceeds through a supermarket, simply picking up the predictor variables that had been mentioned previously in the literature and putting them into our shopping cart, to be included in what we hoped would be a comprehensive regression model capable of explaining a substantial proportion of the variability in children's postdivorce adjustment.

We had noted that most of the existing empirical studies of children's adjustment following parental divorce had considered only a few of the potentially relevant predictors. We had also observed that many of these studies concluded with statements indicating that the relationships identified in the particular study might in fact be more complicated than could be determined on the basis of the available data, due to the possible confounding effects of other, unmeasured predictors. Therefore, our initial goal was to develop as complete a model as possible, in the sense that we did not want to miss or leave out any of the factors that appeared to be relevant.

We were moderately, but not completely, successful in pursuing this goal. We developed a model, described in Chapter 12 of this volume, that comprised ten major predictor domains, including (1) parental conflict during and following the divorce, (2) the custody arrangement, (3) the psychosocial adjustment of the custodial parent, (4) whether or not the custodial parent had remarried, (5) the child's relationship with the noncustodial parent, (6) the age of the child at the time of the divorce, (7) the gender of the child, (8) stressful life changes associated with the divorce, (9) the availability and utilization of social supports, and (10) family systems functioning.

In retrospect, we recognize that we, like prior investigators, failed to include several very important predictors in our model. A major predictor domain we ignored was the effectiveness of the parenting behavior experienced by the child. This would include the parenting behaviors of the custodial parent, the noncustodial parent, and the stepparent(s), if there were stepparents. Also, we did not include the current age of the child as a predictor. This latter omission was really not a problem in either of our two research studies as all the participants were adolescents. However, current age is an important factor in determining children's adjustment to divorce, and it should be included as a predictor or control factor in any study involving children from different age groups. Furthermore, we neglected to include measures of (1) the extent to which the child understands the reasons for the divorce, (2) the length of time that has elapsed since the parental separation, and (3) the characteristic coping styles of the parents and the child. All of these factors appear to be potentially relevant to children's adjustment. Nevertheless, in comparison to previously reported studies in this area, the two research studies we conducted and report on in this volume are fairly comprehensive, representing most of the important domains that may have an impact on children's adjustment following divorce.

Of course, within each of the predictor domains that we included in our model, we needed to make decisions regarding which specific aspects of the domain we would measure, and how we would operationalize those measures. These are important and difficult decisions. For example, when one refers to the domain of parental conflict, the following questions immediately become apparent:

1. How do we define "conflict"? Is conflict limited to physical aggression, or does it include verbal insults and "put-downs" as well? Where verbal or physical abuse is absent, should we include in the definition of conflict the inability of the two divorcing spouses to agree on such issues as visitation, whether and where the child should go to school, and whether or where the child should attend summer camp?

2. Whom do we ask about the conflict? The literature is very clear that reports obtained from children regarding parental conflict are not very closely related to reports obtained from custodial mothers. Few studies have used reports from noncustodial fathers.
3. Does it make sense to attempt to gather objective third-party data on conflict, such as police reports of instances of domestic violence or ratings based on the reports of teachers, friends, or relatives?
4. Do we need to measure conflict just before the separation, immediately following the separation, or some time after the separation?
5. Should we be concerned with the absolute levels of conflict reported, or with the changes in the level of conflict reported as time goes by?

Obviously, questions of this nature must be asked with respect to each of the domains, and the decisions made in response to these questions may have a profound impact on the findings of a study.

In the first research study reported in this volume (Chapter 13), the ten domains identified above were first analyzed and reframed as thirteen different predictors because (1) in considering the adolescent's relationship with the noncustodial parent, the frequency of contact and the predictability of contact with the noncustodial parent were treated as separate variables; (2) the stressful life changes experienced by the adolescent following the divorce were measured by both a single item assessing the child's perception of the adequacy of family income and by a separate checklist of specific stressful life events experienced since the divorce; and (3) family systems functioning was measured by two distinct scales measuring separate dimensions of family systems functioning, the FACES II scales for Family Adaptability and Family Cohesion. Several of the thirteen predictors were operationalized by means of single self-report items, others as multiple self-report items, and still others as scores derived from published multi-item scales.

The second research study reported here (Chapter 14) differed from the first in two important regards. First, based on the greater understanding of the literature derived from writing the first eleven chapters of the book, it was determined that there were at least four variables that absolutely must be controlled for when assessing the predictors of psychosocial adjustment of children of divorce. These are (1) the gender of the child, (2) the stage of life of the child at the time of the divorce (preschool, latency, and adolescence), (3) the custody arrangement, and (4) the child's current age at the time the data on psychosocial adjustment are collected. In reviewing the literature carefully and attempting to reconcile the many contradictory findings that had been reported in different studies, it became clear that these four variables had particularly significant mediating effects on the relationships between many of the other predictors and children's postdivorce psychosocial adjustment. It appears that many of the inconsistencies found in the literature on predictors of adjustment have resulted directly from the failure to control for these factors.

For example, the effects of parental conflict on children's psychosocial adjustment are profoundly different for girls and boys, as are the effect of the remarriage of the custodial parent, the effect of the relationship with the noncustodial parent, and the effect of availability of social support. Therefore, any studies of the relationships between these predictors and postdivorce adjustment that do not report results separately for girls and boys will yield spurious results, applicable to neither girls nor boys. Similar patterns were discovered with respect to the three other major mediating variables noted above: the child's age at the time of the divorce, the child's current age, and custody arrangement.

Therefore, it was concluded that meaningful statements regarding the factors predicting children's psychosocial adjustment following divorce can be reported only on subgroups of children formed by crossing the values of these four key mediating variables. There are fifty-four such combinations (two genders x three age ranges at the time of the divorce x three current age ranges x three possible custody arrangements). Clearly, a study that would include participants representing all of these cells would require a very large number of cases and a sophisticated stratified sampling procedure to obtain adequate numbers of cases in each cell. However, it is not necessary to include all these subgroups in any one study. Valid conclusions may be drawn about a single subgroup or a small number of the subgroups by focusing only on that group or those subgroups, by analyzing the data for each subgroup separately, and by excluding from the study any subjects from other subgroups whose presence might distort the results.

In the second research study we focused our attention on females in mother-custody situations who were currently adolescents. Further, we did not include respondents whose parents had divorced when they were already adolescents, since this would confound the effect of the recency of the divorce with the effect of having the divorce occur when one is an adolescent. Thus the second research study included members of only two of the fifty-four subgroups defined by the four mediating variables noted above. These two groups were (1) adolescent girls in mother-custody situations whose parents had separated while they were in preschool, and (2) adolescent girls in mother-custody situations whose parents had separated while they were in the latency stage. In addition, the study included a control group of adolescent girls from intact families.

Another way in which the second research study differed from the first is that the predictor domains were conceptualized and operationalized somewhat differently. By the time of the second study, we had recognized that it is essential to block on the child's gender, the child's age group at the time of the divorce, the child's current age group, and the custodial arrangement. Thus these factors were eliminated as predictors in the second regression model for predicting postdivorce adjustment.

In addition, all the predictors in the second study were measured using single-item self-report scales, including the following questions:

1. Is your mother depressed? (yes or no)
2. Does your mother have a problem with drugs or alcohol? (yes or no)
3. Is one or both of your parents physically abusive to the other? (yes or no)
4. How satisfied are you with the amount of contact that you have with your dad? (rated from "not at all" to "completely")
5. Does your family have financial problems? (rated from "never" to "all the time")
6. How many of the following events have you experienced since your parents separated? or (when completed by controls from intact families), How many of the following events have you experienced in your lifetime? (checklist: the investigator counts the number of events checked, then codes as "none," "one," or "more than one")
7. How flexible are your parents? (measure of family adaptability, rated from "not at all" to "very")
8. How close are your family members? (measure of family cohesion, rated from "not at all" to "very")
9. Have you someone to confide in? (measure of social support, rated "yes" or "no")
10. If your parents have divorced, has your mom remarried? (yes or no)

The most interesting finding to emerge from the two research studies reported here is that when the two subgroups studied in the second study were compared to the corresponding subgroups in the first study, the correlations between a given predictor and a given measure of psychosocial adjustment in the first study tended to be rather similar to the corresponding correlations in the second study. Moreover, this was true despite differences in the operationalization of the predictors. Certainly the corresponding relationships between predictors and psychosocial outcome factors reported in these two studies were much more consistent with each other than reported in the many previous studies in the literature. This suggests that the decision to report results for these subgroups of children separately was a good one. In fact, it is clear in retrospect that the most important contribution of the present volume is the recognition that it makes no sense to discuss the predictors of postdivorce adjustment unless one treats separately the specific subgroups formed by crossing gender, custody, age group at the time of separation, and current age.

This volume is organized as follows: Chapter 1 considers the disaster and challenge theories of divorce, and establishes that divorce is not necessarily a family disaster that leaves children poorly adjusted. The chapter concludes that it makes far more sense to study the variability in the psychosocial adjustment of children from divorced families rather than to compare the mean scores of groups of children from divorced families to the mean scores of groups of children from intact families. Chapters 2 through 11 constitute a review of the literature on the effect on postdivorce adjustment of each of the ten predictor domains noted above. Chapter 12 presents the model that we developed for predicting postdivorce adjustment, as well as the predictors that should be added in future studies and the operational refinements that should be made with respect to the original predictors. Chapters 13 and 14 present the results of two research studies. Chapter 15 summarizes the findings and presents recommendations for policy and research. Finally, Chapter 16 presents our recommendations to clinicians working with divorcing families.

J.A.T.
January 1998

1

PSYCHOSOCIAL ADJUSTMENT OF CHILDREN OF DIVORCE

IN RECENT YEARS a paradigm shift has occurred in research on the effects of divorce on children. For many years the prevailing view was that divorce is a family disaster that almost inevitably leads to behavioral problems and psychological symptoms among children (Howard and Johnson 1985, Veevers 1991, Wallerstein 1988, Weiss 1976). This view has been supported by a large number of studies that indicate significant group differences in psychosocial adjustment between children whose parents have divorced and children from intact families (Guidubaldi and Perry 1984, 1985, Guidubaldi et al. 1983, Hetherington 1989, 1993, Hetherington et al. 1978, 1985, Isaacs et al. 1985, Kelly and Wallerstein 1977, Skitka and Frazier 1995, Wallerstein 1977, 1988, Wallerstein and Kelly 1974, 1975, 1976, 1980).

Recently, however, several theorists have presented models in which divorce is conceptualized as a family crisis or challenge that may actually have growth-producing potential (Gately and Schwebel 1991, Wolin and Wolin 1993). This view is supported by the results of several recent studies that have indicated no significant differences in adjustment between children from divorced families and children from intact families (Kurdek and Sinclair 1988, Muransky and DeMarie-Dreblow 1995, Tayler et al. 1995). Furthermore, several other empirical studies have demonstrated that children of divorced families actually tend to score higher than children from intact families on some measures of adjustment (Kogos and Snarey 1995, Kurdek and Siesky 1980). Experts have also observed that the population of children from divorced families demonstrates great variability with respect to psychosocial adjustment, and that it probably makes more sense to focus on the factors that predict good and poor outcomes within the population of children from divorced families rather than the group differences between children from divorced and intact families (Emery 1982, Kelly 1988a, Kerr 1981).

In this chapter three bodies of literature are reviewed in some detail: (1) those studies that emphasize the negative effects of divorce on adjustment; (2) those theoretical formulations and empirical studies in which divorce is viewed as a challenge that does not necessarily have long-term negative effects and may even strengthen children; and (3) those studies that identify areas in which children of divorced parents appear to excel. The chapter concludes with a brief review of the research on the factors that may mediate the effects of divorce on children. This final section of the chapter provides an outline for the next eleven chapters, which consider these predictors of postdivorce adjustment in detail.

DIVORCE AS A FAMILY DISASTER

The disaster theory of divorce has been articulated in varying degrees of orthodoxy by numerous investigators. Weiss (1976) argued that "the dissolution of marriage regularly produces emotional distress almost irrespective of the quality of the marriage or desire for its dissolution" (p. 135). Howard and Johnson (1985) concluded that "There can be no doubt that divorce is a life crisis of major proportion for almost all the families who experience it" (p. 483). Veevers (1991) cited the above sources and noted that such pronouncements regarding the stressful nature of divorce are typically followed by the observation that divorced individuals manifest significantly more psychopathology than married individuals. Among the complaints that are depicted as characterizing divorced individuals are loneliness and depression, anxiety, alcoholism, psychotic breaks, and suicide attempts. Disaster theory assumes that these negative parental characteristics are reflected in poor psychosocial adjustment among children.

Wallerstein (1988) presented one of the strongest statements of the disaster theory. Based on her research with Kelly, Wallerstein concluded that even though some divorces work well, "more often than not divorce is a wrenching, long-lasting experience for at least one of the former partners" and that "for virtually all the children, it exerts powerful and wholly unanticipated effects" (Wallerstein 1988, p. 108). Because Wallerstein has stated the theory that divorce is a disaster for children rather recently and in a particularly strong form, her work will be considered in some detail in this section.

In 1971, Wallerstein and Kelly began a longitudinal study of the effects of divorce on middle-class families who continued to function despite the divorce. Their sample consisted of sixty families with a total of 131 children. The investigators purposely selected families in which the parents were not involved in clinical treatment and the children were functioning well. Most of the parents in these families were college educated, and about half attended church or synagogue. This profile led Wallerstein to characterize the sample as representing "divorce under the best of circumstances" (1988, p. 108). Most of these families were followed for ten years, and some of them were followed for fifteen years. Data were collected through in-depth interviews. Wallerstein indicated that the researchers spent many hours with each member of each of the families. The study generated a great volume of data that led to many publications (Kelly and Wallerstein 1977, Wallerstein 1977, 1988, Wallerstein and Kelly 1974, 1975, 1976, 1980).

Wallerstein and Kelly interviewed their families first at the time of the separation and for a second time twelve to eighteen months later. Wallerstein (1988) indicated that during the second interviews they expected to find the families well into the process of recovering from the divorce. This was not what they found at all, however. Instead, they found "family after family still in crisis" (p. 108). The turmoil and stress of the separation had not subsided. Many of the former spouses continued to feel angry and humiliated. Many of the children appeared more poorly adjusted at twelve to eighteen months postseparation than they had been at the time of the separation.

Because of these surprising findings, Wallerstein and Kelly extended their study by interviewing fifty-six of the sixty families for a third time, five years following the separation. At this time they found that only one-third of the children in these families were clearly doing well. They reported that 37 percent of the children were depressed, had difficulty concentrating in school, had trouble making friends, and manifested a wide range of other behavioral problems. Wallerstein (1988) concluded that "It would be hard to find any other group of children—except, perhaps, the victims of a natural disaster—who suffered such a rate of sudden serious psychological problems" (p. 108).

A ten-year follow-up was conducted during 1980 and 1981. At this time the investigators categorized 45 percent of the children as well-adjusted and 41 percent as poorly adjusted. The remainder were placed in an indeterminate category. Wallerstein described the poorly adjusted group as worried, underachieving, self-deprecating, and angry.

At the ten-year point Wallerstein and Kelly identified what they referred to as the "sleeper effect" in some of the children. This phenomenon occurs when children reach the age at which they begin to consider the possibility of entering into a committed relationship with a member of the opposite sex. The primary manifestation of this effect is the sudden emergence of an intense fear of betrayal, which may lead to the avoidance of heterosexual relationships. Another aspect of the sleeper effect is the sudden realization that one is angry with one's parents. This anger is similarly triggered by the prospect of having a relationship of one's own. Wallerstein (1988) reported that 66 percent of the female children in her sample manifested the sleeper effect sometime between the ages of 19 and 23. She did not report the corresponding figure for the males in her sample. However, she did indicate that 40 percent of the 19- to 23-year-old males in the study had no goals, little education, and a sense of having no control over their lives.

Wallerstein (1988) also reported that at the time of the ten-year follow-up one-fourth of the mothers and one-fifth of the fathers had still not gotten their lives back on track. These mothers and fathers were "chronically disorganized and unable to meet the challenges of being a parent" (p. 110). Wallerstein observed that this diminished capacity to parent often led the children to assume the responsibility for ensuring the psychological health of the parent. Wallerstein indicated that 15 percent of the children in the sample conformed to this syndrome, which the investigators referred to as the "overburdened child syndrome." Wallerstein suggested that this is a particularly pernicious aspect of divorce, since few children are capable of actually rescuing a troubled parent. The result is that the children become angry at the parent for making demands on them and for failing to gratify the children's own needs.

Wallerstein (1988) concluded that the children in their sample "weren't dealing simply with the routine angst of young people going through transition but rather that, for most of them, divorce was the single most important cause of enduring pain and anomie in their lives" (p. 112). She suggested that when these children confront the developmental task of establishing love and intimacy, they lack a template for a loving relationship between a man and a woman. She concluded that our divorce-prone society is producing a generation of young adults "so anxious about attachment that their ability to create enduring families is imperiled" (p. 108).

The disaster theory of divorce has been supported primarily by a large number of studies comparing children from divorced and intact families on various measures of adjustment. Abelsohn and Saayman (1991) pointed out that much of this research was flawed methodologically by the use of clinical samples without adequate nonclinical control groups. However, several of these studies were methodologically sound (Guidubaldi and Perry 1984, 1985, Guidubaldi et al. 1983, Hetherington 1989, 1993, Hetherington et al. 1978, 1985, Isaacs et al. 1986). These studies are summarized below.

Guidubaldi et al. (1983) and Guidubaldi and Perry (1985) reported the results of several large-scale surveys comparing children from divorced families to children from intact families on a number of measures of psychosocial adjustment. These authors reported that children from divorced families are significantly more likely than those from nondivorced families to display antisocial, impulsive, acting-out behavior. They also found that children from divorced families had significantly higher means than children from intact families on measures of psychological symptoms, including dependency, anxiety, and depression.

Hetherington and her associates (Hetherington 1989, 1993, Hetherington et al. 1978, 1982) carried out a six-year longitudinal study of divorce and remarriage, based on a sample of 144 well-educated, middle-class white parents and their children. Half of the families represented were divorced, mother-custody families. The other half were intact families. Within each family a target child was identified who was approximately 4 years old at the start of the study. The identification of a single child from each family is a desirable improvement over prior studies that included multiple children from some families, since the use of the single child preserves the independence of observations, which is a requirement of most of the inferential statistics employed in comparing the divorced and intact samples. Within both the divorced and the intact groups in this study, half of the children were boys, half girls.

Hetherington (1989) reported that during the first two years following divorce, "most children and many parents experienced emotional distress; psychological, health, and behavior problems; disruptions in family functioning; and problems in adjusting to new roles, relationships, and life changes associated with the altered family situation" (p. 2).

Hetherington did point out that, by two years after the divorce, the majority of parents and children were "adapting reasonably well" (p. 2), but she noted a number of continuing problems. For example, boys from divorced families were more likely than boys from nondivorced families to display antisocial, acting-out, coercive, and noncompliant behavior. The boys from the divorced families were also more likely than those from nondivorced families to experience difficulties in peer relationships and school achievement. The girls from divorced families in Hetherington's sample did not compare unfavorably to the girls from intact families. Hetherington suggested that the lack of significant differences could be a function of the fact that all the divorced families in her sample were mother-custody families; there is evidence in the literature that suggests that children from divorced families tend to do better when they are in the custody of the same-sex parent (Camara and Resnick 1988, Santrock and Warshak 1979, Zill 1988).

Hetherington and colleagues (1985) reported that six years following the divorce, children's scores on the Child Behavior Checklist (CBCL) (Achenbach 1966, 1978, Achenbach and Edelbrock 1983) scales measuring internalizing and externalizing pathology were correlated significantly with scores on the corresponding scales obtained two years after the divorce. These findings were interpreted as indicating that difficulties in adjustment observed two years after the divorce tend to persist:

> The general pattern of results suggests that daughters in families with a divorced, remarried mother are very similar in adjustment to those in nondivorced families. In contrast, even six years after divorce, sons in divorced families are showing more externalizing behavior and are sometimes reported to be showing more internalizing behavior and less social competence than sons in nondivorced families. The greater externalizing behavior in divorced male subjects is consistently reported by sons, mothers, teachers, and peers. [Hetherington et al. 1985, p. 527]

Isaacs et al. (1986) also reported a study supporting the view that divorce has a significant negative impact on children's psychosocial adjustment. Isaacs and her colleagues sampled 105 children whose families were participants in a larger study of the impact of divorce on children. The children ranged in age from 4 to 16 years. In all but a few cases, the mother had custody of the children. Fifty-six of the children had parents who elected to receive counseling services for divorce-related issues. The other forty-nine children had parents who did not request counseling. Participating parents completed the Child Behavior Checklist with respect to their children.

Isaacs and colleagues (1986) reported that the mean CBCL Problem Behavior score among their total sample was substantially higher (more problems) than the mean of the CBCL norming sample. In addition, mean scores on the CBCL Social Competence Scale and the CBCL School-Related Behavior Scale were substantially lower (less competence) than the corresponding norm group means. The authors indicated that the divorced sample displayed significantly ($p < .01$) poorer adjustment in each of these areas than the norming sample.

Roughly 20 percent of the children sample had scores beyond the recommended clinical cutoff points on these scales (above 70 for the Problem Behavior Scale; below 30 for the Social Competence Scale and the School Related Behavior Scale). Scores falling beyond these cutoff points signify a clinically relevant level of pathology. Isaacs and her colleagues (1986) concluded that the results of their study "support the results of prior research which have indicated the likelihood of emotional or behavior problems for many children in the aftermath of parental separation" (pp. 115–116). However, they also noted that the children in their sample did not appear to be as disturbed as a clinical population:

> There was no indication, however, that clinical levels of disturbance predominated. Rather, there was a tendency for many children in the present study to show difficulties in social relations, and to display behavior indicative of distress to an intermediate extent; that is, more than would be expected in a randomly-chosen normal group, yet not to the degree characteristic of a clinically-disturbed population. These tendencies were obtained when the sample was considered in the aggregate, or broken down into subgroups of those who had requested and those who did not request aid. [pp. 116–117]

The finding that children of families who sought counseling did not differ significantly from children of families who did not seek counseling tends to mitigate the seriousness of the critique of prior research leveled by Abelsohn and Saayman (1991). They argued logically that the use of clinical samples in assessing the psychological adjustment of children of divorced families could bias the results in the direction of making the children of divorce appear less well-adjusted than they really are. However, the lack of significant differences between the clinical and the nonclinical samples in the study by Isaacs and her colleagues (1986) suggest that any such biasing effect may not have been as serious as one might have expected.

A recent study reported by Skitka and Frazier (1995) provides evidence of the negative effects of divorce that is rather similar to the data reported by Isaacs and her colleagues (1986). These investigators sought to evaluate the effects of the Rainbows for Children Program, an intervention aimed at ameliorating the effects of parental divorce. They employed a pretreatment and posttreatment control group design to compare program participants to a control group of nonparticipants on measures of depression (Children's Depression Inventory [CDI]—Kovacs 1982) and academic self-esteem (Behavioral Academic Self-Esteem Scale [BASE]—Coopersmith and Gilberts 1982).

The CDI is a twenty-seven-item self-report measure of depressive symptoms. BASE is used by teachers to rate the academic self-esteem of children from preschool through eighth grade. The BASE yields a Total Academic Self-Esteem score, as well as subscale scores for Social Initiative, Social Attention, Success/Failure, Social Attraction, and Self-Confidence. The Social Initiative subscale measures the extent to which the child is willing to undertake new tasks, make independent choices, show independence and self-direction in activities, and seek help without being coaxed when he or she does not understand something. The Social Attention subscale assesses the degree to which the child is socially appropriate in class (e.g., quiet when necessary, takes turn speaking, talks appropriately). The Success/Failure subscale measures how well the child handles criticism, mistakes, and constructive feedback on classroom performance. The Social Attraction subscale indicates whether the child is popular with peers and gregarious. This scale also contains items concerned with whether or not the child refers to himself or herself in positive terms. Finally, the Self-Confidence subscale measures the extent to which the child readily expresses opinions and whether or not the child has an appreciation of his or her own work.

Skitka and Frazier (1995) reported that at pretreatment the mean scores of both their experimental group of children of divorce ($n = 67$) and their control group of children of divorce ($n = 28$) differed significantly from the means of the general norming samples on both the CDI and each of the five BASE subscales. The children from divorced families tended to be more depressed than children in the general population, and to have lower academic self-esteem. The investigators also reported that their intervention did not significantly improve the status of the children in the experimental group on any of these measures.

In addition to these individual studies suggesting the negative impact of divorce, Amato and Keith (1991a) reported the results of a meta-analysis of the research literature on this subject. They concluded that children from divorced families do tend to manifest significantly more negative outcomes than children from intact families. Their analysis of ninety-two studies led these researchers to conclude that parental divorce is associated with negative outcomes in the areas of academic achievement, problem behaviors, psychological adjustment, self-esteem, and social relations. However, they also noted that these significant group differences tend to be rather small in magnitude.

Amato and Keith (1991b) also reported the results of a meta-analysis of thirty-three studies that led them to conclude that adults who had experienced parental divorce as children, in comparison to adults who were raised in continuously intact families of origin, tend to manifest poorer psychological adjustment, lower socioeconomic attainment, and higher rates of divorce. These findings led Amato (1993) to conclude that:

> the cumulative picture that emerges from the evidence suggests that parental divorce (or some factor connected with it) is associated with lowered well-being among both children and adult children of divorce. However, the differences in well-being between those from divorced and nondivorced families, on average, are not large. This is due to the fact that a great deal of variability is present among children of divorce, with some experiencing problems and others adjusting well or even showing improvements in behavior. [p. 22]

In summary, a substantial body of literature suggests that children from divorced families tend to score lower than children from intact families on a broad range of indicators of psychosocial adjustment. However, there is great variability in adjustment within the population of children from divorced families, and the great majority of these children fall within normal limits on adjustment measures such as the CBCL. The following section of this chapter focuses on theoretical formulations of divorce that represent the event as a challenge to the family system that has the potential for positive as well as negative consequences. The next section also considers several empirical studies that have indicated no significant differences between children from divorced and intact families.

DIVORCE AS A CHALLENGE

There have been critics of the family disaster theory of divorce for some time. Krauss (1979) described the event of divorce in terms of crisis theory. This conceptualization suggests that the divorce may have both pathogenic and growth-producing potential, depending on the nature of the postseparation family system and its influence on the child's response to the divorce.

Kurdek and Siesky (1980) argued that research supporting the disaster theory of divorce had largely ignored the children's own perceptions of the event. Moreover, the few studies that did consider children's views of the meaning of their parents' divorce tended to indicate that the divorce was not typically viewed as a disaster. For example, Rosen (1977) interviewed ninety-two children of divorced families ranging in age from 9 to 28 years. She found that these children typically viewed their parents' separation as preferable to their remaining together and in conflict. The responding children indicated that they did not feel that they had been affected adversely by the divorce, and they also indicated that they felt they had actually benefited from the divorce in terms of developing their understanding of human emotions and developing a sense of maturity and responsibility.

Reinhard (1977) reported the results of a study that was also designed to assess children's perceptions of their parents' divorce. Reinhard surveyed forty-six children of divorced parents ranging in age from 12 to 18 years. Reinhard reported that these adolescents did not have negative reactions to the divorce, but rather viewed it as a reasonable decision on the part of their parents. Furthermore, the responding children did not feel that their social relations had been affected adversely by the divorce. In fact, they tended to indicate that they had developed maturity and a sense of responsibility as a result of their experience.

Kurdek and Siesky (1980) assessed children's perceptions of divorce by administering both an open-ended interview and a structured questionnaire. The subjects were 132 white children of seventy-four divorced, single, custodial parents. Each family had from one to five children. The children, who ranged in age from 5 to 19 years at the time of the study, were recruited through their parents, who were informed of the study at a Parents Without Partners meeting. Clearly, the nature of the sampling limits the generalizability of the findings of this study.

The children completed five measures: (1) an open-ended Divorce Questionnaire that concerned children's perceptions of their parents' divorce, (2) the Nowicki-Strickland Locus of Control Scale, (3) a measure of interpersonal knowledge, (4) a sixty-nine-item Structured Divorce Questionnaire, and (5) the WISC coding subscale. The Structured Divorce Questionnaire was designed to assess the responding child's perceptions of seven aspects of the divorce: (1) initial reactions to the news of the divorce, (2) feelings about losing the noncustodial parent, (3) changes in family relationships, (4) shifts in roles and responsibilities following the divorce, (5) affective reactions regarding the divorce, (6) the desire for counseling, and (7) the extent to which the child had developed independence and responsibility as a result of the divorce.

The results of this study indicated that children did not generally perceive themselves as having been affected adversely by their parents' divorce. The responding children did acknowledge that they had experienced some distress when they were informed of the decision to divorce, and they reported having difficulty dealing with the loss of the noncustodial parent and adjusting to changed family circumstances. However, the children almost universally saw the divorce as preferable to their parents' living in conflict. Kurdek and Siesky (1980) concluded that divorce is certainly a crisis, but "from the child's perspective the crisis need not be a chronic one" (p. 375).

The authors attributed this finding to the increasing prevalence of divorce, as a result of which "the child whose parents are divorced is no longer the social anomaly of a generation ago" (p. 375). Kurdek and Siesky (1980) suggested that these children have a natural peer support system that can buffer the stresses associated with the divorce. They pointed out that many of the children in their study had mentioned that fact that they had friends whose parents were divorced with whom they could discuss divorce-related concerns.

Supporting the view that divorce is not necessarily a disaster are the results of several empirical studies in which no significant differences in psychosocial adjustment were found between children from divorced families and children from intact families. For example, Kurdek and Sinclair (1988) compared seventh- and ninth- grade students from two-parent nuclear families ($n = 160$), stepfather families ($n = 39$), and mother-custody single-parent families ($n = 34$) on goal directedness, psychosocial adjustment, and school-related problems. They reported no significant differences among the three family structure groups on any of these dependent variables, after controlling for the effects of race and number of siblings. Kurdek and Sinclair also noted that there was substantial variability within each of the three groups on the dependent variables. Significant variability in adjustment was explained by a combination of family conflict, availability of social support, and frequency of use of coping strategies involving support from outside the family.

Muransky and DeMarie-Dreblow (1995) compared high school students from divorced ($n = 44$) and intact ($n = 66$) families on a self-concept measure (the Self-Description Questionnaire—Marsh et al. 1983). They found no significant differences between the two groups on this adjustment measure. They also compared the groups on family environment (Family Environment Scale—Moos and Moos 1981) and interparental conflict (Interparental Conflict Scale—Emery and O'Leary 1982), finding no significant differences between the students from divorced families and those from intact families on either of these family process measures. They found that both the family environment score and the interparental conflict score were better predictors of the adolescents' self-concept scores than whether or not their parents were divorced.

Tayler and colleagues (1995) studied differences in intimate attachment between adults whose parents had divorced ($n = 66$) and adults whose parents were still married ($n = 80$). They measured attachment with the Personal Relationship Questionnaire (PRQ), developed originally by Braiker and Kelley (1979) and refined by Heubeck (1987). The PRQ measures four dimensions of the quality of the respondent's relationship with an intimate partner: love, ambivalence, conflict, and maintenance. The maintenance dimension was defined as representing communication, responsiveness, reciprocity, accessibility, and interdependence. Tayler and her associates also measured (1) the participants' readiness for commitment by means of the Intimacy subscale of the Erikson Psychosocial Stage Inventory (Rosenthal et al. 1981) and (2) self-esteem, using eight items from the Shaver and Hazan (1985) self-esteem scale. The results of the study indicated no significant differences between adults whose parents had divorced and adults whose parents had not divorced with respect to the quality of attachment to one's intimate partner, readiness for commitment, or self-esteem.

Thus, despite the fact that many studies do suggest divorce-related differences in psychosocial adjustment between children from divorced and children from intact families, also some studies indicate no difference. Gately and Schwebel (1991) have offered some ideas regarding the possible sources of such inconsistencies in their discussion of the Challenge Model of Divorce. They noted that much of the research on outcomes of divorce has "used conceptual models and methods more likely to detect unfavorable than favorable outcomes" (p. 61). Specifically, they suggested that the traditional pathogenic model of divorce led researchers to use measures that identified weaknesses rather than strengths, and to study clinical samples during the crisis period immediately following the divorce. Further, Gately and Schwebel stressed that studies employing nonclinical subjects indicated that "although most children experience a crisis when their parents divorce, the long-term effects they experience vary" (p. 61). They pointed out that many children from divorced families avoid long-term negative outcomes, especially when continued conflict between parents does not compound the crisis.

The Challenge Model suggests that children's adjustment following divorce is a function of the unique challenges they face during the divorce transition period, the coping strategies employed by the children, and the availability of social support. The model holds that under the right circumstances, the experience of divorce can lead children to develop maturity, self-esteem, empathy, social competence, and androgynous attitudes.

Wolin and Wolin (1993) also presented a "challenge model" to describe the process of adjusting to stressful life events. They suggested that positive outcomes associated with successfully meeting a challenge include the development of positive coping skills and associated gains in self-efficacy and self-esteem. The difference between the formulation presented by Gately and Schwebel (1991) and that presented by Wolin and Wolin (1993) is that the former model is specific to the challenge of divorce, whereas Wolin and Wolin described their model as applicable to any family transition, including divorce. Both models suggest that children faced with parental divorce do not necessarily emerge as damaged, but may well emerge as strong and resilient.

POSITIVE OUTCOMES OF DIVORCE

A number of studies have provided support for the view that divorce can lead to positive as well as negative outcomes. For example, Kurdek and Siesky (1980) reported that 80 percent of the 5- to 7-year-old children of divorced families that they surveyed four years after the divorce had assumed increased responsibilities after the divorce. Similar findings have been reported by Amato (1987), Bohannon and Erikson (1978), and Hetherington (1989).

Santrock and Warshak (1979) and Slater and colleagues (1983) reported that boys from divorced families had higher levels of self-esteem than boys from intact families. This difference did not appear among girls in either study. Gately and Schwebel (1991) attributed this difference to the tendency of custodial parents, most of whom are women, to rely on their sons. As a result, the boys gain a new position of responsibility and status. This new status might logically be expected to result in increased self-esteem.

The notion that children of divorced families show increased empathy is supported by several studies. Kurdek and Siesky (1980) reported that after a divorce children tend to show increased concern for the welfare of other family members. It has also been reported that girls in divorced families are involved more often than girls from intact families in caregiving and play activities with younger sisters (Hetherington 1989).

MacKinnon and colleagues (1984) observed that 3- to 6-year-old children in divorced families tend to have more androgynous sex-role views than children of the same age from intact families. They interpreted this finding according to Bem's theory of psychological androgyny (1974), as reflecting the likelihood that the mother in a divorced home will model more androgynous sex-role behavior and the likelihood that children would assume more nontraditional responsibilities. Based on a meta-analysis of literature on the vocational adjustment of children of divorce, Stevenson and Black (1988) reported that college-age men who had grown up in homes with fathers absent tended to make fewer sex-stereotyped vocational choices.

Kogos and Snarey (1995) measured moral development among samples of 17- to 22-year-old college students from divorced families ($n = 25$) and intact families ($n = 78$). They assessed the students' stages of moral development according to the Kohlberg (1963, 1984) model using the Sociomoral Reflection Measure (SRM—Gibbs and Widaman

1982). They found that among both male and female students those from divorced families scored significantly higher on moral development than those from intact families. They interpreted this finding as indicating that "parental divorce may stimulate adolescents' role-taking which, in turn, promotes their ethical sensitivity and moral autonomy as they seek to comprehend both sides of the dissension" (Kogos and Snarey 1995, p. 184). They also agreed with the argument offered previously by Amato (1987), which suggests that divorced households are more likely than nondivorced households to promote egalitarian decision-making as the adolescents experience less parental control and more autonomy.

CORRELATES OF POSTDIVORCE ADJUSTMENT

Thus it is clear that there is growing recognition that divorce does not *necessarily* have long-term negative consequences for the psychosocial adjustment of children. Emery (1982) summarized the prevailing view of the effects of divorce as follows:

> Although a parental divorce is reliably associated with increased aggression, less success in school, and an increased likelihood of one's own marriage ending in divorce, the differences between children reared in divorced families and married families are small in magnitude. Divorce is a source of considerable distress. However, in and of itself, it is not the cause of lasting maladjustment in children. [p. 142]

Emery argued further that family processes that often begin before and continue after the separation are the best predictors of children's psychological health. He concluded that "the same principles of child development that apply to children in married families also hold for divorced families" (p. 142). Emery suggested that children thrive in a family environment that is warm, consistent, structured, and stimulating. He indicated that, if the family environment remained stable, so would the children.

But Emery's argument really serves to highlight the major issue left unresolved in the recent literature on divorce. If one agrees that divorced families are extremely heterogeneous and that outcomes for children may range from very bad to very good, the next logical question to be asked is, "What are the factors that determine these outcomes?" Emery has suggested that the stability of the family environment is the key. But other investigators have focused on a variety of different predictors.

Several different family-systems theories appear relevant to the identification of factors associated with positive outcomes for children after a divorce. Bowen's (1978) family-systems theory stated that negative outcomes result from chronic anxiety in the individual, and that the antidote to anxiety is differentiation. Bowen defined differentiation as a lifelong process of striving to maintain one's balance through the reciprocal external and internal processes of self-definition and self-regulation. Friedman (1991) has described differentiation as:

> The capacity to become one's self with minimum reactivity to the positions or reactivity of others. Differentiation is charting one's own way by means of one's own internal guidance system, rather than perpetually eyeing the scope to see where others are at. [p. 141]

Bowen suggested that the degree to which a child achieves healthy differentiation is largely a result of the multigenerational transmission of emotional responses. If the mother and father in the family are chronically anxious and undifferentiated, then the children are likely to be anxious and undifferentiated as well. The level of anxiety characterizing both parents and children is critical in terms of adaptation following divorce, because anxiety is related inversely to adaptiveness under stress. Kerr (1988) explained that, according to Bowen's theory, children are more likely to adapt successfully when the members of the family system can "maintain comfortable contact" (p. 47), since such comfort increases the capacity to cope with stress. This theory would lead one to expect that in families of divorce (and intact families as well) the level of adjustment of the children should be related positively to the level of psychological adjustment of the parents and to the degree to which the parents can cooperate comfortably with regard to the raising of the children.

These theoretically based predictions have been supported by empirical studies of children's adjustment following divorce. Kelly (1988a) reviewed the literature on adjustment following divorce, and she noted the following factors that have been shown to be related to the psychosocial adjustment of children in divorced families: (1) the level of conflict between the parents (Crosbie-Burnett 1988, Emery 1982, Johnston et al. 1988); (2) the psychological adjustment of the custodial parent, as indicated by symptoms of depression and alcohol abuse (Guidubaldi and Perry 1985, Wallerstein and Kelly 1980); (3) the nature of the custody arrangement, such that joint custody is associated with the most favorable outcomes; (4) the extent to which children feel that contact with noncustodial parents is regular and predictable (Hess and Camara 1979, Hetherington et al. 1982); and (5) the frequency of contact with noncustodial parents (Hess and Camara 1979, Hetherington et al. 1982).

Clearly these factors reflect both the levels of adjustment of the parents as individuals and their abilities to function cooperatively as parents following the divorce. Another factor cited by Kelly (1988a) as related to children's adjustment following divorce is whether or not the custodial parent remarries (Bray 1988, Crosbie-Burnett 1988). To the extent that remarriage can be viewed as reflecting adjustment, this factor may also be construed as reflecting Bowen's (1978) family-systems perspective. However, it should be noted that the literature on remarriage is mixed, with the more recent studies suggesting that unless the divorce occurred quite early in the life of the child, the remarriage of the custodial parent may be related negatively to children's adjustment (Hetherington 1993).

The Challenge Model of family transitions presented by Wolin and Wolin (1993) also emphasized aspects of the family system that may have an impact on the adjustment of children. Like Bowen (1978), Wolin and Wolin (1993) mentioned cooperation and communication among family members, but they also stressed the importance of flexibility to allow for problem solving. Abelsohn and Saayman (1991) have provided empirical evidence of the importance of family flexibility. They administered the Family Adaptability and Cohesion Evaluation Scales (FACES-III—Olson 1986, 1991) to a sample of forty-five adolescents during the first eighteen months of parental separation. They also had the child's mother complete the CBCL (Achenbach and Edelbrock 1983) to assess the child's adjustment. They found that children in families within the flexible range on the FACES-III Adaptability subscale had significantly lower scores on the CBCL Externalizing Behavior Problems subscale than children in families classified as either rigid or chaotic on the FACES-III Adaptability subscale. They also found that children in families within the connected range on the FACES-III Cohesion subscale had significantly higher scores on the CBCL Social Competence subscale than children in families classified as disengaged or enmeshed on the same subscale.

Kurdek and Sinclair (1988) also reported a significant relationship between family-systems functioning and postdivorce adjustment. These researchers administered the Family Environment Scale (Moos and Moos 1981) to their samples of adolescents from intact two-parent nuclear families, stepfather families, and mother-custody families. The results of their study indicated that two dimensions of family-systems functioning assessed by the Family Environment Scale—family relations and personal growth—were related significantly to adjustment in all three groups.

Variables other than those associated with family-systems theory have also been shown to be related to children's postdivorce adjustment. Gately and Schwebel (1991) reviewed the literature on adjustment following divorce, and they identified the following additional factors that have been shown to be correlated significantly with children's psychosocial adjustment: (1) the child's gender (Guidubaldi and Perry 1985, Hetherington et al. 1982), and (2) the child's age at the time of the divorce (Guidubaldi and Perry 1985, Wallerstein and Kelly 1980).

Several studies have suggested that children's characteristic coping behaviors are also associated with postdivorce adjustment. Kliewer and Sandler (1993) studied 225 children from divorced families. These children ranged in age from 7 to 14 years. The participating children completed the Children's Coping Strategies Checklist (Program for Prevention Research 1991). This checklist measures the frequency of use of each of thirteen different coping strategies. In addition, each child's teacher rated the child on five dimensions of social competence: emotion management, sensitivity/empathy, assertiveness, cooperation, and social acceptance.

The results of the study indicated that children rated high on social competence tended to display specific coping strategies, including reinterpreting stressful situations positively, attempting to understand the reasons for the occurrence of the stressful situation, and behavioral avoidance manifested by leaving or avoiding situations that might lead to trouble.

Kaslow and Hyatt (1982) reviewed the literature on the effects of divorce and concluded that the parents' coping responses during the divorce provide models for children, so that "the mastery of the transitional tasks and the rebuilding of one's life in a productive and independent mode by the divorced person also stimulates growth possibilities in the lives of his/her significant others" (p. 19). This view would suggest that the coping ability and the postdivorce psychological adjustment of the parents may be significant predictors of the children's psychosocial adjustment. Thomas (1982) reported that the postdivorce adjustment of parents is related to enduring personality characteristics, including assertiveness, self-assurance, intelligence, creativity, self-sufficiency, and ego strength.

Simons et al. (1994) identified several significant predictors of the postdivorce adjustment of adolescent children. They studied a sample of 207 divorced women, each of whom rated her adolescent children on scales measuring school problems, delinquency, aggression, depression, hostility, and anxiety. The mothers and their adolescent children also rated the mother's parenting along the dimensions of monitoring their children's behavior and consistency of discipline. In addition, the mothers and the adolescents rated the nonresidential fathers' involvement in parenting, the frequency of contact between the adolescent and the nonresidential father, the level of parental conflict, per capita family income, and paternal child support payments.

The results of this study indicated close correspondence between the ratings of the mothers and those of the children. Accordingly, the ratings were aggregated across mothers and children on those dimensions where they both provided ratings. Simons and his associates (1994) reported significant negative relationships among both female and male adolescents between externalizing problems (school problems, delinquency, and aggression) and both the mother's parenting behavior and the parenting involvement of the nonresidential father. In addition, among females only, there was a significant negative relationship between internalizing problems (depression, hostility, and anxiety) and family income. Among males only, scores on internalizing problems were related negatively to the parenting involvement of the nonresidential father and positively to the reported level of parental conflict.

Thus the psychosocial adjustment of children from divorced families has been shown to be related to a broad range of factors related to family-systems functioning, the adjustment and parenting behavior of both custodial and noncustodial parents, and background and demographic variables. However, no study carried out prior to the empirical studies presented in this book had considered all of these predictors. The work presented here was designed to develop and test a comprehensive model for predicting the postdivorce adjustment of children.

The review of the literature carried out for this work identified ten distinct categories of variables expected to be associated with postdivorce outcomes for children. These domains include (1) the level of parental conflict during and following the divorce, (2) the custody arrangements, (3) the psychosocial adjustment of the custodial parent, (4) the remarriage of the custodial parent, (5) the frequency and predictability of contact with the noncustodial parent, (6) the age of the child at the time of the divorce, (7) the gender of the child, (8) the stressful life changes that may occur as a result of the divorce, (9) the availability and utilization of social supports, and (10) aspects of family-systems functioning. The chapters that follow review the existing research in each of these areas in order to lay the foundation for the model tested in the two empirical studies reported in this book.

2

PARENTAL CONFLICT

THERE IS SUBSTANTIAL evidence of a relationship between the postdivorce adjustment of children of divorced couples and the level of conflict between those couples both prior to the divorce and subsequent to the divorce. This body of literature must be evaluated in the context of a broader body of literature that suggests that parental conflict is related generally to children's adjustment in intact as well as divorced families.

PARENTAL CONFLICT AND CHILDREN'S ADJUSTMENT IN GENERAL

Porter and O'Leary (1980) reviewed the literature on marital discord and childhood behavior problems. They concluded that "Psychodynamic, systems, and behavior therapists have all emphasized marital discord as a determinant and/or maintainer of childhood problems" (p. 287). From the psychodynamic perspective, Love and Kaswan (1974) reported that the parents of children seen in a psychiatric clinic for behavior problems differed from nonreferred control children in that the parents of the clinic children had significantly higher scores on a measure of communication difficulties. Several other empirical studies indicated that children referred to clinics for behavior problems tend to have parents with relatively unhappy marriages or unsatisfactory patterns of communication (Gassner and Murray 1969, Leighton et al. 1971).

From the family systems perspective, Satir (1964) concluded on the basis of her clinical observations that parents who were dissatisfied with their marriages frequently had children who displayed significant behavior problems. She also suggested that parental discord and children's acting-out behavior were mutually reinforcing. Lo (1969) reported that parents who had unsatisfactory emotional relationships with their spouses were more likely than happily married couples to have children who displayed neurotic symptoms.

From the behavioral perspective, Johnson and Lobitz (1974) reported a significant relationship between parental marital discord and children's disruptive behavior. Further, Oltmanns et al. (1977) reported significant correlations between measured marital discord and a variety of childhood problems, including conduct disorders, personality problems, and immature behavior.

Kelly (1988a) noted some additional studies documenting the relationship between marital discord and childhood behavior problems for families in general and for divorced families in particular. She referred to Emery (1982), who studied both intact and divorced families and reported that among each type of family, frequent and intense marital conflict was associated with poor psychological adjustment among children.

Several studies have suggested specifically that it is parental conflict, not divorce, that is the key predictor of poor psychological adjustment among children. Rutter (1970) reported that delinquent behavior among boys is more frequent among children in intact families with high marital discord than among children in divorced families with low marital discord. Hetherington (1979a) reported that children from divorced homes in low-conflict environments tended to be better adjusted than children from intact families with high conflict. Mechanic and Hansell (1989) compared adolescents from divorced low-conflict families to adolescents from intact, high-conflict families on measures of depression, anxiety, self-esteem, and physical symptoms. They reported that the adolescents from the divorced low-conflict families were better adjusted than those from the intact high-conflict families on all four of these measures of psychosocial adjustment. Long (1986) reported that the self-esteem of adolescent girls was related significantly to the marital satisfaction of their parents, but not to the structure of the family (intact versus divorced). These studies really suggest two conclusions: first, the dimension of parental conflict is important to the adjustment of children from all families, intact as well as divorced. In addition, these studies suggest that divorce per se may not be a critical factor leading to poor psychological adjustment among children. Poor outcomes may simply be the result of the fact that the level of conflict between divorced parents is frequently high before and after divorce.

PARENTAL CONFLICT AMONG DIVORCED COUPLES

Several recent empirical investigations have focused on the impact of parental conflict on the postdivorce adjustment of children (Atkeson et al. 1982, Block et al. 1986, Dozier et al. 1993, Emery 1982, Ferri 1976, Forehand et al. 1988, Leupnitz 1979, Long et al. 1987, 1988, Mechanic and Hansell 1989, Simons et al. 1994). These studies are discussed below from two perspectives: (1) establishing the relationship between parental conflict and negative psychosocial outcomes for children, and (2) attempting to explain why parental conflict leads to problems.

Long and his associates (1988) studied the relationship between parental conflict and adolescent adjustment in the school setting. The respondents included thirty-five white adolescents, their mothers, and their social studies teachers. The subjects were recruited through fliers distributed at local schools, newspaper advertisements, and public service announcements on local radio stations. The adolescents ranged in age from 11 to 15 years. Twenty-three of the subjects were from families in which the parents had divorced within the twelve months preceding the study, and the remaining twelve subjects were a comparison group from intact families. All of the students from divorced families were in the custody of their mothers, and none of these mothers had remarried.

The mothers in the twenty-three divorced families completed two measures of parental conflict, the ten-item O'Leary-Porter Parental Conflict Scale (Forehand et al. 1988) and the Divorce Conflict Measure (DCM), a one-item measure developed specifically for this study. The DCM requests mothers to rate the frequency of parental conflict at a specific point in time. The DCM employs a five-point Likert-type rating scale with response options ranging from 1, signifying rare conflict, to 5, signifying frequent conflict.

The O'Leary-Porter Scale was completed once by the divorced mothers, who were asked to respond with respect to conflict with their spouses prior to the divorce. The Divorce Conflict Measure was completed twice, once with respect to the time period prior to the divorce, and once with respect to the period following the divorce. Based on maternal ratings on the DCM, the divorced families were divided into two subgroups: (1) a group in which the level of conflict before the divorce was reduced after the divorce; and (2) a group in which the level of conflict remained high following the divorce. The continued high-conflict group contained eleven adolescents (nine boys and two girls), and the reduced-conflict group contained twelve adolescents (eleven boys and one girl). The mothers in the continued high-conflict group rated the frequency of conflict with their spouses with a DCM rating of either 4 or 5 both before and after the divorce. The mothers in the reduced-conflict group all used a DCM rating of 4 or 5 to describe the frequency of conflict prior to the divorce, but a rating of 1 or 2 to describe the frequency of conflict following the divorce.

Adolescents in all three groups were rated by their social studies teachers on the Revised Behavior Problem Checklist (RBPC) (Quay and Peterson 1983a). Two of the RBPC subscales were employed as dependent variables. The Anxiety-Withdrawal subscale was employed as a measure of internalizing problems, and the Conduct Disorder subscale was used as a measure of externalizing problems. Grade point average (GPA) from the student's most recent report card was also included as a dependent measure.

One-way analyses of variance (ANOVAs) were used to compare the three groups (intact, divorced with reduced conflict, and divorced with continued high conflict) on the two RBPC subscales and grade point average. Significant differences were found on both grade point average and the Anxiety-Withdrawal subscale of the RBPC, and the ANOVA on the Conduct Disorder subscale approached significance ($p < .06$). Post hoc Newman-Keuls comparisons indicated that on grade point average the adolescents in the continued high-conflict group had a significantly lower mean (2.49) than those in either the intact family group (mean = 3.19) or the reduced conflict group (mean = 3.42). The intact group and the reduced-conflict group did not differ significantly on GPA. On the Anxiety-Withdrawal subscale of the RBPC, the continued high-conflict group had a significantly higher mean (5.70) than either the intact family group (mean = 2.58) or the reduced-conflict group (mean = 1.22).

Long and his colleagues (1988) concluded that adolescents from divorced families in which interparental conflict remains high following the divorce are less well adjusted than adolescents from divorced families in which interparental conflict is reduced following the divorce. They acknowledged that "the mechanism by which interparental conflict and young adolescent adjustment are related is unclear" (p. 469), but they speculated that a continued high level of conflict may interfere with the functioning of adolescents by "creating a tense and stressful home environment, by exposing adolescents to dysfunctional models of interpersonal conflict resolution, or by creating an atmosphere of neglect . . . due to poor parent adjustment" (p. 469). They also acknowledged that the relationship between parental conflict and poor adolescent adjustment may be one of mutual causation. That is, acting-out behavior on the part of the adolescent may also generate conflict between the parents.

This study has important methodological strengths and weaknesses that should be considered in evaluating the reported findings. Among the strengths of the study is the authors' attention to the problem of potential confounding background and demographic factors. A one-way ANOVA was run to compare the three groups on age. The two divorced groups were compared with respect to the frequency of contact between the parents, the frequency of adolescent visitation with the noncustodial parent, the time since the marital separation, and the time since the divorce. None of these analyses yielded significant group differences. The two divorced groups did differ in the expected direction with respect to mean postdivorce scores on the O'Leary-Porter Scale. These comparisons bolster the internal validity of the study, since they suggest that differences between the reduced-conflict and continued-conflict divorced groups are in fact attributable to conflict rather than some unknown confounding factor.

Thus the study reported by Long and his associates (1988) clearly establishes the role of interparental conflict following the divorce as a significant mediating variable in the adolescent's response to divorce. However, the design of the study leaves a number of questions unanswered. For example, parental conflict was not assessed within the intact family group, so it was not possible to determine whether the relationship between parental conflict and adolescent adjustment observed among the divorced families pertained among intact families as well. Further, all of the mothers in the divorced families rated interparental conflict as high prior to the divorce. Therefore it was not possible to determine the effect on adjustment of the level of interpersonal conflict prior to the divorce.

In addition, the study examined adolescent adjustment within the first year following the separation. Thus the adolescents were still involved in the short-term crisis period. The effects of conflict on longer-term adjustment might differ substantially from those reported in this study.

A subsequent study by several of the same researchers rectified the problem of not assessing conflict among still married families (Forehand et al. 1988). This study focused on interparental conflict and adolescent sex as predictors of psychosocial adjustment. The study sample included ninety-six white adolescents ranging in age from 11 to 15 years. The study employed a 2 x 2 x 2 factorial design, with the following independent variables: (1) adolescent sex, (2) parental marital status (intact versus divorced), and (3) interparental conflict (high versus low). The adolescents were selected purposively from among a pool of 170 families so as to include twelve families representing each of the eight combinations of the three independent variables. In order to be included in the divorced group, the divorce had to have occurred during the twelve months preceding the study. As in the case of the study by Long and associates (1988), this criterion for inclusion represents something of a limitation on the external validity of the study, since the period immediately following the divorce is typically the most difficult for children and the time during which behavioral disturbances are most likely to manifest themselves. In order to be included in the intact family group, the adolescent had to be living with both of his or her biological parents.

In this study conflict was measured using the ten-item O'Leary-Porter Scale. On this measure the mean conflict score reported for married families is approximately 30 (Long et al. 1987). All the families classified as high conflict in this study had O'Leary-Porter scores above 30, and all the families classified as low conflict had scores below 30. The dichotomization of the sample in this manner, at a single score on the scale, may also be construed as a limitation, since families with quite similar scores around the value of 30 may be artificially separated into different groups. However, Long and associates (1987) reported that the mean conflict scores among each of the four low-conflict groups were in the range of 24 to 25 (SD = 2.13 to 5.23), while the mean conflict score among each of the high-conflict groups was approximately 34 (SD = 1.90 to 2.45). These means suggest that the actual level of conflict within the low- and high-conflict groups was quite different.

As in the study by Long and associates (1987) described above, Forehand and his colleagues (1988) were careful to test for differences in background factors that might represent potential confounding variables. A three-way ANOVA on adolescent age was not significant.

However, a three-way ANOVA on the Hollingshead four-factor index of socioeconomic status yielded a significant main effect due to marital status ($F (1,94) = 11.93, p < .01$), indicating that the divorced families tended to have significantly lower socioeconomic status than the intact families. This is an important potential confounding variable, since several studies have shown that family finances following a divorce may influence the adjustment of the children (Acock and Kiecolt 1989, Baker et al. 1984, Berg and Kelly 1979, Elder and Liker 1982, Hetherington et al. 1978). Forehand and his colleagues sought to control for the effect of socioeconomic status by including this variable as a covariate in their analysis of adolescent adjustment measures.

Forehand and associates (1988) also compared the divorced groups on length of time since the divorce, length of time the parents were separated prior to the divorce, frequency of contact between the two parents following the divorce, and the frequency of visitation between the adolescent and the noncustodial parent. No significant differences were reported among the divorced groups on any of these measures.

The dependent variables in this study included the social studies teacher's ratings of the child's cognitive and social competence, based on the Harter (1982) Teacher Rating Scale of Child's Actual Competence (TRS), and maternal ratings on the Anxiety-Withdrawal and Conduct Disorder subscales of the Revised Behavior Problem Checklist (RBPC) (Quay and Peterson 1983b). The student's academic grade point average for the previous report card was also recorded.

In addition, an observational paradigm was employed to obtain ratings on selected aspects of the mother-child interaction. The mother and child selected an issue from a checklist containing forty-four issues that typically arise between mothers and adolescents. Each dyad discussed their chosen issue for a three-minute period. The discussions were videotaped and rated on several dimensions by raters who were blind to the purpose of the study. Ratings were obtained for (1) dyadic problem-solving ability, (2) positive communication, (3) dyadic conflict, and (4) adolescent depression. The authors reported average interrater reliabilities for these four dimensions ranging from .78 to .84.

Forehand and associates (1988) performed three separate three-way (marital status by adolescent gender by level of interparental conflict) multivariate analyses of covariance (MANCOVAs) for three sets of dependent variables, grouped on the basis of the pairwise correlations among the measures. The three groups of dependent variables were (1) cognitive functioning, comprising grade point average and the TRS Cognitive Competence subscale; (2) social functioning, comprising the TRS Social Competence subscale, the RBPC Anxiety-Withdrawal scale, and behavioral ratings of social problem-solving, positive communication, and depression; and (3) externalizing problems, comprising the RBPC Conduct Disorder scale and the behavioral rating of dyadic conflict. The covariate in these MANCOVAs was socioeconomic status.

The decision to employ three separate MANCOVAs represents a potential limitation with respect to the generalizability of the findings, since several of the significant effects reported by the authors were significant only at the .05 level, and might not have been significant with the differing degrees of freedom that would have pertained had all the dependent variables been included in a single MANCOVA. The use of a single MANCOVA to control for the accumulating probability of Type I error would have represented a more conservative approach to the analysis that would provide the reader with greater confidence that one or more of the findings reported was not in fact a false positive.

In the analysis of the cognitive variables, a significant multivariate main effect due to level of parental conflict was obtained ($F(2,78) = 9.07$, $p < .001$) along with a significant multivariate interaction of level of conflict by marital status ($F(2,78) = 3.91$, $p < .05$). Univariate ANCOVAs yielded significant level of conflict by marital status interactions for both GPA ($F(1,79) = 4.38$, $p < .05$) and the TRS Cognitive Competence subscale ($F(1,79) = 7.85$, $p < .01$). Post hoc Newman Keuls tests indicated that on each of the two cognitive variables the adolescents from divorced families with high interparental conflict were functioning significantly worse than adolescents from any of the other three groups. There were no significant pairwise mean differences among any of the other three groups on either of the two cognitive variables.

The multivariate analysis of covariance performed on the social functioning variables yielded a significant multivariate main effect for level of parental conflict ($F(5,76) = 3.39$, $p < .01$). There were no other significant multivariate main effects, and no significant multivariate interaction tests. Follow-up univariate ANCOVAs yielded significant main effects due to level of conflict for the TRS Social Competence Scale ($F(1,80) = 8.45$, $p < .01$); behavioral ratings of dyadic problem-solving ($F(1,80) = 6.10$, $p < .05$); and depression ($F(1,80) = 4.24$, $p < .05$). On all these measures, the adolescents from high-conflict families were more poorly adjusted than the adolescents from low-conflict families. A trend in the same direction was noted for scores on the Anxiety-Withdrawal subscale of the RBPC ($F (1,80) = 3.15, p < .10$). Thus, on the social functioning measures, adolescents from high-conflict families manifested poorer psychosocial adjustment than those from low-conflict families, regardless of the marital status of the family.

The MANCOVA performed on the two measures of externalizing pathology yielded no significant multivariate main or interaction effects.

Forehand and his colleagues (1988) concluded: "The results provided strong support for a relation between parental conflict and adolescent adjustment, but substantially less support for an association between divorce and adolescent functioning" (p. 625).

Forehand and his associates attempted to explain the difference between the findings obtained on the cognitive measures and those obtained on the measures of social functioning. They argued that both conflict and divorce can reduce the parental attention and supervision provided to adolescents. This can have the effect of disrupting the intellectual environment in the home, the supervision of homework, and effective communication with teachers. They suggested that this might have an immediate effect on the students' academic work, whereas the effect of reduced supervision in the social sphere may be more gradual.

Given the limitation previously noted that all the divorced families in the study had been divorced within the last year, the issue of timing is of some importance. It is possible that adjustment several years postdivorce would have shown the significant level of conflict by marital status interactions for the social variables as well as the cognitive variables, but it is also possible that only the main effect of conflict would be significant for the cognitive variables once the family system had time to adjust to the divorce.

Mechanic and Hansell (1989) reported a study designed to overcome the limitation of including only divorced families in which the divorce had occurred within the last year. These two investigators surveyed a total of 1,193 students from seventh-, ninth-, and eleventh-grade classes in nineteen public schools in five communities in New Jersey. Both inner city and middle-class suburban communities were represented. These students were surveyed on two occasions with a one-year interval between testings. Complete data for both testings were available for 1,067 students. During the first wave of the survey, Mechanic and Hansell asked respondents to indicate whether their parents were still together, whether they had divorced or separated during the last twelve months (recent separation), or whether they had divorced or separated more than one year prior to the survey (earlier separation). Nineteen percent of the responding adolescents indicated that their parents had divorced or separated more than one year ago, and 7 percent indicated that their parents had divorced or separated during the last year. The remaining 74 percent were from intact families.

Conflict at the time of the first wave of the survey was measured by a single dichotomous self-report item asking whether or not there was "a lot of quarreling or fighting where you live in the past year" (Mechanic and Hansell 1989, p. 107). The authors acknowledged that this item did not refer specifically to parental conflict and that it may have tapped quarreling among siblings or between parents and adolescents, but they indicated that they "assumed that all quarreling or fighting contributed to a noxious family environment" (p. 107). However, it should be noted that adolescents who were currently residing with one parent as well as those residing with two parents answered this question, and the question might have a different meaning for adolescents in these two categories. If an adolescent living with one parent responded affirmatively to this question, it is not clear whether the conflict acknowledged was conflict between the parent at home and the parent who had left or conflict among other persons currently residing at home. In any case, the authors indicated that 38 percent of their total sample responded that there had been a lot of quarreling at home during the past year.

Other independent variables assessed at the time of the first data collection were sex, grade level, ethnicity, and parental level of education. Dependent measures of adolescent adjustment assessed at each of the two data collection points included the Center for Epidemiological Studies Depression Scale (CESD) (Radloff 1977), the Rosenberg Self Esteem Scale (RSE) (Rosenberg 1965, 1979), and measures of anxiety and common physical symptoms developed by one of the authors for an earlier study (Mechanic 1979, 1980).

In order to assess the longitudinal effects of family conflict and divorce on the adjustment measures, Mechanic and Hansell (1989) performed four multiple regression analyses. In these analyses, scores on the four dependent variables from the second wave of data collection were regressed on the predictors as assessed at the time of the first data collection. The results of these analyses indicated that family conflict at time one was a significant predictor of depression, anxiety, and physical symptoms at time two. Dummy variables representing recent divorce and earlier divorce were not significant predictors of time two scores on any of the four adjustment measures. Level of parental education was not a significant predictor of any of the time two adolescent adjustment measures. Adolescent gender was a significant predictor of time two scores on all four measures of adjustment. Female adolescents in this study had higher scores than males on depression, anxiety, and physical symptoms. Females had lower self-esteem at time two. Ethnicity was a significant predictor of anxiety only at the time of the second wave of data collection, with black and Asian respondents manifesting relatively high anxiety. Grade level was also a significant predictor of wave two anxiety only, with students in the upper grades having greater anxiety at time two than youngsters in lower grades. The authors interpreted the findings of these regression analyses as indicating that family conflict was a stronger predictor of adolescent adjustment than parental marital status.

Mechanic and Hansell (1989) also sought to test directly the hypothesis that adolescents in divorced families with low conflict will be better adjusted than adolescents in intact families with high conflict. They dichotomized their sample into groups representing those whose parents had separated or divorced at any time and those whose parents were still together. They cross-tabulated this variable by the dichotomous conflict measure to obtain four groups: (1) divorced or separated with low conflict, (2) divorced or separated with high conflict, (3) intact with low conflict, and (4) intact with high conflict. Then they employed independent sample t-tests to compare the divorced low-conflict group to the intact high-conflict group on each of the four adjustment measures at data collection intervals one and two. These tests indicated that "for every measure of well-being in both waves, adolescents in intact families characterized by high family conflict had significantly poorer well-being than adolescents experiencing family divorce who reported low family conflict" (p. 111).

Long (1986) also reported the results of a study indicating that parental discord is a more important predictor of children's adjustment than divorce per se. Long surveyed 199 freshman women in a small private undergraduate college for women. The respondents were primarily middle-class whites. The original subject pool consisted of 215 subjects who represented 91 percent of the entering freshman class.

However, sixteen protocols had to be excluded from the analysis, either because the students omitted items or because they indicated that one or both of their parents had died. Of the 199 students included in the study, 150 indicated that their parents were still living together and forty-nine reported that their parents had separated.

The survey questionnaires required responding students to rate the happiness of their biological parents' marriage on a six-point Likert-type scale with response options ranging from very happy to very unhappy. The survey also included the Rosenberg Self-Esteem Scale.

Long (1986) reported a significant positive correlation between the rated happiness of the parents' marriage and the responding student's self-esteem. No significant relationship was found between family structure (parents together or separated) and the student's self-esteem. Partial correlations indicated that the relationship between the parents' marital happiness and the student's self-esteem remained significant, even after controlling for family structure. However, the correlation between family structure and student self-esteem remained nonsignificant when parental marital happiness was controlled. These findings were interpreted as confirming the hypothesis that it is the quality of the parental relationship, rather than divorce itself, that has an impact on adolescent adjustment. However, it should be noted that the measure of marital happiness employed by Long is certainly not identical to the measures of parental conflict employed in the other studies reviewed here. In addition, the findings of Long's study are limited by the fact that the ratings of the parents' marital happiness were obtained from the student respondents. Anecdotal data and clinical observations are replete with examples of college students who are unaware of the fact that their parents are unhappily married. Often these students learn of the problems with their parents' marriage only after the parents separate, and often the parents separate only after the student has gone off to college.

Another study suggesting the importance of the source of the rating of parental discord is the study reported by Long and colleagues (1987). This study employed forty white adolescents ranging in age from 11 to 15 years. Also participating in the study were the mothers and the social studies teachers of these adolescents. Half of the adolescents were from intact families and half were from families in which the parents had divorced during the past year. Half of the subjects were males and half were females.

Marital conflict was assessed by maternal reports on the O'Leary-

Porter Scale. Within the divorced group, a median split was employed to form high- and low-conflict groups. Within the intact marital group, high- and low-conflict groups were formed by matching the divorced groups with respect to O'Leary-Porter scores, the adolescent's age, the adolescent's sex, and family socioeconomic status. The twenty adolescents from intact families were selected from an available pool of sixty-nine intact families. The matching procedure resulted in comparable conflict scores among the divorced and intact family groups.

The dependent variables in this study included (1) adolescent self-report measures, (2) ratings of the adolescents obtained from parents and teachers, and (3) grade point average obtained from records. The students rated themselves on the twenty-eight-item Perceived Competence Scale for Children (PCSC) (Harter 1982). The PCSC yields self-ratings in the areas of Cognitive Competence, Social Competence, and Physical Competence. Of these scales, only the Cognitive and Social Competence scales were employed in this study. The students' social studies teachers rated the students on the Teacher's Rating Scale of Child's Actual Competence (TRS) (Harter 1982). The TRS is a twenty-eight-item scale that was designed to parallel the PCSC. It yields teachers' ratings of the student on the same three dimensions as the PCSC. In addition, the adolescents' teachers completed the Conduct Disorder subscale of the Revised Behavior Problem Checklist (RBPC) (Quay and Peterson 1983a). Finally, observational ratings were obtained on the basis of videotaped observations of mother–adolescent interactions in which each dyad discussed a standard issue, keeping the adolescent's bedroom clean. Raters viewed the videotapes of these discussions and rated the adolescents on (1) problem-solving ability and (2) positive communication.

The resulting data were analyzed by means of a pair of two-way MANCOVAs. In each MANCOVA, the two independent variables were marital status (intact versus divorced) and level of marital conflict (low versus high). In the first of the two MANCOVAs, the dependent variables were the two measures of self-perceived competence—PCSC-Cognitive Competence and PCSC-Social Competence. In the second of the two MANCOVAs, the dependent variables were the six measures of competence derived from independent ratings: (1) teacher ratings on the TRS-Cognitive Competence subscale, (2) teacher ratings on the TRS Social Competence subscale, (3) teacher ratings on the RBPC Conduct Disorder subscale, (4) student grade point averages, (5) observational ratings of adolescent problem-solving ability, and (6) observational ratings of adolescent positive communication. In each MANCOVA, the covariate was socioeconomic status.

The MANCOVA carried out on the two self-perception scales yielded only a significant multivariate main effect due to marital status ($F (2,34) = 6.63, p < .01$). Univariate tests indicated that with respect to both self-perceived cognitive competence and self-perceived social competence, the adolescents in divorced families scored significantly lower than the adolescents in the intact families.

In contrast, the MANCOVA carried out on the six independent ratings of competence yielded only a significant multivariate main effect due to level of parental conflict ($F (6,28) = 3.41, p < .05$). Univariate tests indicated that the parental conflict factor was significant for both grade point average and teacher ratings of cognitive competence. Adolescents from high-conflict homes tended to have lower grades and tended to be perceived by teachers as being less cognitively competent than adolescents from low-conflict homes. Univariate tests also yielded significant multivariate main effects for each of the two teacher-completed social measures, the TRS Social Competence subscale and the RBPC Conduct Disorder subscale. Adolescents from high-conflict homes tended to be viewed as less socially competent and having more conduct problems than adolescents from low-conflict homes. Finally, a significant univariate test was obtained for one of the two behavioral rating scales, the one assessing problem-solving ability. The adolescents from high-conflict homes tended to have poorer problem-solving skills.

Thus self-ratings were affected by parental marital status, but independent assessments of adolescents' development were affected only by level of parental conflict. The authors interpreted this finding indicating that "divorce per se would be accompanied by an acute distress reaction. Assuming that the young adolescent's cognitive and social competence is an established part of his/her repertoire prior to the divorce, the divorce per se should be associated with an acute lowering of self-perceived competence but not with a lowering of actual competence" (Long et al. 1987, p. 25). The authors suggested that these findings indicate the importance of examining parental conflict level when studying the effects of divorce on children. They also emphasized that the data support the contentions of Atkeson and colleagues (1982) and Emery (1982) that parental conflict is a crucial predictor of adolescent adjustment within both intact and divorced families.

WHY DOES PARENTAL CONFLICT PREDICT NEGATIVE OUTCOMES FOR CHILDREN?

A number of explanations have been offered as to why parental discord is reflected in negative psychosocial outcomes for children. These include (1) the cumulative negative impact of a stressful home environment, (2) the impact of postdivorce parental conflict on the amount and regularity of the child's contact with the noncustodial parent, and (3) the impact of parental discord on the quality of parenting provided. In this section of the chapter, each of these explanations is considered.

Stressful Home Environment

Simons and colleagues (1994) observed that "conflict is apt to be upsetting to children because it increases the probability that they will feel frustration over being caught in the middle, experience distress over the emotional pain that their parents are producing in each other, and experience fear that one of the parents may withdraw from the family in an attempt to avoid altercations" (p. 358). These authors concluded that chronic discord between parents increases the risk that the child will experience feelings of frustration, anxiety, and depression. Thus they linked the stress associated with the conflict itself primarily to internalizing symptoms in children.

Amount and Quality of Contact with Noncustodial Parent

Several studies have suggested that the quality of the postdivorce relationship between the spouses influences the amount and/or quality of the contact between the child and the noncustodial parent, typically the father. It is assumed that this contact may in turn have an impact on the postdivorce adjustment of the child (Hetherington et al. 1982, Isaacs 1988, Kelly 1981, Koch and Lowery 1985, Tepp 1983).

However, Ahrons and Miller (1993) pointed out that the great majority of these studies focused on families in which the divorce had occurred within the last year, when the stress and disequilibrium associated with the divorce are greatest. Ahrons and Miller studied sixty-four divorced families one year, three years, and five years after the divorce. They reported that among these families the quality of the relationship between the parents had a significant influence on both the level of paternal involvement with the child and the quality of the father–child relationship during the period shortly after the divorce. However, they found that the strength of this relationship decreased over time. Moreover, they did not report a direct relationship between either the extent of paternal contact or the quality of the father–child relationship and the adjustment of the child.

Thomas and Forehand (1993) related the quality of the relationship between the former spouses to teacher reports of children's externalizing behavior problems and internalizing behavior problems as measured by the RBPC (Quay and Peterson 1987). They found that within the population of divorced families, neither of these two measures of adjustment was related significantly to the quality of the child's relationship with the father. However, these relationships were significant among the population of intact families. These findings were interpreted by Thomas and Forehand as reflecting the fact that the married fathers typically spend more time with their children than divorced, noncustodial fathers. The investigators suggested that the greater amount of time married fathers spend with their children allows them greater opportunity for involvement with the children. Thus, at this point in time, it cannot be concluded with any great degree of certainty that the relationship between parental conflict and children's adjustment in divorced families is mediated by the frequency or the nature of the interaction between the father and the child.

Parenting Behavior

Simons and his associates (1994) suggested that parental conflict might be associated with externalizing pathology among children by virtue of the impact of conflict on parenting ability. As they pointed out:

> Past research has linked child conduct problems to inept parental monitoring and discipline (Maccoby and Martin 1983, Patterson, Reid, and Dishion 1992). Another line of research has shown that parental conflict tends to disrupt competent parenting practices (Caspi and Elder 1988, Conger et al. 1992, Simons, Lorenz, Wu, and Conger 1993). Hence the contribution of parental conflict to child conduct problems may be indirect through its effect on parenting practices. Caspi and Elder (1988) and Conger et al. (1992) found this to be the case in samples of two-parent families. It may be that the same process operates in single-parent families. If this

hypothesis is valid, controlling for quality of parenting should eliminate any relationship between parental conflict and child externalizing problems. [p. 358]

Simons and his associates (1994) measured parental conflict, effectiveness of maternal parenting, and effectiveness of paternal parenting over a three-year period in a sample of 181 adolescents. Data were collected at each of three points in time. Ratings of paternal parenting were obtained from both the custodial mothers and the adolescents.

The results of the study indicated that parental conflict was related significantly to internalizing pathology among male adolescents, but not among females. Quality of maternal parenting was related to externalizing behavior problems among both boys and girls. Quality of maternal parenting was also related to internalizing problems among boys, but not among girls. Quality of parenting by nonresidential fathers was also related to externalizing behavior problems among both boys and girls, although these correlations varied somewhat depending on the source of the rating of the paternal parenting (i.e., mother or adolescent). Parental conflict was related negatively to both maternal and adolescent ratings of the quality of parenting provided by the fathers, but conflict was not related significantly to the quality of parenting provided by the mothers.

Thus, with respect to fathers, the results of the study support the theory that conflict between the parents affects the adjustment of children, because it has an impact on effective parenting. The study does not appear to support this theory with respect to the parenting behavior of mothers. However, this difference may well reflect the fact that maternal ratings of parenting practices were used to assess the quality of maternal parenting. This is clearly not an unbiased source.

Still another perspective on the possible association between parental conflict and children's adjustment has been offered by Dozier and associates (1993). They studied the postdivorce attachment of former spouses and its relationship to their coparenting relationship. They measured postdivorce attachment by means of a fourteen-item scale that included the ten items in Masheter's (1988) attachment scale, plus four additional items selected from scales developed by Berman (1985, 1988) and Weiss (1975). Based on a factor analysis of the scale, Dozier and associates concluded that their instrument measured two dimensions of postdivorce attachment: friendliness and dependence. The friendliness dimension is described as "the extent to which the respondent considers the divorced spouse a friend all or most of the time and the extent to which the respondent dislikes or gets upset with the divorced spouse" (p. 114). The dependence dimension is described as "the extent to which the respondent has ambivalent feelings toward the divorced spouse or is preoccupied with thoughts about the ex-spouse" (p. 114). Examples of items loading on the friendliness factor are "Though our marriage is over, I like my divorced spouse as a person" and "I can't spend more than a few minutes with my divorced spouse without getting upset." Examples of items loading on the dependence factor are "I can't stop thinking about my ex-spouse" and "I miss my divorced spouse very much."

Dozier and colleagues (1993) used two measures of coparenting. The first was the Quality of Coparental Communication Scale (Ahrons 1981). This is a ten-item scale that measures conflict (four items) and support (six items). An example of a conflict item is: "When you and your former spouse discuss parenting issues how often does an argument result?" An example of a support item is: "Do you feel that your former spouse understands and is supportive of your needs as a custodial (or noncustodial) parent?"

The second measure of coparenting was a ten-item scale measuring the extent to which the former spouses shared parenting responsibilities. Items in this scale included: "Do you and your former spouse share making major decisions regarding your children's lives?"; "Discussing school and/or medical problems?"; and "Making day-to-day decisions regarding your children's lives?"

Based on a sample of ninety-five divorced parents recruited from Parents Without Partners organizations in six cities in the southeastern United States, Dozier and her colleagues (1993) reported that postdivorce friendliness was related significantly to conflict over coparenting ($r = -.77, p < .01$), support in coparenting ($r = .56, p < .01$), and shared parenting responsibilities ($r = .57, p < .01$). Postdivorce dependence was related significantly to support in coparenting ($r = .41, p < .01$) and to shared parenting responsibilities ($r = .31, p < .05$). When these correlations were replicated for male and female children separately, the results obtained with respect to parental friendliness pertained for both boys and girls, while those obtained with respect to dependence pertained for girls only.

These findings suggest that the degree of conflict between divorced spouses may well be related to the extent to which they provide their children with consistent messages regarding appropriate behavior. Such consistency might well be reflected in better psychosocial adjustment among the children.

Further research is required to clarify the relationships between parental conflict, the nature and quality of maternal and paternal parenting, and the psychosocial adjustment of children. It would be useful to replicate the study reported by Dozier and her colleagues (1993) on a larger sample, including measures of the children's adjustment. Then this potential causal chain from conflict to effective parenting to psychosocial adjustment could be examined directly. Such a study would be most useful if it were longitudinal in nature, such that the children's adjustment was measured at a point some time after the assessment of the ex-spouses' relationship. It would also be interesting to obtain rating of the ex-spouses' relationship from both spouses, to determine the extent to which their perceptions of their postdivorce relationship agree, and whether the extent to which they do agree is also related to their children's adjustment.

3

CUSTODIAL ARRANGEMENTS

HISTORICAL BACKGROUND OF CUSTODIAL ARRANGEMENTS

Until the beginning of the twentieth century, fathers tended to be granted the custody of their children in the event of parental separation or divorce. This was based on the ancient tradition of English law. However, around the turn of the twentieth century, the tradition of awarding custody to mothers gradually became established. This new tradition was based on the notion that mothers are better suited than fathers to care for children, particularly young children. This view is referred to as the "tender years" doctrine, which holds that young children will be irreparably damaged if they are separated from their mothers.

Szott (1990) has suggested that the tender years doctrine was supported by a number of different biological, social, and psychological theories. It was assumed that the mother–child relationship has a stronger biological basis than the father–child relationship. Further, because of sex role socialization, it was presumed that fathers tend to lack the necessary preparation for the parenting role. The father simply does not have the skills that are required to care for young children. Finally, it was assumed that because of his limitations, the father's success as a parent was dependent upon his having a successful cooperative relationship with his wife.

Santrock and Warshak (1979) argued: "Many psychologists and child developmental specialists have supported the view that the mother is uniquely suited to rear children, both biologically and psychologically" (p. 113). This view assumes that mothers are endowed with a natural nurturing ability that fathers do not possess. It assumes further that this natural maternal nurturing ability makes mothers more effective than fathers in raising children.

The tender years doctrine led to a legal tradition during the twentieth century that supported the mother's presumptive claim to custody. Santrock and Warshak (1979) have noted that courts have often paid lip service to the contending doctrine of the "best interests of the child," but in fact the courts have generally awarded custody to the mother except in those few cases in which the mother was shown to be grossly unfit.

Most recently, however, changing social and cultural norms and changing economic conditions have begun to erode the strength of the tender years doctrine. Research on psychological androgyny (Bem 1974) and on the defining characteristics of masculinity and femininity (Spence et al. 1979) have indicated that men also have the capacity for nurturance. Women have increasingly entered the workforce and have adopted a dual role as worker and homemaker. At the same time, many men have assumed a more active role in household and child care responsibilities. Hanson (1988) suggested that paternal involvement in parenting activities and even single fatherhood are becoming more acceptable to society.

These social changes have been reflected in legal challenges to the tender years doctrine. Santrock and Warshak (1979) cited a New York State court decision in which it was recommended that the tender years doctrine be discarded, because it was based on outdated social stereotypes rather than on rational consideration of the welfare of the children involved.

Concomitant with these social changes, there has been a great increase in the number of men who seek custody of their children (Santrock and Warshak 1979), and more custody cases have been decided in favor of the father (Szott 1990). The number of cases in which fathers seek custody has also increased simply by virtue of the large increase in the number of divorces. Santrock and Warshak pointed out that there are many reasons why fathers seek custody. In many cases the fathers are genuinely interested in assuming the parenting role. In other cases the issue of custody may be used as a weapon to harass an ex-wife whom they perceive to have wronged them. There may even be cases in which the custody issue is used as a bargaining chip in the overall divorce settlement. Santrock and Warshak suggested that each case should be decided on its own merits, and that these decisions should avoid reliance on "cultural stereotypes and historical biases" (p. 133) and should focus instead on the best interests of the child.

RESEARCH ON CUSTODIAL FATHERS

As the number of father-custody families has increased, a body of research has developed relevant to paternal parenting effectiveness. Of course, there is a long history of theoretical work indicating the importance of fathers in the normal development of children. Freudian theory emphasized the importance of the child's identification with the same-sex parent (Freud 1905). This view may be interpreted as indicating the desirability of father custody for boys. Social learning theory (Bandura 1965) also suggests the need for same-sex models. Parsons' (Parsons and Bales 1965) theory of instrumental and expressive parental roles also suggests the importance of the father's influence and could be interpreted as providing support for father custody. However, actual research on fathers as custodial parents has been limited primarily to the last twenty years.

The earliest studies on father custody were descriptive in nature, typically employing small samples and using either in-depth open-ended interviews or survey questionnaires to obtain data. Gasser and Taylor (1976) administered a survey questionnaire to a sample of forty divorced and widowed fathers. The survey assessed the fathers' perceptions of role conflict, involvement in household activities, and society's attitudes toward single fathers. They concluded that these fathers experienced few problems managing the responsibilities of parenthood, and the fathers all expressed confidence in their ability to raise their children. The investigators also indicated that much more research was warranted on custodial fathers.

Gersick (1979) interviewed custodial fathers and mothers regarding sex role orientation, child-rearing practices, and background variables. Gersick's custodial fathers reported that they experienced problems in a number of areas, including money, child care, visitation, and their social life. However, like Gasser and Taylor (1976), Gersick concluded that these fathers had little difficulty managing their households, and none of the fathers expressed regret regarding their parenting role.

Hanson (1988) interviewed and administered questionnaires to thirty-seven divorced custodial fathers and their children. She assessed the nature of the parent–child relationship, paternal nurturance, availability and utilization of social support, and the background and demographic characteristics of the fathers. She found that three-quarters of these single fathers were professionals or executives. She reported that both the fathers and the children tended to believe that the fathers had become more nurturing following the divorce. Other studies indicating that custodial fathers tend to feel competent as parents have been reported by Chang and Dienard (1982), Orthner and Lewis (1979), and Warshak (1986).

COMPARISONS OF CHILDREN IN MOTHER-CUSTODY AND FATHER-CUSTODY HOMES

Several other empirical studies have made direct comparisons of children in mother-custody and father-custody families. These studies have generally indicated no significant differences in adjustment between children in mother-custody and father-custody families.

Rosen (1979) studied samples of fifty-one individuals whose custody had been awarded to their mothers and forty-one whose custody had been awarded to their fathers. In all cases the parents had divorced in the ten-year period preceding the study. At the time of their parents' divorce, these individuals ranged in age from 3 months to 16 years. At the time of the study, they ranged in age from 9 to 28 years. There were twenty-three boys and twenty-eight girls in the mother-custody group, twenty-one boys and twenty girls in the father-custody group.

The parents and children in each group were assessed on a broad variety of measures of psychosocial adjustment. Clinical interviews were conducted with the custodial parents and the children. Children completed the Incomplete Sentences Blank, the Thematic Apperception Test, and the Human Figure Drawing. Based on the interview and the projective tests, each child was rated in eight areas: (1) family relationships, (2) social relationships, (3) independence, (4) level of aspiration, (5) self-concept, (6) optimism/pessimism, (7) occupational/scholastic adjustment, and (8) sex role functioning. Based on these ratings, an overall global measure of psychosocial adjustment was computed.

The results of the study indicated no significant differences between children in mother-custody and father-custody families in terms of either the overall adjustment measure or any of the eight individual areas rated. Furthermore, the investigators also conducted two-way analyses in which sex of the custodial parent was considered in relation to the sex of the child. These analyses yielded no significant interactions between the sex of the custodial parent and the sex of the child. These findings are particularly relevant in view of other research, considered later in this chapter, that indicates that adjustment may be better when the child is placed in the custody of the same-sex parent.

Santrock and Warshak (1979) studied sixty white, predominantly middle-class families in which the children ranged in age from 6 to 11 years. The families were divided evenly among father-custody families, mother-custody families, and intact families. The three different types of families were matched on the basis of the age of the children, family size, and socioeconomic status. The two groups of children from divorced homes were also matched for sibling status and for age when the parents separated. The parents of these children had been separated for an average of two years and nine months.

These researchers employed a broad range of measures of adjustment obtained through the use of two laboratory observations, structured interviews, and self-report scales. The two laboratory observations were each ten minutes long. In the first observation the parent and the child were asked to plan an activity together. In the second they were asked to discuss the main problems of the family. These exercises were videotaped, and trained graduate students rated the parents and the children on a series of dimensions. Parents were rated on the amount of control they exerted over their child, their attentiveness to the child, and their confidence in themselves as parents. Children were rated on warmth, self-esteem, anxiety, anger, demandingness, maturity, sociability, social conformity, and independence. The ratings were made on nine-point scales, and the authors reported interrater reliabilities ranging from .61 to .92, with a mean of .78.

The children were interviewed to ascertain their perceptions of parental roles and their feelings about their parents. In the case of children from divorced families, the interview also included questions regarding their feelings regarding the divorce and the degree to which the children desired more contact with each parent. Parents were interviewed also, with the focus on parenting style.

Parents completed the Adaptive Behavior Inventory for Children, which measures parents' perceptions of the performance of their children in such areas as family, community, peer, and nonacademic school roles. Parents also completed a number of self-report measures of personality factors, including nurturance, affiliation, aggression, and defensiveness.

When children from mother-custody families were compared to

children from father-custody families on these measures, no significant main effects due to type of custody were obtained. However, significant sex of custodial parent by sex of child interactions were obtained on a number of the variables. These interactions indicated that boys in father-custody homes displayed greater competence in the area of social development than did girls in father-custody homes. In contrast, girls in mother-custody homes were more competent socially than boys in mother-custody homes. The specific variables on which this pattern of results was observed included demandingness, maturity, sociability, and independence. Santrock and Warshak (1979) concluded that their results provide support for "the importance of the same-sex parent in the child's life. Whether psychoanalytic, social learning, or other theories are used to explain these results, it does appear from our data that there is something very important about the ongoing, continuous relationship of the child with the same-sex parent" (p. 121).

Santrock and Warshak (1979) noted that the largest differences between children with same-sex custodial parents and those with opposite-sex custodial parents occurred in the areas of demandingness and maturity. They considered this finding significant, in that it agreed with findings reported previously by Hetherington and colleagues (1978). Those investigators described a coercive relationship that tends to develop between custodial mothers and their sons. Hetherington and her associates suggested that boys are more likely than girls to engage in aggressive and coercive behavior, and therefore they are more likely to become part of such a coercive cycle.

Hetherington and her colleagues also indicated that boys tend to be less mature than girls. Santrock and Warshak (1979) reported that boys with custodial mothers manifested more demanding behavior and less mature behavior than boys with custodial fathers. They concluded that "the friction between sons and their single parent seems to be less in a father custody family than in a mother custody family" (p. 122).

Santrock and Warshak (1979) also noted that the effects of growing up in mother-custody versus father-custody families are mediated by a number of factors. They cited findings reported by Hetherington and colleagues (1978) indicating that in mother-custody families the social development of the child is affected by the mother's behavior, the child's relationship with the noncustodial father, and the availability of external support systems. Santrock and Warshak also observed that the quality of parenting and the use of support systems were important factors mediating the psychosocial adjustment of children in mother-custody and father-custody families. They indicated that the effects of parenting behavior and support systems differed for children in mother-custody and father-custody families.

In their laboratory observation of parent–child interactions, Santrock and Warshak (1979) measured the extent to which each parent displayed authoritative, authoritarian, and laissez-faire parenting styles. Authoritative parenting is characterized by warmth, clearly established rules and regulations, and extensive verbal give-and-take. Santrock and Warshak found that in both mother-custody and father-custody homes, boys and girls whose custodial parents displayed high levels of authoritative parenting tended to score high on self-esteem, maturity, sociability, and social conformity. However, the effect of authoritarian and laissez-faire parenting styles differed, depending on the sex of the custodial parent.

In father-custody families there were significant positive correlations between the father's use of an authoritarian parenting style and the child's anger and lack of independence. These relationships did not pertain in mother-custody families.

In contrast, in mother-custody homes there were a number of significant correlations between laissez-faire mothering and the child's behavior. Specifically, "Mothers who interacted with their child in a laissez-faire manner in the laboratory had children who were rated as showing little warmth, high anger, high demandingness, and little social conformity" (Santrock and Warshak 1979, p. 123).

Santrock and Warshak concluded that their results indicated that laissez-faire parenting strategies are associated with poorer outcomes under mother custody, whereas authoritarian parenting strategies yield poorer outcomes under father custody.

Another factor that appears to mediate the effects of divorce in mother-custody and father-custody families is the availability and use of social support. According to Santrock and Warshak (1979), "To cope with the demands of single parenting, divorced parents were enlisting the aid of additional caretakers, such as the non-custodial parent, babysitters, relatives, daycare centers, and friends" (p. 123). They reported that in general such support systems were used more by custodial fathers than by custodial mothers. The mean number of hours per week of utilization of such support systems was twenty-four among custodial fathers compared to just eleven hours per week among custodial mothers. Moreover, this difference could not be attributed to differences in work status between fathers and mothers. The authors indicated that they could not be certain whether the greater use of support systems by custodial fathers occurred because fathers sought such supports more than mothers, or whether relatives and friends assumed that the father needed such help more than mothers.

In both mother-custody and father-custody families, the use of social support systems was related positively to the child's warmth, sociability, and social conformity. Santrock and Warshak (1979) suggested that the availability of support systems enables children to receive more and higher quality adult involvement from both the additional caregivers and the custodial parent whose resources are less depleted. However, they also acknowledged that there is an alternative explanation. It could be that children who are more sociable to begin with tend to be attractive to other adults, who therefore are more willing to provide care for them.

To summarize, Santrock and Warshak (1979) concluded that the effects of divorce are mediated by a "host of complex factors that include custody disposition, sex of the child, aspects of the custodial parent–child relationship, and availability and reliance on family support systems" (p. 124). They recommended that research be continued to determine the differences between mother-custody and father-custody families in terms of the factors that mediate the effects of divorce on the psychosocial adjustment of children.

Studer (1993) also studied differences between adolescents in mother-custody and father-custody homes. She surveyed 217 students in grades nine through twelve in a predominantly white, middle-class high school. The sample included 138 students from intact homes and seventy-nine students from homes in which a marital dissolution had occurred. Of the adolescents from divorced families, forty-eight were from mother-custody homes and thirty-one from father-custody homes. Participating students completed the Self Description Questionnaire II (Marsh et al. 1983). This is a 150-item instrument that measures various dimensions of self-concept, including reading, physical ability, peers, honesty, parents, general self-concept, math, emotional, school, and physical appearance.

Studer (1993) compared males living in a paternal custodial home to males living in a maternal custodial home on the subscales of the Self Description Questionnaire. She found no significant differences between these two groups on any of the subscales. She also compared females living in paternal custodial homes to those living in maternal custodial homes on the same dimensions. Studer found that adolescent females living in mother-custody homes scored significantly higher than those living in father-custody homes on general self-concept and emotional self-concept. However, female adolescents in father-custody homes scored significantly higher than those in mother-custody homes on the honesty dimension of the Self Description Questionnaire.

Studer (1993) observed that her findings did not support the findings of Santrock and Warshak (1979) with respect to males, but did provide partial support for the findings of Santrock and Warshak with respect to females. Actually, the methods used by Studer do not allow a direct comparison of her results to those of Santrock and Warshak for three reasons: first, Santrock and Warshak assessed a range of personality factors and behaviors based on observations, interviews, and self-report measures. The self-report measures they used assessed the perceptions of both children and parents. In contrast, Studer measured only the students' self-concepts, using the Self Description Questionnaire. It is quite possible that the youngsters in Studer's study would have demonstrated additional significant differences had they been measured on some of the factors assessed by Santrock and Warshak.

Second, the populations employed in the two studies were different. Whereas Santrock and Warshak (1979) studied children ranging in age from 6 through 11 years, Studer (1993) studied high school students in grades nine through eleven. It is quite possible that youngsters in these two different age groups have completely different dynamics in terms of relationships with same-sex versus opposite-sex parents.

Third, the methods of data analysis employed in the two studies were different. Santrock and Warshak (1979) compared male and female children in mother-custody and father-custody homes by means of two-way ANOVAs in which the independent variables were sex of child and sex of custodial parent. This procedure allowed them to test the interaction of these two factors and use post hoc contrasts to determine the significance of all pairwise mean differences among the four groups (boys in mother custody, boys in father custody, girls in mother custody, and girls in father custody). Some of the significant differences they reported compared children of one sex in mother-custody homes to children of the same sex in father-custody homes; others compared boys in a particular custodial arrangement to girls in that same arrangement.

In contrast, Studer (1993) used two sets of t-tests to compare (1) adolescent males living in a paternal custodial home with adolescent males living in a maternal custodial home and (2) adolescent females living in a paternal custodial home to adolescent females living in a maternal custodial home. This method of analysis does not allow the determination of significant differences between males and females having the same custody arrangement. Thus Studer limited the number of group differences that she could evaluate.

The literature comparing children in mother-custody homes to children in father-custody homes is mixed, but the weight of evidence tends to suggest that children fare somewhat better when the custodial parent is the same-sex parent. However, it is not clear that the magnitude of such effects is particularly great. Moreover, a multitude of other factors mediate the effect on children of same-sex versus opposite-sex custody. For these reasons it is doubtful whether there should be a presumption for same-sex custody in any individual case. It may be preferable when all other factors are equal, but it would indeed be rare for all other factors actually to be equal. It would appear that a good deal more research is required on this question, and that in the meantime custody decisions should be made on the basis of a comprehensive evaluation of the particular family.

JOINT CUSTODY ARRANGEMENTS

Kelly (1988a) reviewed the literature on joint custody and concluded, "Although research on the impact of joint physical custody arrangements on child adjustment after divorce is still limited, there are indications that custody agreements that allow youngsters to continue both parental relationships on a frequent and predictable basis are beneficial for many children" (p. 130). Kelly reported that research on joint custody generally defines joint physical custody as an arrangement in which the child spends at least 30 percent of the time with each of the two parents. Joint custody is becoming quite common. It has been estimated that in states where the laws are receptive to joint physical custody, 20 to 30 percent of divorces result in such arrangements (Kelly 1988b, Kline et al. 1988, Maccoby et al. 1988). This proportion is higher among better educated parents.

There is substantial anecdotal evidence that joint physical custody is viewed positively by both children and parents. Leupnitz (1982, 1986) reported that children living in joint physical custody arrangements tend to report feeling loved by both parents and attached to both parents. Leupnitz (1982, 1986) and Handley (1985) reported that children in joint physical custody arrangements were more likely than children in sole custody arrangements to express satisfaction with their living situation.

Numerous studies have suggested that parents tend to express high levels of satisfaction with joint physical custody (Ahrons 1980, 1981, Gardner 1991, Irving et al. 1984, Maccoby et al. 1988, Steinman 1981, Steinman et al. 1985). These findings are particularly clear with fathers, but there is substantial evidence that mothers benefit from joint physical custody as well. Thus Maccoby and his colleagues (1988) reported that both mothers and fathers involved in joint custody arrangements reported greater satisfaction than their counterparts with primary physical custody.

Part of the satisfaction that parents experience with a joint physical custody arrangement appears to be related to respite care. The fact that the other parent has custody of the child for a significant portion of time gives each parent an opportunity to catch up on their other obligations and participate in some activities that are enjoyable. This in turn seems to improve their ability to have "quality time" with their children when the children are with them. Thus Maccoby and his colleagues (1988) reported that parents in joint physical custody arrangements reported significantly less difficulty finding time to engage in meaningful activities with their children than did parents in sole custody arrangements.

Several additional studies have indicated that children from joint custody families may be better adjusted than children from sole custody families. Pojman (1982) studied boys from joint custody families, sole custody families, and intact families. The intact family group was further subdivided into marriages that were happy and those that were unhappy. He assessed the boys on self-esteem and on overall psychological adjustment. Pojman reported that boys from joint custody and intact families with happy marriages did not differ on these outcome variables. Boys in both of these groups had significantly higher self-esteem and significantly higher levels of psychological adjustment than boys in sole custody and intact families in which the marriage was categorized as unhappy. Since joint physical custody arrangements tend to be agreed upon by parents who can establish a reasonable working relationship with respect to coparenting responsibilities, these findings suggest that parental conflict may be a critical factor in determining the adjustment of the child.

Shiller (1986a,b) studied boys between the ages of 6 and 11 from joint physical custody families and mother-custody families. Based on the reports of mothers and teachers, the boys from joint physical custody homes had significantly fewer emotional and behavioral problems than the boys from sole custody homes. In addition, the boys from joint custody homes were better able to accept the reality of the divorce and were less preoccupied with fantasies regarding potential parental reconciliation.

These studies provide considerable evidence for the position that joint physical custody is preferable to sole custody. No studies to date have compared joint physical custody arrangements to sole custody arrangements with the same-sex parent, and more research should be carried out relevant to this issue. Any research conducted on the question of joint custody should take into account the level of conflict between the divorcing parents. It seems obvious that a workable joint custody arrangement is more likely to occur when the spouses have a reasonable working relationship than when they are at odds. Therefore, future studies of the relative benefits of joint custody, sole custody with the same-sex parent, and sole custody with the opposite-sex parent should assess and control for level of parental conflict.

4

PSYCHOSOCIAL ADJUSTMENT OF THE CUSTODIAL PARENT

A SUBSTANTIAL BODY of empirical data suggests that one of the most important predictors of the psychosocial adjustment of children and adolescents from divorced families is the adjustment of the custodial parent (Guidubaldi and Perry 1985, Kline et al. 1988, Kurdek and Berg 1983, Wallerstein and Kelly 1980). Kelly (1988a) argued that "the psychological adjustment of the custodial parent after divorce takes on increasing significance in determining the eventual outcome of the child. Whereas during the marriage one parent can create a buffer and balance the other parent's erratic, angry, neglectful, or disturbed behavior, after divorce the child is more at risk if the custodial parent has significant psychiatric disorders or psychological symptoms" (p. 126).

Wallerstein and Kelly (1980) concluded that being in the custody of a parent with a significant psychological disturbance, or a parent who is neglectful or uninvolved in parenting responsibilities, may lead to serious deterioration in the behavioral, social, and academic functioning of children and adolescents five years after the separation. Kline and his associates (1988) reported the results of a longitudinal study of the relationship between the psychological status of custodial parents during the first year after filing for divorce and the emotional and social adjustment of their children two years later. They found that the depression and anxiety scores of the custodial parent were significant and moderately strong predictors of children's adjustment. Kurdek and Berg (1983) and Guidubaldi and Perry (1985) reported that ratings of children's psychological symptoms made by custodial mothers were correlated significantly with the mothers' self-reports of their own functioning, including such specific variables as depression, lethargy, and increased cigarette smoking.

In addition, Guidubaldi and Perry (1985) found that teachers' ratings of children's inattentiveness and social overinvolvement with peers in the classroom were correlated positively with mothers' self-reports of alcohol abuse. Kelly (1988a) noted that these studies were all done on samples of custodial mothers, but, she concluded, "Presumably such findings would be found among father-custody families, were father-custody families sufficiently normative to be studied in adequate numbers" (p. 123). While most of the research carried out to date has focused on custodial mothers, several studies have been based on samples that included both custodial mothers and custodial fathers (Pett 1982, Santrock and Warshak 1979), or samples comprised solely of custodial fathers (Szott 1990). The sections of this chapter that follow describe the results of studies within these three groups.

PSYCHOLOGICAL ADJUSTMENT OF CUSTODIAL MOTHERS

Kalter (1989) reported the results of a study designed specifically to test the relative predictive strength of six different theories regarding children's adjustment to divorce. These theories included the following: (1) father absence, (2) economic distress, (3) multiple life stresses, (4) interparental hostility, (5) parental adjustment, and (6) short-term crisis. Kalter and colleagues described the parental adjustment theory as suggesting that:

> when parents, especially the primary custodial parent, can adjust well to adversity, they can continue to provide effective care, guidance, and support for their children. It is the continuity of effective parenting that is seen as facilitating healthy child development. Further, a supportive parent–child relationship is seen as buffering the youngster from divorce-related stresses. . . .When the custodial parent is distraught and is not able to continue as an effective parent, the child's developmental progress may be compromised and mental health problems are likely to emerge. [p. 607]

Kalter and his associates (1989) surveyed fifty-six divorced custodial mothers who were recruited in four elementary schools in southeastern Michigan. Of the fifty-six respondents, thirty-seven had not remarried at the time of the study, while nineteen had remarried. The women ranged in age from 29 to 46 years (mean = 35.3 years, SD = 4.0), and the duration of their marriages prior to divorce was between two and sixteen years (mean = 9.0 years, SD = 3.9). The length of time since the divorce ranged from seven months to eleven and a half years (mean = 5.2 years, SD = 2.9). The children in the study were between 7 and 12 years old. There were twenty-seven boys and twenty-nine girls.

The measures of parental adjustment were the Brief Symptom Inventory (BSI) (Derogatis and Spencer 1982), the Social Adjustment Scale (SAS) (Weissman and Bothwell 1976), and the Self-Esteem Inventory (SEI) (Rosenberg 1965). The child adjustment criterion measures included in the study were the Child Behavior Checklist (CBCL) (Achenbach and Edelbrock 1983), the Children's Depression Inventory (CDI) (Kovacs 1983), and the State-Trait Anxiety Inventory (STAI) (Spielberger 1973). Kalter and his associates (1989) reported significant relationships of moderate to strong magnitude among all three measures of parental adjustment and most of the children's psychosocial adjustment measures.

For example, among male children, the global "Total Problems" Scale of CBCL was correlated significantly with maternal scores on the BSI (r = .53, p < .01), the SAS (r = .55, p < .01), and the SEI (r = -.42, p < .05). Thus children tended to exhibit more problematic behaviors when their custodial mothers reported relatively many psychological symptoms (as measured by the BSI), relatively poor social adjustment, and relatively low self-esteem.

Among female children, the Total Problems Scale of the CBCL was correlated significantly with both the BSI (r = .48, p < .01) and the SAS (r = .40, p < .05). However, among female children the Total Problems Scale of the CBCL was not related significantly to the mother's score on the SEI.

These findings clearly suggest that problem behaviors in children from divorced families are related to the psychological adjustment of the custodial mother. The findings suggest further that the relationship between children's problem behaviors and parental adjustment may be somewhat stronger for male children than for female children, at least in the case of children in mother-custody families.

Kalter and his associates (1989) obtained similar results with respect to the children's scores on the CBCL Depression subscale. Among boys, CBCL Depression scores were related significantly to parental scores on the BSI (r = .62, p < .001), scores on the SAS (r = .60, p < .001), and scores on the SEI (r = -.47, p < .05). Among girls, CBCL

Depression scores were related significantly to maternal scores on the BSI Global Severity Scale ($r = .55, p < .01$). However, among the girls there were no significant relationships between CBCL Depression scores and either parental SAS scores or parental SEI scores.

Scores on the Children's Depression Inventory (CDL) were correlated somewhat less strongly with the parental adjustment measures than scores on the CBCL Depression subscale, but the general pattern was similar. The same was true of STAI Trait Anxiety Scores. These findings are particularly impressive in view of the fact that the sample sizes for both the male and female youngsters were rather small. Thus there were instances where correlations in the moderate range ($r = .30$ or above) were not statistically significant, although they would have been had the samples been larger.

Kalter and his associates (1989) concluded that these correlations clearly supported the parental adjustment hypothesis for both girls and boys. They also noted that of the six hypotheses regarding postdivorce adjustment they considered in their study, the parental adjustment hypothesis was the one that received the greatest empirical support. Their results provided no support for the father absence, interparental hostility, or the short-term crisis theories. The results obtained with respect to the economic distress hypothesis were conflicting, in that some of the obtained correlations were in the opposite direction to that suggested by the hypothesis. And the results obtained with respect to the multiple life stresses hypothesis supported this hypothesis, but only with respect to boys.

However, Kalter and associates (1989) did suggest several important reasons why the results of their study had to be interpreted cautiously. For example, they noted a serious limitation associated with measuring children's adjustment by means of maternal reports through the CBCL. They noted that "one possibility is that mothers' reports of child adjustment, as captured by the CBCL scales, are partially attributions to the child of the mother's own difficulties rather than accurate perceptions of the youngster" (p. 615). They suggested that this possibility could explain why the relationships observed between the parental adjustment measures and the CBCL scales were stronger than the relationships observed between the parental adjustment measures and the other psychosocial outcomes for the children, including the CDI and the STAI. The reason for this is that the CBCL is based on mothers' ratings of their children's behavior, whereas the CDI and the STAI are self-report measures completed by the child. On the other hand, Kalter and associates also pointed out the possibility that "children of elementary school age are not particularly adept at observing their own problematic feelings and behavioral difficulties, and would tend to minimize them" (p. 615).

Another question pertinent to the interpretation of Kalter and his associates' (1989) findings is that of the direction of causality involved in the observed relationships. Since the study is correlational in nature, there is no experimental control guaranteeing that it is the mother's psychological adjustment that leads to the psychosocial adjustment of the child. The direction could be the opposite. Problem behaviors displayed by children could result in distress among the mothers. However, Kalter and his colleagues concluded that the most likely causal sequence was in fact from mother to child. To the extent that the mother can remain on an even keel in the face of economic deprivation, interparental hostility, and the burdens of single parenting, the child will tend to do well: "When mothers are psychologically able to provide a loving, effective parent–child relationship, children will be buffered from the stresses divorce can engender and will tend to prosper developmentally" (p. 617).

Stolberg and Busch (1985) studied a sample of eighty-two mother-custody families. They assessed the adjustment of the children using two measures, one completed by the mothers and one self-report measure completed by the children. The mothers completed the Single-Parenting Questionnaire, a global measure of the mother's perception of the child's adjustment. In addition, the children completed the Piers-Harris Self-Concept Scale for Children. The fourteen predictor variables employed included measures of family history, maternal postdivorce psychological adjustment, and maternal parenting style. Multiple regression and path analysis indicated that the postdivorce psychological adjustment of the mothers had a significant indirect influence on children's overall adjustment and self-concept, in that mothers who appeared better adjusted psychologically following the divorce tended to employ more effective parenting styles, which in turn predicted children's adjustment.

Another study focusing on the psychological adjustment of custodial mothers was reported by Copeland (1985). She employed a sample of fifty-nine boys and forty-nine girls from mother-custody families, along with the 108 mothers of these target children. The children ranged in age from 6 to 12 years, and the data were collected between one and eleven months after the actual separation occurred. The data were collected by means of interviews and questionnaires. The mothers and the children were interviewed individually. The interviews assessed perceptions of daily life, the causes and effects of the separation, and the respondents' reactions to the separation.

The mothers completed the Child Behavior Profile (CBP) (Achenbach 1978, 1981, Achenbach and Edelbrock 1978), the Child Health Questionnaire (Copeland 1984), and the Profile of Mood States (POMS) (McNair et al. 1971). The tests orally administered to the children were (1) the Cognitive, Social and General Self-Worth Scales of the Perceived Competence Scale (Harter 1982); (2) a series of one-item rating scales assessing the extent to which the parental separation left the children feeling angry, sad, glad, guilty, confused, surprised, or fearful; (3) and the Children's Social Desirability Questionnaire.

Based on the total score for behavior problems derived from the CBP, the samples of boys and girls were each dichotomized into groups characterized by "more behavior problems" and "fewer behavior problems." These groups were then compared on the other variables assessed in the interviews and questionnaires. Results were reported separately for boys and girls. Among boys, Copeland (1984) found significant differences between the more and fewer problems groups with respect to mothers' scores on several subscales of the POMS, including (1) anger and hostility, (2) confusion, and (3) anxiety. The mothers of boys who exhibited relatively many behavior problems were angry, confused, and anxious in comparison to the mothers of boys who demonstrated fewer problems. Among girls, significant differences were found on these three POMS subscales, as well as on the scale measuring maternal depression. The mothers of girls who exhibited more problems were angrier, more confused, anxious, and depressed than the mothers of girls who demonstrated fewer problem behaviors.

Of course, Copeland's (1985) study has the same methodological problems as the study reported by Kalter and his associates (1989). The study is correlational in nature, so the relationship between the mother's mood states and the child's behavior may not be a causal relationship, or may involve reciprocal causation. Moreover, the CBP behavioral ratings assigned to the children by their mothers may have been influenced by the mother's mood. However, Copeland concluded that the "link between mothers' reports of themselves and their children is probably not exclusively a rater-source artifact" (p. 18). She based this conclusion on the fact that other data from the same project indicated that mothers' adjustment was related to children's adjustment, even when the children's adjustment was rated by their teachers, observers involved in the research project, or the children themselves (Copeland et al. 1984).

Copeland (1985) also observed dyadic interactions between mothers and their children in a subsample of twenty-eight boys and twenty-eight girls. Each mother–child dyad was left alone in a playroom while a partially camouflaged videotape recorder was left running. The dyads played under three conditions. For the first ten minutes of the interaction the mother and child played freely with selected toys, including modeling clay, a puzzle, and a plastic building set. In the next ten minutes the mothers helped their children build a tower of wooden blocks while the children were blindfolded. And in the final ten minutes of the play session the mother and child made a puppet out of a sock or a paper bag. The videotapes of these interactions were rated with respect to the frequency of occurrence of nonresponsive interactions, negative interactions, positive interactions, and commands.

The analysis of these data indicated that the mothers of boys with relatively more problem behaviors displayed significantly more negative interactions and used significantly more commands than the mothers of boys with relatively few problem behaviors. No significant main effects due to problem behavior group were observed among the mother–daughter dyads on the behavioral observation variables. These findings may also reflect reciprocal causation, and Copeland (1985) called for further research in this area to attempt to establish the direction of causality.

Some support for the notion that the mother's mood may lead to differences in the adjustment of her children is provided by the study reported by Propst and associates (1986). These investigators studied 106 single mothers ranging in age from 18 to 53. They administered to the mothers the State-Trait Anxiety Inventory (STAI) (Spielberger et al. 1970), the Depression Adjective Checklist (DACL) (Lubin 1967), and the Ways of Coping Checklist (Folkman and Lazarus 1980). The results of this study indicated that maternal anxiety and depression were related significantly to the mother's use of emotion-focused coping behaviors. Emotion-focused coping includes affective outbursts and denial, and is not likely to result in positive resolutions of stress-inducing situations. Thus it could be argued that the mother who is experiencing psychological distress is likely to employ ineffective parenting behaviors that could contribute to behavior problems in her child. The relationship between parental adjustment and the effectiveness of parenting behavior has been the subject of considerable research, discussed later in this chapter.

STUDIES INVOLVING CUSTODIAL MOTHERS AND CUSTODIAL FATHERS

Santrock and Warshak (1979) conducted a study involving mother-custody families ($n = 20$), father-custody families ($n = 20$), and intact families ($n = 20$). The primary purpose of this study was to compare the overall adjustment of children in each of these three situations, but the study also yielded data relevant to several other issues, including the relationship between parental adjustment and the adjustment of children, as well as the relationship between the parenting style of the custodial parent and the adjustment of the child. With respect to parental adjustment, Santrock and Warshak (1979) concluded that custodial parents who are anxious may focus their anxiety on one or more of their children. When this occurs, the child:

> becomes a more "relationship-oriented" rather than "task-oriented" child. The child's energy is diverted from the developmental tasks appropriate to his or her age, and, instead, that energy is invested in the parent and the parent's problems. When parental anxiety is shared with the child, the more parental anxiety increases, the more the parent–child relationship is defined around mutual concern and worry. Emotional energy and anxiety in the parent are typically matched by an approximately equal amount of emotional energy devoted to worry in the child, and the child may develop a number of symptoms including physical illness and school failure. [p. 144]

This analysis strongly suggests that the relationship between the psychological adjustment of the custodial parent and the adjustment of the child is one involving a direction of causation from the parent to the child.

Pett (1982) studied the correlates of children's social adjustment following divorce in a sample of 206 custodial parents, of whom 185 were women and twenty-one were men. These parents had a total of 411 children ranging in age from 2 through 18 years. She assessed the social adjustment of the children by means of the Personal Adjustment and Role Skills (PARS II) Scale (Ellsworth 1979). The PARS II is a fifty-five-item scale that measures six areas of social adjustment and social skills: peer relations, dependency, hostility, productivity, anxiety/depression, and withdrawal. The scale was completed by the custodial parent, who rated the child on each item.

Pett (1982) recognized the threat to the validity of the study presented by the use of parents as informants, suggesting that parents "have their own particular biases and wishes to appear as 'successful' parents" (p. 28). To assess the degree to which such possible biases might affect the parental ratings, Pett had the 12- and 13-year-old children in the sample ($n = 35$) complete a self-report measure similar to that completed by their custodial parent. The child's self-rating on each item was then compared to the parent's rating of the child on the same item. Pett found significant agreement between the ratings assigned by the parents and the children on "nearly all" of the items of the PARS II Scale, and she interpreted these findings as indicating that the impact of possible parental bias was not substantial.

The parents also completed a self-report measure of parental social adjustment (Weissman et al. 1976), a self-report measure of subjective well-being (Fazio 1977), and "an interview schedule covering those factors identified from the divorce literature as having an impact on the postdivorce adjustment of parents and children" (Pett 1982, p. 31).

Based on a multiple regression analysis in which the social adjustment scores of the children were regressed on all the predictors, the social adjustment of the custodial parent was found to be a significant predictor of the children's social adjustment, along with twelve other predictors: (1) the quality of the relationship between the custodial parent and the child, (2) the residential proximity of the noncustodial parent, (3) the socioeconomic status of the family following the divorce, (4) the child's acceptance of the divorce as final, (5) the number of prior marriages of the custodial parent (negatively related to the child's social adjustment), (6) the frequency of contact with the noncustodial parent's family, (7) the residential proximity of the noncustodial parent's family, (8) the child's positive acceptance of the divorce, (9) the age of the custodial parent, (10) the presence of someone that the custodial parent is considering marrying, (11) the custodial parent's satisfaction with the number of persons available for socializing (negatively related to the child's social adjustment), and (12) a positive change in the nature of the relationship between the child and the noncustodial parent following the divorce (negatively related to the child's social adjustment).

Pett (1982) noted that the thirteen predictors contained in the regression equation together accounted for "only 36 percent" of the variability in children's social adjustment. It should be noted that in reality, explaining 36 percent of the variability in a global variable such as social adjustment is quite impressive. Certainly this proportion of explained variability is greater than one typically finds in studies predicting psychosocial outcomes. However, the findings must be treated with a degree of caution, because Pett used the child rather than the parent as the unit of analysis. She included each of the children represented in families with more than one child. This procedure violates the assumption of independence of observations that underlies the use of multiple regression. Many of the predictor variables included in the analysis would have the same values for all the children from one family. This redundancy could have the effect of inflating the observed multiple correlation and proportion of variability accounted for.

However, Pett (1982) correctly observed that the variability in children's social adjustment left unexplained in her analysis may well have been variability attributable to other factors not assessed in her study. Specifically, she concluded that most of her predictors focused on the relationship between the child and his or her custodial and noncustodial parents. "None of the variables examined the children's relationships with their own network support system (i.e., their peers and siblings) or their level of school adjustment" (p. 38). This is an important observation that suggests a new domain of potentially important predictors that should be considered in future studies. Pett's recommendation to include variables associated with the children's own support network is supported by Hetherington (1991, 1993), who suggested that "for adolescents in particular relationships with siblings and peers and experiences in extrafamilial settings play an increasingly salient role in the adjustment of children in divorced and remarried families" (1993, p. 4). On the other hand, Pett's regression model already included a large number of predictors, and the inclusion of additional predictors would require larger sample sizes than that employed in her study, particularly if the appropriate procedure of using the family as the unit of analysis were employed.

With respect to differences between mother-custody and father-custody families on the social adjustment of the children, Pett's (1982) study is silent. This is because the number of father-custody families included in the study was very small ($n = 21$) relative to the number of mother-custody families ($n = 185$). In reality, the number of father-custody families was too small to permit any meaningful analysis of this group by itself. Pooling the mother-custody and father-custody samples for the purpose of the regression analysis assumes that the correlations between the predictors and the criterion variable were similar for the two groups. Pett does not indicate whether she tested this assumption prior to performing the regression. In the quite likely event that these relationships differed, Pett would have been better advised to drop the father-custody families from the analysis so as to derive meaningful conclusions with respect to the mother-custody families.

PSYCHOLOGICAL ADJUSTMENT OF CUSTODIAL FATHERS

Relatively few studies have focused on custodial fathers, and fewer still have considered the psychological adjustment of these fathers. Most studies of custodial fathers have been small-sample interview studies, which are primarily descriptive in nature. We found only one study that focused specifically on the question of whether the psychological adjustment of the custodial father is related to the psychosocial adjustment of their children (Szott 1990).

Gasser and Taylor (1976) interviewed forty custodial fathers regarding their lifestyle, psychological adjustment, social adjustment, parenting attitudes, and the use of support services such as day care. Gasser and Taylor concluded that these fathers experienced significant role adjustments when they assumed responsibility for home management and the care of small children, but they also concluded that the fathers typically handled these changes quite well. Given the qualitative nature of their data and the apparent lack of variability in the postdivorce adjustment of the fathers, Gasser and Taylor did not specifically test the significance of the relationship between paternal postdivorce psychological adjustment and the psychosocial adjustment of their children. Based on a similar study, Gersick (1979) concluded that custodial fathers generally do not appear to have any significant difficulty in adjusting to their new roles.

Szott (1990) noted the failure of prior research on custodial fathers to investigate the relationship between paternal psychological adjustment and the psychosocial adjustment of their children. She studied fifty-six divorced custodial fathers and one child in each family. The fathers ranged in age from 27 to 57 years, and the children from 6 to 13 years. There were twenty-eight boys and twenty-eight girls in the sample. None of the fathers had remarried. The responding fathers completed the Adjective Checklist (Gough and Heilbrun 1983), the

Child Behavior Checklist (CBCL) (Achenbach and Edelbrock 1983), and the Single Parenting Questionnaire (Stolberg and Ullman 1984). The children completed the Piers-Harris Children's Self-Concept Scale (Piers and Harris 1969).

The Personal Adjustment Scale (P-ADJ) of the Adjective Checklist was used to measure the father's psychological adjustment, and the Nurturing Parent Scale (NP) was used to measure his parenting style. The Personal Adjustment Scale is a thirty-four-item scale that measures an individual's sense of well-being and personal efficacy. Those who score high on this scale are characterized by a positive outlook on life, a prosocial gregarious orientation, and the ability to see projects through to completion. The Nurturing Parent Scale contains twenty-two items and is based on Eric Berne's (1961, 1966) theory of personality development. The NP scale measures supportive, nurturant, and growth-sustaining responses to others.

The Single Parenting Questionnaire assesses six dimensions of single parenting: (1) problem-solving skills, (2) availability of support systems, (3) parental warmth, (4) parent-imposed rules, (5) enthusiasm for parenting, and (6) discipline/control procedures. The scale also yields a total composite score that measures global adaptation to the role of the single parent.

Szott (1990) used parent ratings of the child on the CBCL Total Social Competence score as a measure of the child's adjustment. She used the eighty-item self-report Piers-Harris Children's Self-Concept Scale to measure the children's self-regard. This scale yields six subscale scores measuring (1) behavior (BEH), (2) intellectual and school status (INT), (3) physical appearance and attributes (PHY), (4) anxiety (ANX), (5) popularity (POP), and (6) happiness and satisfaction (HAP). Zero-order correlations and multiple regression analyses were used to assess the relationships between each of the predictors and each of the two primary child adjustment criterion variables, self-concept and social competence. These analyses were conducted separately for boys and girls.

The results indicated that father's psychological adjustment following the divorce was not related significantly to self-concept for either boys or girls. Paternal adjustment was related significantly to the social competence scores of the boys, but not the girls. The sons of fathers with better psychological adjustment tended to manifest greater social competence. Among boys, social competence was also related significantly to fathers' scores on the Nurturing Parent Scale. Thus, for boys, one could hypothesize that fathers who are better adjusted display better parenting behaviors, which in turn are reflected in greater social competence among the children. The results did not support a similar interpretation for girls. These findings are also relevant to the issue of same-sex versus opposite-sex custody, since it appears that the influence of the father's psychological adjustment is greater when the child is a boy than when the child is a girl.

However, it must be noted that the same limitations apply to Szott's (1990) study as have been noted in connection with other studies reviewed in this chapter, namely, the correlational nature of the study and the possible effect of rater bias in ratings of children that are derived from parental reports. Szott's study is another example of a study in which a significant relationship was found between a parental self-report measure of parental adjustment (the Adjective Checklist P-ADJ Scale) and parental ratings of the adjustment of the child (by means of the CBCL Total Social Competence Scale), but no such relationship was found between a child adjustment measure based on children's self-reports (the Piers-Harris Children's Self Concept Scale) and parental ratings of the adjustment of the child. Moreover, the correlational nature of the study obviates conclusions regarding the direction of causation that may be reflected in observed significant correlations.

Szott's (1990) findings with respect to the possible role of nurturing parenting behavior as a possible factor intervening between paternal psychological adjustment and children's social competence is one of several findings already reviewed in this chapter that suggest the importance of parenting style. In the following section of this chapter, the studies relevant to positive parenting behavior are reviewed.

PARENTAL ADJUSTMENT, EFFECTIVE PARENTING BEHAVIOR, AND CHILDREN'S ADJUSTMENT

Based on a review of the literature on custodial parent adjustment and parenting style, Bray and Hetherington (1993) concluded that in both mother-custody and father-custody families "authoritative parenting characterized by high levels of warmth, support, monitoring, communication, and firm, consistent control and low levels of punitiveness and coerciveness [are] associated with positive adjustment in children" (p. 4). Several studies have suggested that the effects on children of a wide range of stressors, including parental distress and psychopathology, are mediated by the quality of parenting provided by the custodial parent (Guidubaldi et al. 1986, Heath and Lynch 1988, Hetherington and Clingempeel 1992, Lempers et al. 1989, Steinberg et al. 1991). In particular, these studies have indicated that authoritative parenting is more likely to be associated with positive psychosocial outcomes among children from divorced families, whereas permissive parenting and authoritarian parenting styles are likely to be associated with negative outcomes.

Permissive parenting is characterized by little control or monitoring of children's behavior and a lack of clearly set behavioral guidelines for the children to follow. Authoritarian parenting on the other hand is characterized by the "Do as I say because I say it" approach to structure and discipline, with little explanation of the reasons for the rules that are established and little or no room for discussion or negotiation between parent and child. Based on a longitudinal study of forty-six elementary schoolchildren from divorced families, Guidubaldi and his associates (1986) found that custodial parents who used authoritative parenting, as opposed to permissive or authoritarian parenting, tended to have better adjusted children. The use of an authoritarian parenting style was associated particularly with poor psychosocial adjustment among boys, although the same relationship was not found to be significant among girls.

A recent study of the mediating role of parenting behavior was reported by Simons et al. (1994). These investigators suggested that "although a few studies have reported an association between family structure and level of parental warmth and support, the dimension of parenting most consistently linked to number of parents in the home is that of control. There is strong evidence that single parents tend to make fewer demands on children and utilize less effective disciplinary strategies than married parents" (p. 357). Specific studies reporting such differences between intact and single-parent families along this dimension of parenting style were Hetherington and colleagues (1982), Furstenberg and Nord (1985), and Astone and McLanahan (1991). Simons and his associates noted, however, that these studies showing significant mean differences between intact and single families with respect to control also reported substantial variability on control within the single-parent samples. They therefore concluded that "it is probably a minority of single parents that account for differences in control between single- and two-parent families" (p. 357), and they set out to determine the extent to which variations in control exerted by single mothers are related to the adjustment of their adolescent children.

Simons and colleagues (1994) conducted a longitudinal study of a sample of 207 mother-custody families recruited through the cohort of eighth- and ninth-grade students in Iowa. The mothers were screened according to the criteria that they must be permanently separated from their husbands, that the separation must have occurred in the last two years, that the husband from whom they were separated is the biological father of the target child, and that the target child has a sibling not more than three years older or younger than the target eighth or ninth grader.

Data were collected annually from each family over a three-year period. The criterion measures of the psychosocial functioning of the adolescent were composite measures of externalizing and internalizing pathology. The measure of externalizing pathology employed was the sum of standardized scores derived from three scales. The first scale was a ten-item self-report measure of school problems. This scale is not attributed to any other author, suggesting that the scale may have been developed specifically for this study. Simons and associates (1994) suggested that the scale items focused on "grades, completion of homework, attendance, and trouble with school authorities" (p. 360). The authors indicated that this scale employed a five-point Likert-type format and had an internal consistency reliability (coefficient alpha) of .85.

The second scale used to measure externalizing pathology was a 28-item self-report scale assessing delinquent behavior. This scale was adapted from the National Youth Survey (Elliot et al. 1985, 1989). Respondents completing this scale indicated on five-point scales how frequently in the last year they had engaged in each of twenty-eight delinquent behaviors. The response options on this scale ranged from zero, signifying never, to 5, signifying five or more times. The acts represented a range of delinquent behaviors ranging from relatively minor offenses, such as using alcohol, to more serious offenses, such as attacking someone with a weapon or stealing something valued at more than $25.

The third component of the externalizing pathology scale was a seven-item measure of aggressive orientation adapted from Velicer and colleagues' (1985) modification of the Buss-Durkee Hostility Inventory. This scale contains statements such as, "I do whatever I have to in order to get what I want," "I don't care much about what other people think or feel," and "When I get mad I say nasty things." The response format for these items ranged from 1, signifying "not at all," to 5, signifying "exactly." The internal consistency reliability for this scale reported by Simons and associates (1994) was .80 for each of the three data collection waves.

The measure of internalizing pathology used consisted of four subscales of the Revised Symptom Checklist (SCL-90-R) (Derogatis 1983). These scales were the depression, hostility, anxiety, and somatization subscales of the SCL-90-R. Together, these four subscales comprised forty-six items, each employing a five-point Likert-type response format. Participating adolescents rated each of the forty-six symptoms with respect to how much discomfort he or she had experienced during the past week because of that symptom. The symptoms contained in the scale included items such as crying easily, restless sleep, and uncontrollable temper outbursts. The response options on these items ranged from 1, signifying "not at all," to 5, signifying "extremely." The four SCL-90-R subscales have all been shown to have good internal consistency (Derogatis 1983), and the alpha coefficient reported for the total forty-six-item scale by Simons and associates was .90.

In relation to these criteria of adolescent adjustment, Simons and colleagues (1994) examined, among other factors, the parenting style of the custodial mother. The specific dimensions of parenting style assessed were setting standards for their children, monitoring their children's behavior, consistently enforcing rules, and refraining from harsh punishment. These dimensions were selected because prior research indicated that these parenting dimensions were associated with effective parenting (Maccoby 1992, Maccoby and Martin 1983). Measures of each dimension were obtained through maternal self-reports, adolescents' reports, and observer ratings of a videotaped family interaction task. The ratings from each source in each area were standardized and summed to obtain an overall measure of maternal parenting behavior. The coefficient alpha reported for this instrument was .70 for each of the first two waves of data collection. This acceptable but modest internal consistency reliability appears to be primarily the result of relatively low correlations between maternal self-reports and adolescent reports on these dimensions. These correlations ranged from .25 to .35.

The data were analyzed separately for girls and for boys. Among girls, the effectiveness of maternal parenting at the first wave of data collection was related negatively to the adolescent's externalizing pathology at the same point in time ($r = -.31$, $p < .05$), but not to adolescent externalizing pathology one year later ($r = .21$, $p > .05$). The maternal parenting effectiveness measure obtained at the second wave of data collection was related significantly to girls' externalizing pathology at both the second data collection interval ($r = -.31, p < .01$) and the third data collection interval ($r = -.36, p = .01$). Thus there is ample evidence of a relationship between maternal parenting skills and externalizing behavior problems among adolescent girls. However, among the girls there was no significant relationship between maternal parenting effectiveness measured at either time one or time two and the adolescent's internalizing pathology measured at any of the three waves of data collection.

Among the boys, the relationships between maternal parenting behavior and the psychosocial adjustment criteria were both stronger and more consistent: The effectiveness of maternal parenting at the time of the initial wave of data collection (time one) was related negatively to boys' externalizing behavior problems at both time one ($r = -.38, p < .01$) and one year later (time two; $r = -.39, p < .01$). Maternal parenting effectiveness at time two was related negatively to boys' externalizing behavior problems at both time two ($r = -.50, p < .01$) and one year later (time three; $r = -.39, p < .01$). Unlike the girls, among the boys internalizing behavior problems were also related significantly to maternal parenting effectiveness. Maternal parenting effectiveness at time one was related negatively to internalizing pathology at both time one ($r = -.39, p < .01$) and time two ($r = -.47, p < .01$). Maternal parenting effectiveness at time two was related negatively to internalizing pathology at time two ($r = -.48, p < .01$) and at time three ($r = -.33, p < .05$).

Simons and associates (1994) correctly noted that their research "avoided the limitations inherent in many prior studies of children's adjustment to divorce by using longitudinal data [and] utilizing multiple sources of information to build measures" (p. 370). The authors concluded that their findings supported the theory that the quality of custodial mothers' monitoring and discipline was related to externalizing problems for both boys and girls. Concerning the observed differences between girls and boys with respect to the relationship between maternal parenting effectiveness and internalizing behavior, the investigators suggested several possible explanations:

> Past research has established that boys have a greater propensity for conduct problems than girls (Loeber and LeBlanc 1990). It may be that young males understood the dangers that low parental control poses for them, and hence are more likely than adolescent

females to interpret low control as an absence of parental control and caring. Or it may be, as past studies have reported, that adolescent males, whether living in a single- or a two-parent family, tend to resist control attempts by their mother (Baumrind 1991). Thus it may be that many of the single mothers in the present study who scored low on effective discipline had reduced their level of monitoring and discipline in response to the anger and resistance shown by their sons. [p. 371]

From the perspective of this chapter, the primary limitation of this study by Simons and associates (1994) is that they did not measure the psychosocial adjustment of the custodial parent.

A study is still needed in which both the adjustment and the parenting behavior of the custodial parent are measured in a longitudinal study, based on large samples of custodial mothers and custodial fathers, and employing multiple sources for ratings of parental adjustment, parenting behaviors, and the psychosocial adjustment of the children. Such a study would provide empirical evidence for the theoretical formulation advanced by Hetherington and her associates (1982) that the psychological adjustment of the custodial parent has an impact on the psychosocial adjustment of the child because the adjustment of the custodial parent alters his or her capacity for effective parenting behavior.

5

REMARRIAGE OF THE CUSTODIAL PARENT

MOST DIVORCED WOMEN and men remarry. Glick (1989) reported that there were 11 million remarried families in the United States. These families accounted for 21.4 percent of all married couples in the United States. Of these remarried families, approximately 20 percent are stepfamilies. A stepfamily is defined as "a family created by remarriage with at least one partner's child from a previous marriage" (Skopin et al. 1993, p. 182). Twelve percent of all children under the age of 18 are living in two-parent stepfamilies. Hetherington (1993) reported that in her longitudinal study of 144 mother-custody families, 75 percent of the mothers had remarried within eleven years of their divorce. The substantial number of stepfamilies in our society has led to growing research interest in this population.

Most of this research has focused on stepfathers, because children from divorced families more frequently reside with their mothers than with their fathers (Cherlin and McCarthy 1985, Hetherington 1993, Spanier and Glick 1981). Several investigators have suggested that the role of stepfather is particularly problematic. Cherlin (1978) suggested that stepfathers experience role ambiguity due to the lack of generally accepted social expectations regarding how stepfathers should behave. For example, it is not clear whether stepfathers are expected to take an active role in such parenting behaviors as rule setting and discipline, or whether such roles should be reserved for the children's mother. Johnson (1980) stated that stepfathers tend to experience problems for several specific reasons, including the complexity of roles and relationships that develop among the various members of past and present families, and conflicts over differences in lifestyles.

Visher and Visher (1978, 1983) suggested that stepfathers who have children of their own may experience substantial guilt concerning the abandonment of their natural children in favor of the stepchildren. This may be reflected in the stepfather's behavior. He may resent the stepchildren and even become psychologically or physically abusive toward them. In addition, the stepfather may not be able to manage the competition for his time and energy that takes place between his natural children and his new wife and stepchildren. Visher and Visher (1978) suggested that many stepfathers attempt to handle such conflicts by becoming overly solicitous of everyone in the family constellation, with the result that children may lack structure and discipline.

These problems are exacerbated by the fact that stepfathers typically tend to enter a family constellation in which there are very close bonds between the divorced custodial mother and her children. It may not be easy for the stepfather to overcome the resentment and jealousy of the stepchildren and penetrate the boundaries of this closed family system. Keshet (1980) suggested that following divorce the relationships between the custodial mother and her children are often very intense, since the mother and the children tend to rely on each other for support and companionship. When a new stepfather enters the system, it may be necessary to reorganize both the power and authority relationships in the family and the patterns of normal social interaction.

Robinson (1984) reviewed the clinical literature on stepfathers. He concluded that the problem areas mentioned most frequently in these studies included (1) issues of authority and discipline with stepchildren, (2) uncertainty regarding the demonstration of affection with stepchildren, (3) concerns regarding the possibility of inappropriate sexual attraction across generations, (4) questions of financial responsibility, (5) issues surrounding the loyalty of children to the noncustodial father, and (6) stress generated by confusion regarding differences in family names. Nelson and Nelson (1982) also concluded that stepfathers tended to experience difficulties in the areas of "discipline, kinship terms, family loyalty, and monetary conflicts" (p. 522).

Remarriage is not only problematic from the perspective of the relationships between children and stepfathers. Research indicates that custodial mothers also tend to experience difficulties with their children following remarriage. For example, Hetherington and colleagues (1985) reported that adolescent boys and girls whose mothers had remarried within the last two years tended to display increased externalizing behavior problems, including acting-out and aggressive behavior. Bray (1988) reported similar results in a study of younger children in stepfamily situations. On the other hand, several relatively recent studies have reported few significant differences in family system functioning among intact families, one-parent families, and stepfamilies (Smith 1992) or a tendency for children in stepfamily situations to demonstrate higher levels of psychosocial adjustment than children in one-parent families (Studer 1993).

Studies of the adjustment of children following the remarriage of their custodial parent have also shown significant differences due to the gender of the child and the length of time since the mother's remarriage. For example, Hetherington and her associates (1985) found that after two years the increased acting-out behavior that characterized both boys and girls during the first two years of the remarriage persisted in girls, but not boys. She noted that after two years boys appeared to benefit from the presence of a stepfather, in that their scores on psychosocial adjustment measures such as the Child Behavior Checklist tended to be similar to the scores of boys from intact families. In contrast, girls with stepfathers continued to demonstrate elevated scores on problem behavior checklists, even after two years. Similarly, Crosbie-Burnett (1984, 1988) reported that girls in mother-custody families reported more problems adjusting to their mother's remarriage than did boys.

Solomon (1995) reviewed the research on the impact of remarriage on custodial mothers' relationships with their children. She concluded that:

> in many remarried families mother–child relations are initially poor, may improve for a time and then deteriorate again as the children reach adolescence. There are suggestions that mother–daughter relations are even more perturbed than mother–son relations. Some researchers and clinicians have suggested that a special relationship exists between mother and child before the mother's remarriage and that it is the rupture of this relationship that is the source of many of the post-remarriage problems. A different suggestion is that perturbed relations are carried from the time of difficult relationships in the original family, through the period of one parent life into the stepfamily. Whatever the sources of the problems, several investigators report that children in remarried families see their mothers less favorably than children in nondivorced families. [p. 95]

In this chapter the research relevant to the effects of the remarriage of custodial mothers has been organized under three major headings, as follows: (1) empirical studies of the effect of remarriage on children's adjustment, (2) studies of the effect of remarriage on the family system and its functioning, and (3) studies of factors that mediate the relationship between the remarriage of the custodial mother and the adjustment of the children.

EMPIRICAL STUDIES OF THE IMPACT OF THE CUSTODIAL MOTHER'S REMARRIAGE

Acock and Kiecolt (1989) reported interesting findings with respect to the effects of the remarriage of the custodial mother in a study that was designed to examine the effects of family structure and socioeconomic status on the adult adjustment of children from divorced and remarried families. Acock and Kiecolt cited the father-absence hypothesis as the basis for the expectation that adults who lived in stepfather families during their adolescence would score higher on psychological well-being as adults than would adults who lived in one-parent mother-custody families. They argued that "a stepfather's presence may mitigate the adverse effects of the biological father's absence, as children sometimes become quite attached to their stepfathers" (p. 555). They also cited several studies that indicated that the loss of income associated with the divorce was the major determinant of adjustment problems among children whose parents had divorced (Desimone-Luis et al. 1979, Elder and Liker 1982). Because of the overreaching effect of changes in socioeconomic status, Acock and Kiecolt (1989) concluded, "To determine the long-term effects of family structure, then, it is necessary to examine its effects on various domains of well-being, to control for adolescent and adult socioeconomic status and other pertinent aspects of location in the social structure, and to test for gender differences" (p. 557).

To ensure a representative sample containing an adequate number of respondents who grew up in mother-headed single-parent families and reconstituted families, Acock and Kiecolt (1989) employed data collected on 20,056 families in thirteen national probability samples collected by the National Opinion Research Center over the period from 1972 to 1986 (Davis and Smith 1986). The actual sample consisted of 1,031 black women, 8,643 white women, 713 black men, and 7,039 white men. All were 18 or over.

Acock and Kiecolt (1989) selected from among the many variables measured in these surveys five indicators of adult adjustment. General happiness was measured by a single item: "Taken all together, how would you say things are these days—would you say that you are very happy, happy, pretty happy, or not too happy." Life satisfaction was measured by the item, "In general, do you find life exciting, pretty routine, or dull." The respondent's sense of control over his or her life was assessed by a three-item scale comprised of the following statements: "In spite of what some people say, the lot of the average man is getting worse, not better," "It's hardly fair to bring a child into the world with the way things look for the future," and "Most public officials are not really interested in the problems of the average man." Trust in people, an indicator of the quality of the respondent's interpersonal relationships, was also measured by a three-item scale, as follows: "Would you say that most of the time people try to be helpful, or that they are mostly just looking out for themselves?" "Do you think most people would try to take advantage of you if they got the chance, or would they try to be fair?" and "Generally speaking, would you say that most people can be trusted or that you can't be too careful in dealing with people?" Satisfaction with friendships was measured by a single item that simply asked the respondents how satisfied they were with their friendships. Responses to this question were made on a seven-item Likert-type scale with response options ranging from "no satisfaction with friendships" to "a very great deal of satisfaction with friendships."

The respondent's socioeconomic status at age 16 was based on a self-report scale that asked the respondent to describe his family income at that time relative to the income of the average American family. Response options for this item ranged from 1, signifying "far below average," to 5, signifying "far above average." An identical scale was used to elicit the respondents' perceptions of their current family income relative to that of the average family. Mother's highest level of education and the respondent's highest level of education were also ascertained. Race, age, and the respondent's present marital status were included as control variables, due to the fact that these variables have been shown to be related to subjective well-being.

Acock and Kiecolt (1989) used the LISREL VI program to estimate the effects on each of the five adjustment measures of family type (intact, single-parent mother-custody, and stepfamily) after controlling for mother's education, family income at age 16, respondent's education, respondent's current family income, age, race, and current marital status. They assessed gender differences by estimating the model for men and women separately.

The results indicated that:

> parents' divorce has negative effects that vary according to whether the adult lived in a mother-headed family or with the mother and a stepfather. Living with one's mother and a stepfather following parents' divorce is associated with significantly less happiness and life satisfaction among both women and men. Thus, rather than improving children's long-term adjustment, parents' remarriage following a divorce may generate different problems. [p. 561]

These findings are noteworthy in view of the large sample size they employed and the fact that the investigators controlled for a number of significant intervening variables that may otherwise have resulted in spurious findings. On the other hand, Acock and Kiecolt (1989) pointed out that the magnitude of the effects of the mother's remarriage were modest. The strongest relationship they observed was that between family structure and the criterion variable of perceived control over one's fate, and they reported that "adults who lived with their mother and a stepfather at age 16 are slightly over one-fifth of a standard deviation lower on the fate control variable than are adults from an intact family" (p. 561). This rather small estimated effect size was statistically significant primarily because of the very large sample the researchers employed. Adults who lived only with their custodial mother at the age of 16 also had a lower mean score on fate control than did adults who had lived in intact families. However, this mean difference was not statistically significant. Acock and Kiecolt did not find any significant gender differences with respect to these relationships. Thus the modest negative impact of the mother's remarriage would appear to apply to males as well as females.

In one of the few studies reported to date to include custodial fathers and stepmothers, Studer (1993) compared the self-concepts of adolescents from four different types of families: (1) mother-custodian, never remarried ($n = 26$); (2) father-custodian, never remarried ($n = 16$); (3) mother-custodian, stepfather in home ($n = 22$); and (4) father-custodian, stepmother in home ($n = 15$). Self-concept was measured by the Self Description Questionnaire (SDQ 11) (Burnett 1988). The SDQ is a 150-item instrument that measures self-concept with respect to various academic and social areas, including reading, physical ability, peer relations, honesty, relations with parents, general self-concept, mathematics, emotional self-concept, school self-concept, and physical appearance.

Studer (1993) compared all the adolescents from reconstituted homes to all the adolescents from one-parent homes on the various dimensions of self-concept measured by the SDQ. She used a series of independent sample t-tests for this purpose. The results indicated that the adolescents from the stepfamilies had significantly higher means than the adolescents from the single-parent families on two of the self-concept dimensions: general self-concept and self-concept of physical appearance. Thus the results seem to suggest that the remarriage of the custodial parent may have some positive benefits for adolescents.

However, these findings must be regarded with great caution, because Studer's (1993) study has some serious methodological limitations. The sample sizes for the four groups of adolescents from divorced families were all quite small. Furthermore, all of Studer's analyses employed a single independent variable. No two-way analyses were performed, which could have addressed the possible interaction of sex of custodial parent by remarriage status. Thus any differences in the possible effects of remarriage that may have existed between custodial mothers and custodial fathers was ignored. Similarly, the gender of the adolescent was not included in similar two-way analyses, and there were no three-way analyses that could have identified possible significant three-way interactions (remarriage by gender of custodial parent by gender of adolescent). Given the differences reported in earlier studies relevant to differential effects of remarriage for girls and boys (Crosbie-Burnett 1984, 1988, Hetherington et al. 1985), these interactions should not be neglected. However, to assess these interaction effects adequately, one would have to employ many more subjects than were available to Studer.

Another limitation of Studer's (1993) study lies in the fact that a rather large number of dependent variables were analyzed by multiple univariate tests, raising the prospect of Type I errors. Indeed, the total number of significant relationships reported by Studer is not very much greater than the number that would be expected by chance, given the total number of univariate tests that she appears to have carried out. On balance, then, Studer's study only suggests the prospect that the remarriage of the custodial parent may have some beneficial effects. The study certainly does not provide strong evidence of such an effect. Moreover, the weight of the evidence available to date on the effect of the remarriage of the custodial parent would favor the general conclusion that the effect is negative. It is clear that much more research needs to be done to determine the impact of remarriage for girls and boys in both mother-custody and father-custody families.

EFFECT OF REMARRIAGE OF THE CUSTODIAL PARENT ON FAMILY SYSTEM FUNCTIONING

Amato (1987) reported the results of a study conducted in Australia comparing family processes in one-parent mother-custody families ($n = 87$), families in which the custodial mother had remarried ($n = 54$), and intact families ($n = 201$). Interviews were conducted with each child and with one parent, typically the mother. The children's interviews were conducted in a private room at the child's school, and the parental interviews were conducted in the participants' homes. The interview schedules for both children and parents were concerned primarily with family relationships and activities.

Items from the interviews with the children were summed to produce eleven scale scores representing family process dimensions. These measures appeared to have good face validity, and Amato (1987) reported acceptable reliabilities for almost all of the scales. Accordingly, they are described in some detail in the paragraphs that follow:

1. *Maternal support* was assessed by means of 12 interview questions, such as, "Does your mother talk to you much?" "Is your mother interested in the things that you do?" "Does your mother ever help you with your homework?" "Does your mother ever help you with personal problems?" The participating children responded to these questions on three-point scales with response options of 0 = never, 1 = sometimes, and 2 = often. Amato (1987) reported that this 12-item scale had an alpha reliability coefficient of .65.
2. *Paternal support* was measured by a 12-item scale identical to that used to assess maternal support, but substituting "father" for "mother" in each item. The internal consistency reliability of this scale was .74.
3. *Maternal control* was measured by five items that asked the child, "In your family, who mostly decides about (a) what jobs you do and when they should be done? (b) your bedtime? (c) programs you watch on television? (d) if you can go out? (e) which new clothes to buy?" (p. 330). Responses to each of these items were open-ended, and each response was coded zero if the response was not the mother and one if the response was the mother. The coded responses were

summed to form a score with a theoretical range of zero to five representing the degree of mother's control. The reliability reported for this scale was .55.

4. *Paternal control* was measured by the same five items, each coded zero if the response was not the father and one if the response was the father. The reliability of this scale was .64.
5. *Child autonomy* was measured by the same five items, each coded one if the responding child indicated that he or she usually made the decisions in this area, and coded zero if the child indicated that anyone else usually made these decisions. This scale had an internal consistency reliability coefficient of .61 in the study sample.
6. *Maternal punishment* was assessed by a five-item scale that asked responding children, "If you are naughty (disobedient) does your mother ever (a) send you to your room? (b) stop you from seeing your friends? (c) hit you? (d) yell at you? (e) stop you from watching television?" (p. 330). Amato (1989) indicated that the five punishments included in this scale are all "coercive, power-assertive" forms of discipline that are quite different from "love oriented" or inductive forms of control. Each item was scored as a dichotomy, with a code of zero assigned if the responding child indicated that his or her mother does not punish in this manner, and a code of one if she does use this form of punishment. Thus scores could range from zero to five. The reliability of this scale score in the study sample was .59.
7. *Paternal punishment* was measured by a five-item scale identical to that used to assess maternal punishment, except that father was substituted for mother in each item. The reliability of the scale for paternal punishment was .70.
8. *Children's responsibility for household tasks* was measured by a list of twenty household chores, each of which the responding child checked if he or she were regularly responsible for completing this task. Included in the list of chores were making your bed, keeping your room clean, setting the table, washing dishes, and taking out garbage. The twenty tasks were combined to form a single score by counting the number of tasks that each child checked. The alpha coefficient for this scale was .71.
9. *Sibling relations* were measured by a question asking the children to indicate, for each of their brothers and sisters, "How well do you get along with _____?" This was an open-ended question, and the children's responses were coded into four ordered categories: (1) "don't get along very well," (2) "sometimes get along well and sometimes fight," (3) "get along most of the time," and (4) "get along well all the time." To obtain a score for each child that adjusted for the number of siblings, responses were averaged across all the siblings

rated by the responding child. In addition, the children were asked, "Overall, how well do you get along with your brothers and sisters?" It was found that responses to this question were correlated highly with the average response regarding the individual siblings, so the two measures were averaged to form a single score for sibling relations. The alpha coefficient for this scale was reported to be .89.

10. *Family cohesion* was measured by an eight-item scale designed to reflect "the frequency of joint family activities and children's feelings of closeness to their families" (p. 330). Amato (1987) provided the following examples of items included in this scale: "How often do you go on family outings together?" "Do you ever play games together as a family?" "Are there times when it feels really good to be together as a family?" Response options for these fixed response items were 0 = never, 1 = sometimes, and 2 = often. This measure had an alpha coefficient of .66.

11. *Marital conflict*. Children who were in intact and stepfamily situations, as opposed to single mother-custody families, responded to two questions: "How do you think your parents get on with each other?" and "How often do your parents get angry with one another or disagree?" Response options for the first of these two items ranged from one, signifying "very well," to four, signifying "not very well." Response options for the second item ranged from one, signifying "never," to four, signifying "all the time." This two-item scale had an alpha of .64 in the study sample.

Amato (1987) noted that the study was designed to focus on children's perceptions of family processes rather than the responding parent's perceptions of these processes. Nevertheless, the parent interview included "similar (but less detailed) measures" of the same dimensions. He reported that the correlations between the children's perceptions of the eleven family process dimensions and the parents' perceptions of the corresponding dimensions were generally "statistically significant but low, although they tended to be higher for adolescents than for primary school children" (p. 331). The correlations that Amato reported ranged from .09 (for sibling relations) to .38 (for household responsibility).

These findings are important because they indicate that parents and children may have quite different perceptions of family processes. This suggests the need for multiple measures of family processes derived from different sources. Observational studies and studies using reports from objective third parties would appear to be particularly informative.

Amato analyzed the children's reports of the eleven family process dimensions by means of a three-way multivariate analysis of covariance (MANCOVA). The independent variables in this analysis were family type (intact, one-parent, and stepfamily), child age level (primary school versus adolescent), and the gender of the child. The covariates included in the analysis were the socioeconomic status of the family, based on the parent's reports of maternal and paternal education, occupational status, and income; the number of siblings living in the household; and the mother's employment status (dummy coded as two dummy variables, not employed versus employed part-time, and not employed versus employed full-time). The inclusion of the additional independent variables and the covariates is very important as several of these factors have been shown to mediate the relationship between custodial-parent remarriage and aspects of children's psychosocial development (see description of the study reported by Acock and Kiecolt [1989] earlier in this chapter).

The MANCOVA yielded a significant multivariate main effect due to family type and a significant multivariate interaction between family type and children's age group. Follow-up univariate ANCOVAs yielded significant main or interaction effects involving family type on eight of the eleven family process dimensions. However, not all of these significant effects involved significant differences between one-parent mother-custody families and stepfamilies. Several of these significant findings involved significant pairwise differences between intact families and either single-parent families, or stepfamilies, or both single-parent families and stepfamilies. Since the focus of the present chapter is on the effect of remarriage, only those findings involving significant differences between one-parent families and stepfamilies will be considered here. Other effects reported in this study will be noted as appropriate in subsequent chapters.

Significant differences between one-parent mother-custody families and stepfamilies were observed on four of the family process measures: maternal control, paternal control, children's autonomy, and paternal punishment. On maternal control, there was a significant interaction between family type and age of the child. Among primary schoolchildren, there was no significant difference between one-parent families and stepfamilies. However, among adolescents, scores on maternal control were significantly higher in stepfamilies than in one-parent families. Amato (1987) noted that this finding confirmed a similar finding reported earlier by Dornbusch and colleagues (1985).

Amato (1987) suggested two possible explanations for this difference. The first and most obvious explanation is simply that single custodial mothers provide less supervision for their adolescent children than do mothers who have remarried. Although Amato did not amplify this observation, one can speculate that a lack of supervision could result from the tendency of single custodial mothers and their adolescent children to establish a close, mutually supportive, and somewhat collegial relationship as opposed to a more clearly defined parent–child authority relationship. If this is the case, the finding could be interpreted as an indication that custodial mothers who remarry are more mature with respect to the parenting role. It could also imply that the presence of a new husband alters the mother–adolescent relationship in the direction of more traditional adult–child authority roles, since the mother's needs for companionship are satisfied in substantial measure by the husband rather than the children. Alternatively, however, Amato pointed out that the finding could be viewed as an indication that adolescents in one-parent mother-custody are simply more mature than adolescents in stepfamily situations, so they require less control.

A significant family type by age of child interaction was also obtained for the paternal control variable. On this measure, however, there was no significant difference between single-mother and stepfather families among the adolescents, but there was a significant difference between these two groups among the primary schoolchildren. The primary schoolchildren in single-parent mother-custody homes had a lower mean score on paternal control than did the primary school children in stepfamilies.

Since the children in the one-parent families would necessarily be responding to this scale with respect to their noncustodial fathers, this finding may be interpreted most parsimoniously as confirming those studies that have indicated that noncustodial fathers tend to have decreased influence over their children following a divorce. The scores assigned by the primary schoolchildren to their stepfather's level of control were roughly equal to the scores assigned by children in intact families to their fathers. This implies that when children are young, stepfathers appear to exert a level of control comparable to natural fathers living with their children.

In contrast, scores on paternal control among adolescents with stepfathers tended to be low. The mean on paternal control among adolescents in stepfamilies did not differ significantly from the mean on paternal control among single-parent mother-custody adolescents. Thus, when the children are adolescents, a stepfather is typically perceived as exercising no more control than a noncustodial father residing away from his children. The obvious explanation for this finding is that stepfathers tend to adopt a relatively passive role with respect to exercising control over their adolescent stepchildren. Amato (1987) suggested that this "may reflect the fact that adolescents tend to have more problems than younger children in accepting the presence of stepfathers and may be touchy about stepfathers exercising authority" (p. 334).

On the dimension of children's autonomy, significant differences were observed between single-parent mother-custody families and stepfamilies among both the primary school sample and the adolescent sample. In each case the mean score on children's autonomy was significantly higher in the single-parent sample. This finding is really a mirror image of the findings obtained with respect to maternal control and paternal control discussed in the previous paragraphs. In fact, the scales measuring maternal control, paternal control, and children's autonomy are actually ipsative in nature, since they are based on the same five questions, and each response can add to the respondent's score on only one of the three scales.

On the paternal punishment dimension, significant differences were observed between the single-parent mother-custody families and the stepfamilies among both primary schoolchildren and adolescents. In each case, the mean score was significantly higher among the stepfamily group than among the single-mother group. This finding may also be interpreted parsimoniously by the virtual absence of discipline exercised by noncustodial fathers. The scores assigned to stepfathers on paternal discipline were lower than the scores assigned to natural fathers in intact families on this dimension, and they were also lower than the ratings of maternal punishment in any of the three family types. Thus it appears that stepfathers are likely to defer to the mother with respect to the role of disciplinarian, although even the stepfathers exercise more discipline than do noncustodial fathers in one-parent homes.

On balance, Amato's (1987) findings suggest that the remarriage of a custodial mother may have some positive effects for primary school-aged children and adolescents alike. With respect to primary schoolchildren, the presence of the stepfather may compensate to some extent for the lack of paternal control that results when fathers no longer reside in the same household as their children. And with respect to adolescents, the presence of a stepfather may help the custodial mother to maintain or restore an appropriate degree of maternal authority, as opposed to adopting a role relationship in which the mother and adolescent are more like companions than mother–child dyads.

Smith (1992) studied family cohesion in a sample of remarried families ($n = 68$). He assessed family cohesion using the Family Adaptability and Cohesion Scales III (FACES III) (Olson et al. 1985). The FACES III is the third version of a scale developed initially in 1978 to measure family adaptability and cohesion as defined in Olson's Circumplex Model of Family Functioning (Olson et al. 1983b). This is a twenty-item scale, with ten items measuring family cohesion and the other ten measuring family adaptability. Smith administered the scale to all the members of each family, and he obtained a total cohesion score for each family by averaging across the cohesion scores of all the members of that family.

Smith (1992) divided his sample of remarried families into two groups, those with and those without an adolescent family member contributing to the overall cohesion score of the family. Smith used a pair of one-sample t-tests to compare the means of each of these two groups to the means of the corresponding FACES III norm groups. He found that his sample of remarried families in which the scores of at least one adolescent in the family were included in the overall score ($n = 20$) had a mean score on Family Cohesion that was significantly lower than the mean of the FACES III norming group sample of families in which at least one adolescent contributed to the Family Cohesion score. In contrast, his sample of remarried families in which no adolescent family members contributed to the measure of Family Cohesion ($n = 48$) had a mean Family Cohesion score that did not differ significantly from the mean of the sample of norm group families in which no adolescent scores were included in the overall measure of family cohesion.

Smith (1992) interpreted these findings as indicating that the remarriage of the custodial mother did not have a significant effect on family cohesion unless the perceptions of adolescent family members were included in the calculation of the Family Cohesion score. Thus the remarriage of the custodial mother is not generally perceived as reducing family cohesion, but it is perceived in this manner by adolescents. Smith concluded, "This finding also offers empirical support to the clinical literature which identified the remarried family with adolescents as the remarried family generally requiring different treatment, especially concerning cohesion" (p. 63). Smith also reported that this pattern of results did not change as a function of the length of time since the remarriage.

Neither Amato (1987) nor Smith (1992) reported any significant main or interaction effects on family processes due to the gender of the child. Amato tested for such effects explicitly and found none. Smith did not test for such effects, since his scores for family cohesion were averaged across all the responding family members. In contrast, Hetherington (1993) did report such effects in her data from the Virginia Longitudinal Study of Divorce and Remarriage. She also noted differences resulting from the length of the remarriage. Her findings are somewhat complex, in that a number of independent variables are examined. Nevertheless, these findings are extremely interesting with respect to the interrelationships among remarriage, the age of the child at the time of the remarriage, the gender of the child, the length of the remarriage, family process variables, and children's problem behaviors. With respect to remarriages involving relatively young children, Hetherington concluded:

> [I]n newly remarried families with preadolescent children, especially with daughters, a close marital relationship was associated with high levels of negative behavior from children toward both the mother and the stepfather. For sons, this relationship was significant in the first two years of marriage but not in the later stages. [p. 43]

She interpreted these findings as indicating that among daughters, who tend to be closer to their divorced mothers than sons, the remarriage is particularly threatening.

However, in those families where the custodial mother's remarriage took place when the children were 9 years old or older, Hetherington found a more positive pattern of outcomes for both boys and girls. In these families a satisfying marital relationship was associated with better adjustment among girls, and in these families also boys were less likely to display acting out behaviors.

Hetherington (1993) interpreted these findings from the perspective of adolescent Oedipus/Electra conflicts:

> At this time, marked physical changes are occurring in children, and they are becoming sensitive to issues of intimate relationships and sexuality. Many nondivorced fathers are disconcerted by their adolescent daughters' burgeoning sexuality (Hill, Holmbeck, Marlow, Green, and Lynch 1985) and are concerned about the proper expression of physical affection at this time. Concerns about affection and sexuality may be more severe in the case of stepfa-

thers and stepdaughters. A close marital relationship may be seen by adolescent daughters and their parents as a buffer against the threat of inappropriate intimacy between stepfathers and stepdaughters. [p. 44]

Christensen and Rettig (1995) studied the relationship between remarriage and indicators of postdivorce coparenting, satisfaction with parenting, and involvement in children's activities. Their sample consisted of 372 women and 277 men from ten counties in Minnesota. The participants were contacted three years following their divorces. All the participants had at least one dependent child in the custody of the respondent, the respondent's ex-spouse, or in a joint or split custody arrangement. Of the women in the study, 106 had remarried during the three years since the divorce (28.5 percent). Of the men, 106 had also remarried (38.3 percent).

The measures of coparenting following divorce were four scales developed in Ahrons' Binuclear Family Research Project (Ahrons and Wallisch 1987): (1) the Coparental Interaction Scale (nine items) measured how often the respondents shared child-rearing activities with their former spouse, such as making major decisions or discussing the children's problems; (2) the Parenting Support Scale (six items) asked respondents how much they helped, supported, or received help or support from their former spouse with respect to parenting activities; (3) the Parenting Conflict Scale (three items) asked respondents how often they argued or disagreed with their former spouse about child rearing; (4) the Parental Attribution Scale (two items) assessed the degree to which the respondents felt that their former spouse was a good and caring parent.

Parental satisfaction was also measured by items developed in the Binuclear Family Research Project. The Parental Satisfaction scale consisted of three items concerned with the amount of satisfaction the respondents felt regarding (1) their custody arrangement, (2) the amount of time they spent with children, and (3) their parenting relationship with their former spouse.

The Involvement with Children Scale (Ahrons and Wallisch 1987) is a seventeen-item scale that measures the extent to which respondents participate in their children's activities.

These scales were examined in a series of two-way analyses of variance (ANOVAs) in which the independent variables were respondent gender and respondent marital status. These ANOVAs yielded significant effects due to marital status on all the variables except involvement in the children's activities. The authors reported that "Single parents, as compared with remarried parents, reported higher levels of coparental interaction, $F(2,649) = 10.12$, $p < .01$; parenting support, $F(2,649) = 9.36$, $p < .01$; attitudes toward former spouse as a parent, $F(2,649) = 6.53$, $p < .05$; and parenting satisfaction, $F(2,649) = 6.63$, $p < .05$, and lower levels of parenting conflict, $F(2,649) = 4.37$, $p < .05$" (p. 80).

Significant gender by marital status interactions were obtained on the Parenting Satisfaction Scale and the Parental Involvement in Children's Activities Scale. Remarried men reported lower levels of parenting satisfaction than single men, whereas remarried women did not differ significantly from single women on this measure. Remarried women reported higher levels of involvement in children's activities than single women, whereas remarried and single men did not differ significantly on this measure.

These findings clearly suggest that remarriage tends to have negative effects. This appears to be the case both for mothers, who typically have custody of the children, and for fathers, who typically do not. Remarriage appears to have had a favorable impact only with respect to women's involvement in their children's activities. However, Christensen and Rettig (1995) pointed out that the generally negative effects of remarriage are moderated by many other variables, including visitation, custody, and household income. Thus remarriage cannot be construed as invariably producing negative outcomes.

It is important to consider factors that promote positive outcomes for children of divorce who are living in stepfamily situations. Hetherington (1993) provided some valuable observations regarding the manner in which stepfathers can facilitate the development of good relationships with their stepchildren. These conclusions are described in the following section of this chapter, which is concerned with factors that predict children's successful adaptation to the remarriage of their custodial mothers.

CORRELATES OF CHILDREN'S SATISFACTORY ADJUSTMENT TO REMARRIAGE OF THEIR CUSTODIAL MOTHER

Hetherington (1993) noted that regardless of the age of the child when the mother remarries, stepfathers tend initially not to feel close to their stepchildren or to believe that they have good rapport with them. Furthermore, stepfathers initially make few attempts to monitor or control the behavior of their stepchildren. Most often stepfathers attempt to build a good relationship with their stepchildren by "self-disclosing and searching for common interests and experiences in spite of the aversive behavior they encountered from their stepchildren" (p. 45). In remarriages that occur prior to adolescence, stepfathers' efforts to control the behavior of stepsons will tend to increase over time. However, this same trend does not characterize the stepfathers' developing relationships with preadolescent stepdaughters.

In remarriages that occur during early adolescence, Hetherington (1993) found that "little adaptation to remarriage occurred in either stepfathers or stepchildren" (p. 45). She concluded that disengaged parenting was characteristic of stepfathers with stepchildren in early adolescence, and, further, that both stepsons and stepdaughters in this age group tended to remain cool and unresponsive to their stepfathers.

Based on her discussions with stepfamilies, Hetherington (1993) concluded that:

> With remarriages that occurred when children were preadolescents, the best method of gaining children's acceptance of the stepfather seemed to be one in which the stepfather attempted to build a close relationship with the child, supported the mother's discipline, but initially did not attempt to independently control or discipline the child; and in which the stepfather only gradually became more authoritative. [p. 46]

However, the best plan of action for the stepfather was quite different when the remarriage occurred during adolescence:

> In contrast, in adolescence, immediate authoritative parenting by the stepfather led to more positive outcomes for the children. Furthermore, although stepfather–stepchild relationships were often difficult, even when a remarriage had occurred in early adolescence, a close relationship with an authoritative stepfather eventually was able to buffer the effects of a hostile or neglecting mother on the development of externalizing behavior in adolescents. [p. 46]

Echoing the conclusion of the previous chapter regarding the mediating effect of authoritative parenting on the relationship between the adjustment of the custodial parent and the psychosocial adjustment of children, Hetherington (1993) concluded that in all family types, for children of all ages, authoritative parenting on the part of the mother, the father, and the stepfather were all related to less externalizing behavior, fewer symptoms of internalizing pathology, and greater academic and social competence in children. Hetherington defined authoritative parenting as characterized by warmth, low coerciveness, high monitoring, firm but responsive control, and expectations for mature and responsible behavior on the part of the child.

Skopin et al. (1993) sought to identify factors that influence the quality of the stepfather–adolescent relationship in a sample of fifty middle- to upper-middle-class stepfather families. The predictors examined in the study included the following dimensions: (1) the closeness of the stepfather to his natural children was assessed by a single item with response options ranging from one, signifying "very close," to five, signifying "distant"; (2) the length of the courtship time between the stepfather and the natural mother was the stepfather's self-report of the number of years that the stepfather dated his current spouse before they married; (3) the amount of agreement between the mother and the stepfather regarding the appropriate way to raise the adolescent was measured by a single item with a five-point Likert-type response format that had response options ranging from "always agree" to "never agree"; (4) the adolescent's relationship with his or her noncustodial parent was measured by a single self-rating made by the adolescent (this item also had a five-point response scale, with response options ranging from "very close" to "distant"); (5) the gender of the adolescent; (6) the number of years that the adolescent lived in a single-parent mother-custody home was measured by the adolescent's self-report of the number of years; (7) the stepfather's satisfaction in the remarriage was assessed by the Marital-Comparison Index (MCI) (Sabatelli 1984), a thirty-six-item questionnaire designed to measure the extent to which the respondent's marital expectations have been met in his or her current marriage. Sabatelli reported an internal consistency reliability of .93 for this scale.

The dependent variable in this study was the quality of the relationship between the adolescent and the stepfather. To measure this variable, Skopin and her colleagues (1993) administered the Parent–Adolescent Communication Scale to both the adolescent and the stepfather. This twenty-item scale measures the positive aspects of parent–adolescent communication (ten items) and the negative aspects of the communication (ten items). Each item has a five-point Likert-type response format with response options ranging from "strongly disagree" to "strongly agree." The responses of the stepfather and the stepchild are summed separately across the items measuring positive and negative aspects of communication to produce a total score for relationship quality as perceived by each respondent that has a theoretical range of twenty to 100. Olson (1980) reported alpha coefficients of .82 for the scale when completed by both parents and adolescents. Skopin and her colleagues did not report alpha coefficients for the scale based on her study sample, nor did she report the correlation between the scores of parents and those of children.

Zero-order correlations indicated that the stepfather's perception of the quality of the stepparent–stepchild relationship was correlated significantly with both the frequency of agreement between the mother and the stepfather regarding how to raise the adolescent ($r = .42, p < .001$) and the stepfather's satisfaction with the marriage ($r = .30, p < .01$). The adolescent's perception of the quality of the relationship was related significantly with the frequency of agreement between the mother and the stepfather ($r = .32, p < .01$), but not with the stepfather's satisfaction with the marriage. Skopin and associates (1993) noted that the findings obtained with respect to the degree of agreement between the mother and stepfather confirmed findings reported previously by Wallerstein and Kelly (1980). Skopin and her associates (1993) interpreted these findings in the light of Bohannon's (Bohannon and Yahraes 1979) assertion that disagreements regarding the raising of children tend to align the children with their mother against the stepfather, a situation that can jeopardize the stability of the remarriage. Based on a review of clinical studies of stepfamily functioning, Mowatt (1972) had concluded similarly that disagreements over the disciplining and punishment of the children were common problems in stepfamilies.

SUMMARY

To summarize the literature on the effects of the remarriage of the custodial parent on the psychosocial adjustment of children and adolescents from divorced families, one can certainly conclude that the relationship is a complex one mediated by a number of factors, including the gender and age of the child, the length of time since the remarriage, and aspects of the relationship between the mother and the stepfather. The weight of the evidence suggests that the effects of remarriage are more likely to be negative than positive, at least in the short term and especially for girls, adolescents, and specifically adolescent girls. However, the magnitude of the negative effects does not tend to be great. Also, there is great variability among stepfamilies in terms of both family process variables and children's psychosocial adjustment. Poor outcomes are certainly not inevitable, and the research provides stepfathers with some indications of how to approach relationships with stepchildren so as to maximize the chances of successful adaptation.

6

ROLE OF THE NONCUSTODIAL PARENT

THE LITERATURE RELEVANT to the relationship between children's postdivorce adjustment and the nature of their postdivorce contact with their noncustodial parent is contradictory. Many of the early studies of this relationship concluded that the frequency and regularity of contact between the noncustodial parent and the child(ren) is a critical determinant of postdivorce adjustment. These studies typically explained this relationship in terms of the father-absence hypothesis, which states simply that children, especially boys, need their fathers to be present in their lives in order to develop in a healthy manner.

However, some of the later studies have reported either no relationship between postdivorce adjustment and the frequency or regularity of contact with the noncustodial parent or even a negative relationship, suggesting that greater contact with noncustodial fathers actually predicts poor adjustment among children. Finally, the most recent studies suggest that it is not so much the frequency of contact that predicts adjustment, but rather the quality of the relationship with the noncustodial parent. In this chapter studies reflecting each of these themes are reviewed.

FATHER-ABSENCE HYPOTHESIS

Kelly (1988a) noted that the primary negative aspect of divorce reported by children in previous studies of psychosocial adjustment following the dissolution of a marriage was the loss of contact with the noncustodial parent, typically the father (Hetherington et al. 1982,

Wallerstein and Kelly 1980, Warshak and Santrock 1983). According to Kelly, "The traditional visiting pattern of every other weekend, most often a maximum of four overnights spent with the father per month, created intense dissatisfaction among children, and especially among young boys" (p. 127). Wallerstein and Kelly observed that youngsters in mother-custody families tended to express profound feelings of deprivation and loss surrounding the loss of contact with their fathers. Wallerstein and Kelly observed that school-age boys in this situation frequently displayed the symptoms of reactive depression.

Amato (1987), who interviewed children in mother-custody families, reported that these children experience less control, less support, and less punishment from their fathers than do children in intact families. Nastasi (1988) reported that children in mother-custody families tend to develop a negative image of the father–child relationship as time goes on following the divorce. Kelly (1988a) described this pattern as the "growing peripherality and loss of support of the father after divorce" (p. 127). She also pointed out that these perceptions on the part of children are mirrored in the distress reported by fathers, who typically recognize that they have become substantially less important in the lives of their children following the divorce. Several studies have indicated that this diminution in the importance of the role of the father is a consequence of their status as visitors rather than regular participants in the lives of their children (Hetherington et al. 1976, Jacobs 1986, Wallerstein and Kelly 1980).

Kalter et al. (1989) suggested that the complete or relative absence of the father has been linked to the adjustment difficulties that may be experienced by children following divorce. The father-absence hypothesis has been used primarily to describe the difficulties experienced by boys:

> [B]oys need a regular, ongoing, positive relationship with their father in order to develop a valued sense of masculinity, internalize controls over behavior, achieve appropriate development of conscience, and perform up to their abilities academically. . . .Failures in these developmental accomplishments are seen as being in large measure responsible for aggressive acting out behavior problems, poor academic work, and social isolation from peers. [p. 606]

More recently, several investigators have argued that the absence of the father may have a significant negative impact on the psychosocial adjustment of female as well as male children (Kalter 1984, Kalter et al. 1985, Wallerstein 1985).

Based on her review of the literature, Kelly (1988a) concluded, "Predictable and frequent contact with the noncustodial parent has been repeatedly demonstrated to be associated with better adjustment unless the father is very poorly adjusted or extremely immature. This is particularly true for boys" (p. 127). Studies supporting this conclusion were reported by Hess and Camera (1979), Wallerstein and Kelly (1980), Hetherington and colleagues (1982), and Warshak (1986).

Isaacs (1986) reported that the regularity of paternal visits was a more significant predictor of children's adjustment than the frequency of these visits. However, a number of studies have indicated that the frequency of visits of noncustodial fathers is associated significantly with a wide range of psychosocial outcomes, including academic achievement measured by scores on standardized achievement tests, self-esteem, depression, and anger (Guidubaldi and Perry 1985, Shook and Jurich 1992, Wallerstein and Kelly 1980).

It has also been suggested that the noncustodial father remains an important role model for children following divorce. Thus Nastasi (1988) reported that the educational level of noncustodial fathers was related significantly to children's academic and behavioral adjustment following divorce, although the educational level of custodial mothers was not.

However, the studies reviewed by Kelly (1988a) that led her to conclude that regular and frequent paternal visitation is an important predictor of children's adjustment all share a methodological limitation that calls into question the notion that it is visitation specifically that accounts for differences in postdivorce adjustment. None of these studies accounted adequately for the possible mediating effect of parental conflict on the relationship between visitation and adjustment.

It appears axiomatic that families in which the divorced mother and father have a reasonable coparenting relationship that is not marked by extreme conflict would tend to be characterized by more regular and more frequent paternal visitation. To the extent that visitation involves conflict with the custodial mother, the noncustodial father may be reluctant to visit. Given the clear relationship indicated in the literature between parental conflict and children's postdivorce adjustment (see Chapter 2), it could be that the relationships observed between visitation and children's adjustment were in fact a function of the mediating effect of parental conflict.

MEDIATING EFFECT OF PARENTAL CONFLICT

The idea that interparental conflict mediates the relationship between children's postdivorce adjustment and contact with their noncustodial parents is supported by Guidubaldi and Perry (1985). They reported that the relationship between the frequency of visitation of the noncustodial parent and the postdivorce adjustment of children was particularly strong when the custodial mother approved of the father's continued contact with the child and viewed the relationship between the father and the child in positive terms.

The mediating effect of parental conflict is further supported by the results of a longitudinal study of noncustodial parents reported by Braver and colleagues (1993). These investigators developed a "social exchange" model for predicting the postdivorce contact between noncustodial fathers and their children, based on the theoretical work of Thibaut and Kelly (1959) and Blau (1964). Social exchange theory holds that people implicitly compute the estimated psychological profit of any potential or actual relationship when deciding whether to enter into or continue that relationship. This theory had already been applied to the general area of divorce in order to predict a spouse's decision to remain in a marital relationship or seek divorce (Levinger 1979, Nye 1979).

Braver and his associates (1993) reasoned that the social exchange perspective was appropriate for predicting the behavior of noncustodial parents following divorce, because "whether to continue the relationship with the child and maintain the parent–child dyad becomes an open question on the decision to divorce. After separation, the noncustodial parent must decide the extent of involvement with the child, in terms of the frequency and quality of the visiting relationship and the level of the fulfillment of the child support obligation" (p. 11). Braver and associates assumed that the noncustodial parent would decide whether or not to continue the relationship on the basis of the anticipated psychological rewards of the relationship versus the perceived costs of the relationship.

Based on the earlier work of Levinger (1979), Braver and his colleagues (1993) identified three different categories of rewards and costs: (1) affectional or interpersonal, (2) material or tangible, and (3) symbolic or moral. Rewards falling into the first category would include "the enjoyment that the noncustodial parent experiences while visiting and the social approval obtained from significant others for being involved" (p. 11). With respect to interpersonal costs, they identified conflict with the ex-spouse, conflict with the child or expressions of anger on the part of the child, and stress derived from third parties, such as the objections of a new spouse or stepchildren. The material or tangible domain contained primarily costs, including economic privations and competing demands on the noncustodial parent's time. Within the symbolic or moral domain, rewards of continued contact include the noncustodial parent's need to remain committed to the parental role, the positive feedback that the noncustodial parent may receive from friends and relatives for his efforts to continue the relationship, and the possible need to assuage feelings of guilt regarding the possible effects of divorce on the child. Costs of remaining committed were conceptualized primarily with respect to regularity of compliance with child support obligations. A noncustodial parent who feels that these arrangements are unfair, or who feels that the child support money is not being used for the benefit of the child, may suffer psychological stress as a result of continuing to adhere to the arrangements.

Braver and his associates (1993) interviewed one or both parents of 378 divorced families. The investigators did not specify the gender breakdown of the noncustodial parents in the sample. As they explained, "Because our emphasis was on the noncustodial parent, an interview with him or her generally needed to be secured before we attempted an interview with the matched custodial parent. Accordingly, our sample has somewhat more fathers ($n = 340$) than mothers ($n = 271$)" (p. 12). Although one cannot determine the exact number of noncustodial fathers and mothers included in the study on the basis of this information, it is clear that there were more noncustodial fathers than mothers. The failure to report the breakdown between noncustodial fathers and mothers is a serious limitation of the study, since one cannot be certain of the population to which the results can be generalized. If, as one might suspect, the noncustodial respondents were heavily weighted toward fathers, then the results might apply to fathers only. On the other hand, if (1) there were a large number of noncustodial mothers in the sample and (2) the relationships between the predictors and the criterion measures differed substantially for noncustodial fathers and noncustodial mothers, then the results reported might not be generalizable to either group. That is, the presence of a number of noncustodial mothers in the sample might distort the relationships reported for fathers. Nevertheless, because the findings were so intriguing, they are reported here with the caveat that the study should be replicated with the results reported separately for adequate samples of noncustodial fathers and noncustodial mothers.

Braver and associates (1993) measured the frequency of visitation of the noncustodial parent by means of six-item self-report measures completed by both the noncustodial parent and the custodial parent, assuming that both members of the couple responded. The six items concerned (1) the number of face-to-face contact hours in the last month between the parent and the child, (2) the percentage of time the child spent with the noncustodial parent, (3) the number of visits in the last month between the noncustodial parent and the child, (4) the number of days in the last month that the child spent with the noncustodial parent, (5) the number of times that the child spent the night at the home of the noncustodial parent, and (6) the longest number of days that the noncustodial parent went without seeing the child. The latter item was reverse-coded. For each responding parent, these items were standardized and summed to obtain a scale score representing the frequency of the noncustodial parent's visitation as perceived by that parent. Braver and his colleagues reported that these scale scores had alpha coefficients exceeding .85 for both the custodial and noncustodial parent's reports at each of the three data collection intervals employed in the study. The authors did not, however, present the correlation between the scores on this measure derived from the reports of the noncustodial parents and the scores derived from the reports of the custodial parents. It would be interesting to see how well the divorced spouses agreed with respect to their perceptions of the frequency of visitation by the noncustodial parent.

The second criterion measure, that of payment of child support, was assessed by asking each parent what percentage of the child support obligation had been paid in the last year. Here again, the reports provided by the noncustodial and the custodial parents were analyzed separately, and the correlation between the reports from the two sources was not presented.

The reward and cost variables used as predictors were assessed similarly by scale scores derived separately from noncustodial and custodial parent responses. Braver and associates (1993) reported that all the scales had internal consistency reliabilities of .60 or above for each parent at each of the three data collection periods. On these scales as well, however, the correlations between the scores of the noncustodial and the custodial parents were not presented.

With respect to the responses of the noncustodial parents, the results of the study indicated that numerous indicators of affectional, material, and symbolic rewards and costs were related significantly to both frequency of visitation and compliance with child support obligations at various data collection periods. Specifically, some significant rewards associated with greater visitation and compliance with child support obligations were social encouragement, quality of communication between the noncustodial parent and the child, the level of enjoyment derived from the visits by both the noncustodial parent and the child, and the sense of obligation that the noncustodial parent felt toward the child. Among the significant costs associated with less frequent contact and compliance were conflict with the ex-spouse, visitation interference, time taken from other social demands, economic hardship, the perception that the visits were harmful to the child, disagreement with the child support decree, and perceived lack of control of the parameters of the parent–child relationship.

With respect to the responses of the custodial parent, there were far fewer significant findings, although there were some significant predictors in each of the areas of rewards and costs. It is not surprising that there would be fewer significant relationships with respect to the responses of the noncustodial parent, since the relationships concern the behavior of the noncustodial parent, who is clearly a more proximate source of data regarding his or her own perceptions and behaviors.

Based on these findings, Braver and his associates (1993) recommended that steps be taken to increase the rewards and decrease the costs associated with frequent visitation by the noncustodial parent. They suggested that clinicians working with custodial parents should employ an approach involving "educating the custodial parents regarding the beneficial effects to the child of the noncustodial parent's visitation, making strong attempts to reduce or resolve postdivorce interparental conflict, and countering the custodial parent's opposition to the noncustodial parent's maintaining a parenting role in the child's life" (p. 21). They suggested further that clinicians working with noncustodial parents should seek to affirm the perceptions of these parents that they can have a meaningful impact on the life of their child in spite of the obvious reduction of influence that accompanies the noncustodial role.

When one considers the mediating effect of interparental conflict on the relationship between visitation by the noncustodial parent and the postdivorce psychosocial adjustment of the child, it is not surprising that studies that have not taken this effect into account have yielded inconsistent and contradictory findings. The following section of this chapter considers several studies that contradict the conclusion of Kelly (1988a) regarding the importance of frequent and regular contact between children from divorced families and their noncustodial parents. In these studies it was reported that contact with the noncustodial parent is either unrelated to children's adjustment or related negatively to children's adjustment.

STUDIES SUGGESTING THE IRRELEVANCE OR POSSIBLE NEGATIVE IMPACT OF FREQUENT VISITATION BY THE NONCUSTODIAL PARENT

Thomas and Forehand (1993), in a review of the literature on noncustodial fathers, concluded: "Findings generally indicate that many fathers rarely or never see their children after divorce and that the effects of visitation on child functioning are negligible" (p. 127). The studies cited by Thomas and Forehand in support of this conclusion were reported by Hess and Camera (1979) and by Hodges and colleagues (1983). In addition, Thomas and Forehand referred to a study reported by Furstenberg and associates (1987) that indicated that frequent visitation may actually have a negative impact on children's postdivorce adjustment. They found that the frequency of visitation by noncustodial fathers was related directly to the number of problem behaviors exhibited by children in school and to the likelihood of the child being retained in grade. Other studies that have failed to find benefits derived from high levels of contact between children and noncustodial fathers have been reported by Clingempeel and Segal (1986), Jacobson (1987), Kurdek and associates (1981), and Leupnitz (1986).

Another study that indicates a possible negative relationship between frequent visitation by the noncustodial parent and the psychosocial adjustment of the child was reported by Shook and Jurich (1992). These investigators studied the relationship between the self-esteem of female and male college students from divorced families and the students' self-reports of the amount of time spent with the noncustodial parent. The sample consisted of eighty-one volunteer undergraduates between 18 and 23 who were enrolled in an introductory course in marriage and family relationships. All had experienced parental divorce during their childhood or adolescence. In addition, all the participants were from families in which the mother had been awarded primary child custody.

The Rosenberg Self-Esteem Inventory (RSEI) (Rosenberg 1965) was used to assess the students' self-esteem. The investigators measured contact with the noncustodial father by means of a single Likert-type item that asked the respondent to indicate the amount of time that the student resided with the noncustodial parent over the previous calendar year. The ten-point response format contained response options ranging from "none at all" (1) to "a great deal" (10). When responses to this question were tallied, it was discovered that the distribution of responses was positively skewed, with the majority of respondents (69.1 percent) endorsing the "none at all" option. This variable was therefore collapsed to a dichotomy, with fifty-six responding students categorized as having "no time spent with non-custodial parent" (p. 164) and twenty-five students categorized as having "some time spent with the noncustodial parent" (p. 164).

Shook and Jurich (1992) also assessed the students' feelings of closeness with the noncustodial parent. This dimension was measured by means of a seventeen-item scale developed by Villwock (1987). The scale contains questions such as, "How confident are you that your father would help you when you have a problem?" "How much do you trust your father?" "How close do you feel to your father?" (p. 164). The authors reported coefficient alphas for this scale of .97 for male respondents and .99 for female respondents.

The data were analyzed separately for female and male students. Multiple regression analysis indicated that among females the amount of time spent in the household of the noncustodial father during the last year was related negatively to self-esteem. That is, female students who had lived with their noncustodial fathers for some time during the past year had significantly lower self-esteem than female students who had not. In addition, girls' scores on the scale measuring perceived closeness to their fathers were unrelated to measured self-esteem. Among boys, neither contact with the noncustodial father during the last year nor self-reported closeness to the father was related significantly to self-esteem.

Of course, this study has several significant methodological limitations that limit the generalizability of the findings. First, one wonders whether contact with the noncustodial father during the previous year is an appropriate predictor for the psychosocial adjustment of students who are already in college. It would seem that contact over the entire period from the parental divorce to the time they entered college would be more relevant to the students' psychosocial adjustment. Furthermore, there was no control for the level of interparental conflict or the quality of the relationship between the custodial mother and the college student at the time of the study. One would suspect that one reason why a student would spend much time with a noncustodial father during the college years is that the student was experiencing some difficulty with the custodial mother. If this were the case, the nature of that difficulty could have contributed to low self-esteem on the part of the student. In that event, the time spent with the father would be the result of other factors rather than the cause of the student's low self-esteem.

Another study reporting no clear relationship between children's adjustment and continued contact between noncustodial parents and their children was reported by Maccoby and colleagues (1993). As part of a longitudinal study of the postdivorce roles of mothers and fathers in the lives of their children, Maccoby and her associates studied a subsample of 522 children between the ages of 10½ and 18 years. These children were from 365 families in which one parent had primary custody, but some time each year was spent in residence with the noncustodial parent. Seventy percent of these children were in mother-custody homes and stayed with the mother from eleven to fourteen nights out of a typical two-week period; nearly 20 percent were in father-custody homes and stayed with the father from eleven to fourteen nights out of a typical two-week period; approximately 10 percent were in de facto joint custody situations. These were defined as arrangements in which the child typically spent from four to ten nights of each two-week period with each parent, regardless of the formal custody arrangements.

The data for this study were obtained through telephone interviews and yielded some interesting findings. First, the children tended to report that they had close relationships with the noncustodial parent. Even in those few cases where visitation with the noncustodial parent was confined to a two-week period during the summer, the responding children tended to report that their relationships were close. Maccoby and her associates also reported that the frequency of visitation with the noncustodial parent did not impact on the relationship between the custodial parent and the child: "The level of monitoring by the primary parent, that parent's household organization, and the involvement of the parent in decision-making with the adolescent were not related to whether the children visited the nonresident parent frequently" (p. 33).

With respect to the relationship between frequency of visitation with the noncustodial parent and the child's postdivorce adjustment, Maccoby and her colleagues (1993) reported mixed results:

> At least minimal contact with the outside parent was necessary for maintaining a close relationship with that parent. Furthermore, when adolescents did have such a relationship, it did not seem to interfere with the child's relationship with the primary parent or with the quality of parenting maintained in the primary household. So far, then, we can say that for children to maintain a relationship with the nonresident parent does no harm. But is it positively beneficial? . . . the answer is yes for children living with their fathers; for them, continued contact with their mother was beneficial. For the much larger group of mother–resident children, we did not find evidence that sustaining a relationship with outside fathers made a difference in adolescent adjustment. [p. 36]

Maccoby and her associates (1993) warned that the zero-order correlations used to reach these conclusions "can conceal opposing trends" (p. 36); they suggested that for some mother–resident children, contact with their fathers very likely had positive effects. However, over the mother–resident group as a whole, they did not find an effect one way or the other.

On balance, it may be concluded that the research suggesting that contact with the noncustodial father may have no relationship or a negative relationship with children's psychosocial adjustment following divorce is at least as flawed methodologically as the research indicating that contact is beneficial. More carefully controlled studies are clearly required to arrive at definite conclusions in this area.

This point was brought home clearly by Amato (1993). He carried out a meta-analysis of the studies that have been reported between the frequency of contact of noncustodial fathers with their children. He identified sixteen studies that reported that the frequency of visitation was related positively to the psychosocial adjustment of children following divorce. However, he identified an equal number of studies that failed to support this hypothesis, seven of which suggested negative relationships between frequency of visitation and postdivorce adjustment. Thus the literature contains conflicting results with respect to the importance of visitation by noncustodial fathers and very little data with respect to the effect of visitation by noncustodial mothers. To sum up the literature with respect to noncustodial fathers, one can cite a substantial number of methodologically weak studies supporting the value of visitation and an equally large number of methodologically flawed studies suggesting that visitation by noncustodial fathers is irrelevant or harmful. With respect to noncustodial mothers, the available data suggest a possible positive relationship, but the limited number of such studies certainly precludes definite conclusions.

CHILD'S RELATIONSHIP WITH THE NONCUSTODIAL PARENT

Thomas and Forehand (1993) suggested that the conflicting findings reported in the literature with respect to the effect of frequency and regularity of visitation by the noncustodial parent may imply a need to "look beyond the amount of contact to the quality of the relationship the child has with the father" (p. 127). However, the literature appears to be contradictory with respect to this dimension of paternal involvement as well. For example, Hess and Camera (1979) reported that in their study the amount of contact between the noncustodial parent and his or her children was not related significantly to children's adjustment, but the quality of that relationship was a significant predictor of adjustment. Similarly, Koch and Lowery (1984) found that the quality of the father–child relationship explained significant variability in children's adjustment.

More recently, Simons and his associates (1994) reported that ratings of noncustodial fathers' parenting ability made by both the children and their custodial mothers were correlated significantly with the children's self-report measures of internalizing and externalizing behavior problems. This longitudinal study was considered in some detail in Chapter 4 of this volume, since another predictor of children's psychosocial adjustment examined by Simons and his associates was interparental conflict. In that chapter the reader will find descriptions of the sample of mother-custody families employed in Simons and colleagues' study, as well as descriptions of the measures used to assess children's psychosocial adjustment.

With respect to the assessment of the parenting behavior of the noncustodial fathers, Simons and his associates (1994) were limited to the reports of the child and the custodial mothers because they did not survey the noncustodial fathers themselves. They developed a fourteen-item scale to be used by the adolescents to rate their father's parenting behavior and an eight-item scale to be used by custodial mothers to rate their ex-spouse's parenting behavior. The items included in these scales were chosen carefully to reflect the reality of the role of the noncustodial parent:

> It is clear that effective parenting practices for nonresidential fathers will differ from those of fathers who live in the home. It would be difficult, for example, for fathers living outside of the home to monitor curfews or enforce punishments such as grounding. Indeed, noncustodial fathers who attempted to engage in such activities might be perceived as intrusive and the consequence might be increased conflict with the children and former spouse. Many nonresidential parents are, however, in a position to monitor their children's school performance and friendship choices, to stress the importance of certain behavior standards, to enforce rules in a fair and consistent fashion, and to support the parenting efforts of the custodial parent. [p. 363]

Therefore Simons and his associates (1994) included items in these scales that they felt reflected actions that the fathers could continue to perform, even though they no longer lived in the same residence as the child.

The questions included in the scale completed by the children were the following:

1. How often does your dad talk with you about what is going on in your life?
2. When your dad tells you to stop doing something and you don't stop, how often does he punish you?
3. How often does your dad punish you for something at one time and then at other times not punish you for the same thing? (reverse coded).
4. When your dad is punishing you, how much does the kind of punishment depend on his mood?
5. How often does your dad disagree with your mom about how or when to punish you? (reverse coded)
6. How often do the same problems seem to come up again and again with your dad and never seem to get resolved? (reverse coded)
7. When you and your dad have a problem, how often can the two of you figure out how to deal with it?

8. How often do you talk to your dad about things that bother you?
9. How often does your dad ask what you think before deciding on family matters that involve you?
10. How often does your dad give you reasons for his decisions?
11. How often does your dad ask you what you think before making a decision that involves you?
12. When you don't understand why your dad makes a rule for you to follow, how often does he explain the reason?
13. How often does your dad discipline you by reasoning, explaining, or talking to you?
14. When you do something your dad likes or approves of, how often does he let you know he is pleased about it? [p. 362]

The adolescents responded to each of these questions on five-point Likert-type scales with response options ranging from "strongly disagree" to "strongly agree."

The eight items on the scale employing the mother's reports of the father's parenting behavior were the following:

1. Knows your children's teachers and how well they are doing in school.
2. Explains to your children the reasons for the rules he expects them to follow.
3. Encourages your children to be responsible in the things they do.
4. Sometimes punishes your children for something and other times doesn't punish them for the same thing (reverse coded).
5. Is clear about what he expects your children to do.
6. Agrees with you about how the children should be raised.
7. Lets your children do things they shouldn't do (reverse coded).
8. Explains to your children the reasons for the rules he expects them to follow. [p. 362]

Simons and associates (1994) reported that the children's report scale had an internal consistency reliability coefficient of alpha = .90 for each of the two data collection intervals during which the children completed the scale (at the start of the study and one year later). The mother report scale was administered only once, at the start of the study. The reliability of the scale was .86. Simons and his colleagues indicated that they planned to combine the scores derived from the adolescent's and the custodial mother's ratings to reduce possible reporting biases on the part of each informant. They reasoned as follows:

Divorced women usually harbor feelings of anger, frustration, and resentment regarding their former husbands. Similarly, children of divorce often possess strong feelings about their nonresidential father, although these emotions may be either positive or negative. One would expect these emotional states to distort the objectivity of the mother and adolescent reports of the father's parenting process. [p. 363]

These considerations would appear to justify the decision to combine the scores on the two scales. This could not be done, however, because the scores derived from the two sources were not even moderately correlated. The correlation between the maternal report at the first data collection interval and the adolescent's report at the same time was only .29 for girls and only .01 for boys. For this reason the scales had to be analyzed separately. This finding underscores the importance of considering the source of ratings for both independent and dependent variables in research on the impact of divorce on children's adjustment.

The results were reported separately for girls and for boys. Among girls, the adolescents' reports of the father's parenting behavior at the first data collection interval were related positively to both externalizing behavior problems at time one ($r = .38$, $p < .01$) and internalizing behavior problems at time one ($r = .26$, $p < .05$). In addition, girls' reports of their father's parenting behavior at time one were related positively to girls' externalizing behavior problems at time two ($r = .42$, $p < .01$). Thus girls who perceived their father's parenting behavior positively at the first data collection period actually tended to have greater psychosocial adjustment problems than girls who perceived their father's parenting behavior more negatively. This pattern was reversed when the adolescents' ratings of paternal parenting behavior were obtained a year later at the second data collection. Adolescent girls' ratings of their father's parenting at time two were correlated negatively with externalizing behavior problems at both time two ($r = -.31$, $p < .05$) and a year later at time three ($r = -.32$, $p < .05$).

With respect to boys, the relationships observed were consistently negative. Boys' perceptions of their father's parenting assessed at time one were related negatively, but not significantly, to both externalizing behavior problems and internalizing pathology measured at time one and time two. Boys' perceptions of their father's parenting assessed at time two were also related negatively to both externalizing and internalizing behavior problems at time two and time three. Three of these four correlations were significant: the correlation between perceived paternal parenting behavior at time two and externalizing behavior problems at time two ($r = -.30$, $p < .05$); the correlation between perceived paternal parenting at time two and externalizing behavior problems at time three ($r = -.35$, $p < .01$); and the correlation between perceived paternal parenting at time two and internalizing behavior problems at time two.

In addition, the reports of the boys' custodial mothers at time one regarding the noncustodial father's parenting behavior were related negatively to (1) the boy's externalizing problems at time one ($r = -.29$, $p < .05$); (2) the boy's externalizing problems at time two ($r = -.30$, $p < .05$); and (3) the boy's internalizing problems at time two ($r = -.30$, $p < .05$).

Simons and his colleagues (1994) interpreted these findings with appropriate caution:

> While overall the findings indicate that involvement by nonresidential fathers diminishes an adolescent's involvement in conduct problems, this conclusion is tempered by the fact that the results varied depending on the reporter used to assess father's parenting.... The finding that the effect of father's parenting varied depending on the reporter used to assess father's parenting is disconcerting and precludes drawing firm conclusions from the analyses concerning the effects of paternal involvement. However, at a minimum, the fact that in four of six tests father's involvement in the role of parent had an effect on conduct problems suggests that it would be fruitful for future studies to focus on the parental behaviors of nonresidential parents rather than merely considering frequency of contact or warmth of the parent–child relationship. [pp. 371–372]

It would appear that the effect of continued contact between noncustodial fathers and their children is in fact mediated by variables other than the level of conflict between the divorced spouses. Future studies must focus not only on the frequency and regularity of contact between noncustodial fathers and their children, but also on the degree to which their father–child relationship is characterized by warmth, affection, and appropriate parenting behaviors. In addition, future studies of this subject must employ multiple rating sources for both the father–child relationship variables and the criterion measures of children's psychosocial adjustment. Such studies should examine these factors separately for female and male children. Similar research is also required to assess the impact of contact with noncustodial mothers on their children.

7

CHILD'S AGE AT THE TIME OF THE DIVORCE

A SUBSTANTIAL BODY of theoretical literature concerns the relationship between the age of a child at the time of parental divorce and the subsequent psychosocial adjustment of the child (Gardner 1976, Hodges and Bloom 1984, Kalter and Rembar 1981, Runyon and Jackson 1988). There is also a substantial body of empirical literature on the relationship between the child's age at the time of divorce and the psychosocial adjustment of the child, both immediately after the divorce and at various points in the lifespan of the child.

These empirical studies have yielded inconsistent results. Some studies have suggested that parental divorce early in the lifespan of the child may be devastating in the period immediately after the separation, but ultimately the children of such divorces are characterized by better long-term psychosocial adjustment than children whose parents divorced when the child was older (Ellis and Russell 1992, Grant et al. 1993, Hetherington et al. 1978). Some other studies suggest exactly the opposite, i.e., that older children are better able to understand divorce and therefore react more positively following this event (Allison and Furstenberg 1989, Borduin and Henggeler 1987, Emery 1988, Zill et al. 1993). Still another group of studies indicate that there may be no overall outcome differences due to the child's age at the time of the divorce, but there may be (1) differences within specific groups of female and male children in different current age groups (Kalter and Rembar 1981) and (2) differences in the specific types of psychosocial outcomes that tend to be affected by divorces occurring at different times in the life of the child (Hodges and Bloom 1984). There is also a small body of literature that deals with the impact of divorces that occur after the child has reached college age or gone off to college (Farber 1980, Kutner 1988, Swartzman-Schatman and Schinke 1993).

This entire body of literature is reviewed below.

RELATIONSHIP BETWEEN CHILD'S AGE AT THE TIME OF PARENTAL DIVORCE AND THE SHORT- AND LONG-TERM PSYCHOSOCIAL ADJUSTMENT OF CHILD

Based on their review of the literature, Kalter and Rembar (1981) concluded that three distinct theories have been used to explain the relationship between the child's age at the time of parental divorce and the child's short- and long-term psychosocial adjustment. The most frequently referred to of these theories is the *critical stage theory*, which suggests that the effects of divorce on children vary as a function of the particular developmental challenges faced by the child at different stages in his or her development. The critical stage theory predicts that the worst possible time for a divorce to occur is when the child is in the oedipal stage. Gardner (1977) has summarized this theory as follows: "Some psychiatrists and psychologists believe that between the ages of three and five—during the so-called Oedipal period—divorce can be particularly devastating" (p. 3).

A second theory is the *cumulative effect hypothesis*, which maintains that the impact of divorce is felt from the time the divorce occurs throughout the lifetime of the child. Thus the earlier the divorce occurs, the more profound its ultimate effects will be. This is the theory favored by Gardner himself: "Generally, I believe that the younger the child the more affected he or she will be by the loss of a parent" (1977, p. 3).

The third theory identified by Kalter and Rembar (1981) is the *Recency Theory*, which holds that parental divorce is traumatic at any time in the life of the child, but the effects of this trauma are relatively transient, such that the child is likely to recover completely within a year or two. This position was expressed by Wallerstein and Kelly (1974), who concluded that "most of the young people whom we studied were able within a year following parental separation to take up their individual agendas and proceed toward adulthood at a more measured pace" (p. 503).

It should be noted that these theories are not mutually exclusive. Furthermore, the critical stage theory and the cumulative effect hypothesis both predict that divorces that occur relatively early in the life of the child should be associated with more negative outcomes. Two of the most complete theoretical discussions of the effects of divorce for children of different ages have been provided by Hodges and Bloom (1984) and Runyon and Jackson (1988). These two discussions share the same framework for their analysis in that they each describe the effects of divorce for children in three different age ranges: preschool (up to 6 years old), latency (6 to 12 years), and adolescence (13 to 18 years). The following sections consider these discussions of the effects of divorce for children in these three age groups.

Preschool Children

Psychoanalytic theory suggests that the impact of divorce is particularly severe on preschool children (Gardner 1976, Longfellow 1979). Toomin (1974) suggested that children whose fathers left the home during the period when the child was between 18 and 36 months were likely to suffer disruptions in the process of separation and individuation. It has also been suggested that for boys the departure of one's father during the first five years of life will interfere with the adoption of appropriate sex roles (Neubauer 1960). Other authors have concluded that the departure of one's father during the oedipal period (between the ages of 3 and 6) may lead to powerful feelings of guilt (Rohrlich et al. 1977, Toomin 1974).

Runyon and Jackson (1988) have described the impact of parental divorce on the preschool child in some detail. They suggested that a child in this age range will be acutely aware of the departure of one parent, typically the father, and consequently the child will fear the possibility of abandonment by the other parent. This fear of abandonment may be manifested in extreme anxiety when the child is temporarily separated from the custodial parent. These children tend to cling to their mothers, and they may suddenly decide that they do not want to go to nursery school, even if they were perfectly happy to go there prior to the separation of the parents. Wallerstein and Kelly (1975) noted that these young children often have difficulty with the separation associated with bedtime. They are afraid to be left alone, and they often experience terrifying nightmares.

McDermott (1968) observed that preschool children whose parents separate may experience disruptions in their normal ability to resolve inner conflicts through play and fantasy. They may cease to engage in play behavior altogether. They may also demonstrate marked behavioral changes in their interactions at nursery school. Runyon and Jackson (1988) described these children as suddenly becoming restless, noisy, and irritable.

Because young children are not able to comprehend fully the issues between their parents that may have precipitated the separation, they may blame themselves for the divorce. They may also assume that the departure of one parent is a sign that they are not worth loving. This can be expected to have a major impact on the subsequent development of their self-esteem. Many young children refuse to accept the reality of the divorce altogether, preferring instead to construct elaborate fantasies of reconciliation. In extreme cases young children may pretend to themselves and their friends that their father is off on a trip from which he will soon return. When a young child develops such a fantasy of reconciliation, it may be very difficult to convince him or her that the divorce is final.

Runyon and Jackson (1988) suggested that the loss of one's father is significant dynamically for preschool children of both sexes, although the dynamic processes are different for girls and boys. Preschool girls typically identify with their mothers and romanticize their fathers. When father departs, young girls may unconsciously assume that he left because their mother was not good enough. This attitude may inhibit the young girl's normal identification with mother, which in turn may disrupt normal acquisition of appropriate sex roles. For boys in this age range, the primary issue involved in the departure of the father is the oedipal conflict. Since the young boy viewed himself as the father's rival for the affection of his mother, the boy may interpret the departure of the father as the result of the jealous and aggressive fantasies he may have had regarding his father. He may experience extreme guilt under such circumstances. Neubauer (1960) suggested that such feelings could lead a young boy to reject normal masculine aggression as dangerous and unacceptable. This could lead to significant anxiety and confusion regarding masculine identification.

Hodges and Bloom (1984) reviewed and summarized some of the empirical studies relevant to the effect of parental divorce on preschool children. They concluded that:

> Preschool children have been found to respond to marital separation with regression, anxiety, tantrums, fantasies of reconciliation, anger, aggression, problems in basic trust, and, for the one to three year age group, loss of recently acquired perceptual-motor skills

(... Klatskin 1972, Santrock 1975, ... Wallerstein and Kelly 1975, 1976). [p. 34]

Another study supporting the conclusions of Runyon and Jackson (1988) regarding the effect of parental divorce on preschool children was reported by Hetherington (1979a), who observed that young preschool children were less able than latency-aged or adolescent children to evaluate their own role in the parental separation, and more likely to perceive the separation as abandonment.

However, the reactions of preschoolers described above are neither uniform nor inevitable. Hodges and colleagues (1979) compared groups of preschoolers from intact and divorced families. When all the families in each of these two groups were compared on psychosocial adjustment, no significant differences were found. However, several important mediating variables were discovered. Among preschoolers from families with relatively young parents, the differences in adjustment anticipated between divorced and intact families were found to be significant. In addition, significant differences in adjustment were found between preschoolers from divorced and intact families among subsets of families who were geographically mobile and families who were of relatively low socioeconomic status.

Latency-Aged Children

Hodges and Bloom (1984) suggested that parental divorce that occurs during the latency period is less likely to have a severe adverse impact on children's psychosocial development:

> From a theoretical point of view, latency age should have less impact on development than those during either the preschool or adolescent periods. Delayed oedipal resolution due to prior marital conflict is a predictable outcome. Academic achievement may be affected and the development of appropriate peer relations may be harmed. [p. 35]

Runyon and Jackson (1988) identified some of the same possible negative outcomes of divorce for latency-aged children, but their description of the reactions to divorce of children in this age range does not suggest that the effects of divorce are as minimal as Hodges and Bloom (1984) suggested.

Runyon and Jackson (1988) conceptualized the effects of divorce on latency-aged children in terms of Erikson's developmental stage typology. According to this developmental framework, early latency is the period during which the child enters school and develops a "work identification" (Erikson 1963). Children at this age typically begin to think of themselves as productive individuals. They are eager to learn and to establish relationships with their peers and in general with the world outside their family. Runyon and Jackson argued that:

> The trauma of divorce disrupts the child's ability to participate freely in the process of learning. A high level of anxiety in the child is expressed through restlessness, inability to concentrate, intrusive thoughts about divorce, and a drop in school performance. Some children may maintain their academic standards but get into difficulty with classmates because of their increased irritability. [p. 102]

Runyon and Jackson (1988) also suggested that children in early latency are particularly overwhelmed by the painful feelings associated with divorce. Children at this age are likely to blame the custodial parent for "kicking out" the other parent. However, they also noted that if "the parents are involved in a bitter, raging battle filled with accusations, the child may be enlisted to become aligned with one parent. Mothers, particularly, may enlist the child to reject the father" (p. 102). Runyon and Jackson argued that such conflict can be extremely stressful to children, who may be completely overwhelmed. Early-latency-aged children of divorce may display open expressions of the pain they are feeling in the form of frequent, uncontrollable periods of crying. Wallerstein and Kelly (1976, 1980) observed that children 5 to 8 years old often react to divorce with compulsive overeating, which they interpreted as a manifestation of the children's fear of going hungry.

Runyon and Jackson (1988) explained the reactions to parental divorce of children in the later stage of latency in terms of Kohlberg's (1972) theory of moral development. By age 8, children will have developed a set of rules defining good and bad behavior, and they will apply these rules in making judgments about the behavior of others. Therefore, parental divorce at this stage:

> produces moral outrage. The child thinks the parents are behaving immorally and irresponsibly and experiences intense anger to-

ward one or both parents. One child may respond with rigid defenses against impulses, assuming the dictatorial stance of an authoritarian. Another child may respond by releasing impulses that he or she normally constrains out of fear of punishment. Two manifestations of the loss of internal controls are the appearance of lying and petty stealing during the initial stress of divorce. The child may get into trouble with authority figures in a variety of settings, as well as with the law. [Runyon and Jackson 1988, p. 103]

Runyon and Jackson also suggested that a divorce that occurs during the later stage of latency may have a profound negative effect on the child's self-esteem, since a major component of self-concept at this time is the sense of belonging to a family. Children between 8 and 12 years old typically experience shame and embarrassment with respect to their parents' divorce, and they may be unable to share this distress with peers. Relationships with peers are especially important during this period of life, because these relationships enable children to "validate their own sense of well-being while identifying with the values and worth of their peers" (1988, p. 103). Children who are unable to share their feelings regarding the divorce with peers may isolate themselves. Such behavior will have the short-term effect of making these children sad and lonely, and the long-term effect of diminishing their sense of self-worth. Runyon and Jackson argued that children from divorced families who are in the later stages of latency have a particular need to be shown that they are loved.

Several empirical studies of clinical populations have provided support for Runyon and Jackson's (1988) description of the reactions to divorce of latency aged children. Kalter (1977) compared latency-aged children from divorced and intact families within the population of children being treated at the University of Michigan Division of Psychiatry Outpatient Clinic. He reported that boys between the ages of 7 and 11 displayed significantly greater aggression toward their peers than boys in the same age range from intact families. Among girls in the same age range, symptoms of anxiety and depression were more prevalent when the parents had divorced than when the parents were still married. Felner and colleagues (1975) also reported that latency-aged children from divorced families tended to display more acting-out and aggressive behavior than comparably aged children from intact families.

In their longitudinal study of children from divorced families, Kelly and Wallerstein (1976) reported that 7- and 8-year-olds typically displayed sadness, grieving, feelings of deprivation, fantasies of responsibility and reconciliation, anger, and conflicts of loyalty. These investigators noted that about half of the latency-aged children they studied showed decrements in school performance. When these children were assessed again a year later, half of the children displayed significant depression, and one-fourth were more distressed than they had been at the initial wave of data collection. Nine and 10-year-old children also tended to be anxious, fearful, and lonely. The 9- and 10-year-olds also appeared to have a shaken sense of identity, and displayed an inordinately large number of somatic symptoms.

Adolescents

Runyon and Jackson (1988) described adolescents at the time of their parents' divorce as:

> angry, upset, and sad. They express concern about their parents' values and are deeply distressed regarding their own futures as adults. Parents' values and judgments are evaluated by adolescents in terms of their own developing concepts and ideals. The process involves gradual devaluation of parents as primary sources of object relationships and opinion leadership. Given the duration of time to separate psychologically from parents, adolescents can view parents as individuals and establish a less dependent relationship with them. Divorce pre-empts the gradual differentiation and devaluation of parents, forcing the adolescent to form judgments prematurely about the parents, which can lead to unrealistic negation of them as role models. [p. 103]

Runyon and Jackson (1988) suggested that the tendency of adolescents from divorced families to make precipitous and premature judgments regarding their parents may lead them to doubt their own future ability to become happily married. This pessimistic outlook may retard the adolescent's development of object relationships outside the family, and it may lead to the development of unhealthy dependence on one parent. Alternatively, Runyon and Jackson maintain that the sudden loss of one's parents as role models may lead some adolescents to effect a premature independence. Such a stance may result in the loss of impulse control, manifested in alcohol and drug abuse, aggression, promiscuity, and truancy.

Runyon and Jackson (1988) expressed particular concern with respect to the developing sexual identity of the adolescent. They argued that adolescents do not typically think of their parents as sexual beings. Instead, they view their parents as "safe objects who do not threaten the adolescent's budding sense of sexuality" (p. 103). However, divorce thrusts upon adolescents the unwelcome knowledge that their parents are in fact sexual beings. This is particularly the case if an extramarital affair was a factor in the decision to divorce. Adolescents may respond to the stress generated by these realizations with extreme anxiety regarding their own sexual competence. They may withdraw from heterosexual relationships entirely, or they may become sexually active prematurely. Runyon and Jackson argued that premature sexual activity on the part of the adolescent is particularly likely if one or both of the parents has been promiscuous.

There is also empirical support for Runyon and Jackson's (1988) description of adolescents from divorced families. Fulton (1979) reported that boys who were adolescents at the time of their parents' divorce were significantly more likely than boys whose parents divorced when they were younger to become truant or to display academic or behavior problems. (This finding, of course, can be interpreted as an effect of adolescence itself, regardless of the possible effects of the divorce.) Kalter (1977) reported that adolescent boys from separated and divorced homes were more likely than those from intact families to display aggressive behavior and to have trouble with the police. Kalter also reported that adolescent girls from separated and divorced families were significantly more likely than those from intact families to manifest aggressive behavior, drug abuse, and promiscuity. Wallerstein and Kelly (1974) reported that the adolescents they studied from divorced families tended either to delay the process of resolving adolescent issues of separation and identity formation or to launch precipitously into a premature "pseudoadolesence" characterized by sexual and aggressive acting-out behavior.

These descriptions of the effects of divorce on preschool, latency-aged, and adolescent children of divorce appear to be theoretically sound, and there is ample empirical evidence for most of the conclusions stated by both Runyon and Jackson (1988) and Hodges and Bloom (1984). However, one is struck by the fact that the descriptions of the problems characterizing children in the three different age groups contain a number of common elements. For example, anger, aggression, disruptions in identity formation, diminished self-concept, and externalizing behavior problems are all included in the descriptions of the difficulties characterizing each of the groups. The lack of specificity in the problems encountered by children in the different groups suggests that psychodynamically based developmental-stage theories do not provide a complete explanation of the relationship between the child's age at the time of the divorce and subsequent psychosocial adjustment.

On the other hand, the basic prediction of the critical stage theory—that children whose parents divorce when the children are preschoolers will experience greater psychosocial adjustment difficulties than children whose parents divorce later in the child's life—is more frequently supported than contradicted in the empirical literature. The following three sections describe the major empirical studies that consider the issue of the effect of the child's age at the time of the divorce.

DIVORCES THAT OCCUR RELATIVELY EARLY IN THE LIFE OF THE CHILD HAVE BETTER OUTCOMES

Several relatively early studies suggested that, although children who are preschoolers at the time of their parents' divorce experience more severe disturbances than older children immediately following the divorce, children who are in latency or adolescence at the time of the divorce may experience greater difficulties later on in life (Hetherington et al. 1978, Kulka and Weingarten 1979, Wallerstein 1984). Unfortunately, these studies do not differentiate between the effects of divorce that might be predicted from the critical stage hypothesis and those that might be predicted from the recency hypothesis. If adjustment is assessed during adolescence, children whose parents divorced during adolescence may exhibit more serious adjustment disorders, either because divorce is truly more traumatic when it occurs in adolescence or because the length of time since the divorce is shorter for this group, affording them less time to recover from the trauma than the group whose parents divorced earlier.

Only two recent studies could be located to support the position that divorces early in the life of the child are less likely than divorces that occur when the child is older to result in maladjustment in later life (Ellis and Russell 1992, Grant et al. 1993). Ellis and Russell set out to compare "older adolescent age undergraduates" (p. 197) from divorced and intact families on dimensions of suicidality. The participants were

286 undergraduates at a southern university. They ranged in age from 17 to 25 years old, and the sample included 168 women and 118 men. More than two-thirds of the participants ($n = 190$, 66.9 percent) reported that their parents were still married, and 27.1 percent of the students ($n = 77$) reported that their parents were divorced. The authors did not indicate the status of the remaining nineteen students in the sample. (Perhaps they did not respond to the question regarding parental divorce.) Among the students whose parents had divorced, the age of the responding student at the time of the divorce ranged from less than 1 to 22 years old. The mean age at the time of parental divorce was 9.9 years.

Ellis and Russell (1992) administered the Expanded Reasons for Living Inventory (RFL) (Linehan et al. 1983) to these undergraduates. The RFL is a seventy-two-item inventory that measures beliefs and expectancies that constitute reasons for NOT committing suicide, should the respondent contemplate doing so. It measures seven dimensions of such beliefs and expectancies: survival and coping beliefs, responsibility to family, child concerns, fear of suicide, fear of social disapproval, moral objections, and responsibility to friends. The RFL subscales can also be summed to yield a total score for reasons for living. With respect to the reliability of the RFL, Linehan and colleagues (1983) reported internal consistency reliability coefficients for the seven subscales ranging from alpha = .72 to alpha = .89. With respect to validity, Linehan and his colleagues reported that the RFL significantly differentiated suicidal and nonsuicidal subjects in both clinical and nonclinical populations.

The primary analyses of the study were a set of 2 x 2 analyses of variance (ANOVAs) in which the independent variables were family status (intact versus divorced) and gender. These analyses yielded only one significant effect due to family status, a significant main effect on the responsibility to family subscale. The students from intact families had a higher mean on this subscale than the students from divorced families.

However, the authors also reported the results of a multiple regression analysis carried out on the students with divorced parents in which total scores on the RFL were regressed on demographic variables considered to have a possible impact on the students' reasons for living. These included current age, age at the time of the parents' divorce, gender, presence of a stepparent in the home, visits by the parent who left home, custodial parent's work status, birth order, and number of siblings. This multiple regression analysis indicated that the student's age at the time of the divorce was a significant predictor of the student's total RFL score. The nature of this relationship was such that younger children tended to have higher scores on the Reasons for Living Scale. Thus the study suggests better outcomes for students whose parents divorced earlier in their lives.

These findings should be treated with caution, however, as the study has several important methodological limitations. First, as was the case with the studies by Hetherington and colleagues (1978), Kulka and Weingarten (1979), and Wallerstein (1984), the significant effect of the student's age at the time of the divorce could reflect the relative recency of the event, as well as the specific stage in the student's life when the divorce took place. Second, the criterion variable employed in the study, suicidality, is a very limited construct. One would have liked to see a broad range of psychosocial development indicators employed as dependent variables. Finally, the size of the sample of students from divorced families was small for a regression analysis employing a rather large number of predictors. Therefore it is quite possible that the findings would not be replicated in another sample.

Grant and colleagues (1993) set out to study the impact of parental divorce on the adjustment of college students. The study was carried out on a sample of 341 freshmen, 99 percent of whom were either 18 or 19 years old. Fifty-six percent of the sample were females. Sixty-five of the responding students were from families in which the parents had divorced. Forty-five of the students from divorced families reported that their custodial parent had remarried. The average length of these remarriages was seven and six-tenths years.

College adjustment was assessed by means of an updated and abridged version of Borrow's (1947) College Inventory of Academic Adjustment (CIAA). This is a ninety-item scale that has six subscales, but Grant and her associates (1993) used only twenty of the CIAA items in their study. These items represented four of the six CIAA subscales: curricular adjustment (two items), maturity of goals and level of aspiration (three items), personal efficiency (nine items), and mental health (six items). The curricular adjustment subscale assesses the student's satisfaction with his or her chosen curriculum. The maturity of goals and level of aspiration subscale measures "the student's educational and life goals, his/her desire to achieve those goals, and his/her sense of values" (p. 188). The personal efficiency subscale investigates the effectiveness with which the student schedules and carries out his or her daily activities. And the mental health subscale assesses the student's emotional well-being. The authors did not report reliability coefficients for any of these abbreviated subscales, nor did they report a reliability coefficient for the total adjustment score obtained by summing all twenty items.

Grant and colleagues (1993) carried out three one-way ANOVAs. The first of these analyses employed the entire study sample. The independent variable in this analysis was family status (divorced versus intact). The other two ANOVAs were limited to students whose parents had divorced. The first of these two ANOVAs employed the age of the student when the parents divorced as the independent variable. The respondent's age at the time of the parental divorce was trichotomized into groups in which the divorce took place: (1) when the respondent was 5 years old or younger ($n = 21$), (2) between 6 and 12 years old ($n = 34$), and (3) between 13 and 18 years old ($n = 10$). These divisions correspond to the division commonly employed in the literature between preschoolers, latency-aged children, and adolescents. The final ANOVA compared the adjustment scores of students from divorced families whose custodial parent had either remarried or not remarried. The dependent variable employed in each of these analyses was the total score for academic adjustment derived from summing all twenty of the CIAA items employed in the study.

The ANOVAs for both family status and the remarriage of the custodial parent were nonsignificant. However, the ANOVA in which the independent variable was the student's age at the time of the divorce was significant ($F = 3.76$, $df = 2$ and 62, $p < .05$). Post hoc Scheffe contrasts carried out at the .10 level of significance indicated that the students who were preschoolers at the time of the divorce had higher adjustment scores than the students whose parents divorced when they were in elementary school. The mean adjustment score of the students whose parents divorced when the students were adolescents did not differ significantly from the mean score of students in either of the other two groups.

The results of this study are best interpreted as providing very weak support for the notion that children fare better when their parents divorced during their preschool years. The results are categorized as "weak" for several reasons. First, the post hoc Scheffe contrast reported as significant was in fact not significant at the generally accepted .05 level of significance, but only at the .10 level. It should more appropriately have been reported as a weak trend in the data, perhaps justifying further study, but certainly not justifying a definite conclusion that earlier divorces are associated with better psychosocial outcomes. Furthermore, the criterion variable in this study, like the criterion variable in the study by Ellis and Russell (1992) described immediately above, is an extremely narrow indicator of overall psychosocial adjustment. Finally, the psychometric properties of the updated and abridged CIAA are totally unknown.

On balance, then, it may be concluded that there is little evidence for the hypothesis that divorces that occur in the child's preschool years are less destructive than those that occur later. The few studies suggesting such a conclusion are methodologically quite weak.

DIVORCES OCCURRING LATER IN THE CHILD'S LIFESPAN HAVE BETTER OUTCOMES

Several relatively recent studies have provided evidence for the hypothesis that the effects of divorce on the psychosocial adjustment of children are less severe when the divorce occurs later in the life of the child (Allison and Furstenberg 1989, Borduin and Henggeler 1987, Emery 1988, Zill et al. 1993).

Borduin and Henggeler (1987) studied the personality characteristics of 12- to 17-year-old boys from three types of families: (1) intact families ($n = 18$), (2) early father-absence families (mother-custody families in which the noncustodial father left the home before the son's 5th birthday; $n = 18$), and (3) late father-absence families (mother-custody families in which the noncustodial father left the home between the son's 5th and 10th birthdays, $n = 18$). Each of these three groups was subdivided equally between well-adjusted boys ($n = 9$ per family status group) and delinquent boys ($n = 9$ per family status group). The well-adjusted boys were identified and referred through local social service professionals, high school principals, and teachers. None of these boys had any history of arrests or psychiatric difficulties. The delinquent boys were all juvenile offenders who had (1) at least one recent arrest for a serious violation of the adult criminal code and (2) a primary classification of conduct problem on the Behavior Problem Checklist (BPC) (Quay and Peterson 1975). The offenses committed by the boys in the delinquent groups included physical assaults, grand larceny, and robbery. The delinquent and well-adjusted groups were matched on age, grade level, race, and family structure. Also, the parents of the delinquent and well-adjusted boys were matched on age and socioeconomic status. The investigators described the families as predominantly black and lower-class.

The participating families were assessed by means of both observational and self-report measures obtained in the homes of the participating families. The parent(s) first completed a demographic questionnaire and the BPC. Each family member was tested using the vocabulary subtest of either the WAIS or the WISC-R (depending on the particular respondent's age) as a measure of the respondent's verbal facility. Then each responding family member completed the following self-report measures: the Eysenck Personality Inventory (EPI) (Eysenck and Eysenck 1963), the Family Relationship Questionnaire (FRQ) (Henggeler and Tavormina 1980), and the Unrevealed Differences Questionnaire (URD) (Henggeler and Tavormina 1980).

The EPI is a psychometrically sound and frequently used personality test that provided measures of both the mother and the son on extraversion, neuroticism, and social desirability.

The FRQ was used to assess both the mother's and the son's perceptions of their relationship with each other. The relationship dimensions assessed by the FRQ include the level of conflict between the mother and the son, the extent of the mother's dominance over the son, and the positive affect displayed between them. The scale employs a five-point Likert-type item format. The FRQ contains items that measure the nature of the child's relationship with both father and mother, but in this study only those items pertaining to the relationship between the mother and the child were used. Borduin and Henggeler (1987) indicated that the FRQ scales "have good face validity and test–retest reliability (mean r = .70 at a two-week interval)" (pp. 279–280).

The URD is an eight-item measure. The first four items focus on expressive (emotional) family issues and the last four on instrumental (practical) family concerns. Each item has three to five alternative choices, which respondents rank in order. Borduin and Henggeler (1987) indicated that each mother and son completed the URD both individually and as a family. The scores obtained from the individual administration of the URD are not discussed further in the report. Instead, the authors focused on scores derived from observing the discussion that took place between the mother and the son in their attempt to respond to the URD as a family.

The mothers and sons were asked to complete the URD jointly:

The interviewer explained that although each family member had *individually* completed the questionnaire, the *family's* opinion or viewpoint was also needed. A pencil and a blank questionnaire were placed on the table in front of the family. At this point, the interviewer turned on the audiorecorder and asked each family member to announce his or her name before beginning the discussion. The interviewer then left the room until the task was completed. [Borduin and Henggeler 1987, p. 278]

Trained raters reviewed the audiotaped discussions and rated the family on a series of twenty quantitative and qualitative measures of family interaction. These measures were derived separately for the tasks of discussing the four expressive questions and the four instrumental questions in the URD. The authors reported acceptable interrater reliabilities for all these ratings across the two tasks.

Based on a factor analysis of URD items reported in a prior study (Henggeler et al. 1985), the authors selected from among the twenty ratings a subset of fourteen ratings they believed to represent three family interaction factors. The first factor, facilitative information exchange, was represented by six observer ratings: (1) the proportion of total talking time during which the two parties were speaking simultaneously; (2) the proportion of the mother's total talking time that involved supportive statements toward the son; (3) the proportion of the son's total talking time that involved supportive statements toward the mother; (4) the proportion of the mother's total talking time that involved conveying explicit information to the son; (5) the proportion of the son's total talking time that involved conveying explicit information to the mother; and (6) the total number of attempted interruptions on the part of both the mother and the son divided by the sum of their total talking times in minutes.

The second factor, conflict-hostility, included five observer ratings: (1) the observer's qualitative rating of conflict; (2) the proportion of the mother's total talking time in which the mother was judged to be communicating defensively; (3) the proportion of the son's total talking time in which the son was judged to be communicating defensively; (4) the proportion of the mother's total talking time in which she was determined to be communicating aggressively; and (5) the proportion of the son's total talking time in which he was judged to be communicating aggressively.

The third factor, maternal dominance, was represented by three ratings: (1) the observer's qualitative rating of the dominance of the mother; (2) the total talking time of the mother divided by the sum of the total talking times of both the mother and the son; and (3) the number of times that the mother made the first or the final statement on a particular question divided by the total number of first and last statements made by either the mother or the son.

Although it did not load on any of the three factors that emerged in the prior study, Borduin and Henggeler (1987) also included in their analysis the observer's qualitative rating of positive affect. Their rationale for including this rating was that prior research (Maccoby and Martin 1983) had demonstrated the importance of affect in parent–child relations. Borduin and Henggeler did not discuss their decision to analyze the separate ratings within each of the three interaction domains suggested by their prior factor analysis rather than calculate factor scores and analyze the resulting more parsimonious set of dependent variables. This is an obvious methodological limitation of the study, since the use of more dependent variables increases the chance of Type I errors. One wonders whether factor scores were not in fact calculated and tested, without yielding significant findings.

The data pertaining to the self-report measures and the observational measures were analyzed separately. The two sets of analyses had different independent variables. Five separate multivariate analyses of variance (MANOVAs) were used to analyze the self-report data. These five MANOVAs pertained to (1) the mother's and son's self-ratings on conflict, (2) the mother's and son's scores on maternal dominance, (3) the mother's and son's scores on positive affect, (4) the mother's scores on the three EPI subscales, and (5) the son's scores on the three EPI subscales. The independent variables in each of these MANOVAs were family structure (intact, early father-absence, and late father-absence) and delinquency status (delinquent boy versus well-adjusted boy). Borduin and Henggeler (1987) do not indicate why they did not employ a single MANOVA for these analyses, which would have provided a more meaningful control for the accumulating probability of Type I errors associated with the analysis of a substantial number of dependent variables. The use of a series of five separate MANOVAs, each including only two or three dependent variables, largely defeats the purpose of using multivariate analysis in the first place. This too must be considered a significant limitation of the study.

The three MANOVAs carried out with relation to the FRQ scales yielded only one significant difference between the early father-absence group and the late father-absence group. This difference occurred on the mother's perceptions of the amount of positive affect involved in her relationship with her son. The direction of this difference was such that mothers in late father-absent families reported more affectionate relationships with their sons than mothers in early father-absent families. The mean score for maternal perception of affection among the late father-absent group was not significantly different from the corresponding mean among intact families. The mean score for maternal perception of affection among the early father-absent group was significantly lower than the mean of the intact family group as well as the mean of the late father-absent group. This finding supports the idea that children who are older at the time of parental divorce ultimately tend to have better relationships with their mothers, at least from the perspective of the mother.

The MANOVAs carried out to analyze the scores of the mother and the son on the EPI also yielded a single significant difference between the early father-absent group and the late father-absent group. This was on the adolescent's score on extraversion. Here again, the early father-absent boys scored significantly lower on extraversion than either the late father-absent boys or the boys from intact families. This finding suggests that a divorce occurring during latency may be less damaging socially than one that occurs during the preschool years.

With respect to the observational data, the Borduin and Henggeler (1987) again performed separate MANOVAs for the sets of ratings grouped under each of the three factors identified in the prior study. They also performed a separate analysis of variance on the single rating for mother–son affect. The same critique applies to this choice of analyses as was applied to the analyses of the self-report measures noted above.

The MANOVA performed on the ratings grouped under the heading of facilitative information exchange yielded a significant multivariate main effect due to family structure. Follow-up univariate tests indicated a significant main effect due to family structure on both maternal supportive communication ($F = 3.14$, $df = 2$ and 48, $p = .050$) and maternal explicit information ($F = 3.65$, $df = 2$ and 48, $p = .033$). In each case, post hoc comparisons indicated that the mean score for the late father-absent group was significantly higher than that for the early father-absent group. On these ratings, however, the means of the late father-absent group were also significantly higher than the corresponding means of the intact family groups. Here again, children whose parents divorced while they were in the latency period appear to fare better than children whose parents divorced earlier.

Borduin and Henggeler (1987) also referred to "marginally significant effects" ($.05 < p < .10$) obtained with respect to the son's supportive statements, the son's explicit information, and the qualitative rating of positive affect between the mother and the son. The pattern of means observed on these variables also indicated better outcomes among boys from late father-absent than from early father-absent families. However, given the already high probability of Type I errors arising out of the large number of dependent variables and the use of multiple MANOVAs, it is certainly not appropriate to deviate from the accepted alpha level of .05. Nevertheless, the results reported by these authors that really were significant do tend to support the idea that divorce during latency tends to have better outcomes than divorce during the preschool years.

Allison and Furstenberg (1989) reported the results of a large sample longitudinal study designed to determine how the effects of marital dissolution are mediated by the gender and age of the child at the time of the separation. They cited two early studies of the effects of divorce (Hetherington et al. 1978, Wallerstein and Kelly 1980) that suggested that "divorce is more traumatic for children who are younger at the time of separation" (Allison and Furstenberg 1989, p. 540). In stating this conclusion, Allison and Furstenberg did not distinguish between the immediate impact of the separation on the child or the long-term effects of divorce on psychosocial adjustment over the lifespan. Presumably their conclusion pertains to the immediate effects of the divorce, since Hetherington and her colleagues (1978) actually reported that children who experience parental divorce at an early age are more likely to overcome the effects of the potentially detrimental experience. Irrespective of this apparent discrepancy, Allison and Furstenberg noted, "Recent reviews of divorce studies reveal considerable inconsistency with regard to the modulating effects of age and gender on the consequences of marital dissolution" (p. 540). They cited the extensive review of the literature presented by Emery (1988) as indicating that:

> age effects may be less clear-cut or easily interpreted than has been previously supposed. Age of the child is frequently confounded with age at the time of separation, length of time since the separation, and even historical period. No study to date has attempted to disentangle these differing temporal dimensions, a task that

requires a longitudinal design and a large sample of children exposed to marital dissolution. [Allison and Furstenberg 1989, p. 540]

Accordingly, they attempted to accomplish this disentanglement by analyzing data from a large national probability sample of children and parents who were measured twice, with five years between the two waves of data collection. Allison and Furstenberg (1989) used the data set collected in 1976 and 1981 in the National Survey of Children (previously collected and used for different purposes by Furstenberg et al. 1983). The children in this sample were 7 to 11 years old at the time of the first wave of data collection. Allison and Furstenberg set out to compare children who experienced a marital dissolution ($n = 328$) to children from intact families ($n = 869$) with respect to measures of problem behaviors, psychological distress, and academic performance derived from the children, their parents, and their teachers. They also sought to determine the impact of the child's gender, age at separation, and years since separation.

The data for the study were gathered by means of personal interviews during the first wave of data collection and by telephone interviews during the second wave. The interviews were conducted with one parent in each family and with either one or two children from each family. Ninety-five percent of the parents interviewed were mothers. It should be noted that the use of two children from some of the same households constitutes a methodological limitation as it results in a violation of the assumption of independence of observations that characterizes each of the inferential statistics used to analyze the data. Of course, Allison and Furstenberg (1989) were using a data set collected earlier, so they were not in a position to change the manner in which the data had been collected. However, one would assume that responding parents and children must have had a family identification number so that, in those cases where two children were sampled from the same family, one could have been chosen at random and the other could have been excluded from the sample. Perhaps this was not done in order to maintain the substantial sample sizes, particularly in the case of the sample from divorced families. However, a more conservative statistical approach would have been to ensure independent observations.

The parent interviews typically lasted more than one hour, and the children's interviews typically lasted about forty-five minutes. Following the interviews, mail questionnaires were sent to one teacher for each child. Allison and Furstenberg (1989) explained that the second-wave interviews "were not a strict replication of the first wave," because "[m]any measures from the first interview had been tailored for very young children and simply were not appropriate for children in early adolescence" (p. 541). From these interviews Allison and Furstenberg developed a series of nine adjustment measures from the 1976 data and a total of ten adjustment measures from the 1981 data. The 1976 measures included parent reports of the child's hyperactivity, problem behaviors, and academic difficulties; teacher reports of the child's problem behaviors in school, adjustment difficulties, and academic difficulties; and the child's own reports of his or her dissatisfaction, distress, and academic difficulty. The 1981 measures included parent reports of the child's delinquency, problem behaviors, distress, and academic difficulty; teacher reports of the child's problem behaviors and academic difficulty; and the child's own reports of his or her delinquency, dissatisfaction, distress, and academic difficulties. The authors explained that the various measures of academic difficulty were typically one-item scales, while all the other measures were multiple-item scales constructed on the basis of a clustering procedure that yields sets of items with high correlations within the set and low correlations with items in other sets. These scales were further refined by testing each scale for unidimensionality using LISREL V (Joreskog and Sorbom 1981). Although Allison and Furstenberg did not report reliability coefficients for each of the scales constructed in this manner, one may presume that the methods they employed would yield internally consistent scales.

Allison and Furstenberg (1989) standardized scores on all the adjustment measures and reported the effect of marital dissolution as the mean difference between the divorced and intact families, expressed in standard deviation units. They reported that these differences were significant on eight of the nine adjustment measures from the 1976 data set and on six of the ten adjustment measures from the 1981 data set. In each case the direction of the difference was such that the children from divorced families had higher problem scores. However, Allison and Furstenberg cautioned that these differences:

> do not necessarily imply that divorce reduces well-being. Families in which a divorce occurs undoubtedly differ in many respects prior to the divorce from families that remain intact, and these prior differences may account for the later differences in the well-being of the children. [p. 541]

To determine the effect of the child's age at the time of the divorce and the effect of the length of time since the separation occurred, Allison and Furstenberg (1989) divided the sample of children from divorced families into three groups with respect to each temporal measure. On age at the time of the separation, the children from divorced families were divided into those whose parents had divorced before they were 6, those whose parents divorced when they were between 6 and 10, and those whose parents divorced when they were between 11 and 16. These groups correspond to the three stages of preschool, latency, and adolescence. On time since the separation occurred, the divorced children were divided into groups whose parents had been separated for less than six years, for six to ten years, and for more than ten years. Children in each of these groups were then compared to the entire sample of children from intact families, using the same method of analysis that had been employed in the overall comparison of children from divorced and intact families. Inferences regarding the effects of the temporal variables were made by comparing the number and magnitude of significant effects due to marital dissolution for the three groups.

With respect to the child's age at separation, the results indicated "a clear tendency for the strongest effects to be concentrated in the youngest age group and the weakest effects to be found in the oldest age group" (p. 543). Among children whose parents divorced before they were 6, the effect of marital dissolution was significant on seven of the nine adjustment measures from 1976 and on six of the ten adjustment measures from the 1981 data collection. Among children whose parents had divorced when they were between the ages of 6 and 10, the effect of marital dissolution was significant on two of the nine 1976 adjustment measures and three of the ten 1981 adjustment measures. The sample size was too small to permit testing the effects of marital dissolution for the 1976 data among those children who were between 11 and 16 at the time of the divorce. When the effects of marital dissolution were tested in this group for the 1981 adjustment variables, only two of the ten tests were significant. The authors concluded that these findings generally support the prevailing professional opinion, that the effects of divorce are worse when the divorce occurs relatively early in the life of the child.

However, Allison and Furstenberg (1989) correctly pointed out that:

> These results are, however, subject to several competing interpretations. Because the interviews occurred at the same time for all the children, whereas the marital dissolutions occurred over a wide

> range of years, there is necessarily a large negative correlation between age at separation and the length of time since separation. In fact, the partial correlation between these two variables, controlling for age at interview, is necessarily 1.0. Thus, a *decline* in the effects of dissolution with increasing age at separation is equivalent to an *increase* in the effects of dissolution with increasing time since the separation. [p. 544]

This was illustrated in the results of the analyses carried out on the three groups of children formed on the basis of years since separation. With respect to the 1981 data, there were no significant effects due to marital dissolution among the sample whose parents had been separated for less than six years. Among the group whose parents had been separated for six to ten years, the effect of marital dissolution was significant for five of the ten adjustment measures, and among the group whose parents had been separated for more than ten years, the effect of marital dissolution was significant for four of the adjustment measures. Thus:

> the dissolution effects are almost completely confined to children whose parents separated at least 6 years prior to the interview. Children whose parents were separated for 5 years or less fare about as well as children in stable marriages. By contrast, their peers whose parents separated 6 to 10 years prior to the interview are doing substantially worse on many of the measures. On the other hand, there does not appear to be any general trend toward further deterioration beyond the 10-year point. [p. 544]

Thus there are clearly two different explanations for these results, one based on the critical stage theory and one based on the cumulative effect hypothesis. Allison and Furstenberg (1989) suggested that focusing on the child's age at the time of the divorce suggests that preschoolers are "especially vulnerable, either (a) because they are more dependent on their parents and, hence, less protected by extrafamilial supports such as teachers or peers, or (b) because they are in a more formative stage of development and are therefore less resilient when faced with a traumatic event" (p. 545). On the other hand, focusing on the length of time since the separation "suggests that marital dissolution is not an isolated event but only the beginning of a continuous exposure to a long-lasting adverse situation that produces cumulative effects on the child" (p. 545).

Allison and Furstenberg (1989) employed a clever analytical strategy to distinguish between these two rival explanations. They looked at adjustment measures that were comparable in the 1976 and 1981 data collection waves, and they eliminated all the children who experienced a marital dissolution after the first wave of data collection in 1976. Then they divided the remaining children into two groups according to whether the separation occurred between 1967 and 1971 or between 1972 and 1976. Within each of these two groups they compared the effects of marital dissolution on the adjustment measures from the 1976 data collection wave and the corresponding adjustment measures from the 1981 data collection waves. They reasoned that if the time since separation were a major factor in increasing the effects of a dissolution, one would expect the effects of dissolution in each group to be substantially larger in 1981 than in 1976.

This was not what they found. There were seven adjustment measures they considered comparable over the two waves of data collection. Two of them were derived from parent reports (problem behaviors and academic difficulties), two from teacher reports (problem behavior and academic difficulties), and three from children's reports (dissatisfaction, distress, and academic difficulties). Among those whose parents had divorced between 1967 and 1971, the effect of marital dissolution measured in 1976 was significant on five of these seven measures. In this same group the effect of marital dissolution measured in 1981 was significant on only three of the seven measures. And among those children whose parents had divorced between 1972 and 1981, the effect of marital dissolution was significant for three of the seven adjustment measures obtained in 1976 and for three of the adjustment measures obtained in 1981.

Allison and Furstenberg (1989) summarized these findings in terms of the source of the rating. They noted that:

> [f]or the teacher's report, the effects are clearly greater in the earlier year. For the parent's report, the effects are approximately the same for each of the two interview years. For the child's report, the effects show a decline with time for those who experienced a separation in the 1967–1971 period and approximate stability for those who experienced a separation during the later interval. [p. 545]

Therefore this study supports the position that children who are younger at the time of the parental divorce tend to fare less well than those whose parents divorce later in their lives, and it concludes that this effect is more likely to reflect the workings of the critical stage theory rather than the cumulative effect hypothesis. Allison and Furstenberg (1989) also threw out one additional explanation for these findings. They suggested that the results could simply reflect a dramatic change in the process of marital dissolution that occurred after 1976, such that "children were completely unaffected by divorce and separation during this historical period and possibly thereafter" (p. 546). However, they concluded that this explanation was unlikely since the increase in the incidence of divorce over that period were not so dramatic that one would expect great differences in the effects of divorce on children.

Zill and colleagues (1993) reported the results of another study utilizing the longitudinal data from the National Survey of Children. Their data included not only the interviews conducted in 1976 and 1981, but also data obtained in 1987, at which point the responding children were between 18 and 22 years old. Zill and his associates indicated that a total of 1,147 youths participated in all three waves of data collection, and that a parent interview was also completed in 1987 for 1,049 of these children. The adjustment measures derived from the 1987 data "were constructed similarly using the 1981 and 1987 waves of the NSC to examine the effects of disruption on the same measures of well-being in both adolescence and young adulthood" (p. 94).

The dependent variables employed in the study were the following: (1) the child's perception of his or her relationship with the natural mother; (2) the child's perception of his or her relationship with the natural father; (3) the parent's perception of the child's behavior problems; (4) the child's self-reported depression; (5) the child's self-report of delinquent behavior; (6) the parent's report of whether the child ever received psychological treatment; (7) the child's self-report of whether he or she had ever received psychological treatment; (8) the parent's report of whether the child had ever been suspended or expelled from school; (9) the parent's report of whether the child ever had to repeat a grade in school; (10) the child's self-report of whether he or she had ever dropped out of school; (11) the child's self-report of high school completion; (12) the child's self-report of class standing; and (13) the teacher's report of the child's class standing. Some of these variables were natural dichotomies and some were scale scores derived from summing the responses to several interview items. The investigators recorded all the dependent variables to dichotomies.

The independent variable in the study was family status, having three values: intact family, divorced family in which the divorce occurred before the child was 6 years old, and divorced family in which the divorce occurred between the ages of 6 and 16. For both the 1981 and 1987 data, multiple classification analyses were performed to determine the significance of differences on the dependent variables between the early divorce group ($n = 133$) and the late divorce group ($n = 107$). Due to the relatively large number of criterion variables employed in the study, Zill and his colleagues (1993) used the Bonferroni correction for significance level to control the accumulating probability of Type I error (Darlington and Carlson 1987).

The results of the multiple classification analysis for the 1981 data indicated that the early and late divorce groups did not differ significantly on any of the adjustment indicators. However, a trend in the expected direction emerged in two adjustment measures. The two areas were behavior problems and whether or not the child had ever received psychological help. The multiple classification analysis actually yielded significance probabilities less than .05 for each of these two findings, but the probabilities were not sufficiently low to be counted as significant, due to the stricter significance level demanded by the Bonferroni correction. The differences between the early and late divorce groups on these two measures were not large. Sixteen percent of the early divorce group fell into the high behavior problems group, compared to 9 percent of the late divorce group. Twenty-six percent of the early divorce group had received some form of psychological treatment, compared to 18 percent of the late divorce group.

The results of the multiple classification analysis for the 1987 data were somewhat stronger. Seventy-three percent of the early divorce group were categorized as having a poor relationship with their father compared to 56 percent of the late divorce group. This difference was significant even allowing for the Bonferroni correction ($p < .006$). In addition, there were two other adjustment measures on which differences were observed with significance probabilities below .05, but not low enough to meet the criterion for significance under the restrictions of the Bonferroni correction. These were the behavior problems measure and the child's self-report of having dropped out of school. Among the early divorce group, 23 percent were classified as having high behavior problems. The corresponding figure for the late divorce group was just 14 percent. Thirty-two percent of the early divorce group reported that they had dropped out of school for a period of time, compared to just 22 percent of the late divorce group.

Thus Zill and his colleagues (1993) provided further support for the notion that divorce has a more deleterious effect during the preschool years than during latency or adolescence. The magnitude of these effects does not appear to be great, but the differences are consistent. Further, Zill and associates demonstrated that these effects appear to persist into early adulthood. The authors concluded that:

> parental divorce in early childhood (i.e., before age 6 years) poses more of a risk to a young person's social and emotional development than does parental divorce at later ages. This reinforces and extends earlier findings by Zill and Peterson (1983) and Allison and Furstenberg (1989). The result may help to explain previous failures to find long-term effects of parental divorce in samples containing adults who experienced disruption at unspecified ages. [p. 101]

On balance, it is clear that the weight of empirical evidence supports the position that divorce occurring during the child's preschool years is more damaging than divorce that occurs later in the lifespan. However, there are also a number of studies that suggest that the impact of divorce is simply different for children of different ages. These studies are reviewed in the section that follows.

EFFECTS OF PARENTAL DIVORCE ARE QUALITATIVELY DIFFERENT FOR BOYS AND GIRLS OF DIFFERENT AGES

Kalter and Rembar (1981) carried out a study aimed at testing the relative predictive validity of the three theoretical explanations of the effects of divorce on children: the critical stage theory, the cumulative effect hypothesis, and the recency theory (described at the beginning of this chapter). Their sample included 144 youngsters whose parents had divorced. These children were selected on the basis of a review of outpatient evaluations of children seen for psychiatric evaluation in the Department of Psychiatry at the University of Michigan from September 1976 through November 1977. These children ranged in age at the time of the study from 7 to 17 years. The sample was categorized into four subsamples based on age and gender: latency-age males (7 to 11.5 years) ($n = 44$); latency-age females ($n = 32$); adolescent males (11.5 to 17 years) ($n = 31$); and adolescent females ($n = 37$).

The age of the child at the time of the parental divorce was available from the case evaluations for 139 of the 144 cases. Sixty-one of these children (43.9 percent) were in the preoedipal stage (under 3 years) at the time of the separation; thirty-four (24.5 percent) were in the oedipal stage (from 3 to 6 years); and forty-four were postoedipal. With respect to the elapsed time between the occurrence of the divorce and the evaluation, sixteen cases (11.5 percent) were referred within two years or less of the separation, thirty-three (23.7 percent) were evaluated between two and five years of the separation, and ninety (64.7 percent) were referred more than five years after the separation.

The dependent variables used in this study included indices of emotional disturbance, a checklist of presenting complaints. The Emotional Disturbance (ED) scale is a single item to be rated by the coder reading the case evaluation. The scale uses an eleven-point response format with response options ranging from zero to ten. On this scale coders are instructed that a zero indicates absolutely no evidence of emotional difficulties; points one and two signify minimal and usually transient problems; points three to five indicate a mild disturbance that is nevertheless clearly present; points six and seven correspond to clear-cut evidence of emotional disturbance on a moderate level; points eight to ten signify a moderately severe to severe range of adjustment problems. The score of ten was reserved for borderline and psychotic disturbances. Interrater reliability for the ED scale was tested by correlating the ratings of two independent coders across a sample of twenty of the case evaluations. The reliability coefficient reported was .92.

The Presenting Complaints Checklist (PCCL) is a list of twenty-eight possible complaints that a patient may present upon evaluation. The complaints included were aggression toward parents, siblings, peers, and inanimate objects; nonaggressive disturbances with parents, siblings, and peers; danger to self; drug and/or alcohol involvement; sexual behavior; running away; school refusal/truancy; academic and school behavior problems; problems with the law; stealing; medical problems, somatization, enuresis, encopresis, sleep disturbances, and eating disturbances; compulsive rituals, subjective psychological symptoms, and bizarre behavior; custody dispute; and prophylactic concern. The raters determined whether each of these categories of presenting complaints was present or absent in a given case. When two independent raters scored a subsample of twenty case evaluations using the PCCL, the median percentage of agreement across the twenty-eight behavioral categories was 93 percent.

To assess the relationship between the children's age at the time of the marital dissolution and emotional disturbance, Pearson correlations were calculated between the total ED score and the child's age at the time of the divorce for each of the four subsamples (latency boys, latency girls, adolescent boys, and adolescent girls) separately. None of these correlations was significant. The investigators also calculated partial correlations between the ED score and age at the time of the divorce in which variability due to the child's current age was controlled. These partial correlations yielded only a single trend toward significance in one of the subsamples, that of adolescent boys ($r = -.32$, $p < .10$). Kalter and Rembar (1981) interpreted these findings as providing "minimal support" for the cumulative effect hypothesis and no support for the recency hypothesis.

To test the critical stage theory, several one-way ANOVAs were performed on the ED scores. The independent variable in each of these analyses was stage at the time of the divorce (preoedipal, oedipal, or postoedipal). One such ANOVA was performed for each of the four subsamples. None of these tests approached statistical significance.

Thus the results obtained with respect to the scores on emotional disturbance provided no support at all for either the critical stage theory or the recency theory, and only the most minimal support for the cumulative effect hypothesis. In fact, if the authors were to adhere to accepted standards for significance, these results would more appropriately be interpreted as providing no support for the cumulative effect theory either. However, Kalter and Rembar (1981) observed that even though "timing is not associated for the most part with *severity* of emotional disturbance, the *forms* of emotional distress and behavior problems that these youngsters developed may be tied to their developmental level at parental separation and divorce" (p. 92).

To investigate this possibility, they analyzed the data from the PPCL both for the total sample and for each of the four subsamples. The analysis of the data for the total sample is somewhat questionable, given the expectation that the results may differ for boys and girls in latency and adolescence. However, in this case the analysis of the total sample and the comparison of this analysis to the analyses carried out for the four separate subsamples yields some interesting insights.

For the total sample, a series of 2 x 3 contingency tables was generated in which the presence or absence of a particular complaint was cross-tabulated by the age of the child (preoedipal, oedipal, and postoedipal) at the time of the divorce. These analyses yielded only two significant findings, on school refusal/truancy ($p < .01$) and academic problems ($p < .04$). Post hoc comparisons indicated that children already in the postoedipal stage at the time of the parental divorce were more likely than either preoedipal or oedipal-stage children to manifest school truancy. On the other hand, children who were in the oedipal stage at the time of the parental divorce were more likely than preoedipal or postoedipal children to manifest academic difficulties. After reporting these few significant findings from the analysis of the total sample, Kalter and Rembar (1981) observed that:

> [t]he paucity of statistically significant findings in the full sample analysis could represent a masking of important relationships that occur within the subsamples. Sex and developmental differences in how psychological problems are manifested can "cancel out" when age-sex controls are not used....[p. 94]

This point was confirmed by the results of the analyses of the PCCL data for each of the four subsamples separately. These analyses yielded different significant ($p < .05$) relationships between the age of the child at the time of the parental divorce and the frequency of occurrence of various presenting complaints.

Among boys in latency at the time of the study, those in the preoedipal stage at the time of the divorce were significantly ($p < .01$) more likely than those in the other two groups to manifest nonaggressive disturbances with their parents.

Among girls in latency at the time of the study, those in the preoedipal stage at the time of their parents' divorce were significantly ($p < .05$) higher than those in the other two groups on both nonaggressive disturbances with parents and aggression toward peers.

Among boys who were adolescents at the time of the study, those in the preoedipal stage at the time of their parents' divorce were significantly ($p < .05$) less likely than those in the other groups to display nonaggressive disturbances with peers.

And among girls who were adolescents at the time of the study, those in the oedipal stage at the time of their parents' divorce were significantly ($p < .01$) more likely than those in the other groups to display academic difficulties. Adolescent girls in the oedipal stage at the time of their parents' divorce were also significantly ($p < .05$) more likely than girls in the other two groups to display aggression toward their parents and peers.

Kalter and Rembar (1981) concluded that this finding "confirms again that the failure to control for sex and current age gives rise to misleading results in studies of children's psychological adjustment" (p. 96). They summarized their findings as follows:

> Perhaps most striking was the relationship between parents parting early in the child's life (0–2.5 years old) and a higher incidence of nonaggressive disturbances with the parents. This was true of both latency-age boys and [latency-age] girls. Since all youngsters in these two groups were between [7] and 11.5 years old when they were evaluated, this result suggests a long-term effect that is in evidence [4] to 11 years after the separation/divorce. [p. 96]

Kalter and Rembar (1981) also noted that male and female adolescents in the oedipal period at the time of their parents' divorce had very different patterns of results. Among the adolescent boys, those in the oedipal period did not manifest more aggression toward their parents and peers than those in the preoedipal or postoedipal stage at the time of the divorce. In fact, there were trends on these two measures (.05 < p < .10) in the opposite direction. In contrast, among adolescent girls, those in the oedipal stage were significantly more likely than preoedipal or postoedipal girls to display problems with aggression toward both parents and peers at the time of the divorce.

The primary lesson to be drawn from this study is that it is unwise to draw conclusions regarding the mediating effects of the child's age at the time of the divorce without considering both the gender and the current age of the child. This conclusion highlights the complexity of the relationships involving the effects of divorce on children's development over the lifespan. It also points to the need for more large-sample longitudinal studies in which numerous background factors can be measured and controlled.

Hodges and Bloom (1984) reported the results of another study designed to determine how the impact of divorce on children's adjustment may be mediated by the age and sex of the child. They complained that:

> Previous research on the relationship of age of the child at the time of the divorce to the impact of that stressful event on adjustment creates problems of interpretation. Retrospective clinical studies have sometimes not looked at diagnosis as a function of the

age of the child at the time of the divorce. The results of other retrospective studies with more careful statistical analysis and greater care concerning time of separation or divorce may be limited to an outpatient population. Several clinical studies have provided a rich source of information for further study, but lead to difficulties of interpretation in terms of small cell sizes for analysis or lack of quantified measures that could be subjected to inferential statistics. [p. 37]

Hodges and Bloom (1984) concluded: "No study has been done that provides a cross-sectional analysis of effects of divorce on children over time as a function of age and sex of the child with a nonclinical population" (p. 37). They set out to rectify this situation by studying parent perceptions of children's adjustment to divorce at two months, six months, and eighteen months postseparation. It is recognized, of course, that the collection of data at three intervals so close to the time of the separation means that the results of the study pertain to adjustment during the "crisis period" rather than long-term psychosocial adjustment.

Hodges and Bloom (1984) recruited a nonclinical sample of recently separated parents by advertising in newspapers, on the radio, and on posters in supermarkets and laundromats, and by direct mailings to attorneys, physicians, clergy, and mental health professionals. Criteria for inclusion in the study required that the responding parents be (1) still legally married, but physically separated because of marital discord; (2) separated from a first marriage; (3) within six months of the date of the separation; and (4) living in Boulder County, Colorado. A total of fifty-one parents who met these criteria were studied. These parents provided data on up to three of their children: the oldest or only child under 18 years, a middle child, randomly selected if there were more than three children in the family, and the youngest child in the family. This process resulted in parental reports on 107 children, 53 boys and 54 girls. Seventy-three percent were in mother-custody homes; 16 percent, in father-custody homes; the remainder were in equal or joint custody situations. The average length of the marriage prior to the separation was nine and four-tenth years.

Hodges and Bloom noted that "each child was treated statistically as a separate case, regardless of family size" (1984, p. 40). This is obviously not the correct procedure, and it constitutes a major limitation of this study. Not only do the inferential statistics used require independent observations, but the problem is confounded in that all the data on the children's adjustment are obtained through parent report. Thus any biases in parent reports that might be associated with the parent's mood or psychological adjustment could be reflected in that parent's reports on several cases in the sample.

The participating parents were interviewed for ninety minutes to two hours at each of the three waves of data collection. Much of this time was spent ascertaining information to be used in connection with other aspects of the much larger study from which the data for this report were drawn. In each session the parents completed the Child Behavior Checklist (CBC) for each child of theirs included in the study. The CBC is a twenty-five-item checklist that was developed for this study. Hodges and Bloom (1984) explained that they chose to develop their own instrument because "no checklist presently available in the literature: (1) included the range of behaviors proposed to be affected by divorce, (2) was short enough to be included in what was already an extensive interview, and (3) was appropriate to a wide range of ages" (p. 39). The CBC employs a four-point Likert-type response format with response options ranging from "never" to "nearly all the time." Its twenty-five items were written to assess aggression, withdrawn behavior, immaturity, socialized delinquency, and shy-anxious problems. A cluster analysis performed on the CBC ratings obtained in this study yielded three item clusters that had internal consistency reliability coefficients adequate to permit their use as dependent variables. These three clusters represented depression (eight items; alpha = .83), disruptive behavior (three items; alpha = .83), and agitation (three items; alpha = .71). The authors also analyzed a total adjustment score based on all twenty-five items. This score had an alpha coefficient of .86.

Scores obtained at each of the three waves of data collection on each of the three clusters as well as the CBC total score were analyzed by means of a two-way ANOVA in which the independent variables were age of the child at the time of the initial interview and gender of the child. Age was collapsed into five categories: birth to 3 years, 4 to 7 years, 8 to 11 years, 12 to 14 years, and 15 to 18 years. The data for the oldest group at the 6- and 18-month data collection intervals were not complete, so the ANOVAs for these intervals included only the four youngest groups.

The analyses of the data from the initial wave of data collection yielded a significant main effect due to the child's age on one of the three clusters, the depression cluster ($F = 8.03$, $df = 4$ and 96, $p <$ .001). The means indicated that depression was highest among the children in the two oldest age groups, and lowest in the youngest age group.

The analyses of the data obtained at the second wave of data collection yielded significant main effects due to the child's age for two of the four dependent variables: the depression cluster ($F = 6.65$, $df = 3$ and 79, $p < .001$) and the disruptive behavior cluster ($F = 4.82$, $df = 3$ and 79, $p < .004$). On depression, the pattern of means at six months was similar to that observed in the initial wave of data collection. Depression was highest among the oldest group (here the 12- to 14-year-old group) and lowest among the youngest group. On disruption, however, the pattern was reversed. Disruptive behavior was highest among the youngest group and lowest among the oldest group.

The analyses carried out for the data obtained in the third wave of data collection yielded one significant main effect due to the child's age, on the disruptive behavior cluster ($F = 5.51$, $df = 3$ and 75, $p < .002$). The pattern of means here was similar to that observed at six months. The mean scores for disruptive behavior were highest among children in the two youngest age groups, and lowest among children in the two oldest groups.

Hodges and Bloom (1984) concluded simply that depression increases with age at both the initial and the six-month interviews, while disruptive behavior decreases with age at both the six-month and the eighteen-month intervals. They noted that they had obtained no significant findings with respect to the age of the child based on the total CBC scores, and they concluded that the use of overall measures of adjustment may obscure age-related differences on specific adjustment factors. They noted further that early studies reported by Hetherington (1979a,b) and Wallerstein and Kelly (1980) had also analyzed a global measure of psychosocial adjustment, and had concluded that the effects of parental divorce were unrelated to the age of the child. Hetherington had suggested that even though the overall *severity* of psychosocial adjustment problems was unrelated to the age of the child, the *pattern* of adjustment might be. Hodges and Bloom interpreted the results of their study as supporting Hetherington's suggestion.

Hodges and Bloom (1984) also looked at each age group separately and analyzed the significance of the changes in each of the problem behavior areas from one wave of data collection to the next. These analyses yielded significant effects due to the time period for the two youngest groups, but not for the three oldest groups. Among the very youngest group, significant effects for time were obtained on the depression cluster ($F = 4.88$, $df = 2$ and 24, $p < .02$) and on the disruptive behavior cluster ($F = 4.15$, $df = 2$ and 24, $p < .03$). Among the 4- to 7-year-old group, significant effects due to time were found on the same two measures: for depression ($F = 4.37$, $df = 2$ and 38, $p < .02$) and for disruptive behavior ($F = 4.55$, $df = 2$ and 38, $p < .02$). In each of the two groups and for each of the two clusters, the direction of the mean differences was such that adjustment difficulties were greater at eighteen months than at two months after the separation. These findings can be interpreted as supporting the cumulative effect hypothesis, but only for children who are young at the time of the divorce, and only for the relatively short term, since eighteen months following the separation is still considered to be in the crisis period.

The aspect of this study most relevant to the discussion in this chapter has to do with the complexity of the relationship between the child's age at the time of the divorce and the effects of the divorce on the child's psychosocial adjustment. The study by Kalter and Rembar (1981) indicated that the effects of the child's age at the time of the divorce on his or her long-term adjustment depends on the current age and the gender of the child. The study by Hodges and Bloom (1984) indicates that the effects of the child's age on the relatively short-term adjustment of children to divorce vary as a function of the specific area of psychosocial adjustment that one studies.

IMPACT OF DIVORCE WHEN THE CHILD IS A YOUNG ADULT

Farber (1980) studied a population of college students from divorced families. She compared the overall adjustment of students whose parents had divorced when the children were between 12 and 17 to that of students whose parents divorced when the children were 17 to 22. She reported that the students whose parents divorced when they were already of college age experienced considerable distress. Being away from home at college did not lessen the adolescents' concerns regarding family conflicts. In fact, being away from home was troublesome for the students whose parents were divorcing at this time because they were unable to obtain adequate information regarding the situation at home to alleviate their apprehensions and unable to use the family support system to help them to adjust.

Kutner (1988) suggested that children of college age have an understanding of their parents that is decimated when the parents suddenly divorce after being together for so long. He argued that the disruption of their concepts of who their parents really are can be quite traumatic. Furthermore, he suggested that because young adults are expected to understand what is occurring, they may get little help or support during this time. This lack of support may exacerbate the difficulties they are experiencing.

Swartzman-Schatman and Schinke (1993) studied sixty college students from divorced families who were attending a large Midwestern university. Thirty of them had parents who had divorced while the student was still in high school; the other thirty had parents who divorced while the student was already in college. The investigators also studied a comparison group of sixty students from intact families. These students all completed the Child's Attitude toward Mother Scale (CAM), the Child's Attitude toward Father Scale (CAF) and the General Contentment Scale (GCS), all developed by Hudson (1982). Each student from a divorced family was also interviewed regarding his or her perceptions of the parental divorce.

The analysis of the quantitative measures indicated no significant differences between the two groups of students from divorced families on any of the three scales, nor did they differ significantly from students in the intact family group with respect to their attitude toward their mothers, but the divorced and intact samples did differ significantly with respect both to their attitudes toward their father and to their general contentment. These findings were interpreted as indicating that the negative impact of parental divorce is just as strong when the divorce occurs after the child has gone off to college as it is when the child is still in high school.

Analysis of the qualitative interview data obtained from the two groups of students from divorced families indicated that students whose parents divorced after they were in college believed that their parents were not helping them to understand what was happening. They felt that their parents assumed that they would adjust easily to the divorce because they were already out of the home. Therefore the parents did not take the time to sit down with them and explain the divorce. In addition, the students whose parents were divorcing while the students were in college were more likely than those whose parents had divorced earlier to perceive their parents as competing with each other for the student's loyalty. This competition was most likely to occur with respect to the students' decisions regarding where to spend their holidays.

The limited amount of research reported with respect to the impact of parental divorce on college students makes it clear that a mid-life parental divorce is troubling for these young adults. Certainly college student personnel workers should be aware of this issue and reach out to provide supportive services to these students.

8

THE CHILD'S GENDER

LIKE THE LITERATURE on the child's age at the time of the divorce, the literature on gender differences in adjustment following divorce is substantial, of uneven methodological quality, and contradictory. The greatest number of empirical investigations have suggested that the adverse impact of divorce is greater for boys than for girls (Emery 1982, Guidubaldi et al. 1983, 1984a,b, Hetherington 1979a,b, Hetherington et al. 1978, 1979, 1985, Hodges and Bloom 1984, Hodges et al. 1979, Kulka and Weingarten 1979, Kurdek and Berg 1983, Santrock 1972). However, a substantial minority of the available studies that have addressed this issue have come to the opposite conclusion, that divorce is more devastating for girls than for boys (Forehand et al. 1988, Furstenberg and Allison 1985, Santrock and Warshak 1979, Santrock et al. 1982a,b).

Predictably, the literature also contains a fair number of studies that indicate no gender differences in children's adjustment to divorce (Acock and Kiecolt 1989, Gregory 1965, Kinard and Reinherz 1984, Kurdek and Siesky 1978, Kurdek et al. 1981, Rosen 1979). In addition, a number of empirical studies and critical reviews have suggested that the presence of lack of significant gender differences in prior studies can be explained to some degree by methodological differences among those studies, and in particular to (1) the nature of the criterion variables chosen to reflect psychosocial adjustment; (2) the source of the data regarding adjustment; and (3) the consideration given by the authors to the effects of important mediating variables, including the age of the child at the time of the divorce and at the time of the study, the amount of time since the parental separation, and the custodial parent's marital status (Baker et al. 1987, Hetherington 1993, Kalter and Rembar 1981, Shook and Jurich 1992, Zaslow 1988, 1989). These studies imply that the effects of divorce may be equally severe, but different, among boys and girls. Furthermore, these differences vary as a function of chronological factors and postdivorce family structure.

The literature in each of these categories is reviewed in this chapter. To keep the length of the chapter reasonable, representative studies have been selected from among the many falling into each of the first three categories (worse for boys, worse for girls, no difference). Detailed attention is paid to those studies emphasizing the complexity of the differential effects of divorce on girls and boys. Particular attention is paid to the role of variables that appear to mediate the relationship between gender and the effects of divorce on adjustment. These variables include the age of the child at the time of the parental separation or divorce and at the time that psychosocial adjustment is assessed, and the length of time between the divorce and the assessment.

Other methodological considerations also appear to influence the nature of research findings reported with respect to gender differences in the effects of divorce. These include the nature of the population sampled for study (clinical versus nonclinical populations), the choice of the variables chosen to represent psychosocial adjustment (especially the choice of externalizing problem behaviors versus internalizing problem behaviors), and the source of the behavioral reports (parents, teachers, or children's self-reports). Special attention is paid to the excellent two-part review and methodological analysis of the literature presented by Zaslow (1988, 1989). These reports indicate clearly the key issues in the research on gender differences in the effects of divorce, and they suggest the factors that should be taken into consideration in future studies.

DIVORCE IS WORSE FOR BOYS

Several of the earlier studies of gender differences in children's reactions to divorce suggested that the effects were more damaging to boys than to girls. Kulka and Weingarten (1979) employed data from a large national probability sample (the Americans View their Mental Health Surveys) to study the effects of marital dissolution on children. They concluded that "coming from a non-intact family of origin does indeed have some significance for psychological well-being in adulthood, especially for men" (p. 73). Hetherington (1979a) concluded that "the impact of marital discord and divorce is more pervasive and enduring for boys than for girls" (p. 853). Emery (1982) studied the impact on adjustment of marital discord in both intact and divorced families. He concluded that "marital turmoil has a greater effect on boys from both divorced and intact, discordant marriages" (p. 316).

In the study described in some detail toward the end of the previous chapter, Hodges and Bloom (1984) examined the impact on children's short-term adjustment to divorce of both the age of the child at the time of the divorce and the gender. For this purpose they employed a nonclinical sample of 107 children under the age of 18 from families in which a separation had occurred within the last two months. They examined parental reports of children's depression, disruptive behavior, and agitated behavior gathered when the families were recruited (generally around two months following the separation), and then again at six and eighteen months following parental separation. They obtained significant main effects due to both the age (considered in the previous chapter) and gender of the child.

With respect to gender, Hodges and Bloom (1984) found that, at the time of their initial wave of data collection, there were significant gender differences on all three adjustment criteria: depression ($F = 5.06$, $df = 1$ and 96, $p < .03$), disruptive behavior ($F = 8.81$, $df = 1$ and 96, $p < .004$), and agitated behavior ($F = 8.09$, $df = 1$ and 87, $p < .006$). In each case the boys in the sample exhibited more problem behaviors than the girls. At the second wave of data collection, six months following the separation, a significant main effect due to gender was obtained on one of the three adjustment measures, agitated behavior ($F = 9.04$, $df = 1$ and 87, $p < .003$). Here again the boys demonstrated greater disturbance. At the eighteen-month data collection interval, there were no significant main effects due to gender. Moreover, the authors reported "no interpretable sex by age interactions" (p. 43) for any of the criterion measures at any of the data collection intervals.

Hodges and Bloom (1984) concluded that the results of their study were consistent with prior studies suggesting that divorce has a greater impact on boys than on girls. However, they appropriately cautioned the reader that their sample consisted primarily (73 percent) of children in mother-custody homes. Thus the effect of gender in their study was confounded with the effect of same-sex versus opposite-sex custodial parent. They suggested that this was important in view of the finding reported by Santrock and Warshak (1979) that boys seem to do better when they are living with their fathers than with their mothers. (This issue is considered in some detail in Chapter 3.)

In addition to the limitation associated with the confounding of the child's gender and the sex match of the custodial parent, it should be noted that Hodges and Bloom (1984) collected data only during the first 18 months following the separation, during which time the family is still attempting to adjust to the shock. This study does not shed any light on the longer-term adjustment of girls and boys following divorce. This observation is particularly relevant in that the findings suggested diminishing gender differences in adjustment with the passage of time. By eighteen months there were no significant gender effects. The results of this study are consistent with the position that boys, possibly boys in primarily mother-custody homes, experience more distress immediately following separation than do girls, but that there are no long-term gender differences in adjustment.

DIVORCE IS WORSE FOR GIRLS

Even among the early works on the effects of divorce, there were dissenters who maintained that girls might be affected as much as or more than boys. McDermott (1968) suggested that the types of changes in the behavior of girls following a divorce may be different from and more difficult to measure than the types of changes among boys. Whereas boys tend to act out, girls may become anxious and withdrawn. Such internalizing behavior problems may not even be noticed by raters such as parents and teachers, but they may have more serious implications for long-term adjustment than the externalizing behavior problems exhibited by boys. Kalter and associates (1985) offered two reasons why the postdivorce difficulties experienced by girls may be less apparent than those experienced by boys. They suggested that girls tend to display difficulties following divorce at different and less frequently studied points in the lifespan, particularly during adolescence and adulthood. In addition, they agreed with McDermott that girls tend to display problem behaviors that are more difficult to monitor than the variables that have been targeted most frequently in research on divorce. Specifically, they noted that girls tend to experience difficulties in the areas of self-esteem and heterosexual adjustment.

Glenn and Kramer (1985) studied the effect of divorce on adult psychological well-being, using data from the General Social Surveys conducted by the National Opinion Research Center (Davis 1982). These data constitute a very large probability sample of the noninstitutionalized population over the age of 18 in the forty-eight contiguous United States. Approximately 1,500 adults were interviewed during each of the eight years during which data were collected. They compared girls and boys from families that were: (1) intact at the time of the child's 16th birthday; (2) one-parent or stepparent families at the time of the child's 16th birthday, due to the death of one of the child's natural parents prior to that time; or (3) one-parent or stepparent families at the time of the child's 16th birthday, due to the separation or divorce of the child's parents prior to that time.

The criterion measures selected by Glenn and Kramer (1985) included eight dimensions of psychological well-being measured by interview items administered as a standard procedure in the National Opinion Research Center interviews. These included (1) overall happiness, (2) self-rated health, (3) excitement in life, (4) satisfaction from health, (5) satisfaction from community of residence, (6) satisfaction from family life, (7) satisfaction from friendships, and (8) satisfaction from family life.

The analyses carried out by Glenn and Kramer (1985) proceeded through several stages. First, for females and males separately, Glenn and Kramer regressed each of these eight indicators of well-being on a series of dummy variables representing family status. They used living with both parents in an intact family as the reference category, and they constructed dummy variables to indicate membership in each of four family categories: (1) living with one parent only because a parent had died, (2) living with one natural parent and a stepparent because a parent had died, (3) living with one parent only because one's parents had divorced, and (4) living with one natural parent and a stepparent because one's parents had divorced. These regressions yielded no significant differences on any of the satisfaction measures between children in one-parent and stepfamily situations. Therefore, the one-parent and stepfamily respondents were combined within each of the two groups of disrupted families (due to death or due to divorce).

The eight regressions for males and the eight females were rerun using intact families as the reference category, and two dummy variables to represent (1) one parent died and (2) parents divorced. A hierarchical regression procedure was employed so that a number of control variables could be introduced before the effect of family status was examined. The control variables were (1) age of child, (2) father's occupational prestige, (3) father's years of school completed, (4) mother's years of school completed, (5) size of the community lived in at age 16, (6) number of siblings, (7) religion in which the respondent was raised, (8) whether or not the respondent's mother worked outside the home prior to the respondent's 6th birthday, (9) respondent's years of education completed, and (10) respondent's marital status. These measures were included because prior research on subjective well-being indicated that they were related constructs.

The results of the regressions for males indicated that after these control variables were partialed, the effect of being from a divorced family was significant for just one of the satisfaction scales: self-reported happiness ($p = .032$). Glenn and Kramer (1985) noted that the effect of divorce was nearly significant in two of the remaining regressions: satisfaction from community of residence ($p = .062$) and satisfaction from friendships ($p = .076$). In all cases the effect of divorce was negative relative to the reference group of intact families.

The results obtained from the regressions for females were stronger. In five of the eight regressions, the effect of being from a divorced family was significant, after variability due to the control variables was partialed. The five satisfaction measures on which divorce had a significant effect were (1) self-reported happiness ($p < .001$), (2) health self-rating ($p = .036$), (3) satisfaction from community of residence ($p < .001$), (4) satisfaction from friendships ($p = .007$), and (5) satisfaction from family life ($p < .001$). Two other regressions yielded effects for divorce that approached significance: excitement in life ($p = .061$) and satisfaction from health ($p = .085$). In all these cases the effect of being from a divorced family was negative.

Glenn and Kramer (1985) interpreted these findings as follows:

> The data reported here, in contrast to those reported by Kulka and Weingarten (1979), provide greater evidence for negative effects for females than for males. The greater number of coefficients estimated to be significant for females is partly a function of a larger N; but the coefficient is distinctly larger for females in the case of self-rated health, satisfaction from health, satisfaction from community of residence, and satisfaction from residence. [pp. 909–910]

Glenn and Kramer (1985) did acknowledge that the magnitude of the effects they reported tended to be rather small. It is clear that some of the significant findings were due to the huge power of the statistical tests associated with the very large sample sizes they employed. Depending on the particular measure of satisfaction, the sample of males from divorced families ranged from 214 to 280, and the comparison group of males from intact families ranged from 2,803 to 3,621. The sample of females from divorced homes ranged from 302 to 423, and the comparison group of females from intact families ranged from 3,295 to 4,505. Given these sample sizes, estimated effect sizes of approximately one-tenth of one standard deviation were statistically significant. Although Glenn and Kramer contended that effects of this magnitude have meaning, they are in fact very small. For example, Cohen's (1988) book on statistical power analysis in social science research describes an effect size of .10 as "small."

Glenn and Kramer (1985) suggested that the magnitude of the effects they observed might have been greater, had a better measure of family status been used:

> [T]he comparison of the children of divorce with persons from intact families of orientation is not a comparison of one category of persons, all of whom had very negative early influences, with another category of persons, all of whom were free of very negative early influences. Rather, since the sample's children of divorce no doubt include some persons whose parents divorced while they were infants or after they reached adolescence, an appreciable proportion probably escaped the more severe short-term effects that seem to be typical when the parental divorce occurs between infancy and adolescence (Longfellow 1979). Moreover, it is likely that many of the persons from intact families suffered from severe and chronic conflict between the parents, child abuse, neglect, and various other negative experiences associated with their early environments. Therefore, the independent variable used for this study is an extremely crude indicator of the quality of preadult family-related formative experiences.... [p. 910]

While these observations are undoubtedly true, they miss the point. The effect that Glenn and Kramer (1985) were testing was that of divorce, not the overall quality of the child's early environment. Of course there will be variability in the early environments of children from divorced families, just as there will be variability in the early environments of children from intact families. The question that matters here is whether differences due to divorce are significant and meaningful in relation to the variability associated with all the other factors that may have an impact on well-being, but that have not been included in the regression model.

In addition, the authors included a substantial number of control variables in their regression model. This step should have resulted in the extraction of substantial variability in well-being from the error term, which would be expected to make the tests for the significance of the effect of divorce even more powerful.

The best way to summarize the findings of this study is simply to acknowledge that the very large sample sizes employed produced many significant effects due to divorce among the females and a single significant effect due to divorce among the males. But the magnitudes of these effects remain small, despite the authors' protestations to the contrary. It would appear that this study does offer some support for the notion that women suffer greater loss of well-being than men as a result of divorce, but such decrements in well-being appear to be small for both females and males.

Furthermore, it should be emphasized that the criterion measures in this study were extremely narrow in scope. Only aspects of subjective well-being were assessed. The findings would have been stronger if similar effects had been shown across a range of psychosocial adjustment factors.

Another study suggesting that the negative effects of divorce might be greater among females than among males was reported by Allison and Furstenberg (1989). Their study was designed to determine the effects of marital dissolution on children's delinquency, problem behaviors, psychological distress, and academic performance. Reports of children's behavior were derived from parents, teachers, and the children's own self-reports. This study was described in some detail in the preceding chapter as Allison and Furstenberg's study focused on the child's age at the time of the divorce as well as on the child's gender. The investigators employed national probability samples of 328 children from divorced families and 869 children from intact families included in the National Survey of Children. Data were collected at two points in time, five years apart. The children were between 7 and 11 years old at the first wave of data collection.

In order to address the question of whether the effects of marital dissolution are greater for girls or for boys, Allison and Furstenberg (1989) regressed each of the criterion measures for each of the two data collection intervals on marital dissolution. These regressions were calculated separately for girls and boys.

Among girls, significant effects due to marital dissolution were obtained on seven of the nine adjustment measures obtained in the first wave of data collection: parent reports of problem behaviors ($p < .05$) and academic difficulties ($p < .05$); teacher reports of problem behaviors ($p < .01$), school adjustment ($p < .01$), and academic difficulty ($p < .01$); and children's self-reports of dissatisfaction ($p < .01$) and psychological distress ($p < .01$). Significant effects due to marital dissolution were also obtained on four of the ten adjustment measures obtained during the second wave of data collection, five years later: parent reports of delinquency ($p < .01$) and academic difficulties ($p < .01$), and the children's self-reports of their dissatisfaction ($p < .01$) and psychological distress ($p < .01$). In all cases the direction of the effect was such that girls from divorced families demonstrated higher problem scores than did girls from intact families.

In contrast, among boys, significant effects due to marital dissolution were obtained on only four of the nine outcomes assessed at wave one and two of the ten measures assessed at wave two. The data from the first data collection yielded significant effects due to marriage on parent reports of hyperactivity ($p < .01$) and problem behavior ($p < .01$), and teacher reports of problem behavior ($p < .01$) and adjustment ($p < .01$). The data from the second data collection yielded significant effects due to marital dissolution only on parent reports of delinquency ($p < .01$) and problem behavior ($p < .01$). These differences all indicated greater problems among the boys from divorced families rather than intact families.

In addition to these differences between boys and girls in terms of the number of areas in which marital dissolution had a significant effect, there were three variables on which tests for the significance of the difference between two independent correlations indicated a significant difference between the girls and the boys with respect to the magnitude of the effect of divorce. These areas were the teacher's report of problem behaviors at the second data collection point, the child's report of dissatisfaction at the second data collection point, and the child's report of psychological distress at the second data collection point. In each case the test indicated that the effect of marital dissolution was stronger among girls than among boys.

Allison and Furstenberg (1989) concluded that the impact of divorce on the psychosocial adjustment of children may be greater on girls than on boys. This study should be given some weight for several reasons. The age of the child at the time of the divorce was controlled by examining this factor as an independent variable in the analyses. The current age of the child was controlled to some extent by the fact that all the participants were within the 7- to 11-year-old (latency) age range at the time of the initial data collection. The study included a broad range of adjustment measures derived from three different sources. Finally, the five-year time interval between the two data collection periods means that the findings pertain to relatively long-term as well as short-term adjustment to divorce.

NO GENDER DIFFERENCES IN THE CHILD'S ADJUSTMENT TO DIVORCE

The early empirical work of Wallerstein and Kelly (1974, 1975, 1976) indicated that boys tended to display more acting-out behavior than girls during the period immediately following the divorce, but that "in the long run neither age nor sex are central factors in determining outcome" (1980, p. 313). Kurdek and colleagues (1981) compared the postdivorce adjustment of girls and boys and concluded that there was no evidence of gender-related differences. Based on a review of the literature on gender differences in adjustment to divorce, Kurdek and Berg (1983) concluded that the results reported were too inconsistent to warrant any firm conclusions regarding the differential impact of divorce on girls and boys.

Forehand and associates (1988) studied the mediating effects of interparental conflict and gender on the short-term adjustment to divorce of adolescents ranging in age from 11 to 15 years. This study has been described in some detail in Chapter 2 of this book, which deals with the effects of interparental conflict. To summarize briefly the most important aspects of the study, Forehand and his colleagues assessed forty-eight girls and forty-eight boys from divorced and intact families characterized by either high or low interparental conflict. The dependent variables in the study included teachers' ratings of the adolescent's cognitive and social competence; maternal ratings of conduct disorder and withdrawn, anxious behavior; and the adolescent's grade point average during the last grading period. The study also included observational measures derived from a mother–child problem–solving task. These measures included dyadic problem-solving ability, positive communication, dyadic conflict, and adolescent depression.

The analysis of these data yielded significant main effects due to level of interparental conflict on several of the criterion variables, but no significant main effects due to family structure (intact versus divorced). Thus the investigators' fundamental conclusion was that conflict, rather than divorce itself, predicts poor short-term adjustment among adolescents. With respect to the effect of adolescent gender, the analyses yielded no significant interactions between gender and either level of conflict or family structure. Thus the study suggested that the impact of conflict did not differ from girls to boys. Forehand and his associates concluded:

> Sex of adolescent did not mediate the effects of divorce or parental conflict. Although preadolescent girls appeared to be more resistant to stress than boys, some adjustment problems increase substantially during adolescence for girls so that girls have as many or more difficulties in some areas as boys (e.g., Peterson and Hamburg 1986). This suggests that adolescent boys and girls may not differ in stress resistance and, thus, that sex differences in reactions to divorce and parental conflict may not exist. [p. 626]

The major limitation of this study is that the adolescent adjustment measures included in the study were all obtained within a year of the parental divorce. Thus the results of the study pertain only to adjustment during the crisis period immediately following the separation. The study does not shed light on the relative impact of divorce on female or male adolescents in the long term. This limitation does not characterize the study of the effects of divorce reported by Acock and Kiecolt (1989), which supports the position that there are few differences between men and women in terms of the effect of parental divorce on adult adjustment. This large sample study was actually carried out to investigate the effects of the remarriage of the custodial parent and postdivorce family socioeconomic status on adult adjustment, and the study has been described in some detail in Chapter 5. However, Acock and Kiecolt analyzed their data for men ($N = 7,752$) and women ($N = 9,674$) separately, so their findings are also highly relevant to the issue of gender differences.

They selected five indicators of adult adjustment from among the interview items included in the National Opinion Research Center interview format. These were (1) general happiness, (2) overall life satisfaction, (3) sense of control over one's life, (4) trust in people, and (5) satisfaction with friendships. The procedures employed to assess these dimensions are described in Chapter 5.

For each of these five dependent variables, Acock and Kiecolt (1989) used the LISREL VI program to perform two analyses of covariance (ANCOVA) structures. One analysis per dependent measure was performed on the data for the men; the second analysis on each measure was based on the data obtained from women. Included as predictors in these analyses were family income at age 16 (representing socioeconomic status) and dummy variables coded to define five family structure categories at age 16: (1) intact (the reference category), (2) living with mother only due to death of father, (3) living with mother only due to divorce, (4) living with mother and stepfather due to death of father, and (5) living with mother and stepfather due to divorce. Also included as control variables in the analysis were the respondent's level of education, family income, age, race (black versus white; other groups excluded), and marital status (married versus not).

The results of these analyses indicated few differences between men and women in terms of the effects on adjustment of either family structure or socioeconomic status: remarriage of the custodial parent was associated with less happiness and lower life satisfaction for both men and women, and family socioeconomic status when the respondent was 16 was associated positively with all five criteria of adult adjustment for both men and women. There were no significant differences between the female and male samples with respect to any of the family structure variables or with respect to family income at age 16. The only differences of note between the results obtained for men and women occurred on the measure of satisfaction with friends. On that measure the participant's level of education and the participant's age were related significantly and positively to satisfaction among women but not among men.

Acock and Kiecolt (1989) concluded that "the long-term effects of family disruption on adult adjustment do not differ by gender" (p. 553). Thus the literature contains several studies suggesting that there are no differences between girls and boys with respect to either short-term or long-term adjustment to divorce. However, these studies do not focus on individuals whose parents divorced when they were very young. The foregoing chapter on the effect of the child's age at the time of the divorce made it clear that the effects of divorce occurring during the preschool years, the latency period, or adolescence may vary as a function of gender. It would appear essential to carry out more longitudinal studies of the adjustment of boys and girls whose parents divorced at various points in the lifespan.

EFFECTS OF DIVORCE ARE QUALITATIVELY DIFFERENT FOR BOYS AND GIRLS

Kalter and Rembar (1981) designed a study to determine the relationship between children's postdivorce adjustment and the period in the child's life during which the parental divorce occurred. This study has been described in detail in the previous chapter, concerned with the age of the child at the time of the divorce. However, the results of the study are also relevant to the question of gender differences in the effects of divorce, because Kalter and Rembar were careful to control for both the gender and the current age of the child when they assessed the effect of the child's age at the time of the divorce.

The study employed a sample of 144 youngsters whose parents had divorced. The sample, recruited from among the patients evaluated at an outpatient psychiatric clinic, consisted of sixty-nine females and seventy-five males who ranged in age from 7 to 17 years old at the time of the study. The children were divided into two groups with respect to current age: a latency-aged group between 7 and 11.5 years old and an adolescent group between 11.5 and 17 years old. Age at the time of the parental divorce was collapsed into three categories: (1) early, from birth to 2½; (2) oedipal, from 2.5 to 5.5; and (3) late, after the child had reached the age of 5½. The children were assessed on the Presenting Problems Checklist, which allows intake workers to indicate the presence or absence of each of twenty-eight possible areas of difficulty.

The data were analyzed separately for latency-aged boys, latency-aged girls, adolescent boys, and adolescent girls. First, for each of these four groups, the percentage of children manifesting each problem was tabled. These figures allowed the comparison of boys to girls within each current age group on each problem behavior.

Among the latency-aged children in the sample, the boys were substantially more likely than the girls to display aggression toward peers (41 percent of the boys versus 25 percent of the girls), school behavior problems (59 percent of the boys versus 28 percent of the girls), and stealing (23 percent of the boys versus 6 percent of the girls). The percentage of the latency-aged girls displaying a particular presenting problem did not exceed the percentage of boys displaying the same problem by more than 7 percent on any of the twenty-eight problems. These findings would lead one to believe that latency-aged boys from divorced families display more aggressive and acting-out behaviors than do latency-aged girls from divorced families.

Among the adolescents in the sample, the boys were substantially more likely than the girls to display seven of the twenty-eight problems. These included aggression toward siblings (45 percent of the boys versus 25 percent of the girls), aggression toward peers (32 percent of the boys versus 11 percent of the girls), aggression toward inanimate objects (29 percent of the boys versus 5 percent of the girls), academic problems (65 percent of the boys versus 54 percent of the girls), school behavior problems (39 percent of the boys versus 16 percent of the girls), stealing (32 percent of the boys versus 14 percent of the girls), and enuresis (13 percent of the boys versus 3 percent of the girls). In this current age range there were four areas in which the proportion of girls displaying the problem was considerably larger than the proportion of boys. These were drug involvement (35 percent of the girls versus 16 percent of the boys), alcohol involvement (22 percent of the girls versus 10 percent of the boys), sexual behavior (32 percent of the girls versus 16 percent of the boys), and running away (22 percent of the girls versus 6 percent of the boys). From these data it would appear that the tendency of boys to display more acting-out, aggressive, and antisocial behavior than girls continues from latency into adolescence. In addition, emerging during adolescence is a tendency for girls to be more likely than boys to display self-destructive behavior. These findings could be interpreted as indicating that divorce affects both boys and girls, but the nature of these effects is different for boys and girls from different age groups. However, it should be noted that this study did not employ an intact family control group, so the differences could also reflect gender differences in problem behaviors in general, irrespective of the divorced family status of these respondents.

Kalter and Rembar (1981) also tested the significance of the effect of the child's age at the time of the divorce among each of the four gender by current age groups. These analyses yielded some interesting patterns of difference as well. For example, among the latency-aged boys, it was found that those whose parents had divorced early in their lives were more likely ($p < .01$) than those whose parents had divorced later to complain of nonaggressive disturbances with their parents. Latency-aged boys whose parents divorced while they were in the oedipal period were more likely than latency-aged boys whose parents had divorced earlier or later to display school behavior problems ($p < .10$), but the oedipal group were less likely ($p < .10$) to report subjective symptoms of psychological distress than the latency-aged boys in the early and late divorce groups. Kalter and Rembar interpreted this as indicating that latency-aged boys whose parents divorced while they were negotiating the oedipal stage were likely to act on their feelings of distress rather than to internalize them. Finally, latency-aged boys whose parents divorced after they had gone beyond the oedipal period were more likely than latency-aged boys whose parents divorced earlier to display nonaggressive disturbances with peers ($p < .10$), and they were less likely than the boys whose parents had divorced earlier to display aggression toward objects ($p < .10$).

Among latency-aged girls, the pattern of differences due to age at the time of the parental divorce was quite different. Latency girls whose parents had divorced early were more likely than those whose parents divorced later to complain of nonaggressive disturbances with parents ($p < .10$). Latency-aged girls whose parents had divorced during their oedipal period did not differ significantly from latency-aged girls whose parents divorced earlier or later on any of the problem behaviors. Similarly, latency-aged girls whose parents divorced after the conclusion of the oedipal period did not differ significantly from latency-aged girls whose parents had divorced earlier on any of the presenting problems.

Kalter and Rembar (1981) suggested that the most interesting aspect of the findings obtained with respect to latency-aged subjects was the fact that both boys and girls whose parents divorced before the initiation of the oedipal period displayed a tendency to complain of nonaggressive disturbances with parents. The authors interpreted this finding as indicating that the effects of early divorce persist over a long time. They based this conclusion on the fact that among the children in the latency-aged group at the time of the study, those for whom the parental divorce had occurred before the age of 2½ had already had between four and eleven years to adjust to the divorce. However, it must be stressed here again that the absence of an intact family control group in this study precludes the attribution of these effects directly to divorce.

With respect to adolescents, the boys and girls also displayed quite different patterns of presenting complaints. Among adolescent boys, those whose parents had divorced early were less likely than boys whose parents had divorced later to display nonaggressive disturbances with their peers ($p < .05$) or academic problems ($p < .10$). Adolescent boys whose parents had divorced during their oedipal period were less likely than adolescent boys whose parents had divorced earlier or later to display aggression directed toward either parents ($p < .10$) or siblings ($p < .10$). Adolescent boys whose parents had divorced after the resolution of the oedipal period were significantly more likely than adolescent boys whose parents had divorced earlier in their lives to display school refusal or truancy ($p < .10$).

Adolescent girls whose parents divorced early did not differ significantly from adolescent girls whose parents divorced during the oedipal or postoedipal period on any of the problems on the checklist. Adolescent girls whose parents had divorced during their oedipal period were significantly more likely than adolescent girls whose parents had divorced earlier or later to present aggression toward parents ($p < .05$), aggression toward peers ($p < .05$), and academic problems ($p < .01$). And adolescent girls whose parents had divorced after the end of the oedipal period were less likely than adolescent girls whose parents had divorced earlier in their lives to present academic problems ($p < .05$).

Kalter and Rembar (1981) noted that the outcomes for adolescents whose parents had divorced during the oedipal period were very different for boys and girls. The adolescent boys whose parents divorced during this period were relatively unlikely to display aggression toward parents and siblings, but the adolescent girls who were of oedipal age at the time of the divorce were relatively likely to display aggression toward parents and peers.

Unfortunately, Kalter and Rembar (1981) did not provide a table indicating the significance of differences in the frequency of occurrence of the various problem behaviors between boys and girls in the same categories with respect to both current age and age at the time of the parents' divorce. It appears that the sample sizes available may have been inadequate for such tests. It would be useful to replicate this study with sufficient cases to make such comparisons possible. In any event, the study by Kalter and Rembar makes it clear that it is well worth investigating the long- and short-term effects of divorce among boys and girls whose parents divorced at different periods in their lives.

Shook and Jurich (1992) studied factors predicting the self-esteem of college students whose parents had divorced during their childhood or adolescence. The predictors they investigated included the students' feelings of closeness with the noncustodial parent. The study has been described already in Chapter 6, which was concerned with the child's relationship with the noncustodial parent. The reader may refer to that chapter for detailed descriptions of the study sample and the measurement procedures employed.

With respect to gender differences, the study by Shook and Jurich (1992) is relevant, because they performed regressions for women and men predicting self-esteem from feelings of closeness to nonresidential father, amount of time spent with nonresidential father over the past year, social class of the postdivorce family, remarriage of the custodial mother, and age of the respondent at the time of the parental divorce. The results of these regression analyses were very different for the female and the male respondents. Among the women in the sample, the only significant predictor of current self-esteem was the amount of contact with the noncustodial father, and this was a negative relationship: women who had more contact tended to have lower self-esteem. Among the men in the sample, the only significant predictor of self-esteem was the age of the respondent at the time of the parental divorce. The older the men were at the time of their parents' divorce, the higher their self-esteem tended to be. Thus one could conclude that the factors that mediate the effects of divorce on adjustment in early adulthood appear to be quite different for men and for women.

Of course, this study has several significant methodological limitations. As in the study reported by Kalter and Rembar (1981), the lack of a comparison group in students from intact families leaves the reader unable to determine whether the differences between the female and male samples have anything to do with divorce at all, or whether they simply reflect general gender differences. Furthermore, the sample sizes of fifty-six females and twenty-five males were far too small for the results of the regression analyses to be reliable. Finally, the single dependent variable, self-esteem, appears far too narrow in scope to provide an adequate assessment of psychosocial adjustment. Nevertheless, the results do suggest that parental divorce may be experienced quite differently by boys and girls.

Hetherington (1993) provided a summary of the findings of the Virginia Longitudinal Study of Divorce and Remarriage. This report considered differences between boys and girls in terms of psychosocial adjustment in various family situations (intact, divorced one-parent, and divorced remarried) at various points in the lifespan. This report has already been discussed from the perspective of the effect of remarriage in Chapter 5 of this book. Here the study is described in somewhat greater detail from the perspective of the gender differences it revealed.

Hetherington (1979a,b) and her associates began their study with a sample of 144 families, each of whom had a target child who was 4 years old at the start of the study. Half of the families were divorced and half were intact. The families in the divorced group had all been separated for between twelve and eighteen months at the time of the divorce. Thus, in interpreting the results of this study, it should be kept in mind that the study is relevant only to the "early divorce" population in which the parental separation occurred during the preschool years. In fact, in the great majority of the families, the initial separation occurred when the target child was between 2½ and 3 years old, around the first onset of the oedipal period. In addition, the families were all white, middle-class families, and almost all of the parents had some education beyond high school. In all the families the mother was the custodial parent.

The children in the divorced group were assessed at five different points in time: at two months following the divorce (fourteen to twenty months after the parental separation; Wave 1); one year after the divorce (Wave 2); two years after the divorce (Wave 3); six years after the divorce, when the children were 10 years old (Wave 4); and eleven years after the divorce, when the children were 15 years old (Wave 5). Over the course of the study 75 percent of the mothers remarried and 33 percent of the nondivorced couples divorced at least once.

Hetherington (1993) and her associates in the Virginia Longitudinal Study employed "multiple measures, methods, and informants to gain information about the adjustment of parents and children and family relationships, including parent (stepparent)–child, marital and sibling relationships, and those with the noncustodial parents and grandparents" (p. 41). They also obtained measures of the children's behavior at school and within their peer groups.

Hetherington (1993) reported that during the preadolescent years there were substantial differences between boys and girls in their responses to divorce and remarriage. The young boys from divorced families showed greater and more enduring adjustment problems when they were living with custodial mothers who had not remarried. In direct contrast, the young girls experienced more substantial problems when the custodial mother remarried, and young girls were more resistant to the presence of a stepfather than were the young boys.

During the early adolescent years, this type of gender difference was not apparent. Hetherington (1993) concluded, "Although throughout the study girls were viewed as more socially competent and until age 15, more academically competent and as having fewer behavior problems than the boys, the Gender X Family Type interactions found with the younger children were no longer found by the age of 15" (p. 49). Thus the differences observed between girls and boys during the early adolescent years were simply differences between girls and boys in general, not differences between girls and boys in terms of the way they reacted to changes in parental marital status. This is an important point, because several of the studies of gender differences that have been reviewed in this chapter did not include comparison groups of children from intact families. Any conclusions regarding gender differences in children's adjustment derived from such studies may similarly be a function of gender itself, rather than gender differences in the effects of divorce.

Hetherington (1993) described the differences between boys and girls from divorced families at each stage following the divorce. Since all the children in this study were the same age, there are also differences between boys and girls at various ages. She suggested that during the first year after the divorce (when the children were between 4 and 5 years old) both boys and girls displayed more anxious, demanding, noncompliant, aggressive, and dependent behavior with peers and adults than boys and girls from intact families. She also noted that these problems were "present in the home and the school, increased over the course of the first year, and declined in the second year as children adjusted to their new home situation" (p. 49).

Hetherington (1993) observed that two years after the divorce the young girls (now about 6) demonstrated no more problems in social and emotional development than girls of the same age from intact families. This was not true for the boys, however. Their behavior had improved somewhat from the first year to the second year after the divorce, but they still exhibited significantly more behavior problems at home and in school than comparably aged boys from intact families. Moreover, Hetherington noted that these differences were still present when the boys were 15 years old.

Furthermore, Hetherington (1993) reported, "By age ten, girls in divorced families, especially early maturing girls who associated with older peers, were showing an increasing number of problems, and by age 15 both boys and girls in divorced families and in remarried families in comparison to those in nondivorced families were exhibiting more externalizing and internalizing behavior and problems in social competence and in school" (p. 49). Hetherington described a cluster of acting-out behaviors including ignoring parental prohibitions, sexual activity, drug and alcohol use, cheating on examinations, truancy, stealing, and loitering. She reported that among adolescents this type of behavior was more prevalent among boys and girls from divorced families and among boys and girls from families in which the mother had remarried after the child had reached the age of 9 than it was among adolescent boys and girls from intact families. Hetherington also noted that between the ages of 10 and 15 internalizing pathology increased more markedly among girls than among boys.

Moreover, Hetherington (1993) reported, "Maturational timing significantly affected the development of externalizing, norm breaking, and internalizing in girls but not boys; early maturers had more problems at ages 10 and 15 years than late maturers, and these effects are most marked in girls in the divorced and stepfather families" (p. 50). This finding suggests the existence of still another factor mediating the relationship between divorce and poor psychosocial adjustment for adolescent girls, that is, the age at which puberty is reached.

Zill and colleagues (1993) examined gender effects in their study of the long-term effects of divorce on parent–child relationships, adjustment, and achievement in young adulthood. This study emphasized the mediating effect of the age of the child at the time of the divorce, and the study has already been described in some detail in the previous chapter, which focused on that predictor. The study employed data from the National Survey of Children collected in 1976, 1981, and 1987 on 1,049 children. During the first wave of data collection all the children were between 7 and 11 years old. During the second wave they ranged from 12 to 16. During the third wave they ranged from 18 to 22. The parents of 240 of these participants separated or divorced before the children reached the age of 16.

The analyses presented by Zill and his colleagues (1993) tested the overall effects of divorce, the effects of gender, the timing of the divorce (before the age of 6 versus between 6 and 16), and the remarriage of the custodial parent. Gender was included as a predictor because prior research had indicated gender differences in children and young adolescents, but the effects of gender had not been tested on a sample that had reached the young-adult age range of 18 to 22.

Zill and associates (1993) noted that the previous research on children and adolescents had indicated that boys are more likely to respond to parental divorce by displaying acting-out behavior at home and in school, whereas girls are more likely to respond with internalizing behavior problems such as depression and "overcontrolled" behavior (see Emery et al. 1985, Hetherington et al. 1982, Zaslow 1988). They also observed that the literature was inconsistent with respect to the overall severity and duration of adjustment reactions among boys and girls. They cited a number of studies suggesting that boys react longer and more intensely to divorce (e.g., Emery 1982, Guidubaldi et al. 1984, Hetherington et al. 1982), but they also cited the study by Allison and Furstenberg (1989) described above in this chapter, which indicated that the effects of divorce may actually be more deleterious among girls than among boys.

When Zill and his colleagues (1993) examined the data from the third wave of data collection (when the participants were between 18 and 22), they found significant main effects due to family status on a number of variables: "Eighteen- to 22-year-olds from disrupted families were twice as likely as other youths to have poor relationships with their fathers and mothers, to show high levels of emotional distress or problem behavior, to have received psychological help, and to have dropped out of high school at some point. For most of the measures, disruption-related problems were at least as evident in adulthood as they had been in adolescence" (p. 96).

Once they had established that the overall negative effects of divorce persisted into adulthood, they addressed the question of gender-related differences. Of nine dependent variables for which significant main effects due to family status had been obtained, only one yielded a significant ($p < .05$) gender by family status interaction. This was the variable measuring poor relationship with mother: "Among young women in Wave 3 of the NSC, 29% of the divorced group had poor relationships with their mothers, compared with 14% of women from nondisrupted families. By contrast, among young men, the proportion with poor relationships with their mothers was roughly the same in divorced and nondivorced families: 19% and 20%, respectively" (Zill et al. 1993, pp. 97–98).

However, Zill and his colleagues correctly noted that since a number of dependent variables were analyzed for each wave of data collection, it was appropriate to employ the Bonferroni correction for significance level. When this correction is applied, the above interaction is no longer significant. Thus the interaction must be evaluated with caution.

In addition, Zill and his colleagues (1993) noted several variables on which apparent differences were observed between boys and girls, but these differences did not yield even a marginally significant gender by family type interaction. For example, 28 percent of the boys from disrupted families had dropped out of high school, compared with only 20 percent of the girls from such families. Also, 23 percent of the boys from disrupted families displayed high behavior problem scores, compared to only 14 percent of the girls from disrupted families. However, they correctly warned that the absence of significant interaction effects with respect to these variables suggested that these observed differences could be accounted for by the main effects of gender alone. Thus the study reported by Zill and his colleagues yields only weak support for the notion of gender-related differences in the effects of divorce among young adults. The effects that he did observe, however, suggested that both females and males may exhibit negative outcomes of divorce when they are young adults, but that the nature of these outcomes is quite different for the two genders.

ZASLOW'S REVIEW OF THE LITERATURE ON GENDER-RELATED DIFFERENCES IN CHILDREN'S RESPONSE TO DIVORCE

Zaslow (1988, 1989) reviewed the research literature on the gender-related differences in children's response to divorce. In an effort to resolve the inconsistencies in the findings reported in this area, she focused on the methodological differences in the studies. She focused her inquiry on six specific questions, as follows: (1) "Are studies that do and do not support a gender difference hypothesis different on methodological grounds?" (2) "Are findings indicating that boys respond less optimally to divorce concentrated in studies involving unremarried mothers with custody?" (3) "Are findings supporting a gender difference concentrated in studies using clinical as opposed to nonclinical samples?" (4) "Are results indicating a gender difference found primarily in studies defining poor adjustment primarily in terms of aggressive, hostile, undercontrolled behavior?" (pp. 356–357) (5) Do boys demonstrate greater adjustment difficulties than girls during the period immediately after the divorce, whereas girls tend to display signs of poor adjustment later on? Or, stated somewhat differently, Do boys manifest more negative effects of divorce only in preadolescence, while girls begin to show new and age-related difficulties when they reach adolescence? (6) Are reports of significant gender differences confined primarily to studies employing school-related indicators of adjustment and/ or teacher reports of behavioral problems?

To address these questions, Zaslow (1988, 1989) reviewed a set of 27 research reports that (1) were quantitative in nature, presenting data on specified child outcome variables; (2) addressed the gender difference hypothesis using a group-comparison strategy involving children of both sexes; (3) defined a family disruption group as involving parental divorce or separation, as opposed to the death or prolonged absence of a parent; and (4) were not repetitious of earlier published reports. Among these twenty-seven studies, twelve supported the hypothesis that boys were affected more severely than girls by parental divorce; four other studies offered qualified support for the hypothesis. In six of the reports no significant differences due to gender were reported. In five of the studies girls demonstrated more negative outcomes than boys. Zaslow (1988, 1989) set out to determine if the studies in these categories differed with respect to the questions stated above.

Methodological Rigor

With respect to methodological rigor, Zaslow (1988, 1989) noted first and foremost that the only studies methodologically adequate to shed light on the gender difference hypothesis were those in which the design made it possible to test for the significance of the gender by family-type interaction, followed by pairwise comparisons of children of each gender to children of the same gender within contrasting family-type groups. In other words, one can only infer a gender difference in the effects of divorce if one can make statements such as this: the boys from divorced families manifested significantly more problems than the boys from intact families, but the corresponding difference for girls was not significant.

Zaslow (1988) noted that six of the studies she reviewed evaluated the gender difference hypothesis using only children from divorced families. Either no children from intact families were included as controls (Kurdek and Berg 1983, Kurdek and Siesky 1978, Kurdek et al. 1981, Reinhard 1977), or data from intact families were available, but not used in the contrasts reported (Hodges et al. 1979, Rosen 1979). When there are no comparisons of same-sexed children from divorced and intact families, it is not possible to differentiate a main effect of gender from an interaction of gender by family type. Zaslow pointed out just how important this distinction can be by referring to the study reported by Guidubaldi and colleagues (1983). In that study the authors contrasted boys from divorced families with girls from divorced families on a series of thirty-four criterion variables; they reported significant gender differences on twenty-four of the thirty-four variables. However, in two-way analyses in which both gender and family type were employed as independent variables, significant interactions were found on only two of the twenty-four criterion measures. In the absence of significant interaction tests, the study might have been interpreted as providing strong support for the gender-difference hypothesis, when in fact the study offered much more limited support.

Zaslow (1988) also pointed out that a study yielding no significant differences between boys from divorced families and girls from divorced families is equally equivocal:

> [I]f no difference is found in a comparison of sons and daughters of divorce, this information is still incomplete: It is again necessary but not sufficient evidence. For example, we cannot determine from such a finding whether the variables chosen for study are insensitive in general in distinguishing between children of divorced and intact marriages, or sensitive, but equally so—across sexes. [p. 368]

Not surprisingly, Zaslow (1988) recommended that in future research, evaluations of the sex-difference hypothesis should be based on data regarding both child gender and family status. She concluded that the most important evidence for testing this hypothesis is that of significant interaction effects and parallel within-gender family-type contrasts. She also suggested that future studies provide estimates of the effect sizes of the interaction terms.

Another methodological issue noted by Zaslow (1989) was the questionable reliability and validity of the measures of psychosocial adjustment employed in some of the studies. She argued that some studies employed data derived from observers' ratings of clinical case records, with no attempts to establish interrater reliabilities. She also pointed out that in some studies observations of brief laboratory interactions were used to indicate adjustment, with no effort to demonstrate that these laboratory observations were related to any other indicators of adjustment.

These observations of Zaslow (1988, 1989) are extremely important, but they did not resolve the question of whether the inconsistencies in the research on gender differences were a function of the relative methodological rigor of the studies that supported or did not support the gender-difference hypothesis. She argued that if methodological problems were the key to the discrepancies, then one might expect that the studies with methodological problems would have failed to support the hypothesis, while the stronger studies would have supported it. She concluded that twenty of the twenty-seven studies did conform to this pattern, but the other seven did not. Three methodologically rigorous studies did not support the hypothesis; four studies with significant methodological weaknesses did. Thus "[I]t does not appear that presence or absence of methodological problems alone suffices to explain the discrepant results regarding the hypothesis" (p. 369).

Custody and Remarriage

With respect to the second question, whether reports confirming the gender-difference hypothesis were confined to those studies involving families with unremarried custodial mothers, Zaslow (1989) cited two theoretical formulations that might lead to the prediction that boys might appear less well adjusted than girls, simply because most studies of the effects of divorce are done on single-parent, mother-custody families. The first explanation is that children fare better when the custodial parent is the same-sex parent. Santrock and Warshak (1979) stated this position as follows: "Parents may know how to interact more effectively and feel more comfortable with a child who is the same sex as they are" (p. 115). In addition, Zaslow pointed out that a custodial parent may identify a child of the opposite sex with the former spouse. This could lead to the development of feelings of emotional distance and anger. Also, as noted by Hetherington (1979a) and by Wallerstein and Kelly (1980), residence with a custodial mother, along the typical pattern of declining contact with the noncustodial father, may involve considerable psychological loss for sons.

The second hypothesis that could account for the greater disruption observed among boys in some studies has to do with the possible remarriage of the custodial mother. This hypothesis states that girls tend to adjust well to divorce in the short term, but may experience considerable distress when their mother remarries. In contrast, boys do not get along very well when they reside with the custodial mother alone, but they often benefit from her remarriage. This theory would imply that studies focusing on families with unremarried custodial mothers would tend to find that girls were better adjusted than boys.

Therefore, Zaslow (1989) asked whether findings reported with respect to the gender-difference hypothesis would differ depending on the nature of the postdivorce family structure. Specifically: (1) Would girls do better than boys in families with unremarried custodial mothers? (2) Would boys do better than girls in families with unremarried custodial fathers? (3) Would boys do better than girls in families with custodial mothers and stepfathers? (4) In studies where the postdivorce family structure was not specified, would there be no significant differences between girls and boys?

Zaslow reported that of the twenty-seven studies she reviewed, fourteen included children who could be identified explicitly as children from families with unremarried custodial mothers. Of these fourteen studies, eleven supported the hypothesis that boys adjusted less well to divorce than girls. The only three reports in this group that did not favor this hypothesis were reported by Santrock and his colleagues, and all these studies were based on laboratory observations. Moreover, the findings from these studies were inconsistent. In the first study (Santrock and Warshak 1979), mother-custody boys were rated as better adjusted than boys from intact families on two of nine categories of behavior observed in mother–child interactions, while mother-custody girls were rated as more poorly adjusted than girls from intact families on two of the same nine behavioral categories. However, in two subsequent reports from the same group of investigators (Santrock et al. 1982a,b), there were no significant differences between children of either sex in divorced versus intact families.

Only two of the twenty-seven studies analyzed by Zaslow (1989) explicitly included a sample of children with an unremarried custodial father (Santrock and Warshak 1979, Santrock et al. 1982a). In each case girls displayed greater disturbance following divorce than did boys.

Three of the twenty-seven studies included samples of children living with remarried custodial mothers (Hetherington et al. 1985, Kalter 1977, Santrock et al. 1982b). In each of these studies the girls did show significantly poorer adjustment than the boys. In the study by Hetherington and her associates, girls in families in which custodial mothers had remarried recently differed significantly from girls in intact families on all three criterion variables examined: internalizing behavior problems, externalizing behavior problems, and social competence. In contrast, sons of recently remarried custodial mothers differed from boys in intact families only with respect to externalizing problems. This pattern differed markedly from that manifested by boys and girls from families with unremarried custodial mothers. In those families, six years after the divorce, daughters did not differ significantly from girls in intact families, but sons did differ from boys in intact families.

Kalter (1977) reported that 22 percent of the girls in an outpatient clinic population came from families with a stepparent. In contrast, only 11 percent of the boys in the same population came from stepparent families. Moreover, relative to adolescent girls in intact families, significantly more adolescent daughters in stepfather families displayed aggressiveness toward parents and peers and became involved in substance abuse or premature sexual relations. Santrock and colleagues (1982b) reported that daughters in stepfather families demonstrated poor social adjustment relative to girls in intact families. In contrast, these investigators found no significant differences in social adjustment between boys from stepfather families and those from intact families.

Finally, Zaslow (1989) examined the twelve studies in her sample that did not either specify or hold constant the custody arrangement or the current marital status of the custodial parent. Most of these studies reported no significant gender differences in children's postdivorce adjustment. Zaslow attributed this to the failure of the studies to examine the effects of divorce separately among boys and girls in mother-custody and father-custody single-parent and remarried parent families. These findings clearly suggest that the idea that boys suffer greater negative effects than girls following divorce is in fact the result of the preponderance of studies involving families with custodial mothers who have not remarried. These findings of Zaslow are also consistent with the two theories that suggest (1) the desirability of custody with the same-sex parent, and (2) the negative impact upon girls of recent maternal remarriage.

Populations Sampled

The third question asked by Zaslow (1989) was whether the studies indicating that boys suffered more than girls following divorce were based on clinical samples. The reason for asking the question had to do with the research reported by O'Leary and Emery (1984) regarding the relationship between marital discord and children's behavior problems in intact families. Based on a review of the literature in this area, O'Leary and Emery concluded that all the studies indicating that only boys were affected adversely by parental discord were studies of (1) children referred to clinics or (2) children from families which displayed indications of psychological disturbance. In contrast, studies employing relatively healthy nonclinical samples tended to indicate that parental discord was related to some categories of psychosocial maladjustment among both boys and girls.

O'Leary and Emery (1984) suggested two possible explanations of why a gender difference in the effects of marital discord would emerge primarily in studies in which clinical samples were used. First, they noted that boys are more likely than girls to respond to marital hostility by displaying conduct problems such as aggression, hostility, and lack of control. Moreover, it is this group of children who manifest such externalizing behavior problems that is most likely to be referred to a clinic for counseling. For this reason the male children of discordant marriages are probably overrepresented in clinical samples. The presence of large numbers of such boys in clinical samples would tend to make the boys in such samples exhibit more behavior problems than the girls.

The second explanation offered by O'Leary and Emery (1984) was that girls simply responded to parental discord differently from boys. Girls may display a delayed reaction to parental conflict, or they may respond with internalizing behavior problems, such as overcontrol. These reactions would not be as likely as externalizing behavior problems to lead to a referral to a clinic.

Emery (1985) suggested that sex differences in response to parental divorce, like sex differences in response to parental conflict, should be concentrated in clinical samples. Among the twenty-seven studies included in Zaslow's (1988, 1989) reviews, only two were based on clinical samples (Kalter 1977, Tuckman and Regan 1966). Both these studies reported that boys were affected more severely than girls by parental divorce. The remaining twenty-five studies, which did not include clinical samples, were "approximately evenly divided between those supporting the sex-difference hypothesis and those failing to support it" (Zaslow 1989, p. 120). Zaslow cautioned that because there were only two studies employing clinical samples in her sample of research reports, she could not conclude flatly that the notion that boys respond more poorly to divorce than girls is due to the presence of studies employing clinical samples. Nevertheless, she did feel comfortable concluding that "findings of a sex difference in response to divorce are consistent in clinic-based samples, and less consistent but not absent in nonclinic-based samples" (1989, p. 120).

Criteria Chosen to Represent Psychosocial Adjustment

Zaslow's (1988) fourth question was whether studies indicating poorer adjustment among boys predominantly defined adjustment in terms of externalizing behavior problems. She referred to McDermott's (1968) contention that there was a sex difference in the relative "visibility" of the problems experienced by boys and girls. The anger and aggression displayed by boys was clear and likely to be noticed. The personality constriction, quarrelsome attitudes, and pseudo-maturity manifested by girls were less likely to be noticed as problems by parents and teachers. Nevertheless, McDermott warned that the types of problems experienced by girls might actually be more damaging in the long run than the brief acting-out episodes displayed by boys.

Similarly, Kalter and colleagues (1985) complained that research on the effects of divorce has relied heavily on standardized measures of adjustment that do not necessarily measure the types of problems that girls tend to experience. These problem areas include (1) internalizing pathology, such as depression, anxiety, and somatic complaints; (2) self-esteem; and (3) adjustment in heterosexual relationships.

Emery and associates (1985) also concluded that externalizing responses were characteristic of boys, while internalizing responses were characteristic of girls. Moreover, it has been argued that problems of overcontrol are much more difficult to assess than externalizing behavior problems (Emery 1982, Hetherington et al. 1985, O'Leary and Emery 1984). For this reason it is possible that gender differences in children's response to parental divorce may simply reflect differences in the reliability of the measures of internalizing and externalizing psychopathology that have been employed in these studies.

In evaluating the impact of the type of criterion measure used to assess psychosocial adjustment, Zaslow (1989) focused first on a subset of studies that included measures of both internalizing and externalizing psychopathology. She focused on this subset of the research reports because the use of these studies would control for other differences among the studies, including differences in methodological rigor. Within this subset she examined the findings of studies that did not distinguish between one-parent and stepparent families and those that did. She concluded that:

> When no stepparent is specified to be present, externalizing reactions tend to be more typical of boys than of girls following di-

vorce, but internalizing reactions are reported in both genders; when a stepparent is present, girls are more likely to show more pervasive differences than boys in both dimensions. [p. 126]

Zaslow (1989) also examined the results of another subset of studies in which a measure of self-esteem had been included as a criterion of psychosocial adjustment. Of fourteen such studies, only five reported that girls from divorced families manifested significantly lower self-esteem than girls from intact families. Furthermore, two of these five studies (Hetherington 1972, Kalter et al. 1985) included only female subjects. The lack of males in these studies leaves open the possibility that the differences observed between girls from divorced and intact families may have been similar for boys. In the remaining three of these five studies, the findings obtained with respect to self-esteem pertained only to girls in father-custody homes (Santrock and Warshak 1979, Santrock et al. 1982a, study 1 and study 2). In nine of the fourteen studies that assessed self-esteem, there were no significant differences between girls and boys in terms of the effect of family type on self-esteem. Zaslow concluded that "self-esteem variables do not appear to show distinctive reactions of girls to parental divorce" (p. 127).

None of the studies included in Zaslow's (1988) sample of twenty-seven studies included an explicit measure of heterosexual adjustment. Therefore she broadened her criteria somewhat to examine the results of several studies that did address the issue. Wallerstein (1985) reported a ten-year follow-up of children of divorce involving 19- to 29-year-olds. Within this group two-thirds of the twenty-four women expressed a conscious fear of marriage, in spite of a desire to be married. One-third of the women were identified as particularly troubled regarding heterosexual relationships. These women, who feared rejection, were reluctant to make any commitment; they tended to be involved in short-term relationships only. Hetherington (1972) compared adolescent girls from divorced and intact families. She reported that the girls from divorced families reported more sexual activity than girls from intact families, but less security in their relationships with men. Kulka and Weingarten (1979) reported that adult women whose parents had divorced were less invested in their marriages than were comparably aged women from intact families. In contrast, adult males from divorced families differed from comparably aged males with respect to comfort with parenthood, but not with respect to investment in marriage. Zaslow concluded that there is some reason to suspect that girls from divorced families do tend to experience difficulties surrounding heterosexual relationships, but that more research was required before firm conclusions could be drawn.

Timing of Adjustment Reactions

Zaslow (1989) referred to Hetherington's (1979a) conceptualization of divorce as a process rather than an event. She suggested that four phases in this process could be noted: (1) disequilibrium in the family prior to divorce, (2) disequilibrium and disorganization after the divorce, (3) efforts to adapt to the new family situation, and (4) the emergence of a new equilibrium. Zaslow also noted that some of the longitudinal studies of the effects of divorce indicate that gender differences in the effects of divorce vary with the amount of time that has elapsed since the divorce. For example, Hetherington and colleagues (1979) reported that both boys and girls manifest behavioral improvements over the first two years following parental divorce. The girls appear to recover more quickly, but eventually the adjustment of boys and girls tends to converge.

These considerations led Zaslow (1989) to suggest that perhaps gender differences in adjustment to divorce are a function of family conflict and disorganization, which will tend to return to equilibrium within two or three years. Therefore Zaslow compared studies in which data on adjustment were gathered within the first three years following the divorce to studies in which data were gathered more than three years following the divorce. Within her study sample of twenty-seven research reports, Zaslow identified eighteen in which the time since the divorce was specified. Of these, data were gathered within three years of the divorce in nine studies and later in nine studies.

Among the studies in which data were collected within the first three years, six indicated that the impact of divorce was greater for boys than for girls, two indicated no significant gender differences, and one showed greater disruption among girls. Among the studies in which the data were gathered more than three years after the divorce, five indicated greater effects for boys than for girls, one indicated no significant gender-related differences, and three suggested that girls experienced greater psychosocial adjustment difficulties than boys. On the basis of these findings, Zaslow (1989) concluded that "specification of time since separation or divorce does not appear to provide a strong basis for clarifying the discrepancy across research reports . . . regarding the sex difference hypothesis" (p. 130). This in turn led Zaslow to suggest that either: (1) Family conflict and disequilibrium are not major factors in the determination of postdivorce gender differences; or (2) perhaps the notion that postdivorce conflict and disequilibrium dissipate after two or three years following the divorce is simply not true.

Sources of Data

The final question addressed in Zaslow's (1989) review was concerned with the source of data employed to assess psychosocial adjustment. Specifically, Zaslow wondered whether studies indicating that the impact of divorce is more severe for boys than for girls were predominantly studies employing teacher reports. She noted that Whitehead (1979) had suggested that teachers are more sensitive to acting-out antisocial behavior than they are to neurotic disorders and internalizing pathology. She also pointed out that in studies reporting significant gender differences in children's learning and school adjustment following divorce, the largest and most pervasive differences were found on teacher ratings, not parent ratings.

To determine whether the source of the data made a difference in findings obtained with respect to the gender-difference hypothesis, Zaslow (1989) focused on the eight studies within her sample of twenty-seven in which ratings from both parents and teachers were employed as criteria of postdivorce adjustment. She examined these studies to identify those in which (1) data from teachers supported the gender-difference hypothesis, but data from parents did not; or (2) data from both sources supported the hypothesis, but the findings derived from teacher reports provided stronger support for the gender-difference hypothesis than the findings derived from parents. Only two of the eight studies fell into one of these two categories. This led Zaslow (1989) to conclude:

> There is no consistent pattern pointing to teachers as the source of the findings that sons of divorce are most negatively affected. Rather, it was more common for parents and teachers to agree as to whether children of one gender were more affected by their parents' divorce, and if so, which gender was more affected. [p. 136]

With respect to her entire review, Zaslow (1989) concluded that the research was quite inconsistent with respect to the hypothesis that divorce has a greater impact on boys than girls. She concluded further that among the six possible explanations for these inconsistencies that she examined in her analyses of the research reports,

> [T]he one that came closest to clarifying the discrepancy was the prediction that boys do indeed respond more to parental divorce, both immediately and over a period of years, *if* they are living with an unremarried mother; whereas in postdivorce families involving a stepfather or father custody, girls fare worse. The major conclusion of this review is that both research and practice with children of divorce must consider gender differences in divorce reactions in relation to postdivorce family forms. [p. 136]

Zaslow put her conclusion in context by noting that, over time, most divorced women do remarry. As this occurs, gender differences are likely to be obscured by the differential effects of remarriage on boys and girls. Thus, in the long run, it is unlikely that boys actually respond more negatively to divorce than girls. This conclusion is supported by the findings of Furstenberg and Allison (1985), who reported that when postdivorce family type was not held constant, the outcomes for children of divorced parents did not differ very much by gender.

Zaslow (1989) also pointed out that her findings suggest that any gender differences in postdivorce adjustment should not be interpreted as indicating that boys are more vulnerable to stress than girls. Rather, the vulnerabilities of both girls and boys appear to be related to family type. Therefore the central issue is not why boys tend to respond more negatively to parental divorce across a variety of situations, but rather what specific aspects of various postdivorce family forms are either stressful or stress buffering for girls and for boys.

9

STRESSFUL LIFE CHANGES

MANY RESEARCHERS HAVE argued that it is not parental divorce per se that leads to adjustment problems among children, but rather the cumulative effect of the stressful life changes that typically accompany divorce (Bloom et al. 1978, Menaghan 1983). This hypothesis has been stated in two different forms. The narrow version of the hypothesis focuses specifically on the typically negative impact of divorce on family income. The broader version is the theory of multiple life stresses. This theoretical perspective encompasses a range of stressors that often accompany divorce, including not only the likely decrement in family socioeconomic status, but also the changes that often occur with respect to place of residence and school system, shifts in family routine and responsibilities that may arise in connection with new maternal educational or employment activities, and changes in one's network of peers and sources of social support.

The multiple life stresses hypothesis represents the application to divorce of Holmes and Rahe's (1967) research on the relationship between stressful life events and the occurrence of physical health problems and psychological symptoms. Within the divorce literature, Rutter (1985) suggested that single traumatic events rarely lead to enduring problems in psychosocial adjustment, but the accumulated stress associated with multiple, stressful, life circumstances does. Thus Rutter suggested that divorce itself does not necessarily result in poor adjustment, but rather the many changes that typically accompany divorce.

Clearly, the two forms of the stress hypothesis are not competing explanations, but complementary. In this chapter the empirical literature relevant to both the narrow model of economic distress and the multiple life stresses hypothesis is reviewed. The literature offers substantial support for both formulations.

ECONOMIC DISTRESS MODEL

Several researchers have provided data indicating that divorce typically does have a major adverse impact on family finances. Flynn (1984) reported that the most significant element in the increased number of United States families below the poverty line is the single-parent family, which are overwhelmingly headed by women. This is due partly to single-mother families in which the parents were never married, but another factor that contributes to this imbalance is that the great majority of custody decisions are still for mother custody. Hodges (1991) reported that, until the recent advent of joint custody laws in some states, approximately 90 percent of custody was mother custody. This fact, coupled with the fact that women earn on the average only 59 percent of what men earn, places the single-mother family at risk for poverty status.

Furthermore, noncustodial fathers typically contribute little. Child support awards typically do not cover anything near the full amount of the expenses associated with raising a child. Furthermore, within three years following the divorce, only 19 percent of noncustodial fathers continue to pay child support. Even in the rare situation in which the noncustodial father does pay child support, the additional expense associated with maintaining two households virtually guarantees some decrease in the family's standard of living. Thus it is not surprising that 75 percent of the poor in the United States are women and children (Flynn 1984).

Hetherington's (1993) report on the Virginia Longitudinal Study of Divorce and Remarriage provided more data relevant to the diminished economic status of single mothers following divorce. She noted that within her sample of divorced mothers, two years after the divorce the average household income was $16,000, including transfer payments received from the noncustodial father. In contrast, the average household income among her intact family sample was $33,000. At eleven years after the divorce, when Hetherington's sample of children were 15 years old, the average household income among divorced mothers who had not remarried had risen to $28,000. At the same time, the average income among the intact family sample was $58,000, and the average income among remarried families was $56,000.

Hetherington (1993) reported that 18 percent of the unremarried divorced women in her study had been on some form of public assistance. She noted that this figure was quite high given the relatively high level of educational attainment that characterized the group. In contrast, only 2 percent of the mothers in intact families had been on public assistance, and only 10 percent of the remarried custodial mothers. Twenty percent of the women in the divorced unremarried sample had resided with parents for some period of time following the divorce due to economic necessity. At the time of the final follow-up study, eleven years following the divorce, more than 95 percent of the divorced nonremarried women were employed. This figure is not quite as startling as it might seem at first, however, because at the same time approximately 90 percent of the women from intact and remarried families were also working. Hetherington also concluded that "[r]emarriage was the most effective route out of economic distress for divorced women" (p. 42).

There are several reasons why a decrement in socioeconomic status following divorce would be expected to be associated with negative psychosocial outcomes for children. Acock and Kiecolt (1989) stated the most obvious reason: "Comfortable economic circumstances provide people with a sense of security that helps them cope with adversity, while strained economic circumstances are a chronic source of stress" (p. 556). This relationship pertains whether or not a divorce has occurred. Based on a general sample of women who were young adults during the Great Depression, Elder and Liker (1982) concluded that socioeconomic status during early adulthood is a strong predictor of psychological well-being in later life.

A number of studies based on general populations have indicated a significant relationship between socioeconomic status and self-esteem (Bloom et al. 1978, Demo and Savin-Williams 1983, Rosenberg 1965, Rosenberg and Perlin 1978). Based on the results of these studies, Shook and Jurich (1992) concluded that:

> a positive relationship exists between social class and self-esteem of individuals of various different ages. Moreover, it appears that social class becomes a stronger determinant of self-esteem as people age. Therefore, it is conceivable that families with high annual incomes can offer their children more privileges than families who report more meager family incomes. This freedom provides children with the opportunities to achieve social competency and

personal goals which lead to self-esteem. Thus, there seems to be evidence to suggest that social class may also be relevant to the study of self-esteem among college offspring from divorced families. [pp. 160–161]

A number of empirical studies have supported the position that loss of income following divorce is a powerful predictor of adjustment problems in children (Bane 1976, Colletta 1979, Desimone-Luis et al. 1979, Espenshade 1979, Hodges 1979, 1984). Desimone-Luis and colleagues (1979) measured the effects of several predictors on postdivorce adjustment, concluding that decreased income was the most important predictor. Hodges and colleagues (1979) found that low income was a significant predictor of child maladjustment among families in which the parents had divorced, whereas low income was not related to maladjustment for children of intact families from the same school. Hodges and associates (1984) reported that parental reports of annual family income were related negatively to parental reports of adjustment problems among preschool children from both divorced and intact families. Specifically, they found that low income predicted withdrawal and anxiety-depression among preschoolers.

However, they also reported a significant interaction between family type and economic distress. The effect of parental perceptions of the adequacy of family income on anxiety-depression was significantly greater among the divorced sample than among the intact family sample. Among children from intact families, rated adequacy of income had no effect on reported levels of anxiety-depression in children. Among children of divorced families with adequate income, scores on anxiety-depression did not differ significantly from the scores of children from intact families. However, among children from divorced families whose parents rated their income as inadequate, scores on anxiety-depression were significantly higher than among children from intact families.

The apparent difference in the magnitude of the effect of economic distress between divorced and intact families may suggest that whatever the general impact of low socioeconomic status may be, an additional effect may be associated with the *decrease* in socioeconomic status that typically follows divorce. It is also possible that part of the problem may be due to the discrepancy in income between the household of the custodial mother and the household of the noncustodial father. Wallerstein and Corbin (1989) reported that when there was a major discrepancy in income between the parents, with mothers more economically disadvantaged than fathers, girls tended to display poor psychological adjustment. This relationship pertained regardless of whether the discrepancy arose from the economic decline of the custodial mother or from a major economic advance on the part of the father.

Another explanation of the adverse effect of economic distress following divorce has to do with the psychological adjustment of the custodial parent. Research has shown that custodial single mothers tend to have higher rates of anxiety and depression than any other marital status group (Bachrach 1975, McClanahan et al. 1981, Radloff and Rae 1979). In addition, single custodial mothers are more likely to seek counseling or other mental health services than women in other marital status groups. As described in Chapter 4 of this book, psychological distress on the part of the custodial parent may limit the parent's ability to provide effective, authoritative parenting, which may in turn lead to inadequate psychosocial adjustment among children. Several investigators have suggested that decrements in the economic status of custodial mothers may lead to the emergence of psychological symptoms that are reflected in inadequate parenting behavior (Brandwein et al. 1974, Bozenzweig 1976).

Evidence of the impact of economic distress has been offered by Acock and Kiecolt (1989) in their large sample study of the effects of family structure and socioeconomic status during adolescence on the adult adjustment of children of divorce. Since Acock and Kiecolt appropriately reported the results of this study separately for female and male respondents, the study has been described in some detail in Chapter 8 of this book, which considers gender differences in adjustment following parental divorce. For the purpose of the present discussion, it should be noted that Acock and Kiecolt included both family income at age 16 and the custodial mother's level of education as predictors of adult psychosocial adjustment, which was operationalized in self-reports of (1) general happiness, (2) overall life satisfaction, (3) sense of control over one's life, (4) trust in people, and (5) satisfaction with one's friendships.

Acock and Kiecolt (1989) reported that for both female and male respondents, family income and maternal educational level were related significantly to all five of the adjustment measures. Furthermore, these results were obtained with respect to each of the four different family types included in the study: (1) single-mother families resulting from the death of the father, (2) single-mother families resulting from divorce, (3) mother and stepfather families resulting from the death of the natural father, and (4) mother and stepfather families resulting from divorce. Acock and Kiecolt concluded: "Socioeconomic status during adolescence has a consistent, independent effect on adult adjustment. The more educated the mother, the better every aspect of adult adjustment. Economic resources during adolescence are important, since family income at age 16 has a significant positive effect on all aspects of adjustment. Together these two indicators of socioeconomic status show significant and positive effects in all 40 tests" (p. 564). The forty tests referred to for each of these predictors represent the five adjustment criteria times two genders times four family structure types. Acock and Kiecolt emphasized that these clear and consistent results for the two adolescent socioeconomic status predictors were much more impressive than the results obtained with respect to family structure, which was a significant predictor in only ten of forty tests.

Kalter and colleagues (1989) also provided some empirical evidence of the importance of economic distress among divorced families. This study was based on a sample of fifty-six divorced custodial mothers recruited from four elementary schools in southeastern Michigan. The study was considered in some detail in Chapter 4 of this volume because it provided strong support for the hypothesis that the psychological adjustment of the custodial mother is an important predictor of children's adjustment.

However, Kalter and his associates (1989) also sought to test the economic distress hypothesis. They used both maternal self-reports of current annual income and the Hollingshead Index of Socioeconomic Status (SES) to predict the adjustment of children, which they defined operationally in terms of maternal reports elicited through the use of the Child Behavior Checklist (CBCL) (Achenbach and Edelbrock 1983), children's self-reports on the Children's Depression Inventory (CDI) (Kovacs 1983), and the State-Trait Anxiety Inventory (STAI) (Spielberger 1973).

Kalter and colleagues (1989) found that, for the total sample (boys and girls pooled), scores on the Hollingshead Index were related negatively to the CBCL subscales for Total Problems, Internalizing Problems, Externalizing Problems, Aggression, and Depression. Hollingshead SES scores were also related negatively to CDI Depression scores and to State and Trait Anxiety. These relationships were not statistically significant, but the authors attributed the lack of significance to the small sample size employed in the study. More conflicting results were obtained with respect to maternal reports of family income. Among girls, the expected pattern was obtained. There were negative relationships between income and almost every adjustment problem measure, although these relationships were not always significant. Among boys, however, family income was actually related positively to the problem measures, and in some cases these relationships were significant. Kalter and his associates suggested that the differences between girls and boys obtained with respect to family income might reflect the fact that a high family income is associated with being in a remarried household in which both parents work outside the home. They indicated that boys may fare less well when their mother works outside the home. This explanation is plausible, since nineteen of the fifty-six families included in this study were remarried families. In this situation, economic distress may not be as important a predictor of adjustment as it is in single-mother families simply because the economic distress is unlikely to be as severe. Nevertheless, even within a sample containing a fairly large proportion of remarried mothers, the economic-distress hypothesis was generally supported.

Mednick et al. (1990) considered the relationships among family socioeconomic status, mother's highest level of education, and children's proficiency in reading and mathematics. Their sample consisted of seventy-seven young adult students who were included in the Danish Perinatal Project, an eighteen-year prospective study begun in 1959 at the state university hospital in Copenhagen. The participants came from divorced homes that had been intact during the first year of the subject's life, but that were broken some time during the subsequent sixteen to eighteen years. The mother was the custodial parent in all cases. The sample contained thirty-four males and forty-three females.

Mednick and her associates (1990) measured academic proficiency by obtaining the ratings of each student from the teacher most familiar with that student. The teachers rated the students on oral language, reading, mathematics, reasoning, work organization, and concentration. Factor analysis of these ratings yielded factor scores for the two domains of reading and mathematics proficiency.

The results of this study indicated that for the entire sample (boys and girls pooled) family socioeconomic status was related significantly to reading proficiency ($r = .26$, $p < .05$) but not to mathematics proficiency ($r = .22$, $p > .05$). Mother's highest level of education was related significantly to both reading proficiency ($r = .34$, $p < .01$) and mathematics proficiency ($r = .27$, $p < .05$). Mednick and her associates (1990) did not present the corresponding correlations for boys and girls separately, perhaps because of the relatively limited sample size they had to work with. Although this is clearly a limitation of the study based on the importance of the gender differences described in Chapter 8, the study nevertheless does provide further support for the notion that the socioeconomic status of children from divorced families is related significantly to postdivorce adjustment.

Blechman (1982) came to an important conclusion on the basis of her reading of the literature on economic distress. She noted that in most of the research reported on the relationship between parental divorce and children's psychosocial adjustment, family socioeconomic status has not been controlled. She suggested that some portion of the adjustment difficulties found in divorced families may result from their diminished capacity to use economic resources to solve problems. Some possible examples of the type of situation that she had in mind would be inadequate funds for day care or babysitting and inadequate funds to provide tutoring in the event of academic difficulties.

Along the same line, Acock and Kiecolt (1989) observed that in studies of the adult psychosocial adjustment of children from divorced families it is critical that researchers measure and control for the respondents' current socioeconomic status. They pointed out that "many indicators of psychological well-being are related to location in the social structure" (p. 557). Campbell (1981) reported that socioeconomic status is related positively to self-reported happiness. Mirowsky and Ross (1986) reported that education and socioeconomic status are related positively to having a strong sense of control over one's life and to the ability to trust other people. Thus it would appear that socioeconomic status should be taken into account in any study attempting to predict adult adjustment, subjective well-being, or life satisfaction.

MULTIPLE LIFE STRESSES MODEL

The multiple life stresses model of adjustment to divorce grew out of the work of Holmes and Rahe (1967) on the relationship between stressful life events and the incidence of physical illnesses and psychiatric symptoms. Holmes and Rahe suggested that the crucial aspect of major life events that made these events stressful was change. Even desirable life changes can be stressful as they often result in significant changes in one's usual activities. The instruments that Holmes and Rahe developed to measure stress—the Social Readjustment Rating Scale (SRRS) and the Schedule of Recent Experience (SRE)—reflect this theoretical viewpoint. These instruments define stress operationally in terms of the weighted or unweighted sum of discrete life changes that have occurred in an individual's life during the recent past. Based on an extensive review of the literature on life changes, Holmes and Masuda (1974) concluded that there is substantial support for the argument that life changes are associated with the onset and severity of disease.

Masuda and Holmes (1967) reported a significant relationship between recent life changes and substance (alcohol and heroin) abuse. Myers and colleagues (1974) found significant relationships in a community sample between the number of recent life changes and a variety of psychiatric symptoms. Other investigators found that recent life events scores significantly differentiated psychiatric populations from the general population. These psychiatric groups included depressives (Paykel 1974), parasuicides (Cochrane and Robertson 1975), and inpatients (Decker and Webb 1974, Ulenhuth and Paykel 1973).

A number of studies have suggested that stressful life changes can have a significant impact on the well-being and adjustment of children. Justice and Duncan (1976) reported that life change scores were related significantly to the incidence of child abuse; Justice and Justice (1979) reported that life change scores were related to child sexual abuse. Several epidemiological studies have yielded significant relationships between stressful life events and children's mental and physical health problems (Coddington 1972a,b, Gersten et al. 1974, Heisel et al. 1974).

Sandler and Block (1979) reported the results of a study that is representative of this body of research. They studied students in kindergarten through grade three in two inner-city elementary schools. Ninety-nine of these students were identified by their teachers as manifesting social or emotional adjustment difficulties in the classroom. Forty-four were controls who were not so identified, but were randomly selected from the same grades at the same schools.

Sandler and Block (1979) measured stress by means of a thirty-two-item recent life event schedule completed by the children's parent(s). Most of the items (twenty-five) were adapted from Coddington's (1972a) scale for assessing stressful life events among elementary school students or from the recent life events schedule developed by Gersten and colleagues (1977) (five items). The remaining two items were developed specifically for this study by Sandler and Block. Item selection was governed by the admonition of Gersten and associates (1977) to select items that are not confounded with the child's adjustment or coping capacities. This means that the events selected should be clearly beyond the child's control and unable to be construed as a consequence of the child's adjustment or behavior.

This life events schedule was scored three ways, reflecting a debate within this area of research regarding the most appropriate manner in which to develop stress scores from these schedules. The first method was to use the simple number of events out of the thirty-two that had been endorsed by the child. A second, weighted life events score was computed using only the twenty-five items developed by Coddington (1972a). This score employed the weights developed by Coddington to represent the relative amount of readjustment required by children in this age range following each one of the various events. In a third scoring procedure raters classified each event in the schedule as desirable, undesirable, or ambiguous, and the numbers of undesirable and desirable events endorsed by each respondent were counted.

The results of this study indicated significant differences between the maladapted and control groups on total life events endorsed ($p < .001$), the weighted life events readjustment score ($p < .05$), and the number of undesirable events endorsed ($p < .01$). In addition, based on the maladaptive sample alone, many significant Pearson correlations were found between the several different life events scores and parental ratings of children's behavior derived from the Louisville Behavior Checklist (LBC) (Miller 1975). The LBC yields subscale scores representing sensitivity, social withdrawal, fear, infantile aggression, hyperactivity, antisocial behavior, academic disability, prosocial behavior, inhibition, and current aggression. The total life events score was correlated significantly ($p < .05$ through $p < .001$) with all of these subscales except social withdrawal and prosocial behavior.

Sandler and Block (1979) concluded that these findings:

> represent an extension of previous research indicating that recent stress is related to the occurrence of physical as well as emotional disorder of children (Gersten et al. 1974, Heisel et al. 1974, Mutter and Schliefer 1966). In the present study, which is correlational in design, the fact that it is highly improbable that an action taken by the children could have caused the occurrence of the stress events strengthens the implication of stress as a contributory cause of children's adjustment problems (Dohrenwend and Dohrenwend 1974). [p. 438]

Thus it may be safely concluded that stressful life events predict the psychosocial adjustment of children from general populations. It would seem logical to investigate the possibility that the relationship between stress and adjustment would likewise characterize children from divorced families specifically. Parental divorce is a stressful event in itself. Also, parental divorce is typically associated with a variety of other stressful life events, including not only diminished financial status, but also relocations and significant changes in the social support network available to the family. Furthermore, divorce has been shown to be associated with a broad range of adjustment difficulties among the divorcing parties, including psychiatric admissions, automobile accidents, substance abuse, suicide, homicide, and disease morbidity (Woody et al. 1984).

Thus the multiple life stresses model of adjustment to divorce, like the narrower economic distress model, can be thought of not only in terms of additional stressful life events that impinge directly on the child, but also in terms of stressful life events that impinge on the custodial parent and may diminish his or her parenting capacity and ultimately affect the child's adjustment. Wallerstein and Kelly (1980) have suggested that children of divorcing parents may be disturbed by the perception that they have no control over major changes in their lives, such as changes in residence and school system, lower family income, and changes in the availability of one or both parents. Hetherington (1993) noted that divorced mothers are frequently confronted with stresses in the form of task overload, household disorganization, child-rearing problems, and loneliness. To these stresses one might add the possible stress associated with entry or reentry into the work force, continuing one's education, and reconstituting one's social network and activities. These stresses on custodial mothers might be expected to lead to diminished parenting ability.

Numerous empirical studies have provided support for the multiple life stresses hypothesis. Stolberg (1980) reported that substantial change in children's physical and social environment following a divorce is related significantly to maternal reports of children's depression, social withdrawal, aggression, and delinquency. Stolberg also noted that environmental change was associated with the perception on the part of children that neither they nor their parents were in control of their lives. Based on a longitudinal study of a birth cohort of children from Hawaii, Werner and Smith (1982) concluded that stressful life changes in the areas of parental health, employment status, and finances were associated with poorer psychosocial adjustment among children. Stolberg and colleagues (1987) found that among children from divorced families, the total number of stressful life changes they reported was related significantly to self-reported psychological symptoms.

In their study referred to earlier in this chapter in the context of the economic distress hypothesis, Hodges and colleagues (1984) measured stressful life events among preschool boys ($n = 44$) and girls ($n = 46$) from divorced ($n = 30$) and intact ($n = 60$) families. They obtained parental reports of stressful life events using the Total Parent Life Events instrument, and they obtained children's reports of stressful events using the Total Child Life Events instrument. They reported that the correlation between the total scores on these two measures was .58, suggesting the convergent validity of the instruments as measures of family stressful life events.

They found that for the entire sample, including both divorced and intact families, the number of reported changes in residence was related positively to increased levels of aggression among children. Also, perceived inadequacy of family income was related positively to teacher ratings of children's anxiety-depression, difficulty staying on task, and global maladjustment. Hodges and his colleagues (1984) reported that the observed relationships were stronger when the measures of stressful life events reflected parental perceptions rather than the perceptions of the preschool children.

Hodges and his colleagues (1984) noted that even though geographic mobility and perceived inadequacy of income predicted children's adjustment independently of family type (divorced versus intact), the families in which a divorce had occurred were more likely to be characterized by such moves and economic distress. Therefore, children from divorced families were more likely than those from intact families to score high on the measures of poor psychosocial adjustment.

The other side of this argument, of course, is that Hodges and his associates (1984) had a very small sample of children from divorced families. The relationships between the stressful life events measures and the psychosocial adjustment measures might not have been significant among the small sample of children from divorced families had the data for these families been analyzed separately. If this were the case, the lack of statistical significance could be the result of lack of power due to the small sample size of the divorced group. However, the lack of statistically significant relationships in the sample of divorced families could also suggest that within the population of divorced families alone the relationships reported for the overall population do not pertain. It is possible that the significant relationships reported for the entire sample between the various stressful life events and the adjustment criteria were simply an artifact of group differences between intact families and divorced families on both stressful life events and psychosocial adjustment. Therefore, it is critically important in research studies of this nature to include samples of children from divorced and intact families that are sufficiently large to permit meaningful within-group analyses as well as analyses carried out on the pooled samples.

Hodges and colleagues (1990) reported the results of a companion study carried out on children in late elementary school. Here again they reported significant relationships between perceived stressful life events and psychosocial adjustment problems. However, in the late elementary school group, both children's and parents' perceptions of stressful life events predicted poor outcomes. The most obvious explanation for this finding is that by the time children have reached the late elementary school years, they have a more accurate perception of the stressful life events that affect their families, and their perceptions are therefore more in line with parental perceptions of stressful life events. However, the same methodological difficulties noted in connection with the 1984 study may have had an impact on the findings reported in 1990.

Sandler et al. (1988) argued that the prediction of postdivorce adjustment among children might best be served by developing a survey of recent stressful life events that included the events most likely to be experienced by this group. Accordingly, these investigators interviewed knowledgeable informants, including divorced parents and their children, mental health professionals, and lawyers, to identify these changes. In selecting the events to be included in this schedule, they sought to (1) eliminate events that were themselves indicators of adjustment problems (such as being retained in grade) and (2) include events that were beyond the child's control. The result was the Divorce Events Schedule for Children, which yields scores for both negative and positive life events. Sandler et al. (1990) administered a revised version of this schedule to a sample of white, middle-class children ranging in age from 8 to 15 years. They reported that the test-retest reliability of the negative events subscale score of the schedule was .83; they also found that the occurrence of negative divorce-related events was related significantly to children's self-reports of adjustment problems.

Farber and colleagues (1985) administered the Hassles of Divorce Survey (HDS) to a sample of sixty-five undergraduates whose parents had separated or divorced subsequent to their 12th birthday. This twenty-three-item measure of stress was adapted from a similar instrument developed by Kanner and associates (1981) designed to measure the types of stress most typically experienced by adolescents whose parents have divorced. Examples of items included in this measure are "difficulty with school work due to increased family demands"; and "caught in a loyalty conflict between parents" (Farber et al. 1985, p. 176). When the items of the HDS were factor analyzed, five factors accounted for nearly 83 percent of the variance in the item set. These factors were named (1) family reorganization/conflict hassles, (2) hassles with siblings, (3) family reconstitution difficulties, (4) increased parental demands, and (5) loyalty conflicts. When scores representing these factors were correlated with scores on the State-Trait Anxiety Inventory (STAI) (Spielberger et al. 1970) and the Multiple Affect Adjective Checklist (MAACL) (Zuckerman and Lubin 1965), it was found that stress associated with divorce-related family reorganization and conflict was a significant ($p < .01$) predictor of state and trait anxiety, depression, and hostility.

Woody et al. (1984) studied a sample of eighty-seven parents recently divorced or in the process of divorcing. The parents were recruited over a fifteen-month period by (1) sending letters to pairs of divorced parents whose names appeared on the divorce records of Douglas County, Nebraska; (2) placing advertisements in local newspapers; (3) publicizing weekend educational workshops for divorced families; and (4) using specific referrals to the workshops from counselors, attorneys, and judges. The recency of the divorce suggests that the results of this study would be applicable only to those families who are still in the crisis period of the divorce. Although some of the parents did participate in a workshop on divorce, the workshop occurred after the data for this study were collected. Thus the findings would not have been influenced by the intervention.

Woody and her colleagues (1984) measured parent stress using the forty-three-item Schedule of Recent Experiences. They measured children's mental health by means of a forty-four-item symptom checklist completed by parents. Each parent completed the checklist for each of his or her children. There were an average of two and one-tenth children in each family, and the total number of children on whom reports were obtained was 181. These children ranged in age from 1 to 17 years old.

Woody and associates (1984) did not state directly whether they had employed the family or the child as the unit of analysis for the study, but the magnitudes of the significant correlations they reported suggest that the family was the unit of analysis. Had the sample size been equal to the number of children included in the study, some of the correlations reported would have had lower significance probabilities than those reported due to the increased statistical power of the tests associated with the larger sample size. In addition, the authors indicated that they calculated a total child symptoms score for each family by averaging the number of symptoms checked for each child across all the children in each family. This constitutes an important methodological strength of this study. Many of the studies on outcomes of divorce have employed multiple children from the same family as if they were independent observations, which violates the assumption of independence of observations that underlies the inferential statistics reported in these studies.

The child mental health checklist included a broad range of psychological or mood states, psychosomatic reactions, and behaviors applicable to children of different ages. Several were divorce-specific reactions that had been observed and reported by Wallerstein and Kelly (1980). Examples of such items include guilt associated with a feeling of responsibility for causing the divorce, attempts to get the parents back together, denial of the reality of the divorce, and statements indicating that the child misses or desires greater contact with the noncustodial parent.

Woody and her colleagues (1984) also measured parental mental health by means of a fifty-three-item checklist of behaviors, moods, and symptoms. Thirty-three of these items were described as "normal reactions for persons in the divorce process—for example, depression, loneliness, confusion, and worrying" (p. 408). Ten other items were indicative of more serious maladaptive problems, including alcoholism, drug use, and suicidal thoughts. The remaining ten items were indications of positive personal growth, including self-improvement activities, finding a new job, and developing a sense of competence. The normal reactions and the maladaptive problems checked were counted to obtain a parent symptom score. In addition, a subscale of psychosomatic symptoms was created by counting the number of items endorsed within a set of ten items that indicated psychosomatic reactions. These included loss of appetite, trouble sleeping, stomach problems, and headaches. (Some additional predictors were included in the domains of social support and family-systems characteristics. These measures and the findings obtained with respect to these measures are considered in the next two chapters of this volume.)

The authors obtained the partial correlation between parent stress and the total child symptoms score, controlling for the number of months since the divorce. This correlation was moderate in magnitude and highly significant ($r = .365$, $p < .001$). This finding strongly supports the notion that parental stress following divorce is associated with children's mental health, at least in the first fifteen months following the divorce. In addition, Woody and colleagues (1984) reported that parental stress was related significantly to parent symptoms ($r = .235$, $p < .05$), which in turn were correlated significantly with the total child symptom score ($r = .261$, $p < .05$). Finally, parental stress scores were related significantly to parent psychosomatic symptoms ($r = .222$, $p < .05$), which were also correlated significantly with the total child symptom score ($r = .234$, $p < .05$). Thus the results of this study suggest that the amount of stressful life change experienced by parents following divorce leads to adjustment problems for the parents, and that these adjustment difficulties may be reflected in the mental health difficulties experienced by children.

The study noted earlier in this chapter by Kalter and his associates (1989) tested not only the economic distress hypothesis, but also the multiple life stresses hypothesis. Kalter and his colleagues measured stressful life events by means of the Negative Change scale of the Life Experiences Survey (LES) (Sarason et al. 1978). The LES is a forty-seven-item self-report instrument that requires respondents not only to indicate whether each event listed has occurred or not, but also to rate each event that has occurred in terms of its desirability or undesirability. The authors reported a six-week test-retest reliability coefficient for this instrument of .88.

Kalter and colleagues (1989) reported different results for the boys and the girls in their sample. Among boys, the LES Negative Change score was related positively to all eight of the psychosocial adjustment criteria they assessed, including the CBCL Total Problems, Internalizing Problems, Externalizing Problems, Aggression, and Depression Scales; the CDI Depression measure; and the STAI State-Trait Anxiety Scales. Three of these correlations were significant ($p < .05$), even in the small sample of boys ($n = 22$). Among girls ($n = 25$), seven of the eight correlations were positive, but none were significant. Kalter and his associates noted that this finding could be due to the fact that the children in the study were elementary school students, and girls from divorced families tend to show few negative effects of divorce at this age. Therefore the range of adjustment scores for the girls could have been somewhat restricted in comparison with the boys, which could have had the effect of attenuating the observed correlations.

The study reported by Mednick and her associates (1990), noted earlier in this chapter in connection with the economic distress hypothesis, also provides some data relevant to the multiple life stresses hypothesis. Based on data derived from social workers' interviews with the mothers, Mednick and her colleagues selected six predictors they described as potential stressor variables:

1. *Mother's disorderliness* was assessed through social workers' perceptions of the order and care that the mother demonstrated with respect to her home and herself. Mednick and her associates indicated that in connection with these ratings, "Every attempt was made to eliminate economic considerations in the perceptions. For example, it made no difference whether furniture or dress was new or fashionable, only that they were clean, functional, etc." (p. 77). The authors reported an internal consistency reliability coefficient of .88 for this scale.
2. *Mother's discontentment* measured how well satisfied the mother was with her general living situation. This scale was based on multiple indicators of satisfaction obtained throughout the interview. The authors reported a reliability coefficient of alpha = .77 for this scale. They also noted that the correlation between the Disorderliness and Discontentment scales in their sample was just .21, indicating that these two variables were reasonably independent.
3. *Maternal employment instability* was a three-item scale based on social workers' clinical judgments of the mothers' responses to interview questions concerned with their employment histories. The three questions concerned employment changes that occurred without reference to the achievement of career objectives, involuntary employment termination, and lack of job satisfaction. The alpha coefficient for this scale was reported to be .72.
4. *Stepfamily unification problems* were assessed on the basis of the social worker's clinical judgment, based on the mother's elaborated response to a single interview item that concerned her perception of the problems that arose with respect to relationships among the family members. This was a dichotomous rating. The social worker made the judgment whether or not stepfamily unification problems were present

in the family.
5. *Poor peer relations* was also a dichotomous variable assessed by the social worker based on the maternal interview data. The child was characterized as exhibiting poor peer relations if the mother described the child as having been teased frequently by peers or having experienced other personal difficulties with peers.
6. *School changes* was a dichotomous predictor included to assess potential stress associated with transferring from one school to another. This stressor was coded as present if more than two such transfers had occurred.

It should be noted at the outset that these six predictors are a somewhat dubious representation of the life stresses that may be associated with divorce. Mother's disorderliness and discontentment would appear to be measures of the psychological adjustment of the custodial mother rather than stressors. It would appear that better representations of stressors would be changing residences, increased demands on the mother with respect to caring for the home and the children, or the loss of significant sources of respite care. The maternal disorderliness and discontentment scales appear to be closer to outcome variables in that they represent the resultant of such stressors with the adaptive and coping capacities of the mothers. Stepfamily unification problems and poor peer relations also appear to be more in the nature of outcome variables than stressors.

Maternal employment instability could qualify as a stressor, but an ideal measure would reflect job instability associated directly with the divorce, such as a change from part-time to full-time work, an employment change following upon a divorce-related change of residence, or an employment change necessitated by the need to alter one's schedule to accommodate employment and increased child care responsibilities. Like the measures of maternal disorderliness and discontentment, the measure of maternal employment instability described by Mednick and her associates (1990) appears to reflect not only external stressors, but also the personality and adaptive capacity of the custodial mother. Finally, while changes in school are certainly stressful events, one wonders why the variable was treated as a dichotomy, and why more than two transfers had to occur before such changes were considered potentially stressful. One would expect that even one change of school would constitute a stressful event for a child.

Mednick and colleagues (1990) also measured the socioeconomic status of the postdivorce family and the mother's education, of course, so they did employ variables relevant to economic distress. However, income or drop in income following the divorce would have been better representatives of the economic distress hypothesis. Furthermore, they conceptualized the Hollingshead Index of Socioeconomic Status (SES) and mother's education as control variables rather than as proxy measures for economic distress.

Mednick and her associates (1990) reported zero-order correlations between each of the six variables they identified as stressors and the two criterion measures of teacher-rated reading and mathematics proficiency. They also reported partial correlations between the stressors and the academic adjustment measures, controlling for SES and mother's educational level. The zero-order correlations indicated significant negative relationships between reading proficiency and mother's discontentment ($r = -.22$, $p < .05$), mother's disorderliness ($r = -.24$, $p < .05$), maternal employment instability ($r = -.25$, $p < .05$), stepfamily reunification problems ($r = -.22$, $p < .05$), and poor peer relations ($r = -.29$, $p < .01$). Mathematics proficiency was related significantly to mother's discontentment ($r = -.31$, $p < .05$), mother's disorderliness ($r = -.32$, $p < .01$), maternal employment instability ($r = -.41$, $p < .01$), and school changes ($r = -.25$, $p < .05$). The partial correlations were generally quite similar to the zero-order correlations, although several of the partial correlations between the stress measures and reading proficiency were slightly smaller in magnitude and were no longer statistically significant.

Given the limitations of the measures of stressors described above, the most important findings of this study are probably those obtained with respect to postdivorce SES and maternal educational level. As noted above, both these predictors were related positively to reading proficiency, and mother's education was related positively to mathematics proficiency. The significant negative relationship between school changes and mathematics proficiency is also relevant to the validity of the multiple life stresses model, although one wonders whether a significant relationship would have been obtained had school changes been treated as a simple count of the number of such changes, which would seem to be a more logical approach to the analysis of this dimension.

Mednick and colleagues (1990) concluded that "stress is related to lower adolescent academic proficiency within this sample" (p. 69). Considering the problems with the measures of the stressors they employed, one is forced to question whether this conclusion is strongly supported by the actual results of the study. There is clearly some evidence that stressors related to family economic status and school changes are associated with poor school performance. However, in order to warrant the conclusion that stress is related negatively to academic performance, one would want to see the study modified to include many more predictors that represent actual stressful life events arising directly from the divorce, and a clear distinction between stressors and outcome measures. Furthermore, one would like to see additional dependent variables in the study, representing a broader range of psychosocial adjustment.

As Mednick and colleagues (1990) also concluded: "Overall, the findings support the general premise that factors describing the developmental milieu and personality characteristics of the child and the divorced custodial parent are significant mediators of the relationship between experiencing parental divorce and a subsequent decline in academic performance" (p. 84). This conclusion appears to be more consistent with the design and results of the study than the conclusion regarding stress. Mednick and her colleagues also suggested that their results indicated the utility of interventions directed toward improving the mother's overall adaptation to her own personal situation. This conclusion also appears to be warranted, but it is clearly a recommendation concerned more with the psychosocial adjustment and coping capacities of the custodial mother than with life stresses.

Wolchik et al. (1993) reported the results of another study supporting the multiple life stresses hypothesis. These investigators studied thirty-five poor children from divorced families. They reasoned that the stressful life changes experienced by poor families following a divorce would likely be more significant than those experienced by more affluent families, and they expected that the relationships between such changes and postdivorce adjustment would be even stronger than the corresponding relationships reported in previous studies that employed middle-class samples. In order to include children born into common-law relationships, they defined divorce both legally, by the filing of a petition for legal separation or the granting of a divorce decree, and functionally, by the physical separation of biological parents who had never been married. The authors noted that the study sample was a subset of participants in a larger study of the efficacy of a school-based divorce education and support group for children (West et al. 1987). They did not indicate whether all the data for the 1993 report were gathered before the start of the group intervention, or whether any steps had been taken to assess or control for the possible influence on the findings of this treatment. Wolchik and her colleagues did note that the children were interviewed individually prior to the child's participation in the intervention, but they also indicated that a second interview was conducted with the parent and child in the home of the child. The time of this second interview is not specified. Wolchik and colleagues (1993) noted: "In families where more than one child participated in the intervention, one child was randomly selected to ensure independence of response" (p. 6).

The participants were in the fourth through eighth grades in two inner-city school districts in a large Southwestern metropolitan area. According to the 1980 census, the mean household income in these census tracts was $14,543, and 32 percent of the children and adolescents in these areas came from families with incomes below the poverty line (U.S. Bureau of the Census 1984). All 35 of the children included in the sample for this study were from families with poverty level household incomes, as defined by the Federal Register guidelines (U.S. Federal Register 1985).

The parents of the participating children had been divorced for periods ranging from four to 134 months, with a mean length of time since separation of fifty-five months. Thus the conclusions of this study would appear to reflect primarily long-term adjustment to divorce. Nearly 85 percent of the children were in mother-custody situations. Fifty-one percent of the children were Hispanic, 17 percent were black, 26 percent were white, and 6 percent were American Indian.

Stressful life events were assessed from the perspective of the children, using the Divorce Events Schedule for Children-Revised described earlier in this chapter (Sandler et al. 1986, 1988, 1990). Stress was defined operationally as the number of negative life changes endorsed by the child out of a total of twelve events in the survey that respondents agreed were negative. Adjustment measures were obtained from both children and parents.

The children's self-report adjustment measures included a thirty-item aggression scale adapted from the Child Behavior Checklist (CBCL) to use a self-report format (Achenbach 1978, Achenbach and Edelbrock 1979, 1983). In addition, Wolchik and colleagues (1993) obtained parental assessments of their children's adjustment using the standard form of the CBCL. Because of the diversity in age of the students in the sample, Wolchik and her associates followed the recommendation of Achenbach and Edelbrock (1979, 1983) to use the Total Behavior Problems Score of the CBCL for the parental reports. All the items from all the questionnaires were read to the participating parents and children so as to control for reading ability.

The results indicated significant correlations between the children's scores for negative divorce events and both the children's self-reports of aggressive behavior ($r = .52$, $p < .001$) and the parents' reports of the children's overall problem behaviors ($r = .50$, $p < .01$). Wolchik and colleagues (1993) noted that these findings "replicate the findings of previous studies with white, middle class children of divorce (Kurdek and Berg 1987, Sandler et al. 1990)" (pp. 14-15). They also pointed out that a strength of their study was the finding that the relationship between negative events and adjustment was significant regardless of whether the reporter of adjustment was the child or the parent. This cross-rater consistency implies that the relationships obtained reflect more than just within-rater biases, such as mood or response style.

The research reviewed in this chapter leaves little doubt that the number of stressful life changes that occur following divorce is a significant predictor of the postdivorce adjustment of children. Several researchers have stated this conclusion flatly. Based on their review of the literature on stressful life events and divorce, Sandler and colleagues (1988) concluded that the number of negative life changes following a divorce may in fact be the best single predictor of postdivorce adjustment. Furthermore, Stolberg and associates (1987) named stressful life events as one of the three most important predictors of postdivorce adjustment, along with marital hostility and parental mental health. What is not clear at this point is whether these negative outcomes are associated with the occurrence of stressful changes per se, or whether the negative outcomes are mediated by downward changes in parental adjustment and parenting ability that may follow from divorce-related stresses. More research employing larger samples is required to answer this question. In all likelihood, both direct and indirect effects of stressful life changes are present.

10

SOCIAL SUPPORT

IF STRESSFUL LIFE changes following divorce are associated with negative psychosocial outcomes for children, it would seem logical that stress buffers such as social support systems would help to mitigate these negative outcomes. Kurdek (1981) reviewed the literature on this issue and concluded, "Although a body of evidence indicates that *adults'* divorce-related stress is mitigated by their turning to friends, counselors, relatives, and self-help organizations (Chiriboga et al. 1979, Raschke 1977, Spanier and Castro 1979), there is no direct evidence that the availability or use of such support systems for parents is beneficial to the children" (pp. 858–59). This conclusion is no longer valid. In the period between Kurdek's review and the present, several studies have demonstrated that the availability and utilization of social supports is associated positively with the psychosocial adjustment of children and adolescents in both the general population (Cauce et al. 1982) and the population of children from divorced families (Drapeau and Bouchard 1993, Farber et al. 1985, Isaacs and Leon 1986).

The literature on social support is reviewed in this chapter. The first part of the review considers the impact of divorce on the availability of social support, showing a tendency for divorce to result in a reduction of the social supports available to both children and divorcing parents. The loss of available supports may be viewed as reducing the capacity of the child to cope with normal developmental tasks as well as stresses arising directly from the divorce. The loss may also reduce the custodial parent's capacity for coping with everyday living and divorce-related stressful life changes. This in turn may affect the psychological adjustment and parenting capabilities of the custodial parent. All of this may be reflected ultimately in the adjustment of children.

The second part of the chapter focuses on empirical studies documenting the relationship between the availability and use of social supports and postdivorce adjustment. It is divided similarly into subsections concerned with the adjustment of children and the adjustment of their custodial parents.

DECREMENTS IN AVAILABLE SOCIAL SUPPORTS FOLLOWING DIVORCE

Among Children

Drapeau and Bouchard (1993) reviewed the literature on the impact of divorce on relationships both within and outside the immediate family. They noted that "the mother who has custody of the child in 80% of the cases tends to be less supportive, less nurturing, and less consistent with her children" (p. 27). This clearly constitutes a loss of social support. This loss is typically more serious for boys than for girls. Girls from divorced families typically tend to confide in their mothers, but boys do not (Guidubaldi and Perry 1985). Boys residing with custodial mothers tend to receive little emotional support from their mothers, and there is frequently a significant level of conflict between custodial mothers and their sons (Hetherington 1979a, Wolchik et al. 1989). As detailed in Chapter 4, the relationship between the custodial mother and her child is an important predictor of the child's academic, social, and psychological adjustment (Guidubaldi and Cleminshaw 1983, Hess and Camara 1979, Hetherington et al. 1979, 1982, Wallerstein and Kelly 1976, 1980). Of course, as described in Chapter 6, the reduction or loss of contact with the noncustodial father can also be viewed as a significant decrement in available support (Hetherington et al. 1976, 1982, Kalter 1984, Kalter et al. 1989, Kelly 1988b, Wallerstein and Kelly 1980). The loss of contact with the noncustodial father appears to have adverse consequences for both girls and boys (Kalter 1984, Kalter et al. 1985, Kelly 1988b, Wallerstein 1985).

Since loss of support within the nuclear family has been considered in detail elsewhere in this book, this chapter focuses more on the loss of social supports outside the immediate household: losses in the availability of members of the extended family, loss of support from peers, loss of status in school, and losses of support from adults who are not members of the family. Several studies have shown that following divorce there is a tendency for children to lose access to relatives other than their parents (Anspach 1976, Cochrane and Riley 1987). The most obvious such loss would be the diminished access to the family of the noncustodial father, which would be expected to occur concomitant with the diminished contact with the father himself. This tendency might be offset to some extent by increased contact with the custodial mother's family, of course, but in fact this does not always occur either (McKenry and Price 1993).

Pett (1982) noted that among the population of children from divorced families there is a significant relationship between the availability of family support and children's postdivorce adjustment. She interpreted the results of her study as indicating that family support affected the postdivorce psychological well-being of the custodial parent, which in turn affected the psychosocial adjustment of the children. However, Isaacs and Leon (1986) noted that the results Pett reported actually indicated that family support had a direct effect on children's adjustment. In the regression of children's postdivorce adjustment on family support and custodial parent adjustment measures, the support received from grandparents was a significant predictor of children's adjustment, even after partialing out variability due to the custodial parent's psychological adjustment.

The research literature also suggests that children whose parents separate tend to be somewhat isolated from their peer groups. Tietjen (1982) and Wyman and colleagues (1985) concluded that children from divorced families tend to be less sociable than their peers from intact families. They also have smaller peer networks than children from intact families, and spend significantly less time with their peers. Stolberg and Anker (1983) reported that children whose parents divorce manifest significantly more behavior problems in social interactions, especially true during the year following the parental separation. When children from divorced families experience a reduction in peer social supports, their adjustment is likely to be placed at risk. A number of empirical studies of children from single-parent families have yielded significant relationships between peer support and psychosocial adjustment following divorce (Kurtzman-Effron 1980, Pedro-Carrol and Cowen 1985, Stolberg and Garrison 1985, Wyman et al. 1985).

Hetherington and associates (1979) reported that parental divorce was stigmatizing for children. They suggested that both teachers and classmates in school tended to hold lower opinions of students from divorced families than they did of students from intact families. Such a reduction in status would be expected to be associated with reduced social contact and therefore reduced availability of social support. Hetherington and her colleagues (1979) also noted that children from divorced families, particularly boys, were significantly more likely than children from intact families to experience conflicts with their teachers. Sandler and colleagues (1984) argued that conflictual relationships anywhere within the child's social network are likely to be associated with poor psychosocial adjustment.

With respect to relationships with adults who are not members of the child's family, Riley and Cochrane (1987) reported that children from single-parent families reported significantly fewer unrelated adults in their social support network than did children from intact families. These unrelated adults may include neighbors, friends of one's parents, coaches, librarians, and child care personnel. Drapeau and Bouchard (1993) noted that relatively little research had been carried out with respect to the impact of nonrelated adults on the psychosocial adjustment of children from either divorced or intact families, but they also suggested that "it is plausible that the child's adjustment is influenced by the presence and actions of these adults" (p. 78).

Among Parents

There is a substantial body of literature supporting the hypothesis that parents who divorce also tend to experience losses in their social support networks. Anspach (1976) confirmed the obvious by reporting that divorced spouses typically lost contact with their former in-laws, who may have been significant sources of support and respite care during the marriage. Kitson and colleagues (1982) found that support received from one's own family could also decrease following divorce, particularly if the family members had philosophical or religious convictions leading them to disapprove of divorce in general or this divorce in particular. Spanier and Castro (1979) found that divorcing spouses who experienced little or no support from their families tended to have a difficult time adjusting to their new status.

Isaacs and Leon (1986) studied the factors that predicted the amount of family support received by a divorcing mother. They found that the most important predictor of emotional support from the family was the general attitude of the family members regarding divorce. With respect to tangible support such as babysitting and respite care, however, the most important predictors were the residential proximity of the family, the ages of the children, and the nature of the predivorce relationship with the family. Leon and Isaacs reported that younger women, black women, and unemployed women are more likely than other divorcing mothers to move back into the family residence.

Spanier and Thompson (1984) reported that many friendships that existed before the divorce either dissolve or decrease in importance following the separation. In the case of mutual friendships shared by spouses before their divorce, there is a tendency for friends to choose one spouse or the other out of a sense that they need to be loyal. When the friend is in conflict with which spouse to choose, he or she sometimes reacts by withdrawing partly or completely from both the divorcing spouses.

When loyalty conflicts do not arise, other problems may cause friends to withdraw from the divorcing spouses. They may feel threatened by the divorce. It may cause them to wonder whether their own marriage will last. It may cause them to reevaluate their relationship with their spouse and to ask if he or she is really happy. In addition, the divorcing friend is now single, and this new status may cause the friend to be viewed as a sexual threat (Goode 1956, Spanier and Castro 1979). Johnson (1977) noted that some people are simply fair-weather friends who may perceive the divorcing individual as too needy or demanding and no longer fun to be with. This perception may also cause friends to withdraw.

Even when none of these issues arise, the frequency and intensity of contact with divorcing friends may diminish simply because married friends are uncomfortable fitting the divorced and now single individual into the established pattern of social activities, which in all likelihood had revolved around activities for couples.

On the other hand, divorced persons sometimes contribute to their own diminished network of friends. They may feel as if they have failed in their marriage, and may be embarrassed by this failure. They may also experience guilt if they initiated the divorce, and may project this feeling onto their friends, leading them to isolate themselves for fear of condemnation (Johnson 1977, Spanier and Castro 1979). McKenry and Price (1993) also suggested that "divorced individuals are often reluctant to contact married friends who are perceived as too busy with their own lives" (p. 4).

Divorced persons may feel depressed and miserable, causing them to experience the apparent happiness of their married friends as discomforting. They may also feel that their married friends cannot really understand what they are going through. This may cause them to form new relationships with other persons who have had the experience of being divorced, and to withdraw from existing relationships with married friends. McKenry and Price (1991) noted that divorced persons typically undergo a period of social withdrawal following divorce. They are likely to view intimate relationships as threatening. They also may feel that they are "too old" or "too out of practice" to participate in the singles scene. If they were left by their former spouse, they may have low self-esteem and a perception that they are unattractive. Brandwein and colleagues (1976) argued that such perceptions can reduce one's confidence and inhibit dating activity.

Finally, a number of practical aspects of divorce can also reduce one's social support network. One or both of the divorcing spouses may move away from the community in which they have been residing and within which their social network has been formed. A newly divorced woman may find it necessary to secure employment or increase the time devoted to employment activities. This can lead to a reduction in the amount of time available for social activities. It may also provide the opportunity for establishing new relationships, of course, but recently divorced individuals may not feel ready to do so. Furthermore, the economic distress engendered by the divorce may necessitate the abandonment of certain activities that the divorced spouses had engaged in prior to the divorce, with the concomitant loss of the social interactions associated with those activities.

Brandwein and colleagues (1974) argued that the reduction in one's social support network constitutes one of the most important sources of stress experienced by single mothers. Several investigators have concluded that single women are at risk for psychological problems by virtue of the fact that they have fewer social supports available to them to buffer the stressful life changes that accompany divorce (Kressel and Deutsch 1979, McLanahan et al. 1981).

On the other hand, it should be noted that divorced individuals do not uniformly experience reduced social contact. Kunz and Kunz (1995) surveyed 500 divorced individuals—293 females and 207 males—from eight western states. The survey included two items relevant to social contact: "Has your participation in organizations and clubs changed since your divorce?" and "How, if any, has the contact (with close relatives including parents, grandparents, brothers and sisters, and aunts and uncles) changed since the divorce?" (p. 114). To the first question, 37.4 percent of the respondents indicated that their participation had increased; 43.4 percent indicated that it had remained about the same; 19.2 percent indicated that it had decreased. Thus, in this sample, divorced persons were almost twice as likely to increase their participation in organizations following their divorce as they were to decrease it.

With respect to contact with family, 31.6 percent of the respondents indicated more contact with relatives after their divorce than before; 55.8 percent indicated no change in the amount of contact; only 12.6 percent indicated reduced contact. These data tend to contradict the accepted view that divorce tends to reduce support. However, it should be noted that Kunz and Kunz (1995) did not really measure support, but only participation and contact. Thus it would appear that more research is required before one can conclude that support tends to increase or decrease. Also, Kunz and Kunz did not report these data broken down by the gender of the respondent. It would be very interesting to see this analysis. It would also be extremely interesting to find out more about the nature of the changes in participation in organizations, contact with family, and actual support received. For example, a divorced woman might well increase her contact with family because she has taken a full-time job and needs to drop off the kids with her mother for babysitting each day. Increased contact of this nature certainly represents support, but this tangible support might be associated with increased moral and emotional support as well, or it might be given in a matter-of-fact fashion with no psychological support. The outcomes associated with these two situations might be quite different.

SOCIAL SUPPORT AND PSYCHOLOGICAL ADJUSTMENT

Among Children

Several empirical studies have considered the relationship between social support and the psychosocial adjustment of children. Some of these studies have been conducted on general populations where separation or divorce had not necessarily occurred; others have focused specifically on children from divorced families. These studies have not always yielded consistent results, but the lack of consistency can be explained in most instances by differences in the populations studied or by differences in the manner in which social support has been operationalized.

Cauce and colleagues (1982) carried out a study of social support and its relationship to the adjustment of adolescents from high-stress, lower-socioeconomic-status, inner-city families. This study was designed to accomplish three purposes: (1) to identify the principal dimensions of social support perceived within this population; (2) to determine the degree to which the perceived helpfulness of each aspect of social support was related to age, gender, and ethnicity; and (3) to examine the relationship between the various aspects of social support that were identified and the personal and academic adjustment of the adolescent. The subjects were 250 high school students, 122 ninth-graders, and 128 eleventh-graders selected randomly from the ninth- and eleventh-grade classes at three inner-city high schools in a large northeastern city. The students were 52.5 percent female and 47.5 percent male. They were 66.8 percent black, 22.4 percent white, 9.6 percent Hispanic, and 1.2 percent other. The authors reported that between 75 and 85 percent of the students in these schools received public assistance in the form of Aid to Families with Dependent Children.

The students completed self-report questionnaires measuring self-concept and social support. The self-concept measure was the thirty-six-item Self-Appraisal Inventory (SAI) (Frith and Narikawa 1972), which measures General Self-Concept as well as self-concept in relation to school, peers, and family. The scale was developed for younger children, and some of the items were modified for the study to make the wording more appropriate for adolescents. Also, Cauce and colleagues (1982) did not use the Family Self-Concept Scale as they felt some of the items were of a very personal nature, which might be perceived as intrusive. The authors also obtained a Total Self-Concept score by summing the School, Peers, and General Self-Concept Scales.

The measure of perceived social support was adapted from the Social Support Rating Scale (SSRS) employed in the National Longitudinal Study of High School Students (U.S. Department of Health, Education, and Welfare 1975). The SSRS is a ten-item scale that assesses the student's perception of the *helpfulness* of a number of different individuals who are potentially available as sources of social support. As suggested in the foregoing section of this chapter, when one evaluates the findings of studies of social support, it is very important to keep in mind the nature of the support measure. Some studies employ measures of the availability of social supports; some employ measures of the utilization of social support; still others, like the Cauce and colleagues (1982) study, focus on the perceived helpfulness of the support received (or the respondent's satisfaction with the support received). These different approaches to the measurement of social support may yield quite different results.

In the SSRS, respondents rate the helpfulness of the support received from a number of individuals: parents, teachers, friends, other relatives, the school principal or assistant principal, guidance counselors, state employment service officials, other adults, and members of the clergy. Each category of individual is rated on a three-point scale with response options ranging from "not at all helpful" to "a great deal helpful."

In addition to self-concept, two measures of children's adjustment in school included in this study were (1) grade point average across English, mathematics, science, and social studies; and (2) attendance during the school year.

Cauce and her colleagues (1982) factor-analyzed the ten-item SSRS. They found three principal components that together accounted for 95.3 percent of the variability in the item set: (1) family helpfulness, which accounted for 63.1 percent of the variability; (2) the helpfulness of formal sources of support, which accounted for 22.2 percent of the variability; and (3) the helpfulness of informal sources of support, which accounted for 10.0 percent of the variability. The items loading on family helpfulness were parents (loading = .39) and other relatives (.60). The items loading on the helpfulness of formal sources of support included guidance counselors (.53), teachers (.61), principal or assistant principal (.56), and state employment service official (.43). The items loading on the helpfulness of informal supports were friends your own age (.59) and other adults (.45). Factor scores were generated for each of these three factors, and a total support score was obtained by summing the items loading on the three factors.

These social support scores were broken down by gender, grade, and ethnic group. The analyses indicated that blacks perceived family support as significantly more helpful than did whites or Hispanics. A significant gender by grade interaction on family support indicated that, among males, the ninth-graders perceived family as more helpful than did eleventh-graders; among girls, eleventh-graders perceived family as more helpful than did ninth-graders. On helpfulness of formal supports, a significant grade by ethnic group interaction indicated that among whites and blacks there was no difference between ninth- and eleventh-graders. Among Hispanic students, however, the eleventh-graders perceived formal supports as more helpful than did the ninth-graders. Girls perceived informal supports as more helpful than did boys, and black and white students perceived informal supports as more helpful than did Hispanic students. Scores on total support were higher among black students than among white or Hispanic students.

Cauce and associates (1982) employed median splits to obtain high and low perceived social support groups for each of the four categories of support. Four multivariate analyses of variance were run, one for each of the social support dimensions. In each MANOVA, grade point average and absences were the dependent variables. Grade, gender, and ethnic group were independent variables in each MANOVA, along with one of the four social support dimensions. No significant main or interaction effects were obtained with respect to the MANOVAs employing Family, Formal, and Total Social Support. In the analysis employing Informal Social Support as an independent variable, a significant multivariate main effect due to perceived level of support was obtained. Post hoc univariate tests indicated that, contrary to expectation, grade point averages were significantly lower and absences were significantly higher among the high informal social support group than among the low informal social support group.

Univariate analyses of variance were used to determine the effects of grade, gender, ethnic group, and each of the social support dimensions on each of the SAI self-concept measures. In the analyses of the Peer Self-Concept Scale, two of the four ANOVAs yielded significant gender by social support level interactions. These were the analyses that included perceived helpfulness of informal social support and perceived helpfulness of formal social support. In each case males in the high perceived social support group had significantly higher Peer Self-Concept scores than did males in the low perceived social support group. However, among girls, there was no significant difference in Peer Self-Concept between the high and low perceived support groups for either informal or formal support. The ANOVA employing family social support did not yield any significant effects with respect to Peer Self-Concept. The ANOVA employing total social support as an independent variable yielded a significant main effect for that factor. Students in the high group on perceived helpfulness of total social support had significantly higher scores on Peer Self-Concept than did students in the low group on total social support.

In the analyses carried out on School Self-Concept scores, only the ANOVA employing perceived helpfulness of family social support yielded any significant main or interaction effects. A significant main effect due to level of perceived family support was obtained. In general, students who perceived family support as relatively helpful had higher School Self-Concept scores than students who perceived family social support as less helpful. However, on this Self-Concept Scale there was a significant three-way interaction of gender by ethnic group by level of perceived family support. The nature of this interaction was such that among black females only, the main effect of perceived family support was reversed. Black females who perceived family support as relatively helpful tended to have lower School Self-Concept scores than those who perceived family support as less helpful.

No significant main or interaction effects were obtained in any of the analyses carried out with respect to General Self-Concept or Total Self-Concept.

Cauce and her associates (1982) concluded that the differential results obtained with respect to the various dimensions of social support suggested that research findings based on global, unidimensional measures of social support could be misleading. They focused on the surprising findings that grade point average and attendance were related negatively to the level of perceived helpfulness of informal social supports. They attributed these findings to conformity to peer pressure. They suggested that:

> for this population of adolescents, which is a generally low-achieving system, those students with closer ties to informal sources of support such as peers, while feeling better about themselves socially, may also be subject to greater pressure to conform and thus have poor attitudes toward school and do less well. [p. 426]

On the other hand, given the correlational nature of this investigation, one could argue that the direction of causality is the reverse. Perhaps those who do well in school do not have as great a need for peer support as those who perform poorly. This is particularly plausible when one considers that the measures of social support employed in this investigation did not, in fact, measure "closer ties" to informal sources of support, but rather the perceived helpfulness of the various categories of support. In spite of this caveat regarding the authors' interpretation of their findings, the study is important to understanding research on social support because it correctly identifies the need to differentiate among various types of social support.

In the study described in the foregoing chapter in the context of the multiple life stresses model of postdivorce adjustment, Farber and colleagues (1985) also considered the possible mediating role of social support. Their study sample consisted of sixty-five undergraduates, ranging in age from 17 to 23, whose parents had separated or divorced sometime since their 12th birthday. Their measure of stress was the Hassles of Divorce Survey, but they also measured social support using an adapted version of the SSRS employed by Cauce and her colleagues (1982). The measure employed by Farber and her associates, referred to as the Survey of Social Support (SSS), reflected substantial changes from the SSRS.

First, the list of categories of individuals who could provide social support was expanded from ten to sixteen. Among the categories added are siblings and mental health professionals. Second, the respondents to the SSS are asked to indicate not only the perceived degree to which each category of individuals is helpful, but also the frequency with which they seek support from each of these sources. This change reflects the assertion of Heller and Swindle (1983) that both the frequency of support and the perceived helpfulness of social support are important predictors for assessing the effect of social support as a buffer to life stress. A third difference between the SSRS and the SSS is that on the SSS respondents rated the frequency of support seeking and the helpfulness of support received from each source with respect to two different types of support: (1) information, guidance, and specific assistance; and (2) emotional support in dealing with their parents' divorce or separation. Finally, a fourth change from the SSRS to the SSS was a change in the response format from three-point to four-point Likert-type response scales.

In a prior study of the factor structure of the SSS, Farber (1980) had reported that ratings of the frequency of support-seeking behavior represented four principal domains of support: frequency of seeking peer support (three items), frequency of seeking formal supports (two items), frequency of relying on the self (one item), and frequency of seeking family support (three items). Ratings of the perceived helpfulness were found to represent three primary domains: perceived helpfulness of formal supports (eight items), perceived helpfulness of peer supports (three items), and perceived helpfulness of family supports (three items).

The criterion variables used to assess postdivorce adjustment included the State and Trait Anxiety Scales of the State-Trait Anxiety Inventory (STAI) (Spielberger et al. 1970), the Depression and Hostility Scales of the Multiple Affect Adjective Checklist (MAACL) (Zuckerman and Lubin 1965), and the Tennessee Self-Concept Scale (Fitts 1965).

The results of the analyses carried out to determine the mediating effect of social support on postdivorce adjustment indicated that ratings of the frequency of utilization of family support to cope with the parental divorce were related significantly to both State Anxiety and Trait Anxiety. Those who reported that they frequently sought support from family members tended to have *high* levels of State and Trait Anxiety. Ratings of the perceived helpfulness of family support were also related significantly to both State and Trait Anxiety. Here, however, the direction of the relationship was the opposite. Those who perceived social support received from their family as relatively helpful tended to have lower scores on State and Trait Anxiety.

These findings clearly provide support for the notion that social support can indeed buffer the impact of the stressful life changes that so often follow upon divorce. Moreover, the findings reported by Farber and her associates (1985) reconfirm the observation of Cauce and colleagues (1982) that one must distinguish between various types of social support to evaluate the stress-buffering effect of social support. In the study by Farber and associates, the operationalization of support in terms of frequency of support seeking leads to the conclusion that support seeking is associated with more negative outcomes, while the operationalization of support-seeking in terms of the perceived helpfulness of support leads to precisely the opposite conclusion.

The study reported by Woody and colleagues (1984) was also considered in some detail in the previous chapter on the relationship between stressful life changes following divorce and the psychosocial adjustment of the children. Woody and her colleagues measured social support by several questions addressed to parents measuring both the extent to which they used various helping resources and the extent to which they perceived these resources to be helpful. The authors reported a significant negative relationship between the parent's use of helping resources and the number of maladaptive behaviors reported in the child. They also reported a significant negative relationship between the parent's subjective estimation of the value of these helping resources and the number of symptomatic behaviors reported in the child. These findings support the position that social supports can be important determinants of children's postdivorce adjustment. In addition, the authors found that both the extent of use of helping resources and the value placed on these resources were related negatively to the stress experienced by the parent, as measured by the Schedule of Recent Experience. This finding supports the contention that the utilization and perceived helpfulness of social support may have its effect on children's postdivorce adjustment by buffering the impact of divorce-related life stresses on the parents. Several other empirical studies have provided evidence that social support is associated with the adjustment and coping ability of divorced parents.

Among Parents

Propst and colleagues (1986) studied the impact of external and internal coping resources on the adjustment of divorced single mothers. Their sample consisted of 106 women who were divorced and/or separated from their husbands and who had at least one child living with them at least part of the time. The women were recruited from several different sources, including a chapter of Parents without Partners, a community youth services center, a woman's resource center, and child care centers. The women ranged in age from 18 to 53. Elapsed time since their separation ranged from zero to 204 months, with an average of sixty months. The mothers were predominantly white and middle class.

Social support was measured by several different questionnaire items. The most direct measure of social support was a one-item rating scale that asked respondents to indicate how many people they felt cared for them and with whom they could discuss their problems. Responses to this item were made on a five-point scale with response options ranging from "none" to "six or more." Other survey items that appear to be related to the use of supports were questions concerned with whether the mother was receiving public assistance, whether she had sought professional help from a counselor or other mental health professional, and the extent to which she felt that her religious faith had contributed to her coping. The latter item had a four-point Likert-type response format with response options ranging from "not at all" to "very much."

The authors also administered the Ways of Coping Checklist (WCC) (Folkman and Lazarus 1980) to the responding mothers to determine the extent to which they tended to use problem-focused coping strategies and emotion-focused coping strategies to handle stressful situations. Problem-focused coping refers to efforts or behavioral strategies aimed at altering or managing the source of the problem. Emotion-focused coping refers to cognitive or behavioral efforts aimed specifically at managing emotional distress. An example of problem-focused coping would be "made a plan of action to solve the dilemma." An example of emotion-focused coping would be "tried to forget about it." The parent adjustment criterion measures were the State Anxiety Scale of the STAI (Spielberger et al. 1970) and the Depression Adjective Checklist (Lubin 1967).

Propst and her colleagues (1986) analyzed their data by performing median splits on scores on State Anxiety and Depression, then discriminant analyses to determine whether one could significantly differentiate high and low anxious persons or high and low depressed persons on the basis of demographic factors, social support factors, and scores on problem-focused and emotion-focused coping.

The results obtained with respect to anxiety indicated that seeking help was related significantly to membership in the high State Anxiety group. Receiving public assistance, self-reported number of individuals in the social support network, and value placed on religion were not significant predictors of anxiety. Scores on both problem-focused and emotion-focused coping were significantly higher in the low State Anxiety group than in the high State Anxiety group. The results obtained with respect to Depression were identical.

These findings are consistent with findings reported by Farber and associates (1985) and Woody and associates (1984) in that the use of external coping resources, in the form of seeking professional help, was associated with greater adjustment difficulties. On the other hand, the availability of social supports, measured by the self-reported number of people who cared for the respondent, was not related significantly to adjustment. Once again we see how important is the manner in which social support is defined and operationalized.

Isaacs and Leon (1986) studied the types of support that divorcing mothers receive from their parents and the effects of such support on the adjustment of both the mothers and their children. Their sample consisted of 124 divorced mothers and one target child of each of these mothers. Thus "each child therefore constitutes an independently drawn sample element, which would not have been the case if more than one child per family were included" (p. 7). The mothers were interviewed shortly after their separation: 87 percent within a year of that event; none of them had been separated for more than twenty months. The median period of separation was six months. The mothers ranged in age from 23 to 48. The target children ranged from 2 to 17 years old. Eighty-eight of the 124 mothers had parents still living.

In the course of an in-depth structured and semistructured interview lasting approximately two hours, each mother was asked a number of questions related to the amount of help she had received from her parents since the separation. She was asked to rate the overall help they had offered her since the separation, and to indicate whether or not they had provided her with each of six specific categories of help: (1) if she had moved back into their house; (2) if they provided her with financial support; (3) if they gave her advice; (4) if they babysat for her; (5) if they provided emotional support; and (6) if they provided other, unspecified forms of help. In addition, the interviews ascertained data on five demographic characteristics of the relationship between the mother and her parents: (1) residential proximity, (2) the frequency of interaction between the mother and her parents during the last year of her marriage, (3) the frequency of interaction between the mother and her parents at the time of the interview, (4) the degree to which the parents were either critical or accepting of the separation, and (5) how much advice she had asked of them. In addition, the mother was asked to indicate on ratings scales how helpful she felt that her parents were overall, and "whether she felt that the current amount of contact with her parents was too little, just right, or too much" (Isaacs and Leon 1986, p. 8).

Isaacs and Leon measured the mother's emotional adjustment by means of the Hopkins Symptom Checklist (Derogatis et al. 1974). This checklist comprises a large number of specific symptoms that yield scale scores for anxiety, depression, and several other psychological problems. In this study the total Hopkins index score was employed as a measure of maternal adjustment. The authors assessed the adjustment of the target child by maternal reports on the Child Behavior Checklist (CBCL) (Achenbach and Edelbrock 1983). The CBCL yields a large number of scores for various aspects of children's psychosocial adjustment, but in this study only the overall Behavior Problems Scale and the Social Competence Scale were employed as adjustment criteria.

The authors factor-analyzed the various items concerned with help received from the parents. This analysis yielded four principal components. Factor one, referred to as "local," is characterized by close residential proximity to the parents as well as high frequency of interaction between the mother and her parents during both the last year of the marriage and the period following the separation. Mothers having high scores on this factor also tended to perceive their parents as quite helpful, particularly with respect to babysitting. However, they also tended to feel that there was too much contact with the parents, indicating that they may have been somewhat overwhelmed by their parents' active roles in their households. Factor two, referred to as "helpful," is characterized by the mother's perception that her parents are not at all critical of the separation, that they provided financial and emotional support, and that they were helpful in an overall sense. Factor three, referred to as "directing," was characterized by the parents' allowing their daughter to move back in with them, by daughters who actively solicited their parents' advice, and by parents who freely gave advice. Factor four, referred to as "detached," was characterized primarily by a perception on the part of the mother that the parents were not helpful in other, unspecified ways. Factor scores were obtained on each of these factors, and the maternal and child adjustment measures were regressed on these factor scores.

The results indicated that there was a significant negative relationship between scores on the helpfulness factor and the mother's overall symptom score on the Hopkins index (beta = -.21, $p < .05$). Scores on the helpfulness factor were also related significantly and negatively to the child's overall Behavior Problems score from the CBCL (beta = -.26, $p < .05$). Moreover, factor scores on the "local" factor were correlated significantly and positively with the child's Social Competence score (beta = .32, $p < .05$). Thus it is clear that maternal perceptions of specific aspects of social support from the mother's parents were related to both her postdivorce adjustment and the postdivorce adjustment of the child.

Isaacs and Leon (1986) added another element to their analysis by regressing each of the two child adjustment measures on both the parental social support factor scores and the mother's score on the Hopkins index. In the analysis of the child's CBCL overall Behavior Problems score, the inclusion of the maternal adjustment measure as a predictor resulted in a decrease in the beta for the Helpfulness factor such that this parent support factor was no longer significant. This suggests that the impact of parental helpfulness on the child's postdivorce behavior problems is primarily an indirect effect that operates through the improved adjustment of the mother that results from the social support provided by her parents. This was not the case in the second regression of the child's CBCL Social Competence scores. The mother's Hopkins index was not a significant predictor of the child's social competence, nor did the inclusion of the mother's Hopkins score in the regression result in a reduction of the significance of scores on the "local" factor.

Isaacs and Leon (1986) interpreted their findings as indicating that "the child's adjustment with respect to behavior problems is related to the mother's ability to receive support from her own parents while not relinquishing her instrumental role. It is the helpful parents, those who support the divorcing mother without usurping her management of the children, that are most beneficial in terms of the mother's adjustment as well as the child's behavior problems" (p. 14). On the other hand, Isaacs and Leon suggested that "the child's social competence is tied less to the mother's adjustment than it is to frequent and nurturant interaction with a 'local' family network" (p. 14).

In the study by Kunz and Kunz (1995) previously referred to, responding divorced men and women were asked, "Compared to the time immediately after the divorce, how are things now?" To this question the overwhelming majority of respondents indicated that things were "better" (91.9 percent); only 8.1 percent indicated that things were "the same or worse." In spite of the lopsided distribution on this criterion measure, Kunz and Kunz reported that responses to this item were related significantly to both change in participation in organizations and change in contact with one's family following the divorce. In each instance the proportion of respondents who felt that things were better now than before the divorce was lowest among those who indicated that they experienced a decrease in participation (or contact). Thus the results of this study also indicated a positive relationship between support and adjustment, even using the rather crude assessment devices they employed. (In fairness to Kunz and Kunz on this point, it should be noted that their data were derived from another study designed for a different purpose, so they had to make do with what they had.)

In summary, it would appear that there is considerable evidence for the hypothesis that certain types of social support are associated with better postdivorce adjustment both of the divorcing parents and the children in the families. On the other hand, a number of cautions are in order. As Rutter (1985) described,

> a straightforward social support buffering hypothesis is inadequate. In the first place, what seems to be important is people's satisfaction with their relationships, rather than the frequency or range of social contacts (Schaefer et al. 1981). Clearly, this is likely to re-

> flect their own personal qualities, to an appreciable extent. Secondly, social support can be a two-edged sword, with the prolonged interdependence of friends and kin during times of stress creating bitterness and hostility as well as love and trust (Belle 1982). Thirdly, with single parents, increased social contacts may mean less time with children, who may respond by being more demanding and resistive when they are together (Weinraub and Wolf 1983). Similarly, both going out to work and remarriage may provide effective support for divorced women, but yet create additional difficulties for their children (Hetherington et al. 1982). [p. 604]

It is clear that the role of social support as a predictor of children's postdivorce adjustment is complex, like that of most of the other predictors we have considered so far in this volume. The mediating factors noted by Rutter (1985) must certainly be considered. Furthermore, the literature in this area has barely begun to take account of the possible interactive effects of the child's gender, the age of the child at which the parental separation occurred, the length of time since the separation, and the child's current age. All of these factors have been demonstrated to mediate the effects of other predictors of children's psychosocial adjustment, and there is no reason to think that they will not similarly affect the relationships between various forms of social support and adjustment criteria. The more predictors of children's postdivorce psychosocial adjustment one considers, the clearer it becomes that large sample studies are required in which large numbers of predictors can be considered, along with the many potential interactions among these predictors.

11

FAMILY SYSTEMS

THE POSTDIVORCE ADJUSTMENT of children has been viewed as a function of the status of the family system. This focus has emerged from two different perspectives. The first is derived from some of the landmark studies of adjustment following divorce, which emphasized that the event of divorce typically results in a number of significant changes in both family organization and in the relationships that exist among family members (Hetherington et al. 1978, Rosen 1977, Wallerstein and Kelly 1980, Weiss 1979a,b). For example, Hetherington and her associates (1978) observed that during the two years following divorce, custodial mothers of preschoolers tend to become more restrictive and controlling, whereas noncustodial fathers tend to become more permissive and indulgent, but less available. In addition, Hetherington and her colleagues noted that, following a divorce, both parents tend to (1) make few demands on children for mature behavior, (2) communicate poorly with children, (3) show diminished levels of affection, and (4) maintain inconsistent disciplinary practices. It is logical to expect that changes of this nature would be associated with poor psychosocial adjustment among children.

Wallerstein and Kelly (1980) came to similar conclusions with respect to adolescents from divorced families. They suggested that, following divorce, parenting competence suffers as a result of the parents' own emotional turmoil. Weiss (1979a,b) noted that divorce tends to cause shifts in the relative power of parents and children. In two-parent families the parents typically share in the decision making, and children are expected to abide by the decisions the parents agree upon. Single parents, however, are likely to incorporate the children into the decision-making process. Weiss suggested that this tendency toward a partnership relationship results in the development of reciprocal friendship and confidant roles between parent and child, which may affect the child's self-concept, maturity, and peer relations.

This perspective on the relationship between the postdivorce family system and the adjustment of children has already been considered to some extent in Chapter 4, which focused on the importance of the postdivorce psychological adjustment of the custodial parent as well as the relationship between parental adjustment and the ability of the parent to provide effective parenting. Accordingly, this approach to family systems will not be reconsidered in detail here.

The second perspective that leads to consideration of the relationship between family-systems functioning and the postdivorce adjustment of children is that of family-systems theory in general. It has been argued that the adjustment of individual family members can be predicted from the family-systems dimensions of cohesion, adaptability, and communication (Green et al. 1991, Olson et al. 1979, Russell 1979). It has also been argued that individual adjustment is related to family structure, the availability of information, and flexibility (Beavers 1976, 1977, 1981, 1982, Beavers and Voeller 1983). If such relationships pertain to families in general, then it is logical to suspect that they may pertain to families in which a divorce has occurred as well.

In this chapter the basic premises of the major family-systems theories are outlined. Then the available empirical studies of the relationship between individual adjustment and family systems functioning are considered. These include studies carried out on general populations and on families in which a divorce has occurred.

FAMILY-SYSTEMS THEORIES

The best known and most widely researched model of family systems functioning is the Circumplex Model of Marital and Family Systems developed by Olson and colleagues (1979). This model specifies that two crucial dimensions of family functioning are family adaptability and family cohesion. Adaptability refers to "the ability of a marital/family system to change its power structure, role relationships, and relationship rules in response to situational and developmental stress" (p. 12). Developmental stress refers to the demands associated with normal development, while situational stress refers to demands associated with a specific event. Clearly, a divorce could constitute one such event. The dimension of cohesion has two components, including "the emotional bonding members have with one another and the degree of individual autonomy a person experiences in the family system" (p. 5).

The Circumplex Model suggests that each of these dimensions is related to family functioning in a curvilinear manner. Thus it is hypothesized that the optimal adjustment of family members is most likely to be achieved when families are characterized by moderate levels of adaptability and cohesion rather than extremely low or extremely high levels.

Olson and his colleagues (1979) identified four levels of family adaptability, ranging from "rigid" through "structured" and "flexible" to "chaotic." The extreme categories of rigid (not enough room for change) and chaotic (too much change) are considered maladaptive. The middle categories of structured and flexible adaptability represent a balance between too little change and too much change. Families with balanced adaptability are viewed as better able to cope with the demands of living.

Olson and associates (1979) also identified four levels of cohesion, ranging from "enmeshed" through "connected" and "separated" to "disengaged." Enmeshed families are too closely connected. There is an overidentification with the family that results in extreme bonding and limited individual autonomy. Disengaged families are characterized by low bonding and high autonomy.

The combinations of the four levels of adaptability and the four levels of cohesion result in the possibility of sixteen different types of families. Of these, the best adjusted families are those with balanced classifications with respect to both adaptability and cohesion—structurally separated, structurally connected, flexibly separated, and flexibly connected. The worst adjusted families are those having extreme classifications on both dimensions—chaotically disengaged, chaotically enmeshed, rigidly disengaged, and rigidly enmeshed. The eight family types characterized by a balanced classification on one dimension and an extreme classification on the other are said to fall in the "mid-range family zone."

The Circumplex dimensions of family adaptability and cohesion are measured by the Family Adaptability and Cohesion Evaluation Scales (FACES). This self-report assessment tool has undergone several revisions over the years. The original FACES is a 111-item measure (Olson et al. 1979). FACES II is a thirty-item version of the measure designed to be more convenient for clinical assessment (Olson et al. 1982). FACES III is a twenty-item measure (Olson et al. 1985). There is also a FACES IV, but this measure has received less attention (Green et al. 1991). In addition to the various self-report FACES measures of adaptability and cohesion, Olson and Lavee (1989) developed the Circumplex Assessment Package (CAP), which includes measures of dyadic communication and family satisfaction. Furthermore, Olson and Killorin (1984) developed the Clinical Observer Rating Scale (CRS), which allows clinicians to record ratings of the Circumplex dimensions based on observations of actual family interactions.

Green and colleagues (1991) pointed out that primarily because of the existence of these measures a large number of studies have been carried out relevant to the validity of the Circumplex Model. Many were conducted to test the curvilinear hypothesis by determining whether individuals from families with balanced scores on adaptability and cohesion tend to function more adequately than individuals from families with more extreme scores on the FACES instruments. However, Green and his colleagues noted that these studies have produced very inconsistent results, suggesting, in fact, that they have yielded four distinct patterns of findings, only one of which supports the Circumplex Model.

The studies that supported the curvilinear hypothesis tended to be studies in which control families who did not have any previously identified problems were compared to families in which there was a reasonably serious identified problem. For example, the proportion of families with extreme scores on adaptability and cohesiveness was significantly lower among nonproblem families than among families with (1) an alcoholic member (Olson and Killorin 1984), (2) a member with a psychiatric diagnosis of schizophrenia or neurosis (Clarke 1984), (3) a member who had a record of juvenile delinquency (Roderick et al. 1986), or (4) a member who was a sex offender (Carnes 1987).

However, when families in nonproblem comparison groups were compared to families having a member or members with a less serious identified problem, the curvilinear hypothesis tended to be disconfirmed. For example, Walker and colleagues (1988) found no significant differences on FACES II scores on adaptability or cohesion between families of adolescents having a functional illness and families of healthy adolescents. Moreover, Green and associates (1985) found that, among families of individuals on probation, there was no significant difference between balanced and extreme families on measures of individual or family well-being.

Another group of studies found linear rather than curvilinear relationships between the FACES adaptability and cohesion scales and indicators of individual or family functioning. For example, Miller and colleagues (1985), who studied randomly selected members of a Canadian university community population, reported significant linear relationships between FACES II scores on adaptability and cohesion and scores on family functioning derived from the McMaster Family Assessment Device (FAD). Similarly, Beavers and associates (1985) reported significant linear relationships among college students between scores on the FACES II dimensions of adaptability and cohesion and adjustment scores derived from the Self-Report Family Inventory (SFI). Moreover, Thomas and Cierpka (1989) reported significant linear relationships between FACES II scores on adaptability and cohesion and overall scores on the Family Adjustment Measure (FAM III).

Finally, several studies have reported significant relationships between the cohesion scale of the FACES and some measure of individual or family functioning, but no significant relationship between the FACES adaptability scale and the same criterion variable. Thus Green (1989) reported that families of adolescent psychiatric inpatients differed from the families of a nonpatient comparison group on cohesion, but not on adaptability. Similarly, Beavers and colleagues (1985) found that college students' scores on the FACES cohesion dimension were correlated significantly with their scores on the Self-Report Family Inventory (SFI), but scores on the adaptability dimension of the FACES were not.

Green and his colleagues (1991) pointed out that the conflicting findings reported with respect to the validity of the Circumplex Model can be attributed to differences in methodology, including the selection of measures of individual and family functioning, the populations sampled, the methods of data collection, and the techniques of data analysis employed. The changes in the FACES make it difficult to compare the results of studies employing different versions of the instrument. It appears that FACES II and the Circumplex Model's Clinical Rating Scale are more likely to support the curvilinear hypothesis, whereas FACES III is more likely to yield linear relationships between indicators of psychosocial adjustment and the Circumplex dimensions of adaptability, cohesion, and communication (Olson 1991). There is some evidence, in fact, that FACES II and FACES III measure quite different constructs. Hampson and colleagues (1988) reported that when they correlated scores on the two FACES measures with scores on the

Self-Report Family Inventory (SFI), the results were very different.

Another factor that helps to explain the differences among studies of the validity of the FACES model is that the ratings of family functioning employed in these different studies come from different sources. As noted by Olson and colleagues (1983), research on family-systems functioning has demonstrated repeatedly that different members of a given family tend to view family processes quite differently. This is why Olson and his colleagues recommended administering the FACES to all the members of a family and analyzing the data for each family member separately. However, researchers have not always followed this recommendation. They often use ratings obtained only from mothers, an unspecified parent, or a child. In some instances investigators obtained ratings from the various members of each family, but computed total scores by averaging ratings across two parents or across all the members of the family. The use of single sources of ratings that differ from study to study is likely to result in contradictory findings, and the use of average ratings is likely to obscure any relationships.

The use of different methods of data analysis has also contributed to the inconsistency of findings with respect to the Circumplex Model. Some investigators have simply correlated raw FACES scores with adjustment criterion measures (Beavers et al. 1985, Hampson et al. 1988). Some have applied transformations to allow the detection of curvilinear relationships through linear correlation and regression analysis (Green et al. 1985, Olson et al. 1982). Some have used a combination of these techniques (Olson and Lavee 1989, Thomas and Cierpka 1989). Obviously, the use of these different approaches to data analysis will tend to result in different findings from study to study. Olson and colleagues (1985) have suggested that due to the curvilinear nature of the model, only inferential statistics assuming nominal level data should be used to test the model. However, they have not always followed their own suggestion.

Green and associates (1991) have also noted correctly that even if the curvilinear hypothesis is correct, it will not necessarily be manifest in every sample. In samples that are homogeneous with respect to family cohesion and adaptability such that few families fall into the extreme classifications on these dimensions, no significant relationships may emerge between the Circumplex dimensions and individual or family adjustment criteria. It is also possible that within samples that have restricted ranges on adaptability and cohesion, the relationships between the Circumplex dimensions and adjustment criteria may be linear rather than curvilinear, even though these relationships are curvilinear across the full theoretical ranges of adaptability and cohesion. Thus, when Olson (1989) studied a national sample of 1,000 "normal" families, he found significant linear relationships between adaptability and cohesion scores derived from the FACES II and indicators of family adjustment.

Green and his associates (1991) administered the FACES III to a sample of 2,440 male members of the Virginia National Guard. All the participants were married and were living with their spouse at the time of the study. The men ranged in age from 17 to 68 years, with a mean of 34.8 years. The men also completed the Hudson Generalized Contentment Scale (GCS) (Hudson 1982) and the Kansas Marital Satisfaction Scale (KMSS) (Schumm et al. 1983). The GCS is a twenty-five-item scale that measures the respondent's overall contentment with his or her life and surroundings. The scale employs a five-point Likert-type response format with response options from zero to four. Respondents rate the amount of time that they feel the way each item indicates. For example, they evaluate the amount of time that they "feel blue," the amount of time that they "feel that the future looks bright," and the amount of time that they "feel great in the morning." Green and his associates reported that the alpha coefficient for this scale was .91 in the National Guard sample. The GCS has a theoretical range of zero to 100, and higher scores indicate lower levels of contentment. Hudson demonstrated that individuals who score above thirty on the GCS are likely to have a clinically significant problem with depression.

The KMSS is a three-item measure of marital satisfaction. The three items require respondents to rate (1) their satisfaction with their spouse as a wife, (2) their satisfaction with their relationship with their wife, and (3) their satisfaction with their marriage. The five-point Likert-type response options range from "very dissatisfied," scored as one, to "very satisfied," scored as five. Thus total scores for marital satisfaction have a theoretical range of three to fifteen. Scores are reverse coded so that higher scores indicate greater dissatisfaction. Green and his associates (1991) indicated that there is substantial evidence of the reliability and validity of the KMSS in the literature (Grover et al. 1984, Schectman et al. 1985, Schumm et al. 1983a,b). Green and colleagues reported an alpha coefficient of .96 for the KMSS within their sample.

Green and his colleagues (1991) reported that the FACES III resulted in the classification of 812 respondents as members of "balanced" families (33.3 percent); 1,151 as members of "mid-range" families (47.1

percent); 477 as members of "extreme" families (19.6 percent). Two one-way analyses of variance were used to compare the respondents in each of these three categories with respect to their scores on the GCS and the KMSS. Each ANOVA was highly significant ($p < .0001$), and in each case the results were in the expected direction. Of course, given the large sample size, the ANOVAs were very powerful, so it is important to evaluate the effect of size as well as the significance probability.

On the GCS the mean for the men from balanced families was 21.2 ($SD = 12.8$); for the men from mid-range families, 27.8 ($SD = 15.9$); and for the men from extreme families, 32.3 ($SD = 18.9$). Thus the magnitude of the difference between the means of the balanced and the extreme groups was in the range of two-thirds of a standard deviation. This is a large difference. On the KMSS the mean for the men from balanced families was 4.2 ($SD = 2.0$); for the men from the mid-range families, 4.8 ($SD = 2.7$); and for the men from the extreme families, 5.3 ($SD = 3.0$). Here the difference between the means of the balanced and the extreme groups was between one-third and one-half of a standard deviation, which is also a moderately large difference. Green and colleagues (1991) concluded: "These results certainly appear supportive of the curvilinear hypothesis" (p. 63).

However, Green and his colleagues did not stop their analysis at this point. They went on to test the curvilinear hypothesis using a different analytic strategy. They computed "distance from center" scores for the FACES by subtracting the sample mean from each cohesion and adaptability score, squaring the resulting differences, adding the squares, and taking the square root of the sum. This procedure results in a set of scores on which higher scores represent more extreme (i.e., further from the mean in either direction) scores on adaptability and cohesion. Pearson correlations were calculated between the distance from center score and scores on the GCS and the KMSS. The curvilinear hypothesis would be supported by positive correlations.

Results indicated that the correlations were significant ($p < .001$) and in the expected direction. However, the magnitudes of the correlations were not large. The correlation between the distance from center score and the GCS was .17; from center score and the KMSS, .06. Squaring these correlation coefficients indicates the proportion of variability in each satisfaction measure that can be explained by the FACES distance-from-center score. These figures are 2.9 and 0.3 percent, respectively. This demonstration made the point clearly that the use of different methods of data analysis can result in quite different findings.

The first method of analysis indicated strong relationships between FACES classifications and satisfaction, but the second method indicated only very weak relationships. Green and colleagues (1991) interpreted these contradictory findings as indicating that "the relationship between FACES III and the indicators of marital and individual well-being is more complex than hypothesized" (p. 65).

Based on this conclusion, Green and his colleagues went on to examine the significance of the differences among men from families in the four balanced combinations of adaptability and cohesion, the four extreme combinations of adaptability and cohesion, and each of the eight mid-range combinations of adaptability and cohesion. Contrary to what would be expected on the basis of the curvilinear hypothesis, the six ANOVAs used to make these three sets of comparisons on the GCS and the KMSS were all significant. In fact, the mean differences observed among the subgroups within the broader groups of balanced, mid-range, and extreme family types were generally larger than the differences that had been observed among the three major categories.

Furthermore, the differences observed fell into a clear pattern. Among the four "balanced" subgroups, men in the two groups categorized as "connected" with respect to cohesion were clearly more satisfied with their lives and their marriages than those categorized as "separated" on that dimension. The adaptability classification made no difference.

Among the eight "mid-range" subgroups, men in the four subgroups whose families had been classified as either "connected" or "enmeshed" with respect to cohesion were more satisfied than those whose families had been classified as "separated" or "disconnected" on cohesion. Here too the classification of families with respect to adaptability was irrelevant to satisfaction.

Among the four "extreme" subgroups, men in the two subgroups whose families had been classified as "enmeshed" were more satisfied than those whose families had been classified as "disengaged" with respect to cohesion. And once again the adaptability classification meant little.

The results of these analyses suggest that individual and family adjustment may be related only to cohesion, and that the whole adaptability dimension of the Circumplex Model may be irrelevant. To further test this notion, Green and colleagues (1991) rank-ordered the sixteen FACES subgroups in terms of their mean scores on the GCS and the KMSS. This analysis indicated that the four most satisfied groups on both measures comprised men from families classified as enmeshed. The four groups ranked from five through eight in terms of both measures of satisfaction were from families classified as connected. The four groups ranking 9 through 12 on both measures of satisfaction were from families classified as separated. And the four least satisfied groups of men were from families classified as disengaged.

Green and his colleagues (1991) concluded that "because the FACES III adaptability subscale was unrelated to measures of family well-being and because the cohesion subscale was related to these measures in a linear manner, balanced families were no more likely than mid-range or even extreme families to receive high scores on the well-being measures" (p. 69). This caused them to question whether the results of previous studies supporting the curvilinearity hypothesis might not have reflected incomplete data analysis or sampling artifacts. They did not conclude that the entire Circumplex Model was erroneous, but they did recommend discontinuing the use of FACES III for family assessment. They suggested that the most likely interpretation of their findings was that FACES III was really not a very good measure of the Circumplex Model. They also noted, however, that their results tended to support previous work reported by Beavers and associates (1985) and by Friedman and colleagues (1987) that suggested that the adaptability dimension of the model "may need some conceptual as well as measurement attention" (Green et al. 1991, p. 71).

The second major theoretical conceptualization of family systems is the Beavers Systems Model (Beavers 1976, 1977, Beavers and Voeller 1983). Beavers and his colleagues have criticized the Circumplex Model of family functioning on four distinct grounds: (1) that the model has logical defects that make it confusing; (2) that it does not match clinical reality; (3) that it omits an extremely important dimension of family functioning known as the negentropic continuum, which is a dimension of functional ability related to family functioning in a linear rather than a curvilinear manner; and (4) that it ignores developmental theories. These criticisms are described in the paragraphs that follow.

With respect to the logical defects of the Circumplex Model, Beaver and Voeller (1983) noted that Olson and his colleagues (1979a,b) defined their cohesion dimension as having two components: the emotional bonding members have with one another and the degree to which the individuals in the family system experience autonomy. They argued that "Olson et al. have linked and confounded cohesion, a variable defining the interaction among family subsystems, with autonomy, a developmental concept defining the functioning of self" (p. 86). They argued that the development of the self is actually determined by family interaction. In well-functioning families the developing individual family members are progressively offered greater and greater levels of autonomy. Because each family member is encouraged to differentiate, the family is more capable of adapting to new situations. This is a linear relationship, however, not a curvilinear one. The more autonomous the members of the family are, the greater the adaptive capacity of the family. Cohesiveness on the other hand does appear logically to have a curvilinear relationship to family functioning, since either too little or too much cohesion can be maladaptive. Thus Beavers and Voeller suggested that the Circumplex Model mixes apples and oranges by attempting to include in a single dimension of cohesiveness two components that are related to family functioning in essentially different manners, one curvilinear and the other linear.

Beavers and Voeller (1983) also argued that the Circumplex Model's adaptability dimension is logically flawed. Olson and colleagues (1979a) defined adaptability in terms of the ability of the system to "change its power structure, role relationships, and relationship rules in response to situational and developmental stress" (p. 12). But Beavers and Voeller noted that change per se is not necessarily adaptive. Thus the chaotic families in the Circumplex Model are the most adaptive, but not the most capable. Previous investigators have defined adaptiveness essentially as capability, and accordingly they have viewed moderately adaptable families as less capable than very adaptable families (Angell 1936, Beavers 1976, Bowen 1960, Kafka 1971, Mishler and Waxler 1968). Beavers and Voeller suggested that by altering the definition of adaptability in this manner, Olson and his colleagues (1979a,b) obfuscated the dimension. As evidence of the confusion resulting from this change, Beavers and Voeller noted that in order to make their 16-cell grid fit, Olson and his associates had to define the most adaptable families, the chaotic families, as families with no leadership and poor problem-solving ability. This does not sound like a definition of adaptable.

Beavers and Voeller (1983) argued further that the Circumplex Model does not fit clinical reality very well. Thus, when Olson and associates (1979b) attempted to describe a chemically dependent family in terms of the Circumplex Model, they were forced to describe them as "chaotic flippers" who vacillated between low cohesion and high cohesion. Beavers and Voeller suggested further that some of the cells in the Circumplex Model that are described by Olson and his associates (1979a,b) as diametrically opposed may in fact be closely related. For example, they argued that chaotic families are clinically much more similar than dissimilar to families characterized by rigid control. Beavers and Voeller interpreted these apparent contradictions as indicating the inconsistencies of the model.

Beavers and Voeller also criticized Olson and his colleagues (1979a,b) for not building into their model a clear dimension representing family competence, a simple linear dimension ranging from ineffective to outstanding. This failure was viewed as resulting in a number of anomalies within the Circumplex Model. Thus Beavers and Voeller (1983) argued:

> It seems unwise to teach clinicians that chaotic families are poles apart from families with rigid interpersonal controls, that chaos is extreme adaptiveness, and that moderate autonomy is optimum. The orderly progression in family systems differentiation is lost. Autonomy, maturity, even degrees of health or illness, are concepts best placed on an infinite continuum, not a curvilinear dimension. [p. 88]

Finally, Beavers and Voeller argued that from a developmental perspective chaos and authoritarian rigidity are viewed more appropriately as one step away from each other rather than poles apart. They suggested that an infant begins life with absent boundaries and fantasies of omnipotence (in Freudian terms, the oral stage). This is followed most proximately by a period during which the child is likely to experience rigid control from his or her parents, during the "terrible twos" (the anal stage). After this tumultuous period of struggling against control, the developing individual has more or less defined his or her boundaries, and an accommodation with parents will be reached. At this point the rigid control will gradually lessen, and the growing individual will learn to accept a degree of uncertainty and ambivalence.

Beavers (1976) maintained that families display an adaptability/competence continuum analogous to the developmental progression of the young child. At the lowest end of the adaptability continuum are severely disturbed families, characterized by chaotic relationships with respect to both communication and an overt expression of power. These chaotic systems are actually the most inflexible, and the least capable of making any adaptive change. From this level the family may move up a notch in the competence continuum by achieving a dominance/submission mode of functioning. In this mode one family member typically recognizes the need for the family to get organized, and he or she takes control. Beavers and Voeller (1983) noted that the authoritarian mode is painful, but nevertheless more likely to produce adaptive change than chaos. Finally, after experiencing the pain associated with an authoritarian order, the family may move in the direction of reducing power differences and increasing the flexibility of role relationships to allow for discussion, debate, and compromise.

The Beavers System Model reflects these criticisms of the Circumplex Model by positing two linear dimensions of family systems functioning. The first is a stylistic dimension ranging from centripetal to centrifugal. This dimension is described by Beavers and Voeller (1983) as equivalent to Olson's (1979) cohesion dimension, but without the component of autonomy. The second dimension is a simple linear dimension of adaptability, ranging from severely disturbed to optimal. Beavers and Voeller described this continuum by reference to five stages that can be thought of as progressing from dysfunctional to optimally healthy.

1. Severely disturbed families are characterized by poor boundaries, confused communication, lack of shared attentional focus, stereotyped family processes, cynicism, and the denial of ambivalence.
2. Borderline families display shifts from chaotic relationships to efforts at tyrannical control. Boundaries in such families fluctuate from poor to rigid. These families are characterized by distancing, depression, and outbursts of rage.
3. Mid-range families typically display relatively clear communication and constant efforts at control. They tend to turn out "same but limited offspring" (1983, p. 90), and display distancing, anger, anxiety, and depression. Ambivalence is handled by repression.
4. Adequately healthy families are characterized by relatively clear boundaries. There is some negotiation, but it is painful. Ambivalence is recognized, but reluctantly. There are periods of warmth and sharing interspersed with struggles over control.
5. Optimally healthy families display capable negotiation. Individual choice and ambivalence are respected. These families are characterized by warmth, intimacy, and humor.

Among severely disturbed families, the stylistic dimension is noteworthy, because disturbed centrifugal families tend to produce sociopathic offspring whereas disturbed centripetal families tend to produce schizophrenic offspring. As one moves up the adaptability dimension, the stylistic dimension becomes less important, and stylistic differences less noticeable.

The theoretical arguments made by Beavers (1976, 1977, 1981, 1982) and by Beavers and Voeller (1983) make sense. As noted earlier, however, there has been less empirical research carried out based on the Beavers Systems Model than on Olson's Circumplex Model. The following section describes some of the empirical research that has been reported relevant to the relationship between family-systems functioning and the psychosocial adjustment of family members.

FAMILY-SYSTEMS FUNCTIONING AND PSYCHOSOCIAL ADJUSTMENT

A number of empirical studies have been carried out to determine the relationships between aspects of family-systems functioning and the adjustment and well-being of individual family members. Some studies have been carried out using general samples of families. Others have compared intact and divorced families on aspects of family-systems functioning. Still others have focused exclusively on divorced families and on the relationship between family-systems functioning and the adjustment of the children in divorced families.

Barnes and Olson (1985) studied the relationship between parent–adolescent communication and the dimensions of the Circumplex Model among a sample of 426 intact families. The mother, father, and one adolescent from each family were assessed separately using the Parent–Adolescent Communication Scale (Barnes and Olson 1982), the FACES II (Olson et al. 1982), a Family Satisfaction Scale, a Quality of Life Satisfaction Scale, the Family Inventory of Life Events (FILE), the Family Strengths Scale, and the F-COPES, a measure of family coping strategies.

The Parent–Adolescent Communication Scale measures two dimensions of communication. One subscale measures the degree of openness in family communication; the other subscale measures the extent of communication problems experienced by the family. Each scale comprises ten items selected on the basis of factor analysis of data derived from an earlier study (Olson et al. 1983). The alpha coefficients reported for these scales in that earlier study were .87 and .78, respectively. Examples of the items in the Open Family Communication Scale are: "My mother (father/child) tries to understand my point of view"; "It is easy for me to express all my true feelings to my mother (father/child)"; and "My mother (father/child) is always a good listener" (Barnes and Olson 1985, p. 441). Examples of items from the Problems in Family Communication Scale are "My mother (father/child) has a tendency to say things to me which would be better left unsaid"; "I don't think I can tell my mother (father/child) how I really feel about some things"; and "When we are having a problem, I often give my mother (father/child) the silent treatment" (Barnes and Olson 1985, p. 441).

The Family Satisfaction Scale used in the study "assessed satisfaction related to cohesion and adaptability on the Circumplex Model" (Barnes and Olson 1985, p. 441); the Quality of Life Satisfaction Scale was "used to assess satisfaction with various domains of a person's life" (p. 442). Barnes and Olson did not describe either of these scales in any greater detail. The FILE was described simply as "a stress scale" (p. 442). The Family Strengths Scale was described only as consisting of two subscales, one measuring Family Pride, the other measuring Family Accord.

The F-COPES measure of family coping contains five subscales related to: (1) acquiring social support for the family; (2) reframing incidents to give them a more positive interpretation; (3) seeking spiritual support; (4) mobilizing the family to acquire and accept help, and (5) passive appraisal, which measures the tendency of the family to adopt a fatalistic attitude.

The results of the study showed first of all that mothers, fathers, and adolescents differed significantly in their perceptions of the nature of communication in the family. The adolescents viewed family communication much more negatively than did either their mothers or their fathers. The adolescents rated communication between themselves and their mothers as significantly less open and significantly more problematic than did the mothers. Similarly, the adolescents rated communication between themselves and their fathers as significantly less open and significantly more problematic than did the fathers. The mothers reported greater openness of communication with their adolescents than the fathers reported. The adolescents were in agreement with their mothers on this point. The adolescents' ratings of the degree of openness of communication with their mothers were significantly higher than the corresponding ratings with respect to their fathers.

It seems clear from these initial results that the only appropriate manner in which to analyze the data for this study would be to treat the communication scores of the three family members separately. Barnes and Olson (1985) did this, classifying the total communication score of each family member as low, medium, or high on the basis of a rough trichotomization of the distribution of total communication scores for that family member. Thus each family was classified as low, medium, or high on family communication three times, once for each of the responding family members.

However, when Barnes and Olson (1985) sought to determine the relationship between the communication dimensions and the FACES II dimensions of cohesion and adaptability, they did not employ the same procedure with respect to the FACES scores of the various family members. Instead they used family mean scores on both adaptability and cohesion to classify entire families as either balanced, mid-range, or extreme. The authors explained that they used the family means to determine the location of the families on the Circumplex Model "so that all members of a particular family had the same family type for this analysis" (p. 443).

Why they chose to do this is unclear since (1) they did not report the significance of differences among the various family members on the dimensions of cohesion and adaptability (as they had done for the communication scales); (2) they did not report the intercorrelations among the family members with respect to scores on these dimensions; and (3) in the earlier study by Olson and colleagues (1983) the same research group had specifically recommended against using this procedure as they had found that family members tended to have very different perceptions of family-systems functioning. Moreover, Barnes and Olson (1985) acknowledged that this procedure is fraught with dangers:

> One problem using family means scores is that families with very discrepant scores end up being misclassified as a Balanced type because of the averaging procedure. Another more serious problem is classifying these normal families as Extreme on the Circumplex Model, since this is a characteristic more frequently found in problem families. [p. 443]

Nevertheless, they did use family means for the classification of families with respect to the Circumplex Model.

Thus Barnes and Olson (1985) presented the results of a hybrid set of analyses in which families were classified as low, medium, or high on family communication based on the separate scores of mothers, fathers, and adolescents, but the families were classified only once with respect to the Circumplex Model, based on the family mean scores on Cohesion and Adaptability.

Moreover, when they compared the Circumplex classifications to the classifications of communication based on the parents' perceptions of communication with their children, they combined the classifications of mothers with those of fathers to produce a sample size for the chi-square test almost twice as large as the number of families in the sample! This additional methodological anomaly renders the results reported even more suspect, since the investigators violated the assumption of independence of observations that underlies the chi-square test they employed.

With these extreme cautions in mind, it is noted that Barnes and Olson (1985) reported that families classified as balanced on the Circumplex Model were significantly more likely than families classified as extreme to be viewed by parents as having high levels of family communication (chi-square = 29.48, $df = 4$, $p < .001$). They concluded that this finding supported the major hypothesis of the study, that balanced families would demonstrate better communication.

However, when the classification of families on the Circumplex Model was cross-tabulated by family communication as rated by the adolescents, very different results were obtained. Here Barnes and Olson (1985) chose to do two separate chi-square analyses. In the first analysis Circumplex classifications were cross-tabulated against family communication classifications based on the adolescents' perceptions of communication with their mothers; in the second analysis the same Circumplex classifications were cross-tabulated against family communication classifications based on the adolescents' perceptions of communication with their fathers.

The chi-square analysis employing the adolescents' responses regarding their mothers was highly significant (chi-square = 13.14, $df = 4$, $p < .001$). However, in this cross tabulation, results indicated that families classified as balanced with respect to the Circumplex Model were more likely than those classified as extreme to have low communication scores, and those classified as extreme with respect to the Circumplex Model were more likely than those classified as balanced to have high communication scores. The chi-square analysis employing the adolescents' responses with respect to father was also significant (chi-square = 26.87, $df = 4$, $p < .001$). This cross tabulation was in the same direction as that based on adolescents' perceptions with respect to communication with mothers, but the results were even more extreme. Balanced families tended to have low communication; extreme families, high communication.

A final analysis reported by Olson and Barnes (1985) was described as being shifted from an individual level to the "family level" (p. 444). While the foregoing critique of the treatment of FACES II data would certainly lead one to question whether the results reported above were in fact based on "individual reports," it is not necessary to belabor that point here. However, it should be pointed out that Olson and Barnes did not describe adequately how they treated communication scores in this "family level" analysis. They simply stated: "A step-wise discriminant analysis was conducted to determine the extent to which several variables could distinguish between a group of families who scored high on parent-adolescent communication and a group that scored low" (p. 444). One might assume that in this analysis family mean scores were used with respect to ratings of family communication as they had been used previously with respect to ratings of cohesion and adaptability. This would mean that each family had a single classification for communication as did each family previously with respect to the Circumplex Model. This uncertainty notwithstanding, these groups of high and low parent-adolescent communication families were compared on twelve predictor variables: family cohesion, family adaptability, family satisfaction, family stress, the five subscales of the F-COPES, the two subscales of the Family Strengths Scale, and Satisfaction with the Quality of Life. Presumably these scores were also averaged across the three responding family members, although the authors do not state this explicitly.

Barnes and Olson (1985) reported that five of the predictors discriminated significantly between the high and low communication groups: family cohesion, family adaptability, satisfaction with the quality of life, family satisfaction, and the passive appraisal subscale of the F-COPES measure. The high communication families had significantly higher scores on all of these measures except the passive appraisal measure, in which the high communication families had significantly lower scores.

The authors concluded that "the Circumplex Model has been supported for adults but not for adolescents" (1985, p. 445). They suggested that the discrepancy between the results obtained for parents and adolescents might be a function of the fact that the sample consisted of "normal" rather than dysfunctional families. In a general population the label "extreme" with respect to the Circumplex Model may actually be somewhat misleading. In other words, they suggested that in a normal sample the group classified as extreme may actually consist of high balanced levels of cohesion and adaptability rather than extremely dysfunctional levels of these dimensions. Obviously, this conclusion would be consistent with the notion that within relatively normal populations the relationships between criterion measures of adjustment and family cohesion and adaptability may well be linear rather than curvilinear.

Barnes and Olson (1985) also commented on the differences they observed between the responses of the two parents and the adolescents with respect to both family cohesion and adaptability and family communication. They asked whether these differences were due to a problem with the measures, or whether they represented real differences in the perceptions of the several family members. If the differences they reported did represent real differences in perceptions, they asked "how does one obtain an adequate family level score?" (p. 446). This is an excellent question, but one that may not have an easy answer.

Holdnack (1992) reported the results of a study in which adults from divorced families were compared to those from intact families with respect to their perceptions of family-systems functioning. Holdnack surveyed 147 full- and part-time students at a large Northeastern university, including 107 females, thirty-eight males, and two individuals who did not indicate their gender. The sample comprised 61 percent individuals whose parents were still married, 18 percent whose parents had divorced, 3.5 percent whose parents had separated but not divorced, and 13.5 percent in families in which one parent had died. Among the divorced group, the average age of the respondent when the parents divorced was 12.5 years, with a range of 2 years to 37 years. The respondents themselves ranged in age from 18 to 72 years, with mean of 25 years. The sample was 85 percent Caucasian.

To this group Holdnack administered the Family Environment Scale (FES) (Moos and Moos 1981). This is a ninety-item scale that yields scores on ten dimensions of family functioning: cohesion, conflict, expressiveness, independence, achievement orientation, active recreational orientation, moral-religious emphasis, organization, control, and intellectual/cultural orientation. Internal consistency subscale reliabilities on this measure reported by the authors of the FES ranged from alpha = .54 to alpha = .84.

Holdnack (1992) also administered the Tennessee Self-Concept Scale (TSCS), a well-validated and frequently used measure of self-concept that yields scores for three global self-concept dimensions and eight subscales. The three global dimensions are Total Self-Esteem, Self-Criticism, and Definiteness about the Self. The eight subscales are identity, self-satisfaction, behavior, physical self, moral-ethical self, personal self, family self, and social self. Buri and colleagues (1987) reported a test-retest reliability for the Total Self-Esteem Score of the TSCS of .94. Holdnack (1992) reported internal consistency reliabilities for the global and subscale scores based on his own sample. These ranged from .54 to .84.

To reduce the number of predictors employed in the data analysis, Holdnack factor-analyzed the ten subscales of the FES. Image factor extraction yielded three factors that had eigenvalues greater than one and conform to the screen plot criterion. Varimax rotation was applied. The three were (1) positive family interactions, (2) structural family cohesion, and (3) parental control. The subscales loading heavily on the first factor were cohesion, expressiveness, independence, intellectual and cultural activity, and active recreational interactions. On the structural family cohesion factor, the cohesiveness subscale had a high positive loading, while the conflict subscale had a large negative loading. The parental control factor was characterized by the respondent's perception that his or her parents were controlling, that they had high expectations for the respondent to achieve, and that there was a high degree of conflict in the family as the child was growing up.

Holdnack used multivariate analysis of covariance to compare the respondents whose parents had divorced to those whose parents were currently still married, separated, or widowed on factor scores representing the three FES factors. The covariates employed in this analysis were gender, respondent age, ethnicity, respondent's marital status, respondent socioeconomic status, birth order, and whether or not the respondent has children. This MANCOVA yielded a significant multivariate main effect due to marital status ($p < .001$). Follow-up univariate tests indicated that the respondents from divorced families differed significantly from respondents in the other groups with respect to both positive family interactions ($p = .034$) and structural family cohesion ($p = .003$). The respondents from the divorced families had significantly lower scores on both the positive family interaction factor and the structural family cohesion factor. There was no significant univariate main effect due to parental marital status with respect to the parental control factor ($p = .216$).

MANCOVAs were also run comparing the parental marital status groups on the TSCS global self-concept measures and the TSCS subscales. These analyses employed the same covariates as the analysis of the three FES family-systems functioning factors. Neither of these analyses yielded significant differences. Thus the respondents from divorced and nondivorced families differed with respect to perceived family functioning but not with respect to the criterion measures of self-concept.

Holdnack (1992) ran zero-order correlations and hierarchical multiple regressions to determine the relationship among each of the three global self-concept measures and the measures of family-systems functioning derived from the FES. In these analyses the demographic variables included in the first step as control variables were gender, age, socioeconomic status, race, parents' marital status, whether or not the respondent has children, birth order, and several terms representing the interactions among these factors. The scores representing the three family environment factors were introduced after variability to these factors was partialed. The results of these analyses indicated that, after controlling for the demographic factors, the FES factor representing positive family interactions was a significant predictor of each of the three global self-concept scales. Thus, for the entire sample, positive family interaction did predict various domains of self-concept. This effect was observed after variability due to parents' marital status was controlled. This could be interpreted as suggesting that this relationship between perceived family environment and self-concept pertains for individuals with divorced and nondivorced parents alike.

However, the sizes of the sample for the four parental marital status groups did not permit Holdnak (1992) to test these relationships for each of the marital status groups separately. This would have allowed a more definitive conclusion regarding the existence of this relationship among individuals with divorced parents as a group, and among individuals from intact families as a group. In addition, Holdnack pointed out that the results of this study were limited as the study sample included a disproportionately large percentage of female and Caucasian respondents, which certainly limits the generalizability of findings.

Several studies have been carried out to determine the relationships between family-systems functioning and indicators of psychosocial adjustment among the population of children from divorced families specifically. The study by Farber and colleagues (1985) reviewed in Chapter 10 in connection with the role of social support in mediating the effect of divorce was designed to assess the effect of family-systems functioning as well. These authors administered the Family Environment Scale to the sixty-five adolescents in their sample, along with the measures of social support, state and trait anxiety, depression, hostility, and self-concept (described above).

Farber and her colleagues (1985) performed regression analyses predicting the psychosocial adjustment variables from the FES family functioning scales, social support, and divorce-specific stressors. They found that the FES measure of family cohesion was related negatively to anxiety, while the FES measure of family conflict was related positively to anxiety, as measured by the State-Trait Anxiety Inventory. They also found that the FES measures of family independence and control were related positively to hostility, as measured by the Multiple Affect Adjective Checklist. These findings support the notion that dimensions of postdivorce family functioning are related to adolescents' psychosocial adjustment.

Ellwood and Stolberg (1991) studied thirty-six divorced or legally separated families having at least one child between the ages of 6 and 16 living in the home of one of the actual parents. All the families had been separated for at least six months, and none had been separated for longer than thirty-four months. The families were recruited through three different sources: psychologists, lawyers specializing in divorce mediation, and social workers. Custodial parents completed an extensive survey instrument. These parents included twenty-three with sole custody and thirteen who shared custody. There were thirty women and six men in the sample.

The responding parents completed a survey package with the following measures: the Single Parenting Questionnaire (SPQ) (Stolberg and Ullman 1984), the Hopkins Symptom Checklist (SCL-90) (Derogatis 1983), the Life Experiences Survey (LES) (Sarason et al. 1978), the Divorce Events Schedule for Children (DES-C) (Sandler et al. 1986), the Child Behavior Checklist (CBCL) (Achenbach 1981), and the Family Functioning Scales (Bloom 1985).

The Single Parenting Questionnaire (SPQ) is an eighty-eight-item survey that measures the single parent's perceptions of six dimensions of parental interactions with a single target child. These dimensions include problem solving, support systems, parental warmth, discipline/

control, parental rules, and enthusiasm for parenting. The SPQ also yields a total parenting score, which can be interpreted as an overall measure of parenting skills. Only the latter global score was used in this study. The authors reported an alpha coefficient of .86 for this score.

The SCL-90 is a ninety-item measure that yields scores for nine symptom dimensions, plus a global General Severity Index (GSI). The GSI was employed as a measure of the psychological symptoms of the responding parent in this study. Test-retest reliabilities reported by Derogatis (1983) for the GSI have ranged from .78 to .90.

The Life Experiences Survey (LES) was used to measure the stress experienced by the custodial parent. The LES is a fifty-seven-item measure of life stress in which respondents indicate both the occurrence of and the perceived impact of each of a series of life events, including potentially positive as well as potentially negative events. The LES yields scores for both negative and positive life changes. Sarason and his colleagues (1978) reported very low correlations between the scores for negative and positive life changes. The authors reported test-retest reliabilities for the two scales ranging from .56 to .88 in several different samples. They also reported significant correlations between scores on negative life changes and measures of depression in several samples.

The Divorce Events Schedule for Children (DES-C) was used to assess the stress experienced by the children following the divorce. This scale was described briefly in Chapter 9, in connection with a study reported by Wolchik and associates (1993). As noted above, the DES-C assesses the child's perceptions of his or her exposure to critical divorce events that are essentially out of the child's control. The child indicates the occurrence of each event and the extent to which it was positive or negative. Two-week test-retest reliabilities reported by Sandler and associates (1986) for the positive and negative events scores were .87 and .77, respectively. Sandler and colleagues (1984) reported that scores on the negative divorce events were correlated significantly with measures of depression, child anxiety, and hostility. In the study by Ellwood and Stolberg (1991), DES-C scores for positive, negative, and total divorce events were used. Although the DES-C was designed to assess the stressful events experienced by children, the scale was completed by the responding custodial parent, who selected a target child from among his or her children on whom to complete the DES-C, CBCL, and SPQ.

The Child Behavior Checklist (CBCL) (Achenbach 1981) is a 118-item checklist completed by an adult to assess the social competencies and behavioral problems of a child between the ages of 4 and 16. The CBCL, described in detail earlier in this book, yields scores on Internalizing Pathology and Externalizing Pathology, as well as scores for social competency in three areas (Activities, Social, and School). In the study by Ellwood and Stolberg (1991), only the two scales measuring pathology were used.

The measure of family-systems functioning employed by Ellwood and Stolberg (1991) was the Family Functioning Scales (FFS). The measure resulted from a series of factor analytic studies of four separate measures of family functioning: the Family Environment Scale (Moos and Moos 1981), the Family Concept Q-Sort, the Family Adaptability and Cohesion Evaluation Scale (FACES) (Olson et al. 1979b), and the Family Assessment Measure. From among the factors obtained in these prior factor analytic studies, five dimensions of family systems functioning were selected by Ellwood and Stolberg (1991) for use as predictors of adjustment in their study: Cohesion, Conflict, Democratic Style, Idealized Family, and Laissez-Faire Style.

Ellwood and Stolberg (1991) reported the results of a multiple regression analysis that indicated that scores on the Internalizing Pathology scale of the CBCL were related significantly to six predictors, including four of the five family-systems functioning measures. The significant predictors were Laissez-Faire Family Style, Democratic Family Style, Family Cohesion, Family Conflict, the gender of the identified child, and the age of the identified child. Internalizing pathology was greater among families in which the custodial parent tended to characterize the family as relatively high on laissez-faire style and conflict, but relatively low on democratic style and family cohesion. Additionally, internalizing pathology was higher among boys than among girls, and higher among older children than among younger children.

A second multiple regression analysis indicated that scores on the CBCL Externalizing Pathology Scale were predicted significantly by four variables, including one of the family-systems functioning measures. The four significant predictors of Externalizing Pathology were Family Cohesion, the DES-C score for children's negative divorce-related events, the parent's Negative Life Events score from the DES-C, and the overall parent–child interaction score from the SPQ. Children who were rated by their parents as demonstrating relatively large amounts of acting-out behavior tended to come from families where cohesion was low, be rated by their custodial parents as experiencing relatively large numbers of negative divorce-related events, have custodial parents who reported experiencing relatively large amounts of life stress themselves, and have custodial parents who perceived themselves as having relatively poor parenting skills with respect to the target child.

These findings reported by Ellwood and Stolberg (1991) indicate clearly that aspects of postdivorce family system functioning are related to the adjustment of children from divorced families. The major limitations of this study are the extremely small sample size, particularly for a study employing multiple regression analyses, and the fact that all the measures were based entirely on parental perceptions.

The study reported by Abelsohn and Saayman (1991) was discussed briefly in Chapter 1. These investigators focused on the relationship between family-systems functioning and the adjustment of adolescents from divorced families. The investigators set out to rectify a specific methodological problem that characterized many prior studies of adolescent children of divorce. This is the problem of studying samples drawn from families who have reported for psychological treatment. Obviously the use of such samples is problematic, because by definition such families have some problem of adjustment that brings them into treatment. Abelsohn and Saayman (1991) therefore differentiated between adolescents from families who had reported for treatment and those who had not.

These investigators studied forty-five adolescents from thirty families. They ranged in age from 12 to 16.8 years, with a mean age of 14.2. There were twenty-four males and twenty-one females. On the average, the parents of these adolescents had been separated for ten months. Abelsohn and Saayman (1991) did not specify the range on this variable, but a criterion for inclusion in the study was that the parents had to have separated within the last eighteen months. The marriages had lasted from eleven to twenty-three years, with a mean duration of sixteen and seven-tenths years. All the families were classified in the second category of the Hollingshead Index of Social Class, which includes the owners of medium-sized businesses and minor professionals. There were twenty-three white and seven black families. An additional criterion for inclusion in the study was that the adolescent's living arrangement was not time-equalized. These adolescents either lived most of the time with their mothers or they did not see their fathers at all.

Of the thirty families, nineteen were categorized as aided families who had applied for treatment to the Families of Divorce Service of the Philadelphia Child Guidance Clinic. This agency provides child-focused family help in negotiating the process of separation and divorce.

The remaining eleven families were categorized as unaided. They met the criteria of being separated within the last eighteen months and having the child(ren) spend most or all of their time with the mother, but they had not sought treatment. These unaided families were recruited through advertisements in the local newspapers. The mothers in the unaided families were paid $25 for their participation; the adolescents, $5.

Obviously, there are a number of serious methodological problems with this study. The use of multiple adolescent respondents from some families clearly violates the statistical assumption of independence of observations. The authors recognized the limitation and compensated for it in some of their statistical analyses by employing only one adolescent from each family. In other analyses, however, they employed the entire set of forty-five adolescents. In addition, the fact that the aided group had applied specifically for assistance in working through the divorce process makes them a unique group, although it is not clear in what way. It could be argued that they were more disturbed than the average divorcing family and therefore required psychological intervention, or it could be argued that they were more enlightened and therefore sought help to preclude possible difficulties. The volunteer status and payment of the unaided group raises questions of their motivation. The authors also noted that the families in the unaided group were first offered the assistance of the Families of Divorce Service, and were included in the unaided group only after they refused these services. This could imply that the unaided group were particularly resistant to psychological assistance.

The mother in each family completed the Child Behavior Checklist (CBCL) (Achenbach and Edelbrock 1983) on each adolescent in the study. Abelsohn and Saayman (1991) employed as criteria of adolescent adjustment the three CBCL scales for Social Competence (Activities, Social, and School), the two scales for Internalizing and Externalizing Behavior Problems, and the Total Behavior Problems Scale derived from adding the Internalizing and Externalizing Behavior Problems Scales.

Each adolescent in the study completed the Family Adaptability and Cohesion Evaluation Scales (FACES) (Olson et al. 1978). Abelsohn and Saayman (1991) indicated that they had the adolescents complete the FACES because they wanted to "avoid the possibility that mother's bias in evaluating the adolescent's adjustment would contaminate and skew her view of the family, or vice versa" (p. 181). Following the curvilinear hypothesis of the Circumplex Model, Abelsohn and Saayman employed as measures of family adaptability and cohesion the absolute value of the distance of each score from the mean on the respective scale reported by Olson (1979) for a norming sample. They referred to these measures as the "Deviation from the Mean Cohesion" and the "Deviation from the Mean Adaptability."

The adolescents also completed the Postseparation Generational Hierarchy Questionnaire (GHQ). *Generational hierarchy* implies that the family is a hierarchical, nondemocratic organization run by the parent(s). Abelsohn and Saayman (1991) sought to measure this construct as they felt that in many divorced families there is a role reversal in which "children consistently parent their parents by controlling and/or nurturing them" (p. 180). The GHQ contains an unspecified number of items developed specifically for this study to assess: (1) the maintenance of the generational hierarchy in the home following the separation; or (2) its opposite, the compromise or collapse of the generational hierarchy. The only example of an item from this questionnaire that Abelsohn and Saayman provide is: "How often does your mother cry in your presence?"

A factor analysis of responses to the GHQ indicated two meaningful and coherent concepts. The items having high loadings on the first factor "suggest a process of the adolescent being exposed to, or being involved with the mother's distressed affect, problems, or difficulties" (Abelsohn and Saayman 1991, p. 183). This factor was named "Access to Mother's Distressed Affect." The items loading heavily on the second factor pertained to the importance of rules in the household and to the strictness or consistency of their enforcement. This factor was named *hierarchical control*.

The correlation between the FACES Deviation from the Mean Cohesion Score and the CBCL Social Competence Scale was significant ($r = -.48$, $p < .01$). Thus adolescents who saw their families as either relatively enmeshed or relatively disengaged tended to be rated by their mothers as manifesting relatively poor social competence. The Deviation from the Mean Cohesion score was not related significantly to any of the other CBCL scores.

The correlation between the FACES Deviation from the Mean Adaptability Score and the CBCL Internalizing Behavior Problem Scale was also significant ($r = .37$, $p < .05$). Abelsohn and Saayman (1991) indicated that no adolescents in their sample rated their families as rigid on the FACES adaptability scale. Therefore, the positive correlation between the Deviation from the Mean Adaptability Scale and Internalizing Behavior Problems was interpreted as indicating that adolescents who saw their families as chaotically organized tended to be rated by their mothers as displaying internalizing behavior problems such as anxiety and withdrawal. The Deviation from the Mean Adaptability Score was not related significantly to any of the other CBCL scores.

Abelsohn and Saayman (1991) also reported a significant positive correlation between scores on the GHQ factor measuring Access to Mother's Distressed Affect and the CBCL Social Competence Scale ($r = .38$, $p < .05$). This GHQ factor was not related significantly to any of the other CBCL scales, and the GHQ factor measuring hierarchical control was not related significantly to any of the CBCL scales. Independent sample t-tests indicated no significant differences between adolescents from the aided and the unaided groups on any of the CBCL behavior scales.

These findings suggest that the psychosocial adjustment of children from divorced families is related to dimensions of family-systems functioning, including cohesion and adaptability. Moreover, the findings provide some support for the Circumplex Model curvilinear hypothesis. Abelsohn and Saayman (1991) did not test for linear relationships between the two FACES dimensions and the CBCL behavior scales, so it is not possible to evaluate the relative merits of the curvilinear hypothesis and the linear hypothesis in this data set.

Brown and colleagues (1991) obtained data on postdivorce family functioning and children's psychosocial adjustment from seventy-six divorced, unremarried custodial parents and 111 of their children (forty-five boys and sixty-six girls). The authors were not clear with respect to the unit of analysis employed in the study, but at one point they refer to a sample size of ninety-five. Thus the unit of analysis could not have been the family, and we must assume that the findings of the study are limited by the lack of independence of observations.

The children ranged in age from 6 to 16. The custodial parents ranged in age from 24 to 50, with a median of 34 years. Parental reports of the time since the divorce ranged from less than one year to fifteen years. About three-quarters of the sample had been divorced for more than two and one-half years. The average income of the sample was $13,000 per year.

Brown and his colleagues (1991) measured children's adjustment by means of parental reports using the Child Behavior Checklist. They focused their analyses on the Total Problem Behavior Score. The investigators measured family-systems functioning using the McMaster Family Assessment Device (FAD), which measures six dimensions of family functioning: problem solving, communication, family roles, affective responsiveness, affective involvement, and behavior control. The FAD also yields a global score for general family functioning. Brown and his colleagues indicated that they selected this measure of family systems functioning, because "the dimensions measured are closely aligned with the risk factors known to be present in the divorcing family" (p. 85). Brown and associates did not provide data on the reliability or the validity of the FAD, either from prior studies or from their own data set. However, the FAD is a well-known instrument that is used frequently in research on families.

Brown and colleagues (1991) also employed the Divorce Adjustment Inventory (DAI), a thirty-one-item "parental self- report instrument designed specifically to identify children at risk for divorce-related maladjustment" (p. 84). This instrument was developed by Portes and associates (1991) based on a discriminant analysis employing an initial item pool of 143 items and two groups of divorced families (N = 102 and N = 98, respectively). The authors stated; "A discriminant analysis of the DAI produced 31 items (out of 143 items) that were found to be statistically associated with both family functioning and child adjustment. A subsequent factor analysis produced four factors that were retained for further analysis in the present study" (p. 85).

In the 1992 study, the thirty-one DAI items identified in the earlier study were factor-analyzed once again in order to compare the two factor structures and obtain factor scores to be correlated with child adjustment. A principal-components analysis yielded four factors the authors described as "similar" to those obtained in the prior study: (1) external support systems, representing the amount of time that the custodial parent spends in outside activities and with support people outside the family system; (2) child reaction and insight into divorce, which reflects the child's level of understanding of the divorce; (3) postdivorce conflict between the parents; and (4) family stability, which reflects primarily the emotional stability of the custodial parent.

Brown and his colleagues (1991) regressed the child's total problem behavior score from the CBCL on the factors measured by the family-systems functioning factors measured by the FAD and the DAI. Although they did not state their method of regression or the significance criterion for inclusion that they employed, it seems apparent from the results they reported that they employed a stepwise analysis, and that the criterion for inclusion was probably that of statistical significance. Three predictors were included in the regression (in order of entry into the regression equation): (1) the FAD factor measuring family roles, accounting for 34 percent of the variability in total problem behavior; (2) the DIA factor measuring the child's insight into the divorce, accounting for an additional 9 percent of the variability; and (3) the DIA factor measuring postdivorce conflict between the parents, accounting for an additional 5 percent of the variability. All three predictors were highly significant ($p < .001$) at the step when they were introduced.

The FAD roles construct was described by Brown and colleagues as "a comprehensive factor with important implications for the healthy functioning of the family. Included in this factor is the family's ability to maintain family rituals, provide a sense of security to its members, support each other emotionally, and overall, maintain the organization of the family system" (p. 91). Brown and his colleagues noted that the importance of this factor in the prediction of children's adjustment:

> strongly underlines the importance of providing resources, nurturance and support, life skills development, and systems management and maintenance (Epstein et al. 1978). Healthy families are characterized by adequate fulfillment of all family functions, appropriate allocation of responsibility, and clear accountability. It would appear that maintaining family rituals and providing emotional support helps stabilize the family following divorce. [pp. 91–92]

Brown and his colleagues (1991) also suggested that this finding supported previous studies that indicated the importance of the parents' postdivorce adjustment for the satisfactory psychosocial adjustment of the child (e.g., Emery 1982, Guidubaldi and Perry 1984, Wallerstein and Kelly 1976, 1980). Brown and associates pointed to Wallerstein's (1989) report that the children of divorce whom she interviewed frequently indicated a need for family structure and protection. Brown and associates (1991) concluded: "Children yearned for clear guidelines for moral behavior, thus placing central importance on this family function for healthy postdivorce adjustment" (p. 92). With respect to the other significant predictors, Brown and his associates concluded that in addition to the maintenance of family organization, it is important that (1) the relationships between the ex-spouses and between the parent and child remain open and there is a minimal level of conflict; and

(2) the child understands the reasons for the divorce and avoids taking responsibility for it.

The theoretical and empirical literature described in this chapter make it clear that aspects of postdivorce family-systems functioning are clearly related to the psychosocial adjustment of the children. The controversy surrounding the most appropriate models and measures of family-systems functioning simply makes it clear that a good deal more theoretical work and psychometric research needs to be carried out relevant to the issue of the nature and measurement of family-systems functioning, especially those aspects affected by marital discord and dissolution. This body of literature also makes it clear that professionals working with separating and divorcing families should assess family-systems functioning and work toward improving dysfunctional patterns of behavior.

12

MODEL FOR PREDICTING CHILDREN'S ADJUSTMENT TO DIVORCE

THE FOREGOING CHAPTERS have made clear the complexity of relationships between the psychosocial adjustment of children following the divorce of their parents and the many variables that investigators have used to attempt to predict adjustment. In reviewing the research associated with each of the predictors to which a chapter of this book has been devoted, one frequently finds conflicting research results. These discrepancies can sometimes be explained by differences in the populations studied, the manner in which predictors and criterion measures are defined conceptually and operationalized, and other differences in the methodological strengths and weaknesses of the studies.

To understand these issues and their implications for conducting meaningful research on children's adjustment following parental divorce, this chapter begins by considering each of the predictors discussed in Chapters 2 through 11 so as to identify (1) the complexities of defining and operationalizing the predictor, which frequently leads to the conclusion that "the" predictor is not a single variable at all, but rather a complex domain that can be represented only by multiple measures derived from several different respondents; (2) variables that have been shown to mediate the relationship between the predictor and psychosocial adjustment; and (3) any other important methodological issues that have been identified in research using that predictor. In the course of this review, a number of additional predictors are identified that should be included in future research on children's outcomes following parental divorce.

PARENTAL CONFLICT

The review of research on the effects of parental conflict clearly established that this variable is related negatively to children's postdivorce adjustment. Several studies that employed children from both divorced and intact families indicated that it might actually be the level of parental conflict that predicts poor psychosocial outcomes among children rather than the divorce itself. This observation leads to a basic principle of research on the adjustment of children following divorce: always include a same-age and same-gender comparison group of children from intact families. Without such groups one cannot be certain that the relationships one observes with respect to the prediction of psychosocial adjustment are unique to divorced families. They might pertain to the general population as well.

The literature on parental conflict highlighted the question of attribution of causation in correlational studies. As Long and colleagues (1988) pointed out, parental conflict may cause a child to experience psychological symptoms or to display acting-out behavior, but the presence of symptoms and/or conduct disorders on the part of children may also lead parents to quarrel. The best solution for the problem of establishing causality is to conduct longitudinal research. This is frequently difficult to do, particularly for individual investigators with limited resources. Nevertheless, the existing literature does in fact contain a number of large-scale longitudinal studies, indicating the awareness of the importance of such studies within the research community.

The literature on parental conflict made it clear that the length of time since the parents separated is an important variable that mediates the relationship between parental conflict and children's postdivorce adjustment. Much of the early research on parental conflict employed samples in which the families were still in the first year following the parental separation. But it is during this period that parental conflict is likely to be greatest, and that children are most likely to display psychological symptoms or behavior problems. Furthermore, the first year or two following the initial parental separation represents a critical period of adjustment during which the members of the family struggle to adjust to new roles.

Therefore it is not surprising that the relationships between parental conflict and adjustment that pertain during the critical adjustment period may be very different from the corresponding relationships after the family has had an opportunity to restore equilibrium. Mechanic and Hansell (1989) employed two techniques to assess the possible effects of the amount of time passed since the divorce: (1) they included in their study and differentiated between groups of adolescents whose parents had divorced within the last year and those whose parents had divorced more than a year ago; and (2) they collected data at two points in time, a year apart. This combination of cross-sectional and longitudinal design is highly recommended.

The research on parental conflict also indicated that the relationships between predictor variables and adjustment criteria may be very different for female and male children. Thus the gender of the child is not only a predictor of adjustment in its own right, but also a mediating variable that affects the relationships between other predictors and postdivorce adjustment. It is questionable whether relationships between predictor variables and measures of psychosocial adjustment should ever be reported for pooled samples of male and female children.

The research on conflict made it clear that investigators must be aware that relationships observed between parental conflict and children's adjustment may vary greatly, depending on the sources of the ratings. This applies both to the ratings of the degree of parental conflict present in the family and to the ratings of the children's adjustment. In many cases, particularly studies of older children, there is very little relationship between parental perceptions and children's perceptions of marital conflict. Most studies of outcomes of divorce have employed parental (generally maternal) ratings of children's adjustment. Some researchers have used teacher ratings; others, self-rating scales completed by the children themselves. The study of adolescents reported by Long and colleagues (1987) employed ratings of children's adjustment derived both from the students and their social studies teachers. When the criteria of adjustment employed were behavioral ratings of children obtained from teachers, significant main effects were observed for both the marital status of the parents (divorced versus intact) and the level of parental conflict (low versus high). However, when children's self-report measures were employed as criteria of adjustment, level of parental conflict was not a significant predictor.

It is probably advisable whenever possible to use multiple rating sources for both predictors and criteria of children's adjustment. This may not always be possible, of course. However, it is always possible for researchers to be aware of the importance of the sources of the ratings they do use so as not to make inappropriate comparisons between their results and the results of other studies that may have used different sources to rate the same constructs.

The literature on the relationship between parental conflict and children's adjustment also brings home the point that the observation of a statistically significant relationship between a predictor and an outcome measure does not necessarily imply that the investigator understands the dynamics behind this relationship. This pertains not only to the issue of causal direction noted above, but also to the possibility of multiple competing or mutually compatible theoretical explanations of the relationships observed. The review of the literature on the effect of parental conflict revealed three different schools of thought with respect to the question of why parental conflict may lead to poor psychosocial outcomes for children: (1) parental conflict produces a stressful home environment that can lead to feelings of frustration, anger, and anxiety; (2) conflict between the custodial and noncustodial parents may cause the latter parent to stay away, reducing the regularity and frequency of his or her contact with the child, which may in turn lead to poor adjustment on the part of the child; and (3) conflict between the parents can lead to ineffective parenting on the part of one or both parents, which may also lead to poor psychosocial adjustment in the child.

Each of these three explanations is logical; in fact, all three may well contribute to the observed negative relationship between parental conflict and children's adjustment. The existence of multiple possible explanations for this relationship suggests that it may well be useful to supplement empirical research in this area with in-depth interviews and clinical case studies that describe the perceptions of the various family members about the manner in which parental conflict actually impacts on parenting behavior, visitation, and children's symptoms.

CUSTODIAL ARRANGEMENT

The literature reviewed with respect to the impact of the custody arrangement on children's adjustment made it clear that most research on outcomes for children following divorce has been carried out on populations comprised entirely or almost entirely of mother-custody families. This is relevant because the research indicates significant interactions between the sex of the custodial parent and that of the child, such that children tend to be better adjusted when they are in the custody of the same-sex parent (Santrock and Warshak 1979). Thus one should be careful in interpreting the results of studies of the effect of mother custody versus father custody. It is imperative that such studies report separate results for female and male children.

The literature on custody arrangement also made clear the mediating role of social support with respect to children's adjustment. Santrock and Warshak (1979) reported that custodial fathers tended to make greater use of social support than custodial mothers. They also indicated that in both mother-custody and father-custody homes the use of support systems was related positively to children's adjustment.

The literature on joint custody is limited. What literature there is tends to suggest that joint custody is associated with better outcomes for children. However, this relationship may well be an artifact due to the mediating effect of parental conflict. Families in which the parents are able to agree to and coordinate joint custody arrangements are certainly more likely to manifest lower levels of parental conflict and better coparenting relationships than sole-custody families.

PSYCHOSOCIAL ADJUSTMENT OF THE CUSTODIAL PARENT

The literature suggests that the adjustment of the custodial parent is a key predictor of the adjustment of children from divorced families. Indeed, the literature suggests that parental adjustment predicts children's adjustment in intact as well as divorced families (Maccoby 1992, Maccoby and Martin 1983).

A key methodological issue pertaining to this relationship is that of the source of the ratings of adjustment of the parent and the child. If both ratings are derived from the parent, it may well be that the ratings of children's adjustment are in part attributions to the child of the difficulties that the parent may be experiencing. This might explain the findings reported by Kalter and associates (1989), who reported strong relationships between parental self-report measures of adjustment and parent reports of children's behavior by means of the Child Behavior Checklist, but relatively weak relationships between parental self-reports of adjustment and children's self-reports of symptoms of depression and anxiety.

The issue of direction of causality is also relevant here, since an acting-out child could contribute to the stress experienced by the custodial parent, which might eventually be expressed in the form of physical or psychological symptoms.

Most of the research on the psychological adjustment of the custodial parent has been based on mother-custody families. As noted above, this means that the results reported are meaningful only if they are reported separately for female and male children. The one empirical study of custodial fathers that examined the relationship between the father's own adjustment and that of his children (Szott 1990) reported very different results for female and male children. Thus it would appear that regardless of whether the population under study comprises mother-custody or father-custody families, results must be reported separately for boys and girls. Also, investigators should not pool groups of mother-custody and father-custody families since the results obtained in such samples will most likely not represent either type accurately.

The literature on the adjustment of the custodial parent, like that on parental conflict, makes clear the potentially important mediating role of parenting skills. Poorly adjusted custodial parents, like custodial parents who are experiencing extreme stress due to conflict with their former spouses, may well display inadequate parenting behavior. Several studies have shown that quality of parenting mediates the relationship between parental adjustment and children's adjustment (Guidubaldi et al. 1986, Heath and Lynch 1988, Hetherington and Clingempeel 1992, Simons et al. 1994). These findings suggest that quality of parenting should always be assessed when studying children's adjustment following divorce. Large-scale longitudinal studies will be required to establish such possible causal sequences as (1) conflict, leading to (2) poor adjustment on the part of the custodial parent, leading to (3) inadequate parenting behavior, leading to (4) poor psychosocial adjustment among children.

REMARRIAGE OF THE CUSTODIAL PARENT

Most of the research on the remarriage of the custodial parent has focused on stepfathers, since most divorces lead to mother-custody situations. More research is required on father/stepmother families. For the same reasons cited in connection with parental conflict, custody arrangements, and the adjustment of the custodial parent, samples of families with mother-custody and father-custody should not be pooled when the effects of remarriage are investigated. Similarly, the results of research on impact of remarriage should always be reported separately for female and male children.

The literature on remarriage indicates that the relationship between remarriage and children's adjustment is mediated by a large number of factors, including not only the genders of the custodial parent and the child, but also the current age of the child, the age of the child at the time of the remarriage, the length of time since the remarriage, the extent to which the mother and stepfather agree on appropriate parenting practices, and the nature of the relationship between the stepfather and the child. One is forced to conclude that adequate studies of the effects of remarriage would have to include measures of these variables. Furthermore, one would assume that the ideal situation would be to have measures of all these variables derived from the reports of the child, the parent, and the stepparent.

Hetherington (1993) concluded that the best approach for stepfathers to take in seeking to establish good relationships with their stepchildren differed dramatically, depending on the age of the stepchild. Whereas a laid-back approach involving little more than support for the mother's decisions was best when the children were preadolescents, a much more authoritative approach appeared desirable for use with adolescents. Based on these observations, it would appear that studies of the effect of remarriage should also include measures of parenting style and effectiveness.

CHILD'S RELATIONSHIP WITH NONCUSTODIAL PARENT

The literature on the child's relationship with the noncustodial parent is perhaps the most contradictory body of literature reviewed in this book. Many studies, particularly the early ones, indicated that the frequency and regularity of contact with the noncustodial parent was related positively and strongly to the child's postdivorce adjustment (Hetherington et al. 1982, Kelly 1988a,b, Wallerstein and Kelly 1980a,b). Although this relationship was initially thought to be stronger among boys than among girls, other investigators have concluded that the absence of the noncustodial parent, generally the father, is damaging to girls as well (Kalter 1984, Wallerstein 1985).

In some more recent studies, however, results have indicated that frequency of contact with noncustodial fathers may be irrelevant to the child's adjustment (Clingempeel and Segal 1986, Jacobsen 1987, Kurdek et al. 1981, Leupnitz 1982) or might even be related negatively to children's adjustment (Shook and Jurich 1992).

One of the most obvious methodological issues in this body of literature is that most of these studies did not measure and control for the effect of parental conflict. As noted above, conflict may cause noncustodial parents to avoid visits. Any sound study of the relationship between frequency and regularity of visitation by the noncustodial parent must include a measure of conflict. Ideally, the perceptions of the parents and the child should be assessed.

Another methodological issue that arises in the context of the child's relationship with the noncustodial parent is the choice of measures of this relationship. Thomas and Forehand (1993) suggested that frequency and regularity of contact might not be adequate measures of the relationship between children and their noncustodial parents, that we need to ascertain the quality of the relationship as well. Simons and associates (1994) suggested that the quality of a noncustodial father's parenting ability was likely to mediate any relationship between contact and the child's adjustment. It should also be pointed out that the relationships reported between the parenting behaviors of noncustodial fathers and the adjustment of their children were quite different for boys and girls. Thus, once again, we see the need to report results separately for boys and girls.

CHILD'S AGE AT TIME OF DIVORCE

Results reported with respect to the effect of the child's age at the time of the divorce, like those reported with respect to the effect of the child's relationship with the noncustodial parent, are conflicting. Some studies suggest that although the immediate impact of the divorce is worse for younger children, the long-term adjustment of this group may tend to be better than that of children whose parents divorced when they were older (Ellis and Russell 1992, Grant et al. 1993). Other studies suggest that children fare better when they are older at the time of the divorce, since they are better able to understand it (Allison and Furstenberg 1989, Zill et al. 1993). This group of studies suggests an additional predictor that one might wish to include in a comprehensive model aimed at predicting children's postdivorce adjustment: the degree to which the child has a realistic understanding of the reasons for the divorce. A closely related predictor is the amount of responsibility or guilt experienced by the child in connection with the divorce. Children who lack information regarding the reasons for the divorce may attribute the divorce to something they did or failed to do. This perception could engender guilt.

Still another group of studies suggests that there are no overall differences due to age at the time of the divorce, but there are differences due to age at the time of the divorce among specific subgroups of children of different genders and different current ages. Thus it seems clear that research on the effect of the child's age at the time of the divorce should measure and control for both gender and current age.

It has also been suggested that the nature of the postdivorce adjustment difficulties experienced by children may vary, depending on the child's age at the time of the divorce (Hodges and Bloom 1984). This implies that research on the relationship between long-term adjustment and the age of the child at the time of the divorce should include a variety of different outcome variables, preferably derived from different sources. Certainly studies should include measures of both internalizing pathology—such as anxiety, depression, and social withdrawal—and measures of externalizing acting-out behavior—including physical and verbal aggression, substance abuse, truancy, and premature or promiscuous sexual activity. In addition, objective measures of school performance are useful criteria of adjustment. It is desirable to obtain such measures at several points in time so that changes can be noted.

It should also be noted that in studies using children who are similar with respect to current age, the child's age at the time of the divorce is correlated nearly perfectly (r approaching -1.0) with the amount of time that has elapsed since the divorce. Thus, in studies that do not include children of different current ages, the effects of age at the time of the divorce and since the divorce are completely confounded. Therefore it is recommended that research on the psychosocial outcomes of children from divorced families should include children of different ages, and that current age should be employed as a factor in the analysis. Unless this is done, the researcher who discovers a significant relationship between age at the time of the divorce and one or more of the outcome measures will not be able to conclude that the relationship was not really due to the relative recency of the divorce rather than the child's age at the time of the divorce.

On the basis of theoretical considerations regarding the nature of relationships between children and their same- and opposite-sexed parents during the oedipal, latency, and adolescent stages, it is recommended that future studies include children whose current age falls into each of these three age ranges (preschool, elementary school years, and adolescence), and that within each of the older groups children should be represented whose parents separated at various points in the past. Longitudinal studies may also be used to differentiate between the effects of age at the time of the divorce and the effect of the amount of time that has elapsed since the divorce.

CHILD'S GENDER

The research on gender differences in adjustment to divorce is also contradictory. The majority of studies on this predictor suggest that boys experience greater difficulties than girls (for example, Emery 1982, Guidubaldi et al. 1984, Hetherington 1979a,b, Kurdek and Berg 1983); other studies suggest that the impact of divorce is actually more devastating for girls (for example, Furstenberg et al. 1987, Santrock et. al. 1982a,b). Predictably, there have also been a number of other studies that have indicated no significant differences between boys and girls with respect to the long-term impact of divorce (Acock and Kiecolt 1989, Kinard and Reinherz 1984, Kurdek and Siesky 1978). These contradictory findings can be explained by some of the same factors considered earlier in the chapter in relation to research on the other predictors of adjustment.

The tendency for most samples to comprise mother-custody families entirely or primarily would be expected to bias studies in the direction of making it appear that girls adjust better to divorce than do boys, since girls in mother custody are residing with the same-sex parent. The relationship of the child's gender to postdivorce adjustment cannot be assessed adequately without reporting results separately for mother-custody, father-custody, and joint-custody families. Further, since we have seen that the custody arrangement may well be related to the level of conflict between the former spouses, parental conflict should be measured and controlled as well.

The nature of the criterion variables selected to measure postdivorce adjustment is also extremely important. Since boys in general tend to display more aggressive, acting-out behavior than girls, one would expect that studies in which the outcome measures tapped primarily externalizing behavior problems would be likely to find that boys tend to be more poorly adjusted than girls following divorce. Kalter and associates (1985) pointed out that much of the research on the impact of divorce has employed standardized measures of adjustment that do not measure the types of adjustment problems that girls experience, such as anxiety, depression, somatic complaints, low self-esteem, and poor adjustment with respect to heterosexual relationships. Thus research on gender differences in children's adjustment following parental divorce should always include a broad range of measures of social and psychological adjustment relevant both to females and to males.

The issue of the source of the ratings of adjustment is also pertinent here. Teachers, who may be particularly concerned with classroom order, may be much more sensitive to manifestations of acting-out behavior than are the parents of the children. Teachers may not be as likely to identify withdrawn, internalizing behavior problems, since these do not typically result in class disruptions. Thus studies using teacher ratings of adjustment might be expected to indicate that divorce has a greater impact on boys.

Other factors that mediate the relationship between gender and adjustment following divorce include whether the custodial parent remarries and the age of the child at the time of the assessment of the outcome variables. Girls in mother-custody families tend to be affected adversely by the remarriage of their mother, and their relationships with their mothers tend to be particularly problematic when the girls reach adolescence. Thus it appears essential to control for both remarriage and current age in assessing the relationship between gender and the impact of parental divorce on adjustment.

STRESSFUL LIFE CHANGES

The literature on stressful life changes following divorce makes it clear that children's adjustment can be affected negatively by decreased family income (Bane 1976, Espenshade 1979, Hodges et al. 1984, Mednick et al. 1990) as well as other life changes that frequently accompany divorce, such as moving, changing schools, and mother's returning to full-time work (Sandler and Block 1979, Stolberg 1980, Stolberg and Busch 1985, Werner and Smith 1982). Such stressful life changes have been shown to be related to adjustment difficulties in the general population (Demo and Savin-Williams 1983, Rosenberg 1965, Rosenberg and Perlin 1978, Shook and Jurich 1992), but it appears that these changes are related more strongly to adjustment among children from divorced families than from intact families (Hodges et al. 1984).

The fact that socioeconomic status is positively related to adjustment suggests that SES should be included as a control variable in all studies of children's adjustment following divorce, regardless of the particular set of predictors under scrutiny.

Wallerstein and Corbin (1989) suggested that, separate and distinct from the effect of SES in general, there is a negative impact on psychosocial adjustment associated with the *downward change* in family finances following the divorce. In addition, they suggested that there is a negative relationship between children's adjustment and the *discrepancy in income* between the mother and the father following the divorce. This effect appears to pertain regardless of whether the discrepancy arises as a result of decreased maternal income or new financial gains on the part of the father. These considerations suggest that studies of the impact of divorce on children's psychosocial adjustment should routinely include not only measures of the income of the custodial parent following the divorce, but also measures of family income prior to the divorce and of the noncustodial parent following the divorce, at the time children's adjustment criteria are assessed.

The relationships between family socioeconomic status variables and children's postdivorce adjustment may be particularly important among adolescents, since they are heavily invested in peer relationships. A significant drop in disposable resources at this time might result in the adolescents' not being able to have the same clothes or material possessions as their friends, or it could force them to abandon certain activities in which they had participated with a group of their peers (e.g., going to a particular summer camp or being a member of a particular club). Thus the child's current age should also be measured and controlled when evaluating the relationship between stressful life changes and postdivorce adjustment.

The relationships among socioeconomic status, stressful life events, and postdivorce adjustment may also be mediated by the psychological adjustment of the custodial parent (typically the mother), who may experience anxiety regarding financial matters that may preoccupy her thoughts and cause her to become less attentive to any problems that her children may be experiencing at home or in school. Income discrepancies between the custodial and the noncustodial parent may also exacerbate conflict between the former spouses, which in turn may have an impact on the visitation patterns of the noncustodial parent. Thus research on the effect of stressful life changes on the postdivorce adjustment of children should measure and control for the adjustment of the custodial parent, interparental conflict, and the parenting style and effectiveness of both the custodial parent and the noncustodial parent. Another factor that would appear relevant to the effect of stressful life changes is the characteristic coping style of both the custodial parent and the children themselves. Families characterized by problem-focused coping strategies may well adapt to stressful life changes better than families characterized by emotion-focused coping styles. Thus it would appear to be desirable to measure the characteristic coping styles of the custodial parent and the children when studying the effect of stressful life changes following divorce.

SOCIAL SUPPORT

The literature indicates that the availability and utilization of social supports is related positively to adjustment among children within the general population (Cauce et al. 1982) and within the population of children from divorced families (Drapeau and Bouchard 1993, Farber et al. 1985, Isaacs and Leon 1986). The literature made it clear that social support can be defined and measured in very different ways: in terms of the number of persons in the respondent's social network, the actual provision of support services by individuals in that network, the respondent's perceptions of the degree to which the support received had actually been helpful. It is recommended that studies of the relationship between social support and children's postdivorce adjustment include all three types of social support measures.

Furthermore, it is recommended that the availability of, utilization of, and satisfaction with social support be assessed from the perspectives of both the custodial parent and the child. More research needs to be carried out with respect to the stress-buffering effects on children of supports available in their world of school and peer relationships.

Finally, the research on the role of social support has not adequately considered the possible mediating roles of the child's gender, the child's age at the time of the parental separation, and the length of time between the separation and the time data are collected with respect to children's psychosocial adjustment.

FAMILY-SYSTEMS FUNCTIONING

Family-systems functioning may be viewed broadly, in terms of the general pattern of relationships among family members, or very specifically, in terms of one of the theoretical models of family-systems functioning that have been developed, such as the Circumplex Model of Marital and Family Systems (Olson et al. 1979) or the Beavers Systems Model (Beavers 1976, 1977, Beavers and Voeller 1983). Certain aspects of general family systems functioning have already been noted, including the level of postdivorce conflict between the former spouses, the quality of the coparenting relationship between the former spouses, and the parenting style and effectiveness of both the custodial and the noncustodial parent. There is no doubt that these factors are relevant to adjustment and should be included in any models used to predict adjustment.

The specific models of family-systems functioning that have been studied in relation to children's postdivorce adjustment include family cohesiveness, family adaptability, family competence, and family communication. As indicated in the previous chapter, there are numerous issues with respect to the best instruments to measure these concepts and the best statistical analysis approaches to take when assessing the impact of these factors. Nevertheless, there appears to be sufficient empirical evidence in the literature to warrant the inclusion of one or more of the available family-systems assessment instruments in studies of children's postdivorce adjustment. Although much work has been done with the Circumplex Model and the Beavers Family System Model, the Family Environment Scale (FES) (Moos and Moos 1981) may be the most comprehensive, straightforward, and psychometrically unambiguous measure of family functioning. This ninety-item scale assesses ten dimensions of family functioning that are conceptually clear: cohesion, conflict, expressiveness, independence, achievement-orientation, active recreational orientation, moral-religious emphasis, organization, control, and intellectual/cultural orientation.

Research on children's postdivorce adjustment should assess these dimensions. Ideally, family-systems functioning should be assessed from the perspectives of each parent and the target child in the family. Given the differences noted in the foregoing review with respect to the source of the rating, these ratings should not be pooled to obtain a single score for the whole family on any of these dimensions. Typically, correlations between the ratings derived from parents and children are not sufficiently high to warrant combining their scores. Further, the ideal study would be a longitudinal study in which these dimensions could be assessed before the parental separation, during the crisis period immediately following the separation, and again after one to two years, when the family has had a chance to regain its equilibrium.

COMPREHENSIVE MODEL FOR PREDICTING CHILDREN'S POSTDIVORCE PSYCHOSOCIAL ADJUSTMENT

As indicated by the chapter outline of this volume, this work was begun with the plan to employ a ten-predictor model of children's adjustment following parental divorce. The model was developed during the course designing the two empirical studies reported in the next two chapters. These studies, for which data were collected several years ago, included the following predictors of children's postdivorce adjustment: (1) level of parental conflict, (2) nature of the custody arrangement, (3) psychosocial adjustment of the custodial parent, (4) remarriage of the custodial parent, (5) frequency and regularity of contact between the child and the noncustodial parent, (6) age of the child at the time of the divorce, (7) gender of the child, (8) number of stressful life changes associated with the divorce, (9) availability and utilization of social support, and (10) family-systems functioning. It was assumed that separate variables would be used to represent (1) the frequency and (2) the regularity of contact with the noncustodial parent. It was assumed further that stressful life changes should be assessed in terms of two variables as well: (1) adequacy of family finances following the divorce and (2) total number of stressful life changes experienced following the divorce. Finally, it was assumed that family-systems functioning would be measured as two variables derived from the Circumplex Model: (1) family cohesion and (2) family adaptability. Thus the model employed in designing the two empirical studies described below envisioned thirteen independent variables predicting postdivorce adjustment.

In comparison to previous efforts aimed at the prediction of postdivorce adjustment, this thirteen-predictor model is fairly comprehensive. Few studies reported to date have considered such a broad range of predictors. However, the extensive literature review carried out for this volume by the senior author between March 1996 and September 1996 has made it abundantly clear that a truly comprehensive model of children's adjustment to divorce would have to contain many predictors not included in our original thirteen-predictor model. Moreover, many of the predictors included in our original research model are clearly far more complex than we had realized, such that multiple dimensions of particular predictor domains are required to assess those domains adequately. In addition, it is clear now that measures of many of the predictors that we included initially really need to be obtained on the basis of the perceptions of the various family members, which should not be aggregated for the whole family. Finally, in the ideal study of the factors associated with positive psychosocial outcomes for children following divorce, the predictors really need to be measured at several points in time so that we can assess the effects of changes in these dimensions from preseparation to the crisis period, and from the crisis period to the long term. The following sections summarize (1) the major methodological recommendations regarding research on children's postdivorce adjustment, (2) the predictors that should be added to our original model in future studies, and (3) new dimensions within the general domains of several of the predictors already in the model that should be included so as to represent those domains adequately.

METHODOLOGICAL RECOMMENDATIONS FOR RESEARCH ON CHILDREN'S PSYCHOSOCIAL ADJUSTMENT FOLLOWING DIVORCE

The review of the research in this area leads to the following general recommendations:

1. In sampling, select only one target child per family so as to preserve independence of observations.
2. Always employ a comparison group of children from intact families so that you will be able to distinguish between relationships unique to children from divorced families and relationships that obtain for the general population of children. The comparison group should be comparable to the group of children from divorced families with respect to gender, current age, and socioeconomic status.
3. Employ multiple measures of children's adjustment. In particular, make certain to include measures of acting-out, aggressive behavior, which tends to be more common among boys, and anxious, depressed, or withdrawn behavior, which is more common among girls.
4. Use multiple sources for measures of predictors and adjustment criteria. Where relevant, as in the case of reports of parental conflict, frequency and regularity of visitation, and parenting skills, ratings should be obtained from both the custodial and the noncustodial parents and from the child. Where possible, third-party ratings, such

as the teacher's ratings of the child's classroom behavior and academic adjustment, should be used. The teacher is generally more aware of the child's school behavior, and is more likely than the parent(s) to provide objective ratings. Where possible, behavior samples can be obtained and rated by trained judges, which is particularly useful in the assessment of family-systems functioning.

5. Do not aggregate ratings derived from different sources within the family to come up with a single score for the whole family. Ratings obtained from the various family members are typically not correlated strongly enough to justify their combination.

6. Always measure and control for the child's gender, current age group (preschool, elementary, adolescent, adult), custody arrangement (mother-custody, father-custody, joint custody), and child's age at the time of the divorce (preschool, elementary, adolescent, adult). Interactions among these factors, observed frequently in previous research, suggest that any relationships between other predictors of adjustment and psychosocial outcome variables should be reported separately for each group formed by crossing these four variables.

It should be stressed that it is not necessary that every study include all fifty-four combinations of the child's gender, current age, custody arrangement, and age at the time of the divorce. A study focusing on a single group among the fifty-four (e.g., female adolescents in mother-custody situations whose parents had divorced while they were in elementary school) could be methodologically sound, and its results could be perfectly valid for that one group. However, it is very important not to pool samples across any of these four variables since the results obtained with respect to such pooled samples may actually not describe any of the specific groups accurately.

7. Measure and control for socioeconomic status, measured at the time of collection of the data indicating the child's psychosocial adjustment.

8. Obtain longitudinal data whenever possible. Prospective studies are best of all. Ideally, data should be obtained before the decision to divorce, at the time of that decision, during the "crisis period" that may last for a year or two following the initial separation, and then again after about five years, when equilibrium has been restored. Longitudinal data can be used to help establish causal relationships. It can also be used to disentangle the effects of age at the time of the divorce, current age, and time elapsed since the divorce.

9. Use clinical case study material and qualitative data derived from in-depth interviews to inform the findings obtained in empirical investigations. Often the reports of family members can provide researchers with clues to the psychological and social dynamics underlying significant statistical relationships.

ADDITIONAL PREDICTORS FOR FUTURE STUDIES OF CHILDREN'S POSTDIVORCE ADJUSTMENT

The literature review indicated at least six additional predictors of children's adjustment following divorce that should be included in future research in this area:

1. *Parenting behavior* should be measured. Parenting style is one dimension of parenting behavior. Parents may have authoritative, authoritarian, or permissive styles. Parenting can also be measured in terms of the extent of involvement of the parent. This dimension of parenting appears to be particularly relevant with respect to the behavior of noncustodial fathers. Parenting behavior is particularly important as a factor that may mediate the effects of parental conflict, stressful life changes, and poor psychosocial adjustment in the custodial parent.
   Parenting behavior should be assessed in both the custodial and the noncustodial parent. It should also be assessed as it is perceived by the parent himself (herself), by the former spouse, and by the child. It should be assessed at several different points in time so that changes can be measured and related to outcome variables.
2. *Current age of the child* was not included as a predictor in our original model, primarily because the two studies we designed focused on adolescents in high school. In studies focusing on broader age ranges, however, current age should be measured and treated as an independent variable, as described in methodological recommendation No. 6 in the previous section of this chapter.
3. When the custodial parent has remarried, aspects of *the stepparent's behavior* should be measured. His or her parenting style and parenting involvement should be assessed. Also relevant is the extent to which the natural custodial parent and the stepparent agree on such parenting issues as determining appropriate discipline. The nature of the relationship between the stepparent and the noncustodial natural parent may also affect the adjustment of children.
4. The *child's understanding of the reasons* for the divorce should be assessed. One expects that children who do understand the real reasons for the divorce will not tend to blame themselves. *Guilt on the part of the child* can also be measured directly.
5. The *length of time since the separation* should be measured. In particular, families in the crisis period—the first year or two after the separation—should not be pooled with families in which the parents have been separated for a longer period.

6. The *characteristic coping styles* of parents and children should be assessed. Measures of coping may be fairly global, simply yielding general scores on problem-focused coping and emotion-focused coping. Or more specific dimensions of coping may be assessed, such as the dimensions measured in the Ways of Coping Questionnaire (Folkman and Lazarus 1988).

PREDICTORS INCLUDED IN THE ORIGINAL MODEL THAT REQUIRE FURTHER ELABORATION

1. *Parental conflict* should be measured on the basis of the perspective of the child as well as the parents. Ideally, the level of conflict between the family should be measured before the decision to divorce, at the time of the decision, during the first year following separation, and about five years after the initial separation.
2. The *child's relationship with the noncustodial parent* should be assessed in terms of frequency and regularity of contact, but also in terms of subjective reports of feelings of closeness and objective measures of the extent of the parent's involvement in the life of the child. Reports from both parents and from the child are desirable.
3. In addition to measuring and controlling for family socioeconomic status, one should measure (1) the *change in income* that accompanies the separation and (2) the *discrepancy in income* between the households of the custodial and the noncustodial parents.
4. *Social support* should be measured in terms of availability, utilization, and satisfaction with support received. It should be assessed for both the custodial and the noncustodial parents. In addition, the social support of the child should be assessed, including support from peers and school personnel.
5. *Family-systems functioning* must be measured from the perspectives of both the custodial and the noncustodial parents and the child.

13

RESEARCH STUDY I

THE STUDY REPORTED in this chapter was designed to identify the predictors of psychosocial adjustment among adolescents from divorced families in New York City. Based on our original thirteen-predictor model described in Chapter 12, the study included measures of the following predictors: (1) parental conflict; (2) nature of the custody arrangement; (3) psychological adjustment of the custodial parent; (4) marital status of the custodial parent; (5) frequency and (6) predictability of contact between the child and the noncustodial parent; (7) child's age at the time of the divorce; (8) child's gender; (9) adequacy of the income in the custodial family following the divorce; (10) number of stressful life changes following the divorce; (11) availability of social support following the divorce; (12) family adaptability; and (13) family cohesion.

The psychosocial adjustment of the child was represented by measures of internalizing pathology, externalizing pathology, and social problems. These variables were assessed by means of a survey instrument that incorporated several published measures and other items developed or adapted specifically for this study.

The data for Research Study I were analyzed originally by treating the group of children from divorced families as a single sample. The gender of the child, the custody arrangement, and the age of the child at the time of the divorce were included as predictors of adjustment, along with the other predictors in the original model. Thus, in the original analysis of these data, we did not follow the recommendation included in the previous chapter to report results separately for children of different genders, children with different custody arrangements, children whose parents divorced at different stages in the child's life, and children of different current ages.

To illustrate the effect of these recommendations on the nature of the results reported, it was decided to present first the results obtained on the basis of the original analysis, and then the results obtained when following the recommendation to report findings for the several groups of children separately. By comparing the two sets of results, we can get an idea of the degree to which the results of previous studies may have been spurious due to the pooling of data from unlike populations.

The three major sections of the present chapter pertain to (1) the methods employed in the study, (2) the results obtained in the original analysis, and (3) the results obtained when several groups of children from divorced families are viewed separately.

METHODS

Subjects

The participants in the study were high school students from families in which the parents were divorced ($n = 221$) and from intact families ($n = 215$). The students were recruited at five high schools in New York City: three day high schools, one in Queens and two in Staten Island; and three evening high schools, two in Brooklyn and one in Staten Island. The evening division students at these schools came from various parts of New York City, since enrollment in evening high schools is open to students from any borough. The largest numbers of students in the evening high schools were from Brooklyn or Staten Island, however, since they attend schools close to their homes, if possible.

The criteria for participation in the study required students in grades ten through twelve between the ages of 15 and 18. Thus all participants were in the adolescent category with respect to current age.

As an additional criterion, the adolescents in the divorced group had to come from families in which the parents were divorced (or separated) for at least two years. The latter criterion was included to eliminate adolescents in the difficult postseparation transitional period. The length of time since the parental divorce or separation was determined by responses to questionnaire items assessing the respondent's current age and age at the time of the divorce. Respondents who indicated their parents had divorced or separated within the last two years were simply excluded from the study. There were thirty-seven such students, who are not included in the sample size of 221 reported above.

The sample of 221 adolescents actually used in the analysis was adequate to accommodate Edwards's (1980) recommendation to employ a minimum of fifteen subjects for each predictor variable to be used in a multiple-regression analysis. With respect to tests of the bivariate relationships between psychosocial adjustment and each predictor, a power analysis indicated that with the $N = 221$ divorced group, tests for the significance of a Pearson correlation at the .05 level had a power in excess of .99, assuming a moderate effect size (true population correlation = .30) (Cohen 1988).

Procedure

The investigators received permission to conduct the study from the New York City Board of Education and from the board of education of a suburban community in New Jersey from which a sample of twenty students was recruited for the purpose of piloting the survey instrument. The investigators also obtained permission from the principals of the specific schools to be included in the study. The purpose and requirements of the study were explained to the principals, as well as the provisions to guarantee anonymity of respondents.

Once permission to conduct the study had been granted, the investigators solicited respondents in health education classes during the school day and evening. The investigators or their assistants went to each class and described the study requirements to students. Students were informed that their participation would be completely voluntary and that there would be absolutely no penalty should the student choose not to participate in the study or to withdraw after beginning to participate.

The investigators explained that the study had been designed to identify the factors associated with the adjustment of children following parental divorce, but that respondents from intact families were needed as well to provide a comparison group. American Psychological Association (APA) ethical standards required that participants be fully informed regarding the nature of the study, so that those from divorced families realized that they were the primary focus of the study and those from intact families were serving as a comparison group. This knowledge may have resulted in some motivational differences between the two groups, which could in turn have influenced responses. This possibility must be noted as an unavoidable potential limitation of the study.

The investigators assured the students that their responses would be completely anonymous. To ensure uniformity in this explanation from class to class, the investigators and their assistants read from a prepared document. Following the reading of the study description, the investigators answered students' questions and distributed student assent forms and parental consent forms to be signed and returned to the classroom teacher.

Parental consent forms were returned within two weeks of their distribution, and the investigators returned to each class to distribute the survey. At that time the investigators collected any remaining consent forms and distributed the actual survey, which also contained an assent form to be signed by the student. The student assent forms were separate from the actual questionnaire packet, so that responses could not be linked directly to specific individuals.

Students who agreed to participate were immediately given copies of the survey instrument, which they completed during the class and returned to the investigators before they left. Utilization of a class period for the completion of the survey instrument was justified by the improvement in the response rate associated with this form of administration in comparison with students' being allowed to complete the instrument at home. The students obtained some educational benefit from the study because the investigators reported the results to them in their classes when the findings became available.

Instruments

The questionnaire packet consisted of four published, validated measures that had been adapted for the study and a series of items developed specifically. A pilot study was carried out to assess the reliability of the measures. The next section describes the measures developed specifically for this study and the pilot study that was carried out to determine the reliability of the measures. Subsequent sections describe the several published measures.

Researcher-Developed Measures

The investigators developed items to assess the adolescent's report of his or her age at the time of the divorce, perceptions of parental conflict prior to the divorce and in the first two years following the divorce, depression and substance abuse in the custodial parent, frequency and predictability of contact with the noncustodial parent, and adequacy of family finances.

A pilot study was conducted to determine the reliability of these measures, to identify any items or scales that students might find vague or difficult to understand, and to make certain that the survey could be completed within a single class period. Twenty high school students from divorced families completed the entire survey questionnaire twice, with a two-week interval between testings. These twenty were recruited from a high school in suburban New Jersey rather than from the schools used in the study proper. The pilot sample was recruited in New Jersey as the original plan for the study was to recruit respondents in both New York and New Jersey. In fact, permission to conduct the study was obtained from the school boards of several suburban and urban school districts in New Jersey. When the time came to actually collect the data for the study, however, the New Jersey districts could not participate, primarily because of time constraints associated with an excessive number of snow days that had been taken over the winter.

Based on the test-retest sample of twenty, the reliability coefficients for the researcher-developed measures ranged from .75 to 1.00, with a median of .96. Thus the scales had adequate reliability. The pilot study respondents were asked to indicate any items that were unclear or ambiguous. No such items were identified. Finally, it was found that the survey could be completed easily within a class period.

Youth Self-Report (YSR)

This scale was developed by Achenbach to take the place of his Child Behavior Checklist (CBCL) (Achenbach 1966, 1978, 1991) in research situations in which the child rather than the parent was surveyed. The YSR yields an overall measure of psychosocial adjustment in the form of the total problem score. It also yields subscale scores representing specific problem areas. In the proposed study the subscales for internalizing psychopathology, externalizing psychopathology, and social problems were employed. The manual for the YSR indicates that the test requires only a fifth-grade reading level. The manual provides recent (1991) norms for adolescents in age ranges 11–12, 13–14, 15–16, and 17–18. The manual also provides extensive data relevant to the reliability and validity of the YSR.

With respect to reliability, Achenbach (1991) reported the following one-week test-retest reliabilities for the three subscales of the YSR to be included in this investigation: Internalizing Pathology, .91; Externalizing Pathology, .83; and Social Problems, .87. The manual also reports Cronbach's alpha internal consistency reliability coefficients for the subscales. The coefficients reported for the scales are Internalizing Pathology, .91; Externalizing Pathology, .89; and Social Problems, .68.

Achenbach (1991) reported several forms of validity data. In the area of concurrent validity, Achenbach reported significant ($p < .001$) correlations between each of the YSR subscales and the corresponding subscales of the parent report CBCL upon which the YSR was modeled. These correlations ranged from .63 to .92. Further evidence of the validity of the YSR is provided through the method of group differences. Weinstein and colleagues (1990) reported that adolescents having different DSM-III diagnoses were differentiated reliably by YSR subscales. Achenbach reported that the YSR Externalizing Pathology subscale, Internalizing Pathology subscale, and Social Problems Scale significantly ($p < .01$) differentiated groups of referred and nonreferred adolescents.

Family Adaptability and Cohesion Evaluation Scales-II (FACES-II)

This thirty-item, self-report scale (Olson et al. 1978) measures the perceptions of an individual family member regarding the adaptability and cohesion of the family. The FACES-II employs a five-point, Likert-type response format, with response options ranging from "almost never" to "almost always."

The FACES-II is based on the Circumplex Family Systems Model as described originally by Olson and colleagues (1979). It measures the two key dimensions of family-systems functioning of the Circumplex Model: Family Cohesion and Family Adaptability. The former refers to the emotional bonding that members have with one another and the degree of individual autonomy a person experiences in the family system. It is viewed as a continuum ranging from a low extreme, disengagement, to a high extreme, very connected. Family adaptability refers to the ability of the family system to change its power structure, role relationships, and relationship rules in response to situational and developmental stress. Family adaptability is viewed as a continuum ranging from a low extreme, rigid, to a high extreme, very flexible.

As originally conceptualized in the Circumplex Model (Olson et al. 1978), extreme scores on both cohesion and adaptability were viewed as dysfunctional, while mid-range scores on each dimension were viewed as balanced and conducive to effective family functioning and optimum individual development. However, empirical findings reported in studies using FACES-II have led Olson and his associates (Olson 1991, Olson and Tiesel 1991) to modify the original curvilinear formulation to a linear model in which greater cohesion and greater adaptability are viewed as associated with more positive outcomes.

Olson and Tiesel reported internal consistency reliability (alpha) coefficients of .87 for the cohesion scale of FACES-II and .78 for the adaptability scale. Walker and colleagues (1988) reported alpha coefficients for the two scales of .76 for cohesion and .78 for adaptability, based on a sample of 123 adolescents.

Social Support Questionnaire—Short Form (SSQ6)

The SSQ6 (Sarason et al. 1987) is a six-item version of the previously validated twenty-seven-item Social Support Questionnaire (SSQ) (Sarason et al. 1983). The six items in the SSQ6 were selected from among the twenty-seven items of the SSQ based on the results of a principal-components factor analysis of the SSQ based on a sample of 182 undergraduates. The items with the highest loadings on the first principal component were selected for inclusion in the abbreviated questionnaire. The SSQ6 employs a four-point response scale with response options ranging from "a lot" to "not at all."

Sarason and his colleagues (1987) reported the internal consistency reliability (coefficient alpha) of the resulting six-item questionnaire for two additional undergraduate samples of 217 and 146 students, respectively. These reliability coefficients were .90 and .93, respectively. Evidence of the concurrent validity of the SSQ6 was provided by the authors in the form of significant correlations between SSQ6 scores and several variables logically expected to be related to social support, including anxiety, depression, hostility, social competence, and loneliness. These variables were measured using the Multiple Adjective Affect Checklist (anxiety, depression, and hostility), the Social Reticence Scale (social competence), and the UCLA loneliness scale (loneliness). These correlations were all significant and in the expected direction. The correlations ranged in absolute value from .15 to .63.

The SSQ has been employed in studies carried out on a diversity of populations, from preschoolers (Newcomb 1990) through senior citizens (Blazer 1982).

Children's Recent Life Events Questionnaire (CRLEQ)

The CRLEQ (Sandler and Block 1979) is a thirty-two-item checklist on which respondents indicate the number of changes in their lives over a two-year period. Some of the change areas included are "moving to a new house," "changing schools," and "Mom beginning work." The validity of the CRLEQ was indicated by several findings reported by Sandler and Block. The authors compared groups of maladapting and nonmaladapting elementary school students on the CRLEQ, finding that the former group had significantly more stressful life changes than the latter. In addition, within the maladapting group, Sandler and Block compared students whose families were on welfare with those who were not. They found that the nonwelfare, maladapting children had significantly higher CRLEQ scores than the maladapting children from welfare families.

In the study reported here, the CRLEQ instructions were modified so that respondents did not check events of the last two years, but events in the two years immediately following the divorce. In addition, due to the time constraints imposed by the necessity of administering all the survey instruments in a single class period, the questionnaire was shortened to include only the twelve items that appeared most relevant to families undergoing divorce.

Since the CRLEQ was modified substantially for the present study, the scale was included in the pilot study described above. The two-week test-retest reliability coefficient obtained for the stressful life events measure was .91.

Social Desirability

Social desirability was measured by a ten-item short form of the *Marlowe-Crowne Social Desirability Scale (M-C SDS)* (Crowne and Marlowe 1964). The original M-C SDS consisted of thirty-three items. Strahan and Gerbasi (1972) developed two homogeneous ten-item forms of the MC-SDS M-C 1(10) and M-C 2(10). The first of these two forms was used in the study. The authors reported that the twenty items used to form the two ten-item scales were selected from among the thirty-three original items on the basis of a factor analysis of an item set consisting of the 33 M-C SDS items and an additional forty items representing extroversion-introversion and neuroticism. The first principal component that emerged from this analysis represented the social desirability dimension. All thirty-three M-C SDS items loaded in the appropriate direction on this factor. The loadings for the thirty-three items ranged in absolute value from .11 to .54 with a mean of .35. The twenty items having the highest loadings were selected to be used on the ten-item scale. These twenty items had loadings that ranged from .28 to .54, with a mean of .42.

Strahan and Gerbasi (1972) reported internal consistency reliabilities for each of the two ten-item scales. The K-R 20 reliabilities reported for the MC-1(10) were .70 for a sample of sixty-four university males, .66 for a sample of thirty-four university females, and .61 for a sample of 130 college females. Reliabilities were similar for the MC-2(10).

With respect to validity, Strahan and Gerbasi (1972) reported correlations in the .80s and .90s between the MC-1(10) and the MC-SDS. In the study reported here the response format for the MC-1(10) was changed from a true-false format to a six-point Likert-type item format to maintain a consistent response format throughout the survey instrument. To make the purpose of the MC-SDS less transparent to the subjects, the ten items were interspersed with the six items of the Acquiescence Response Set Scale (described below). The total set of sixteen items was labeled with the acronym SACQ.

RESULTS: ORIGINAL ANALYSIS

The results of the original analysis were organized in six sections: (1) description of samples of adolescents from divorced and intact families, (2) scale reliabilities, (3) bivariate relationships between predictors and measures of psychosocial adjustment, (4) multivariate relationships between predictors and measures of psychosocial adjustment, (5) comparison of adolescents from divorced and intact families on measures of adjustment, and (6) comparison of adolescents from divorced and intact families on the relationships between predictors and measures of adjustment.

Description of Sample

The entire sample (of children from divorced and intact families) consisted of 436 adolescents from 15 through 18 years (mean = 16.25): 226 males (52 percent) and 209 females (48.0 percent). One respondent did not indicate his or her gender. There were 215 adolescents from intact families (49.3 percent) and 221 whose parents had divorced. Among the latter group, the self-reported age of the child at the time of the divorce ranged from birth through 16 years, with a mean of 6.8 years ($SD = 4.3$ years).

Table 13-1 presents frequency distributions of responses to background questions answered by the adolescents in the divorced group. The majority (59.5 percent) of respondents indicated some level of agreement with the statement indicating that the family had enough money since the parents had split up. Substantial majorities indicated some level of agreement with statements indicating that their parents had displayed anger (64.2 percent) and made insulting remarks (60.2 percent). On these two items approximately one-fourth of the sample indicated strong agreement. A substantial minority (37 percent) indicated there had been some form of physical abuse.

Table 13-1. Self-Reported Background Data, Divorced Family Group

Variable	Value	N	%
Since my parents split up, my family has had enough money	strongly disagree	23	11.0
	disagree	28	13.3
	slightly disagree	34	16.2
	slightly agree	42	20.0
	agree	51	24.3
	strongly agree	32	15.2
Before my parents split up and during the two years after the separation, my parents displayed anger toward each other	strongly disagree	19	9.3
	disagree	28	13.7
	slightly disagree	26	12.7
	slightly agree	43	21.1
	agree	39	19.1
	strongly agree	17	24.0
Before my parents split up and during the two years after the separation, one or both parents made insulting remarks about the other	strongly disagree	25	12.1
	disagree	24	11.7
	slightly disagree	33	16.0
	slightly agree	41	19.9
	agree	27	13.1
	strongly agree	56	27.2

Table 13-1. (continued)

Variable	Value	N	%
Before my parents split up and during the two years after the separation, one or both parents were physically abusive toward the other	strongly disagree	72	35.0
	disagree	39	18.9
	slightly disagree	19	9.2
	slightly agree	29	14.1
	agree	24	11.7
	strongly agree	23	11.2
What is the custody arrangement?	mother	140	69.7
	father	29	14.4
	joint custody	32	15.9
Has your mother remarried?	yes	126	57.0
	no	95	43.0
Has your father remarried?	yes	103	46.6
	no	118	53.3
Custodial parent[1] seems sad	strongly disagree	54	25.7
	disagree	51	24.3
	slightly disagree	32	15.2
	slightly agree	33	15.7
	agree	25	11.9
	strongly agree	15	7.1
Custodial parent[1] has a problem with alcohol or drugs	strongly disagree	115	54.5
	disagree	34	16.1
	slightly disagree	17	8.1
	slightly agree	22	10.4
	agree	14	6.6
	strongly agree	9	4.3
I spend as much time as I want with noncustodial parent	strongly disagree	39	18.6
	disagree	32	15.2
	slightly disagree	30	14.3
	slightly agree	23	11.0
	agree	54	25.7
	strongly agree	32	15.2
The times I spend with my noncustodial parent are regular and predictable	strongly disagree	42	20.0
	disagree	39	18.6
	slightly disagree	22	10.5
	slightly agree	38	18.1
	agree	49	23.3
	strongly disagree	20	9.5

1. Question reads, "parent with whom you spend the most time."

Most (69.7 percent) of the adolescents were in the custody of their mothers. Most (57 percent) of the mothers had remarried, but most

(53.5 percent) of the fathers had not. Among the respondents in this group, 34.7 percent reported that their custodial parent seemed sad, and 21.3 percent indicated that their custodial parent had a drug or alcohol problem. The majority of respondents from divorced families (51.9 percent) indicated some level of agreement with the statement: "I spend as much time as I like with my noncustodial parent." The majority of these adolescents (50.9 percent) also indicated some level of agreement with the statement: "The times I spend with my noncustodial parent are regular and predictable." However, nearly as many of the adolescents in this group disagreed with these statements.

Table 13-2 presents frequency distributions on self-report background variables for the adolescents in the intact family group. Over three-quarters (75.7 percent) of them agreed that their families had enough money. The majority of respondents in this group disagreed that their parents displayed anger toward each other (59.6 percent) or made insulting or sarcastic remarks (62.3 percent). Only 8.1 percent of the intact family group indicated any physical abuse between their parents; only 16.6 percent indicated agreement with the statement that their mothers were depressed; only 9.1 percent felt that their fathers were depressed. Small proportions (2.9 percent) of these respondents indicated their mothers (2.9 percent) or fathers (4.8 percent) had a problem with drugs or alcohol. The adolescents from divorced versus intact families responded to different questions, but no inferential statistics were run to determine the significance of group differences on these background factors.

Table 13-2. Self-Reported Background Data, Intact Family Group

Variable	Value	N	%
My family has had enough money	strongly disagree	9	4.3
	disagree	20	9.5
	slightly disagree	22	10.5
	slightly agree	46	21.9
	agree	72	34.3
	strongly agree	41	19.5
My parents displayed anger toward each other	strongly disagree	46	21.9
	disagree	48	22.9
	slightly disagree	31	14.8
	slightly agree	42	20.0
	agree	30	14.3
	strongly agree	13	6.2

Table 13-2. (continued)

Variable	Value	N	%
One or both parents made insulting or sarcastic comments about the other	strongly disagree	62	29.7
	disagree	38	18.2
	slightly disagree	30	14.4
	slightly agree	35	16.7
	agree	30	14.4
	strongly agree	14	6.7
One or both parties were physically abusive toward the other	strongly disagree	155	74.2
	disagree	29	13.9
	slightly disagree	8	3.8
	slightly agree	8	3.8
	agree	5	2.4
	strongly agree	4	1.9
My mom is sad or depressed	strongly disagree	110	52.4
	disagree	44	21.0
	slightly disagree	21	10.0
	slightly agree	19	9.0
	agree	9	4.3
	strongly agree	7	3.3
My dad is sad or depressed	strongly disagree	113	53.8
	disagree	53	25.2
	slightly disagree	25	11.9
	slightly agree	15	7.1
	agree	2	1.0
	strongly agree	2	1.0
My mom has a problem with drugs or alcohol	strongly disagree	184	88.5
	disagree	15	7.2
	slightly disagree	3	1.4
	slightly agree	2	1.0
	agree	1	0.5
	strongly agree	3	1.4
My dad has a problem with drugs or alcohol	strongly disagree	177	84.7
	disagree	17	8.1
	slightly disagree	5	2.4
	slightly agree	4	1.9
	agree	1	0.5
	strongly agree	5	2.4

Scale Reliabilities

Scale scores were calculated for three scales of the Youth Self-Report, the FACES Adaptability and Cohesion Scales, and the SSQ6 Social Support Scale. Internal consistency reliability coefficients were calculated for each of these scales based on the sample data. These alpha coefficients are presented in Table 13–3. The reliabilities are acceptable.

Table 13–3. Scale Reliabilities

Scale	Alpha
YSR—Social Competence	.75
YSR—Externalizing Pathology	.89
YSR—Internalizing Pathology	.88
FACES-II Cohesion	.88
FACES-II Adaptability	.78
SSQ6—Social Support	.91

Predictors of Adolescent Adjustment in Divorced Families

Preliminary scatter diagrams depicting the relationships between the FACES scales and the YSR measures of psychosocial adjustment did not indicate any curvilinear relationships. Nevertheless, as a precaution to ensure that the largest possible correlations would be obtained between the FACES scales and the outcome measures, the scales were analyzed for both linear and curvilinear relationships. The latter were assessed by transforming each scale, first standardizing it (so that the mean = 0) and then taking the absolute value of the standardized scores. This transformation results in the more extreme FACES scores having higher numerical values; the scores nearest the mean, lower values.

Table 13–4 presents the correlations for the divorced family sample between the predictors (including both the untransformed and the transformed FACES scores) and the YSR scales measuring psychological adjustment. The raw YSR scores rather than scaled scores were used in calculating these correlations.

Psychological Adjustment of the Custodial Parent

The data in Table 13–4 indicate that the depression of the custodial parent was related significantly ($p < .001$) to YSR raw symptom scores for social competence ($r = .30$), internalizing pathology ($r = .36$), and externalizing pathology ($r = .33$). Substance abuse in the custodial parent was also related significantly ($p < .001$) to symptom scores for social competence ($r = .31$), internalizing pathology ($r = .30$), and externalizing pathology ($r = .29$). Since the YSR scores are symptom scores, higher numerical scores represent more problems or greater pathology. Therefore the positive correlations indicate that greater depression and more substance abuse on the part of the custodial parent are associated with greater pathology.

Table 13-4. Correlations between Predictors and YSR Scales
(Adolescents from Divorced Families)

Predictor	YSR Scale					
	Poor Social Competence		Internalizing Pathology		Externalizing Pathology	
	n	r	n	r	n	r
Depression of custodial parent	210	.30***	210	.36***	210	.33***
Substance abuse of custodial parent	211	.31***	211	.30***	211	.29***
Parents displayed anger	204	.15*	204	.15*	204	.25***
Parents made insulting remarks	206	.17*	206	.15*	206	.28***
Parents physically abusive	206	.43***	206	.34***	206	.40***
Joint custody?[1]	201	-.05	201	-.06	201	-.06
Frequency of contact with noncustodial parent	210	.05	210	.01	210	-.09
Predictability of contact with noncustodial parent	210	-.09	210	-.07	210	-.13
Respondent gender	220	-.18	220	.06	220	-.15
Age at time of parents' separation	219	.02	219	.04	219	.08
Stressful life changes	221	.38***	221	.41***	221	.32***
Adequacy of finances	210	-.14*	210	-.14*	210	-.21**

1. Question reads, "parent with whom you spend the most time."

Table 13-4. (continued)

Predictor	YSR Scale					
	Poor Social Competence		Internalizing Pathology		Externalizing Pathology	
	n	r	n	r	n	r
Remarriage	221	.00	221	-.01	221	-.14*
Social support	218	-.38***	218	-.25***	218	-.32***
FACES-Adaptability	220	-.23***	220	-.36***	220	-.35***
FACES-Cohesion	220	-.22***	220	-.31***	220	-.29***
Transformed Adaptability	220	-.06	220	-.01	220	-.07
Transformed Cohesion	220	-.17	220	-.11	220	-.09
Social desirability	211	-.23***	211	-.18**	211	-.44***
Acquiescence	209	-.06	209	.01	209	-.25***

* $p < .05$
** $p < .01$
*** $p < .001$

These relationships were moderate in magnitude. Cohen (1988) defined a moderate correlation as one having a magnitude of .30. The magnitude of the relationship is distinct from the significance level, which depends on the sample size as well as the actual calculated value of the sample correlation. In this study, the large sample sizes of both the divorced and intact family group mean that a correlation that is moderate in magnitude ($r = .30$) will be extremely significant ($p < .001$). The correlation of .30 between parental depression and social competence indicates that 9 percent of the variability in social competence can be explained by parental depression.

Factors Affecting the Adolescent's Relationship with Noncustodial Parent

The factors affecting the adolescent's relationship with the noncustodial parent included hostility between the parents as manifested in displays of anger, insults, and physical abuse; frequency of contact with the noncustodial parent, and predictability of contact with the noncustodial parent. It was expected that adolescents whose parents had joint custody arrangements would be better adjusted than those from single-parent custody families.

The data in Table 13-4 indicate that this hypothesis was confirmed only in part. All three measures of parental conflict were related significantly to each of the YSR symptom scales. Parental display of anger was related weakly to poor social competence ($r = .15$, $p < .05$), internalizing pathology ($r = .15$, $p < .05$), and externalizing pathology ($r = .25$, $p < .001$). Parental insulting remarks were also related weakly or moderately to poor social competence ($r = .17$, $p < .05$), internalizing pathology ($r = .15$, $p < .05$), and externalizing pathology ($r = -.28$, $p < .001$). Physical abuse on the part of one or both parents was related moderately to each of the YSR symptom scales: poor social competence ($r = .43$, $p < .001$), internalizing pathology ($r = .34$, $p < .001$), and externalizing pathology ($r = .40$, $p < .001$). However, no significant relationships were found between any of the psychosocial outcome measures and the frequency or predictability of visits by the noncustodial parent. Furthermore, no significant relationships were found between a joint custody arrangement and any of the YSR symptom scales.

Demographic Characteristics

It was anticipated that female adolescents would be better adjusted than males, and that children who were older at the time of the divorce would be better adjusted than those who were younger. The correlations in Table 13-4 indicated that this expectation was supported with respect to gender but not to age at the time of divorce. Gender was related both to poor social competence ($r = -.18$, $p < .01$) and externalizing pathology ($r = -.15$, $p < .05$). Since gender was coded as 1 = male and 2 = female, the negative correlations signify a tendency for boys to manifest more symptoms than girls. Age at the time of divorce was not related significantly to any of the YSR symptom scales.

Stresses of Divorce

The data in Table 13-4 indicate that significant relationships were found between stresses associated with the divorce process and the indicators of adjustment. Stressful life changes were related moderately to poor social competence ($r = .38$, $p < .001$), internalizing pathology ($r = .41$, $p < .001$), and externalizing pathology ($r = .32$, $p < .001$). Weak negative relationships were found between adequacy of family finances and the YSR symptoms scales: poor social competence ($r = -.14$, $p < .05$); internalizing pathology ($r = -.14$, $p < .05$); and externalizing pathology ($r = -.21$, $p < .01$). Weak to moderate negative relationships were found between availability of social support and the symptom scales. Social support was related significantly to poor social competence ($r = -.38$, $p < .001$), internalizing pathology ($r = -.25$, $p < .001$), and externalizing pathology ($r = -.32$, $p < .001$). The remarriage of the custodial parent was not related significantly to poor social competence or internalizing pathology. Remarriage, however, was related weakly to externalizing pathology ($r = -.14$, $p < .05$). Since remarriage was coded such that 1 = yes and 2 = no, this positive correlation indicates a weak tendency for adolescents whose custodial parents have remarried to display less externalizing pathology. (Higher numerical scores on remarriage, i.e., not remarried, are associated with higher numerical scores on externalizing pathology, i.e., more pathology.)

Family Cohesion and Adaptability

The data in Table 13-4 provided no support for a curvilinear relationship between adjustment and family adaptability and cohesion. As indicated in Chapter 12, the curvilinear hypothesis was tested by transforming the FACES adaptability and cohesion scales before computing the correlations between these scales and the YSR adjustment measures. Scores were transformed by standardizing them and then taking the absolute value of each standardized score, which has the effect of making the most extreme scores in the distribution have the highest values.

The transformed adaptability score was not related significantly to any of the YSR symptom scales. The transformed cohesion scale was related weakly to one of the outcome measures, poor social competence ($r = -.17$, $p < .05$). However, since higher scores on the transformed FACES scale represent more extreme scores, the direction of this relationship was opposite to the one hypothesized.

The correlations of the untransformed FACES scores with the adjustment measures were significant, however, supporting the hypothesis that relationships between adjustment on the one hand and family adaptability and cohesion on the other are in fact linear. Adaptability, correlated weakly to moderately with the symptom scores, was related significantly to poor social competence ($r = -.23$, $p < .001$), internalizing pathology ($r = -.36$, $p < .001$), and externalizing pathology ($r = -.35$, $p < .001$). Family cohesion was similarly related weakly to moderately to the symptom scales: poor social competence ($r = -.22$, $p < .001$), internalizing pathology ($r = -.31$, $p < .001$), and externalizing pathology ($r = -.29$, $p < .001$). Greater adaptability and greater cohesion were associated with better adjustment.

Multivariate Relationships

In the original analysis, three hierarchical multiple regression analyses were used to assess the multivariate relationships between the predictors and each of the three YSR symptom scales. In each analysis one of the three symptom scales was the dependent variable. Social desirability and acquiescent response set were control variables introduced into the regression at step 1. The predictors were introduced in a stepwise manner starting at step 2. Due to the finding reported by Zill and associates (1993) that the remarriage of the custodial parent could have a positive impact on the adjustment of the child if the child was very young at the time of the divorce, one of the predictors included in these regressions was a product term representing the interaction of the remarriage of the custodial parent and the age of the child at the time of the divorce. Furthermore, the findings reported by Braver and colleagues (1993) suggested that conflict between divorced parents was related negatively to the frequency of visits by the noncustodial parent, so a second product term was included to represent the interaction of parental abuse and frequency of visitation by the noncustodial parent. Finally, three product terms were included representing the interactions between custody arrangement and the respondents' reports of parental anger, insults, and physical abuse.

Table 13–5 presents the results of the regression of YSR social competence on the predictors. The table data indicated that five predictors were included after social desirability and acquiescence, based on a criterion of a probability-to-enter of .05. The predictors making significant ($p < .05$ or beyond) contributions on the successive steps were social support, stressful events, perception of parent(s) as physically abusive, perception of spending enough time with the noncustodial parent, and the respondent's current age. The betas indicated that symptoms of poor social competence are related negatively to social desirability response set and to the availability of social support. Symptom scores were related positively to stressful life events, to the perception of parent(s) as physically abusive, to satisfaction with the amount of time spent with the noncustodial parent, and to the respondent's age.

Table 13-5. Regression of YSR Social Competence Score

Step	Variable(s)	R	R-Squared Change	F[1]	Beta[2]
1	Social desirability				-.11
	Acquiescence	.27	.07	6.64***	[3]
2	Social support	.45	.13	27.35***	-.28
3	Stressful events	.54	.09	22.18***	.27
4	Physical abuse	.57	.03	7.56**	.20
5	Enough time with noncustodial parent	.58	.01	4.80*	.14
6	Age	.60	.01	4.04*	.22

1. Significance of change in R-squared at entry
2. In final regression equation
3. Acquiescence removed at step 2, due to probability-to-remove > .95

* $p < .05$
** $p < .01$
*** $p < .001$

Table 13-6 presents the results of the regression of scores on YSR internalizing pathology on the predictors. Five predictors explained significant ($p < .05$ or beyond) proportions of the variability in internalizing symptoms at successive steps, after partialing out social desirability and acquiescence response set. These were stressful events, family adaptability, gender, physical abuse, and sadness or depression in the custodial parent. The betas indicated that internalizing pathology was related positively to stressful events, being female, perceived physical abuse by parents, and sadness or depression in the custodial parent. Family adaptability was related negatively to internalizing symptoms.

Table 13-6. Regression of YSR Internalizing Pathology Score

Step	Variable	R	R-Squared Change	F[1]	Beta[2]
1	Social desirability				-.08
	Acquiescence	.22	.05	4.21*	.17
2	Stressful events	.43	.13	25.84***	.23
3	Adaptability	.51	.07	16.89***	-.25

Table 13-6. (continued)

Step	Variable	R	R-Squared Change	F[1]	Beta[2]
4	Gender	.54	.03	7.62**	.18
5	Physical abuse	.56	.02	6.56*	.17
6	Custodial parent sad	.58	.02	5.57*	.17

1. Significance of change in R-squared at entry
2. In final regression equation
* $p < .05$
** $p < .01$
*** $p < .001$

Table 13-7 presents the results of the regression of YSR externalizing symptoms on the predictors. In this regression four variables explained significant ($p < .05$ or beyond) portions of the variability in externalizing pathology at successive steps after partialing out the effect of social desirability and acquiescence response set. These were stressful events, age, social support, and physical abuse by parent(s). Social support was related negatively to externalizing pathology. Stressful life events, respondent age, and perceived physical abuse were related positively to externalizing pathology. These positive relationships indicated that symptoms of externalizing pathology tended to be more severe among older respondents, those who experienced more stressful events in connection with the divorce, and those who perceived their parent(s) as relatively abusive.

Table 13-7. Regression of YSR Externalizing Pathology Score

Step	Variable	R	R-Squared Change	F[1]	Beta[2]
1	Social desirability				-.26
	Acquiescence	.47	.22	23.75***	-.10
2	Stressful events	.55	.08	20.52***	.21
3	Age	.59	.05	12.96***	.22
4	Social support	.62	.04	10.63**	-.18
5	Physical abuse	.64	.02	6.86**	.18

1. Significance of change in R-squared at entry
2. In final regression
** $p < .01$
*** $p < .001$

Psychosocial Adjustment among Adolescents from Divorced and Intact Families

Psychosocial adjustment among adolescents from intact families was compared to that among adolescents from divorced families by means of a one-way multivariate analysis of variance in which the dependent variables were the three YSR symptom scores. The results of this MANOVA are presented in Table 13–8.

Table 13–8. YSR Symptom Scores among Adolescents from Divorced and Intact Families

Variable	Divorced (n = 221)		Intact (n = 215)	
	mean	SD	mean	SD
Social competence	6.36	3.99	5.17	3.44
Internalizing	14.04	8.86	10.06	6.33
Externalizing	17.90	9.77	13.79	8.19
Significance tests:				
		df		F
Multivariate test		3 and 432		12.73***
Univariate tests				
Social competence		1 and 434		11.18***
Internalizing		1 and 434		28.99***
Externalizing		1 and 434		22.59***

*** $p < .001$

The table data indicated that adjustment was better among adolescents from intact families than from divorced families. The multivariate test was significant ($p < .001$), as were each of the three univariate tests ($p < .001$). On each adjustment measure symptom scores were higher among adolescents from divorced families than from intact families.

Predictors of Adjustment among Adolescents from Divorced and Intact Families

Table 13–9 presents correlations between predictors and measures of psychosocial adjustment for the intact family group. Here, as in the correlations for the divorced family group presented in Table 13-4, the raw YSR symptom scores were used in the calculation. The Fisher z-transformation method was used to determine the significance of differences between corresponding correlations in the two groups.

Table 13-9. Correlations between Predictors and YSR Scales
(Adolescents from Intact Families)

Predictor	YSR Scale					
	Poor Social Competence		Internalizing Pathology		Externalizing Pathology	
	n	r	n	r	n	r
Depression of mom	210	.16*	210	.21**	210	.24
Depression of dad	210	.13	210	.25**	210	.21**
Substance abuse of mom	211	.31***	211	.30***	211	.29***
Substance abuse of dad	209	.10	209	.11	209	.24***
Parents displayed anger	210	.25***	210	.20**	210	.32***
Parents made insulting remarks	209	.27*	209	.15*	209	.31***
Parents physically abusive	209	.20	209	.12	209	.25***
Respondent gender	215	-.23***	215	.01	215	-.17
Stressful life changes	215	.22***	215	.34***	215	.27***
Adequacy of finances	210	-.01	210	-.24***	210	.05
Social support	215	-.04	215	-.13	215	-.14
FACES-Adaptability	215	-.20**	215	-.26***	215	-.29***
FACES-Cohesion	215	-.28***	215	-.35***	215	-.39***
Transformed Adaptability	215	-.08	215	.01	215	-.09
Transformed Cohesion	215	-.18*	215	-.12	215	-.11
Social desirability	208	-.29***	208	-.15**	208	-.46***
Acquiescence	207	-.01	207	-.06	207	-.14*

* $p < .05$
** $p < .01$
*** $p < .001$

These tests indicated significant differences on only four correlations. The relationship between adequacy of finances and externalizing behavior was negative in the divorced group ($r = -.21$) and near zero in the intact family group ($r = .05$). These correlations differed significantly ($t = 2.66$, $df = 414$, $p < .01$). Also, the groups differed significantly with respect to the relationship between perceived physical abuse and social competence ($t = 2.35$, $df = 409$, $p < .05$). This correlation was higher within the divorced family group ($r = .43$) than within the intact family group ($r = .20$).

The two groups also differed significantly with respect to the relationship between perceived physical abuse and internalizing pathology ($t = 2.25$, $df = 409$, $p < .05$). Here again, the relationship was stronger among the divorced family group ($r = .34$) than among the intact family group ($r = .12$). Finally, the negative relationship between social support and poor social competence was significantly ($t = 3.42$, $df = 417$, $p < .01$) stronger among the divorced group ($r = -.38$) than among the intact family group ($r = -.04$).

Conclusions Regarding Predictors of Postdivorce Adjustment Based on the Original Analysis

The analysis of the data employing the entire sample of adolescents from divorced families indicated that children's adjustment following parental divorce was related positively and moderately to the psychological adjustment of the custodial parent, as manifested in ratings of depression and substance abuse. The adolescent's perception of the adequacy of family finances was related positively to adjustment, although the relationships were weak. Moderate positive relationships were observed between the psychosocial outcome variables and the availability of social support. Family adaptability and cohesion were also related positively to the adjustment measures; the magnitudes of these correlations were weak to moderate.

Adjustment following divorce was related negatively to the level of conflict between the parents prior to and immediately after the divorce. Physical abuse was the strongest predictor of adjustment difficulties. The number of divorce-related stressful life changes was related positively to the adjustment measures. These correlations were moderate in magnitude. Postdivorce adjustment was not related significantly to the custody arrangement, nor to the frequency or predictability of contact with the noncustodial parent. The remarriage of the custodial parent was not an important predictor of postdivorce adjustment.

RESULTS OBTAINED WHEN SUBGROUPS WITHIN DIVORCED SAMPLE ARE ANALYZED SEPARATELY

Based on the review of the literature reported in the first twelve chapters of this volume, it is recommended that samples of children from divorced families be broken down into subsamples based on the gender of the child, custody arrangement, the child's current age, and the age of the child at the time the parental separation occurred. The literature review suggested that these variables had both direct and interactive effects on children's psychosocial adjustment, and that the relationships between other predictors and children's adjustment might well vary among the groups formed by crossing these factors.

Accordingly, it was decided to reanalyze the data for the first research study, looking at each group separately. In this study the participants were adolescents at the time the psychosocial outcome variables were measured. Therefore, current age did not have to be included among the factors used to establish the groups. In addition, there were too few adolescents from father-custody or joint-custody families to provide statistically adequate samples when further subdivided on the basis of the adolescent's gender and age at the time of the divorce. Accordingly, six subsamples of adolescents in mother-custody situations were identified for reanalysis:

1. Males, parents divorced when in preschool ($n = 32$)
2. Females, parents divorced when in preschool ($n = 45$)
3. Males, parents divorced when in latency ($n = 31$)
4. Females, parents divorced when in latency ($n = 29$)
5. Males, parents divorced when in adolescence ($n = 14$)
6. Females, parents divorced when in adolescence ($n = 18$)

Several of the samples are rather small for the calculation of correlations, but the findings obtained in these analyses are intended to be suggestive rather than confirmatory, and are aimed primarily toward providing guidance with respect to sample selection and data analysis procedures for future investigations.

Within each of these groups, correlations were calculated between each of the three YSR adjustment criteria and the following predictors: (1) custodial parent sad or depressed, (2) substance abuse by custodial parent, (3) parents displayed anger, (4) parents made insulting remarks, (5) parents were physically abusive, (6) satisfaction with frequency of contact with noncustodial parent, (7) satisfaction with the predictability of contact with noncustodial parent, (8) perceived adequacy of family finances, (9) whether of not the mother had remarried, (10) total number of divorce-related stressful life changes, (11) social support, (12) the FACES adaptability score (untransformed), and (13) the FACES cohesion score (untransformed).

To facilitate the comparison of these correlations to each other and to the corresponding correlations obtained for the total sample of adolescents from divorced families, the correlations have been arrayed in Tables 13-10 through 13-48 in such a way that each combination of predictor variable and adjustment criterion is represented in a single table, with the correlations for the total sample and the six subgroups on successive lines. These tables are described under subheadings corresponding to the twelve predictors.

Depression of Custodial Mother

Table 13-10 indicates the correlations obtained for the various groups between depression of the custodial parent and the YSR Poor Social Competence Scale. The correlation of .30 ($p < .001$) obtained for the total sample of children from divorced families suggested a moderate positive relationship between maternal depression and Poor Social Competence. However, when we analyze the several subgroups separately, we see that this relationship actually pertains only to female adolescents whose parents separated when they were in the preschool (oedipal) period ($r = .41$, $p < .01$). A weaker relationship between this predictor and social competence may also pertain to males whose parents divorced during their oedipal years but the observed correlation did not reach statistical significance, given the sample size involved.

Table 13-10. Correlations between Adolescent's Rating of Depression of Custodial Mother and Adolescent's YSR Score for Poor Social Competence

Group (Subgroup)	n	r
Total sample from divorced families	210	.30***
Males, parents separated when in preschool	31	.24
Females, parents separated when in preschool	43	.41**
Males, parents separated during latency	31	.16
Females, parents separated during latency	29	.04

Table 13-10. (continued)

Group (Subgroup)	n	r
Males, parents separated during adolescence	14	.23
Females, parents separated during adolescence	18	.04

** $p < .01$
*** $p < .001$

Table 13-11 shows that when the sample is analyzed as a whole, there is a moderate positive relationship between the depression of the custodial mother and the adolescent's score on the YSR Internalizing Pathology Scale. The subgroup analysis indicates that this relationship is consistent only for females, however. Among females the correlations are moderate (.30 or above) for all three groups with respect to age at the time of the parental separation (although not always statistically significant, given the sample sizes). On the other hand, among the males a moderate correlation between these variables is observed only among those whose parents divorced when the child was in latency, and there is no relationship at all between these measures among males whose parents divorced during adolescence.

Table 13-11. Correlations between Adolescent's Rating of Depression of Custodial Mother and Adolescent's YSR Score for Internalizing Pathology

Group (Subgroup)	n	r
Total sample from divorced families	210	.36***
Males, parents separated when in preschool	31	.26
Females, parents separated when in preschool	43	.36**
Males, parents separated during latency	31	.38*
Females, parents separated during latency	29	.32
Males, parents separated during adolescence	14	-.03
Females, parents separated during adolescence	18	.30

* $p < .05$
** $p < .01$
*** $p < .001$

Table 13-12 presents the correlations for the several groups between the adolescent's report of the depression of the custodial mother and the adolescent's score on the YSR Externalizing Pathology Scale.

Here again, the moderate positive relationship observed for the total sample ($r = .33$, $p < .001$) does not remain consistent across the subgroups. It holds up well for males ($r = .40$, $p < .05$) and females ($r = .48$, $p < .01$) whose parents divorced when they were in the oedipal stage. The correlation also remains moderate among females whose parents separated during the latency stage ($r = .32$), although the latter correlation was not statistically significant, given the relatively small sample size. Thus it appears that the relationship between maternal depression and the psychosocial adjustment of adolescents is generally stronger for girls than for boys, and generally stronger among children whose parents divorced while they were in preschool.

Table 13-12. Correlations between Adolescent's Rating of Depression of Custodial Mother and Adolescent's YSR Score for Externalizing Pathology

Group (Subgroup)	n	r
Total sample from divorced families	210	.33***
Males, parents separated when in preschool	31	.40*
Females, parents separated when in preschool	43	.48**
Males, parents separated during latency	31	.01
Females, parents separated during latency	29	.32
Males, parents separated during adolescence	14	.16
Females, parents separated during adolescence	18	.09

* $p < .05$
** $p < .01$
*** $p < .001$

Substance Abuse of Custodial Parent

Table 13-13 presents the correlations between the child's rating of the substance abuse of the custodial parent and the child's YSR score for Poor Social Competence. The moderately significant relationship observed for the total sample ($r = .31$, $p < .001$) was also moderate ($r > .30$) among the subsamples of males whose parents had divorced when they were in preschool ($r = .51$, $p < .01$), females whose parents had divorced while they were in latency ($r = .43$, $p < .05$), and males whose parents had divorced while they were in adolescence ($r = .31$, $p > .10$). On this combination of predictor and dependent variable, however, all the correlations were positive and greater than or equal to .20. Had all the subsamples been large ($n = 50$ or more), the correlations would have been significant. Thus there was some degree of consistency across the subgroups with respect to the relationship between the custodial mother's substance abuse and the adolescent's Poor Social Competence.

Table 13-13. Correlations between Adolescent's Rating of Substance Abuse of Custodial Mother and Adolescent's YSR Score for Poor Social Competence

Group (Subgroup)	n	r
Total sample from divorced families	211	.31***
Males, parents separated when in preschool	31	.51**
Females, parents separated when in preschool	43	.22
Males, parents separated during latency	31	.20
Females, parents separated during latency	29	.43*
Males, parents separated during adolescence	14	.31
Females, parents separated during adolescence	18	.23

* $p < .05$
** $p < .01$
*** $p < .001$

Table 13-14 presents the correlations between ratings of mother's substance abuse and the adolescent's scores on the YSR Internalizing Pathology Scale. Here there is no consistency. Moderate ($p > .30$) positive relationships were observed between these two variables only among males whose parents had divorced when they were in preschool ($r = .34$, $.10 > p > .05$) and among females whose parents had divorced while they were adolescents ($r = .55$, $p < .05$). In several of the other subsamples the observed relationships were very weak.

Table 13-14. Correlations between Adolescent's Rating of Substance Abuse of Custodial Mother and Adolescent's YSR Score for Internalizing Pathology

Group (Subgroup)	n	r
Total sample from divorced families	211	.30***
Males, parents separated when in preschool	31	.35**
Females, parents separated when in preschool	43	.18
Males, parents separated during latency	31	.03
Females, parents separated during latency	29	.25
Males, parents separated during adolescence	14	.15

Table 13–14. (continued)

Group (Subgroup)	n	r
Females, parents separated during adolescence	18	.55*

* $p < .05$
** $p < .01$
*** $p < .001$

Table 13–15 presents the correlations between ratings of maternal substance abuse and the adolescents' scores on the YSR Externalizing Pathology Scale. Here the results were extremely erratic from group to group. Rather strong positive relationships were observed among males whose parents had separated when they were in preschool ($r = .51$, $p < .01$) and when they were adolescents ($r = .54$, $p < .05$). However, among males whose parents had divorced while they were in latency, there was a nonsignificant negative relationship between mother's substance abuse and Externalizing Pathology. No correlations of moderate or strong magnitude ($r > .30$) were observed among any of the female subsamples.

Table 13–15. Correlations between Adolescent's Rating of Substance Abuse of Custodial Mother and Adolescent's YSR Score for Externalizing Pathology

Group (Subgroup)	n	r
Total sample from divorced families	211	.29***
Males, parents separated when in preschool	31	.51**
Females, parents separated when in preschool	43	.20
Males, parents separated during latency	31	-.08
Females, parents separated during latency	29	.15
Males, parents separated during adolescence	14	.54*
Females, parents separated during adolescence	18	.21

* $p < .05$
** $p < .01$
*** $p < .001$

Parental Anger

Table 13–16 contains the correlations observed between the adolescents' ratings of the extent to which their parents had displayed anger before the separation and in the two years following the separation and the adolescents' YSR scores for Poor Social Competence. A weak relationship had been observed between parental displays of anger and Poor Social Competence for the total sample ($r = .15$, $p < .05$). Weak relationships were also observed for most of six subsamples. However, for females whose parents separated when the girls were adolescents, the observed relationship was moderate ($r = .36$, $p > .05$). This finding might reflect a recency factor, since the parents would not have separated very long ago for some of these adolescents. However, no such relationship was observed among males whose parents had separated when they were adolescents.

Table 13-16. Correlations between Adolescent's Rating of Parental Display of Anger and Adolescent's YSR Score for Poor Social Competence

Group (Subgroup)	n	r
Total sample from divorced families	204	.15*
Males, parents separated when in preschool	31	.04
Females, parents separated when in preschool	43	-.03
Males, parents separated during latency	31	.08
Females, parents separated during latency	29	.24
Males, parents separated during adolescence	14	.05
Females, parents separated during adolescence	18	.36

* $p < .05$

Table 13-17 presents the correlations between parental display of anger and the adolescents' scores on the YSR Internalizing Pathology Scale. Whereas the relationship between these two variables was weak for the total sample ($r = .15$, $p < .05$) and for most of the subsamples, it was moderate among females whose parents had separated during latency ($r = .43$, $p < .05$).

Table 13-17. Correlations between Adolescent's Rating of Parental Display of Anger and Adolescent's YSR Score for Internalizing Pathology

Group (Subgroup)	n	r
Total sample from divorced families	204	.15*
Males, parents separated when in preschool	31	.06
Females, parents separated when in preschool	39	.08
Males, parents separated during latency	31	.12

Table 13-17. (continued)

Group (Subgroup)	n	r
Females, parents separated during latency	29	.43*
Males, parents separated during adolescence	14	.18
Females, parents separated during adolescence	18	.05

*$p < .05$

Table 13-18 shows the correlations between parental display of anger and the adolescents' scores on the Externalizing Pathology Scale of the YSR. A weak to moderate positive relationship had been observed between these two variables for the total sample ($r = .25$, $p < .001$). This relationship was moderate among males whose parents had separated when they were in preschool ($r = .33$, $.10 > p > .05$), as it was among females whose parents had separated while they were in the latency stage ($r = .45$, $p < .05$). Among the remaining subsamples the relationship was very weak. Thus, across the three criteria of psychosocial adjustment, the impact of parental anger appears to be greatest on female adolescents whose parents separated when they were in latency.

Table 13-18. Correlations between Adolescent's Rating of Parental Display of Anger and Adolescent's YSR Score for Externalizing Pathology

Group (Subgroup)	n	r
Total sample from divorced families	204	.25***
Males, parents separated when in preschool	31	.33
Females, parents separated when in preschool	43	-.13
Males, parents separated during latency	31	.19
Females, parents separated during latency	29	.45*
Males, parents separated during adolescence	14	.01
Females, parents separated during adolescence	18	.16

*$p < .05$
***$p < .001$

Parental Insults

Tables 13-19 through 13-21 present the correlations observed for the total sample and each of the six subsamples between the adolescents' ratings of the extent to which their parents had made insulting remarks toward each other and the three YSR psychosocial outcome measures. Because the patterns of the correlations in these three tables are quite similar, they will be discussed together. In each case a weak but significant positive relationship was between the predictor and the criterion variable for the total sample. When the subsamples were examined separately, however, this relationship tended to hold up in only one of the six groups, females whose parents had separated when the daughter was in her latency stage. The relationship with insulting remarks was particularly strong for this group with respect to YSR Internalizing Pathology ($r = .39$, $p < .05$) and Externalizing Pathology ($r = .52$, $p < .01$). Here again, parental discord appears to have the greatest long-term impact on girls whose parents divorced while the child was in latency.

Table 13-19. Correlations between Adolescent's Rating of Parents Making Insulting Remarks and Adolescent's YSR Score for Poor Social Competence

Group (Subgroup)	n	r
Total sample from divorced families	206	.17*
Males, parents separated when in preschool	32	.01
Females, parents separated when in preschool	39	.10
Males, parents separated during latency	31	.08
Females, parents separated during latency	29	.28
Males, parents separated during adolescence	14	.06
Females, parents separated during adolescence	18	.30

* $p < .05$

Table 13-20. Correlations between Adolescent's Rating of Parents Making Insulting Remarks and Adolescent's YSR Score for Internalizing Pathology

Group (Subgroup)	n	r
Total sample from divorced families	206	.15*
Males, parents separated when in preschool	32	-.04
Females, parents separated when in preschool	39	.20
Males, parents separated during latency	31	.01
Females, parents separated during latency	29	.39*
Males, parents separated during adolescence	14	.10
Females, parents separated during adolescence	18	-.09

* $p < .05$

Table 13-21. Correlations between Adolescent's Rating of Parents Making Insulting Remarks and Adolescent's YSR Score for Externalizing Pathology

Group (Subgroup)	n	r
Total sample from divorced families	206	.28***
Males, parents separated when in preschool	32	.11
Females, parents separated when in preschool	39	.06
Males, parents separated during latency	31	.22
Females, parents separated during latency	29	.52**
Males, parents separated during adolescence	14	.21
Females, parents separated during adolescence	18	.14

** $p < .01$
*** $p < .001$

Parental Physical Abuse

Tables 13-22 through 13-24 consider the relationships between adolescents' reports of parental physical abuse and the YSR measures of adolescent adjustment. As one might expect, the impact of actual physical abuse was greater than that of parental displays of anger or parental insulting remarks, both for the overall sample of adolescents from divorced families and for the subsamples. The correlations for the total sample fell between $r = .34$ and $r = .43$ (all $p < .001$). Parental physical abuse was correlated at least moderately ($r > .30$) with both Poor Social Competence and Internalizing Pathology among female respondents in each of the three categories of age at the time of the divorce. Among males, parental physical abuse was correlated moderately with both Poor Social Competence and Internalizing Pathology only when the parents had separated during latency. This finding confirms the idea developed in the foregoing literature review that the impact of parental conflict on females may be different from the impact on males in that girls are more likely to display internalizing symptoms such as depression, withdrawal, and anxiety.

Table 13-22. Correlations between Adolescent's Rating of Parents Being Physically Abusive and Adolescent's YSR Score for Poor Social Competence

Group (Subgroup)	n	r
Total sample from divorced families	206	.43*
Males, parents separated when in preschool	32	.24

Table 13-22. (continued)

Group (Subgroup)	n	r
Females, parents separated when in preschool	39	.36*
Males, parents separated during latency	31	.38*
Females, parents separated during latency	29	.56**
Males, parents separated during adolescence	14	.09
Females, parents separated during adolescence	18	.48*

* $p < .05$
** $p < .01$

Table 13-23. Correlations between Adolescent's Rating of Parents Being Physically Abusive and Adolescent's YSR Score for Internalizing Pathology

Group (Subgroup)	n	r
Total sample from divorced families	206	.34***
Males, parents separated when in preschool	32	.21
Females, parents separated when in preschool	39	.32*
Males, parents separated during latency	31	.38*
Females, parents separated during latency	29	.35*
Males, parents separated during adolescence	14	.18
Females, parents separated during adolescence	18	.54*

* $p < .05$
*** $p < .001$

Table 13-24. Correlations between Adolescent's Rating of Parents Being Physically Abusive and Adolescent's YSR Score for Externalizing Pathology

Group (Subgroup)	n	r
Total sample from divorced families	206	.40***
Males, parents separated when in preschool	32	.18
Females, parents separated when in preschool	39	.12
Males, parents separated during latency	31	.41*
Females, parents separated during latency	29	.39*
Males, parents separated during adolescence	14	.47
Females, parents separated during adolescence	18	.46

* $p < .05$
*** $p < .001$

The impact of parental physical abuse with respect to Externalizing Pathology among adolescents was similar among females and males. Moderate relationships were observed between physical abuse and Externalizing Pathology among males and females whose parents had separated during latency and among males and females whose parents had separated after they had entered adolescence. These findings suggest that girls as well as boys may manifest externalizing pathology in response to parental conflict, although the girls did not have as high mean scores as the boys on the Externalizing Pathology Scale in the group whose parents had divorced during latency or the group whose parents divorced when they were already adolescents. Once again, however, the importance of separating adolescents into groups on the basis of gender and the stage in their life when the parental separation occurred is manifest.

Frequency and Regularity of Contact with Noncustodial Parent

Tables 13-25 through 13-27 contain the correlations between the adolescents' ratings of satisfaction with the frequency of their contact with their noncustodial parent and the YSR adjustment measures; Tables 13-28 through 13-30 contain the correlations between the adolescents' ratings of the predictability of contact with their noncustodial parent and the adjustment measures. Neither frequency nor predictability of contact was a significant predictor of any of the three YSR scales in the total sample of adolescents from divorced families. However, when the six subsamples are examined separately, several moderate and several strong relationships are observed. With respect to satisfaction with the frequency of contact, moderate negative relationships were observed among females whose parents divorced after they had already entered adolescence on both Internalizing Pathology ($r = -.35$, $p > .10$) and Externalizing Pathology ($r = -.31$, $p > .10$). The small size for the females whose parents divorced after they had reached adolescence kept these correlations from reaching statistical significance.

Table 13-25. Correlations between Adolescent's Rating of Satisfaction with Frequency of Contact with Noncustodial Parent and Adolescent's YSR Score for Poor Social Competence

Group (Subgroup)	n	r
Total sample from divorced families	210	.05

Table 13-25. (continued)

Group (Subgroup)	n	r
Males, parents separated when in preschool	31	.13
Females, parents separated when in preschool	39	.15
Males, parents separated during latency	31	.22
Females, parents separated during latency	29	-.21
Males, parents separated during adolescence	14	.08
Females, parents separated during adolescence	18	-.01

No significant relationships

Table 13-26. Correlations between Adolescent's Rating of Satisfaction with Frequency of Contact with Noncustodial Parent and Adolescent's YSR Score for Internalizing Pathology

Group (Subgroup)	n	r
Total sample from divorced families	210	.01
Males, parents separated when in preschool	32	.01
Females, parents separated when in preschool	39	.05
Males, parents separated during latency	31	-.10
Females, parents separated during latency	29	.00
Males, parents separated during adolescence	14	.18
Females, parents separated during adolescence	18	-.35

No significant relationships

Table 13-27. Correlations between Adolescent's Rating of Satisfaction with Frequency of Contact with Noncustodial Parent and Adolescent's YSR Score for Externalizing Pathology

Group (Subgroup)	n	r
Total sample from divorced families	206	-.09
Males, parents separated when in preschool	32	-.07
Females, parents separated when in preschool	39	-.07
Males, parents separated during latency	31	.13
Females, parents separated during latency	29	-.25
Males, parents separated during adolescence	14	.04
Females, parents separated during adolescence	18	-.31

No significant relationships

With respect to the predictability of contact with the noncustodial parent, the correlations are more dramatic. Among females whose parents divorced after the daughter had reached adolescence, a strong negative correlation was observed between predictability and poor social competence ($r = -.60, p < .01$). These findings did not emerge in the initial correlation observed between predictability of contact and scores on the YSR Poor Social Competence Scale. Moreover, this correlation was not greater than .20 in absolute value in any of the other subsamples. Also, among adolescent girls whose parents had not divorced until after the girl had reached adolescence, a moderate negative relationship was observed between predictability of contact with the noncustodial father and Internalizing Pathology ($r = -.35, p > .10$). This correlation was no greater than .10 in absolute value in any of the other subsamples.

Table 13-28. Correlations between Adolescent's Rating of Predictability of Contact with Noncustodial Parent and Adolescent's YSR Score for Poor Social Competence

Group (Subgroup)	n	r
Total sample from divorced families	210	-.09
Males, parents separated when in preschool	31	-.09
Females, parents separated when in preschool	39	.05
Males, parents separated during latency	31	.09
Females, parents separated during latency	29	-.20
Males, parents separated during adolescence	14	.00
Females, parents separated during adolescence	18	-.60**

** $p < .01$

Table 13-29. Correlations between Adolescent's Rating of Predictability of Contact with Noncustodial Parent and Adolescent's YSR Score for Internalizing Pathology

Group (Subgroup)	n	r
Total sample from divorced families	210	-.07
Males, parents separated when in preschool	32	.00
Females, parents separated when in preschool	39	.03
Males, parents separated during latency	31	-.05
Females, parents separated during latency	29	-.05
Males, parents separated during adolescence	14	-.10
Females, parents separated during adolescence	18	-.35

No significant relationships

Table 13-30. Correlations between Adolescent's Rating of Predictability of Contact with Noncustodial Parent and Adolescent's YSR Score for Externalizing Pathology

Group (Subgroup)	n	r
Total sample from divorced families	206	-.13
Males, parents separated when in preschool	32	-.38
Females, parents separated when in preschool	39	-.16
Males, parents separated during latency	31	.09
Females, parents separated during latency	29	-.19
Males, parents separated during adolescence	14	-.71**
Females, parents separated during adolescence	18	-.19

** $p < .01$

In contrast, the correlation between predictability of contact with the noncustodial father and Externalizing Pathology was moderate to strong among several subsamples of males. Among male adolescents whose parents had divorced when they were in preschool, the relationship was moderate ($r = -.38$, $p > .10$); and among those who had already reached adolescence when their parents separated, the relationship was strong ($r = -.70$, $p < .01$).

Thus we find that if the data on contact with the noncustodial parent are analyzed on the basis of pooling the entire sample of adolescents from divorced families, there appears to be no relationship to postdivorce adjustment. However, if one follows the recommended procedure to analyze the subsamples separately, one finds that in fact moderate to strong relationships exist for specific combinations of gender and age of child at the time of the parental separation. In the case of females whose parents separated after the child had reached adolescence, the frequency of contact, the predictability of contact, or both were related moderately to Poor Social Competence, Internalizing Pathology, and Externalizing Pathology. In the case of males who were adolescents at the time of the parental separation, a strong negative relationship ($r = -.71$, $p < .01$) was observed between satisfaction with the predictability of contact with the noncustodial father and the level of externalizing pathology.

Adequacy of Family Finances

Tables 13-31 through 13-33 present the correlations between the psychosocial outcome measures and the adolescents' perceptions of the adequacy of family finances. For the total sample the adolescents' perceptions of the adequacy of family finances were related weakly but significantly to all three adjustment criteria. The correlations ranged from -.14 to -.21. When the correlations were calculated for the subsamples separately, however, moderate to strong relationships were again found for the females whose parents had not divorced until they reached adolescence. In this group the correlation of perceived adequacy of finances with Poor Social Competence was $r = -.50$ ($p < .01$); with Internalizing Pathology, $r = -.63$ ($p < .01$); and with Externalizing Pathology, $r = -.39$ ($p > .10$).

Table 13-31. Correlations between Adolescent's Rating of Adequacy of Family Finances and Adolescent's YSR Score for Poor Social Competence

Group (Subgroup)	n	r
Total sample from divorced families	210	-.14*
Males, parents separated when in preschool	32	-.25
Females, parents separated when in preschool	42	-.16
Males, parents separated during latency	31	-.16
Females, parents separated during latency	29	-.02
Males, parents separated during adolescence	14	.00
Females, parents separated during adolescence	18	-.50**

* $p < .05$
** $p < .01$

Table 13-32. Correlations between Adolescent's Rating of Adequacy of Family Finances and Adolescent's YSR Score for Internalizing Pathology

Group (Subgroup)	n	r
Total sample from divorced families	210	-.14*
Males, parents separated when in preschool	32	.00
Females, parents separated when in preschool	42	-.06
Males, parents separated during latency	31	-.30
Females, parents separated during latency	29	-.18
Males, parents separated during adolescence	14	.23
Females, parents separated during adolescence	18	-.63**

* $p < .05$
** $p < .01$

Table 13-33. Correlations between Adolescent's Rating of Adequacy of Family Finances and Adolescent's YSR Score for Externalizing Pathology

Group (Subgroup)	n	r
Total sample from divorced families	210	-.21**
Males, parents separated when in preschool	32	-.14
Females, parents separated when in preschool	42	-.24
Males, parents separated during latency	31	-.19
Females, parents separated during latency	29	-.24
Males, parents separated during adolescence	14	-.12
Females, parents separated during adolescence	18	-.39

** $p < .01$

Remarriage of Custodial Parent

Tables 13-34 through 13-36 present point-biserial correlations between the remarriage of the custodial parent and the YSR measures of psychosocial adjustment for the total sample of adolescents from divorced families and for the subsamples. The correlations for the total sample were near zero in the case of Poor Social Adjustment and Internalizing Pathology, and a weak negative correlation was observed between remarriage and Externalizing Pathology ($rbs = -.14, p < .05$). Since remarriage was coded as yes = 1 and no = 2, this weak negative relationship signified a slight tendency for adolescents whose custodial parents had remarried to show few externalizing behaviors. Based on the original analysis, this was interpreted as possibly reflecting the benefits of the presence of a male role model. This explanation would appear to apply primarily to the male adolescents in the sample. An alternative explanation offered on the basis of the original analysis was that custodial parents who remarry are themselves better adjusted than those who do not. The well-adjusted custodial parent might be a better parent, and good parenting might reduce externalizing pathology in adolescents.

When the data are analyzed separately for the subsamples formed by crossing the gender by the age of the child at the time of the divorce, however, these conclusions do not hold. Among female adolescents whose mothers did not separate until their daughter had reached adolescence, a moderately strong positive relationship was found between the remarriage of the mother and Poor Social Competence (rbs

= .47, $p < .05$). Given the coding of the remarriage variable, this finding suggests that among this group the remarriage of the custodial mother is associated with greater social competence.

Table 13-34. Correlations[1] between Remarriage of Custodial Parent and Adolescent's YSR Score for Poor Social Competence

Group (Subgroup)	n	r
Total sample from divorced families	221	.00
Males, parents separated when in preschool	32	.10
Females, parents separated when in preschool	45	-.06
Males, parents separated during latency	31	.08
Females, parents separated during latency	29	.26
Males, parents separated during adolescence	14	.00
Females, parents separated during adolescence	18	.47*

1. Point-biserial correlation: yes coded 1, no coded 2
* $p < .05$

Table 13-35. Correlations[1] between Remarriage of Custodial Parent and Adolescent's YSR Score for Internalizing Pathology

Group (Subgroup)	n	r
Total sample from divorced families	221	-.01
Males, parents separated when in preschool	32	-.07
Females, parents separated when in preschool	45	-.18
Males, parents separated during latency	31	.25
Females, parents separated during latency	29	.10
Males, parents separated during adolescence	14	-.01
Females, parents separated during adolescence	18	.05

1. Point-biserial correlation: yes coded 1, no coded 2
No significant relationships

Table 13-36. Correlations[1] between Remarriage of Custodial Parent and Adolescent's YSR Score for Externalizing Pathology

Group (Subgroup)	n	r
Total sample from divorced families	210	-.14*
Males, parents separated when in preschool	32	.12
Females, parents separated when in preschool	45	.06

Table 13-36. (continued)

Group (Subgroup)	n	r
Males, parents separated during latency	31	.27
Females, parents separated during latency	29	.27
Males, parents separated during adolescence	14	-.19
Females, parents separated during adolescence	18	.12

1. Point-biserial correlation: yes coded 1, no coded 2
* $p < .05$

In addition, when the subsamples are analyzed separately, it turns out that the weak negative relationship between remarriage and externalizing pathology is actually an artifact that does not does not correspond at all to the relationships observed among five of the six subsamples, in which the observed correlations are actually positive. Thus, in the analysis of the relationship between remarriage and the Poor Social Competence Scale, the pooling of all the children from divorced families obscured a moderate relationship that did exist in one of the subsamples; in the case of the Externalizing Pathology subscale, the pooling of the samples led to the emergence of a spurious relationship.

Divorce-Related Stressful Life Events

Tables 13-37 through 13-39 present the correlations between the adolescents' reports of the stressful life changes that followed from the divorce and the YSR psychosocial outcome variables. The data in these three tables indicate that in the pooled sample moderate relationships exist between stressful life changes and each of the three outcome measures. These relationships are fairly consistent throughout the subsamples with the exception of males whose parents separated after they had already reached adolescence. Within that group the relationships between stressful life events and the adjustment measures were weak.

Table 13-37. Correlations between Divorce-Related Stressful Life Events and Adolescent's YSR Score for Poor Social Competence

Group (Subgroup)	n	r
Total sample from divorced families	221	.38***
Males, parents separated when in preschool	32	.28

Table 13-37. (continued)

Group (Subgroup)	n	r
Females, parents separated when in preschool	45	.31*
Males, parents separated during latency	31	.55***
Females, parents separated during latency	29	.43*
Males, parents separated during adolescence	14	.13
Females, parents separated during adolescence	18	.31

* $p < .05$
*** $p < .001$

Table 13-38. Correlations between Divorce-Related Stressful Life Events and Adolescent's YSR Score for Internalizing Pathology

Group (Subgroup)	n	r
Total sample from divorced families	221	.41***
Males, parents separated when in preschool	32	.28
Females, parents separated when in preschool	45	.21
Males, parents separated during latency	31	.54**
Females, parents separated during latency	29	.44*
Males, parents separated during adolescence	14	.21
Females, parents separated during adolescence	18	.30

* $p < .05$
** $p < .01$
*** $p < .001$

Table 13-39. Correlations between Divorce-Related Stressful Life Changes and Adolescent's YSR Score for Externalizing Pathology

Group (Subgroup)	n	r
Total sample from divorced families	210	.32***
Males, parents separated when in preschool	32	.32
Females, parents separated when in preschool	45	.36
Males, parents separated during latency	31	.50**
Females, parents separated during latency	29	.39*
Males, parents separated during adolescence	14	.19
Females, parents separated during adolescence	18	.62**

* $p < .05$
** $p < .01$
*** $p < .001$

Social Support

Tables 13-40 through 13-42 present the correlations between the adolescents' perceptions of the social support available to them and the YSR outcome measures. When the total sample is analyzed, the correlations with all three YSR scales are weak to moderate and negative, ranging from -.25 to -.38 (all $p < .001$). When the subsamples are analyzed separately, the observed correlations are moderate in some groups but not in others. The correlation between social support and Poor Social Competence is negative in all subsamples, but there is a great range in the magnitude of the correlation from one subsample to the next, with particularly strong correlations observed among the participants whose parents had separated after the children had reached adolescence, both males ($r = .74$, $p < .01$) and females ($r = .60$, $p < .01$). The strength of these two correlations may reflect the recency of the separation.

Table 13-40. Correlations between Social Support and Adolescent's YSR Score for Poor Social Competence

Group (Subgroup)	n	r
Total sample from divorced families	218	-.38***
Males, parents separated when in preschool	32	-.23
Females, parents separated when in preschool	45	-.43**
Males, parents separated during latency	31	-.28
Females, parents separated during latency	29	-.54**
Males, parents separated during adolescence	14	-.74**
Females, parents separated during adolescence	18	-.60**

** $p < .01$
*** $p < .001$

Table 13-41. Correlations between Social Support and Adolescent's YSR Score for Internalizing Pathology

Group (Subgroup)	n	r
Total sample from divorced families	218	-.25***
Males, parents separated when in preschool	32	-.09
Females, parents separated when in preschool	45	-.37*
Males, parents separated during latency	31	-.14
Females, parents separated during latency	29	-.36
Males, parents separated during adolescence	14	-.73**

Table 13-41. (continued)

Group (Subgroup)	n	r
Females, parents separated during adolescence	18	-.25

* $p < .05$
** $p < .01$
*** $p < .001$

Table 13-42. Correlations between Social Support and Adolescent's YSR Score for Externalizing Pathology

Group (Subgroup)	n	r
Total sample from divorced families	218	-.32***
Males, parents separated when in preschool	32	-.49**
Females, parents separated when in preschool	45	-.23
Males, parents separated during latency	31	-.18
Females, parents separated during latency	29	-.06
Males, parents separated during adolescence	14	-.49
Females, parents separated during adolescence	18	-.58*

* $p < .05$
** $p < .01$
*** $p < .001$

The negative correlations observed between social support and the Internalizing Pathology subscale also varied considerably from one subsample to the next, ranging from $r = -.09$ ($p > .10$) for males whose parents separated when they were preschoolers to $r = -.73$ ($p < .01$) for males whose parents separated after their sons had reached adolescence. The negative correlations between social support and the Externalizing Pathology Scale ranged from $r = -.06$ ($p > .10$) for female adolescents whose parents separated while their daughters were in the latency stage to $r = -.58$ ($p < .05$) for girls whose parents did not separate until their daughters had reached latency. Thus the correlations obtained with respect to social support at least had the same negative sign, but those obtained for the total sample were not often representative of the relationships within some of the specific subsamples.

Family Adaptability and Cohesion

Tables 13-43 through 13-48 contain the correlations between the YSR psychosocial adjustment criteria and the FACES adaptability and cohesion subscales. The pattern of correlations observed with respect to the family system measures was similar to that observed with respect to social support. When the entire sample of children from divorced families was analyzed as a pooled sample, low to moderate negative correlations were observed (all $p < .001$). When the subsamples were examined separately, the correlations were all negative, but there was rather substantial variability in these correlations from one subsample to the next. This again suggests that it is not appropriate to pool data across groups formed by crossing gender and age at the time of the separation.

Table 13-43. Correlations between Family Adaptability and Adolescent's YSR Score for Poor Social Competence

Group (Subgroup)	n	r
Total sample from divorced families	220	-.23***
Males, parents separated when in preschool	32	-.02
Females, parents separated when in preschool	45	-.30**
Males, parents separated during latency	31	-.04
Females, parents separated during latency	29	-.30
Males, parents separated during adolescence	14	-.35
Females, parents separated during adolescence	17	-.50*

* $p < .05$
** $p < .01$
*** $p < .001$

Table 13-44. Correlations between Family Adaptability and Adolescent's YSR Score for Internalizing Pathology

Group (Subgroup)	n	r
Total sample from divorced families	220	-.36***
Males, parents separated when in preschool	32	-.33
Females, parents separated when in preschool	45	-.37*
Males, parents separated during latency	31	-.24
Females, parents separated during latency	29	-.47**
Males, parents separated during adolescence	14	-.47
Females, parents separated during adolescence	17	-.55*

* $p < .05$
** $p < .01$
*** $p < .001$

Table 13-45. Correlations between Family Adaptability and Adolescent's YSR Score for Externalizing Pathology

Group (Subgroup)	n	r
Total sample from divorced families	220	-.35***
Males, parents separated when in preschool	32	-.41*
Females, parents separated when in preschool	45	-.12
Males, parents separated during latency	31	-.04
Females, parents separated during latency	29	-.49**
Males, parents separated during adolescence	14	-.14
Females, parents separated during adolescence	17	-.57*

* p < .05
** p < .01
*** p < .001

Table 13-46. Correlations between Family Cohesion and Adolescent's YSR Score for Poor Social Competence

Group (Subgroup)	n	r
Total sample from divorced families	220	-.22***
Males, parents separated when in preschool	32	-.41*
Females, parents separated when in preschool	45	-.26
Males, parents separated during latency	31	-.19
Females, parents separated during latency	29	-.52**
Males, parents separated during adolescence	14	-.16
Females, parents separated during adolescence	17	-.43*

* p < .05
** p < .01
*** p < .001

Table 13-47. Correlations between Family Cohesion and Adolescent's YSR Score for Internalizing Pathology

Group (Subgroup)	n	r
Total sample from divorced families	220	-.31***
Males, parents separated when in preschool	32	-.01*
Females, parents separated when in preschool	45	-.52***
Males, parents separated during latency	31	-.35*
Females, parents separated during latency	29	-.37*
Males, parents separated during adolescence	14	-.24

Table 13-47. (continued)

Group (Subgroup)	n	r
Females, parents separated during adolescence	17	-.55*

* $p < .05$
*** $p < .001$

Table 13-48. Correlations between Family Cohesion and Adolescent's YSR Score for Externalizing Pathology

Group (Subgroup)	n	r
Total sample from divorced families	220	-.29***
Males, parents separated when in preschool	32	-.48**
Females, parents separated when in preschool	45	-.26
Males, parents separated during latency	31	-.19
Females, parents separated during latency	29	-.52**
Males, parents separated during adolescence	14	-.16
Females, parents separated during adolescence	17	-.43*

* $p < .05$
** $p < .01$
*** $p < .001$

Conclusions Based on Separate Analyses of Subsamples of Adolescents from Divorced Families

The analyses in which the six subsamples established by crossing adolescent gender and age at the time of the parental separation yielded results that are often quite different from those obtained in the original analysis based on the total sample of adolescents from divorced families. These differences were especially important in the areas of satisfaction with the frequency and regularity of visitation by the noncustodial father. While these relationships appeared nonexistent or very weak in the analysis of the total sample, the subsample analysis indicated that for adolescents whose parents had separated after the children were already adolescents, the relationships were often strong.

The implication of these findings is that the results reported for studies in which all children from divorced families were analyzed as a total sample may actually not apply at all to any of the subsamples defined by crossing the child's gender and stage in life when the separation occurred. Although the data for the present study were not such as to allow us to test the possible effects of the custodial arrangement and the child's current age on the relationships between psychosocial adjustment and the predictor variables, the literature suggests that the custodial arrangement and the child's current age may also influence the nature of these relationships.

Thus research on children's postdivorce adjustment should always be reported for groups of children representing a single combination of the four demographic and background factors: (1) child's gender, (2) stage in life at the time of the parental separation (preschool, latency, or adolescence), (3) custodial arrangement (mother, father, or joint), and (4) current age of the child at the time of the data collection. Our second research study, which is reported in Chapter 14, follows this recommendation. It focuses on female adolescents in mother-custody situations whose parents had divorced during the children's preschool years or during latency. The results are reported separately for respondents whose parents divorced when they were in preschool, during latency, or in adolescence.

14

RESEARCH STUDY II

THE SECOND RESEARCH study reported in this volume was carried out after the review of the literature on children's adjustment to divorce. It reflects the conclusion that meaningful conclusions can be reported only on subsets of children established on the basis of the child's gender, stage of life at the time of the divorce, custody arrangement, and current age at the time the data were collected. This study focused on females in mother-custody situations who were currently adolescents (aged 13 to 18).

METHODS

Subjects

The sample included girls whose parents had separated when the girls were in the preschool age group and the latency stage (elementary school years). Girls whose parents had separated after the child had reached adolescence were not included to eliminate ambiguity regarding the confounding effects of the stage of life when the separation occurred and the recency of the separation. This question must be investigated by employing samples of adult children from divorced families who can be broken down with respect to age at the time of the divorce and length of time since the divorce. To comply with our recommendation not to pool respondents whose parents had separated at different stages in the lives of the children, the data from this sample were analyzed separately for respondents whose parents had separated during their preschool and elementary school years. Consistent with our general recommendations for research on children from divorced families, we included a comparison group of adolescents from intact families.

The sample reported on here consists of thirty-eight females whose parents had divorced when they were in the preschool period, forty-three females in the latency stage, and 151 females from intact families. The data were collected in high schools in suburban communities in northern New Jersey. The sample is uniformly middle and upper middle class. As indicated in Table 14-1, the sample was quite diverse with respect to ethnicity, birthplace, and religious affiliation.

Table 14-1. Background and Demographic Characteristics of Adolescent Females Included in Research Study II

Variable	Value	Number	%
Age	13	15	6.5
	14	12	5.2
	15	90	38.8
	16	78	33.6
	17	19	8.2
	18	18	7.8
Ethnicity	white	94	40.5
	black	62	28.5
	Asian	34	14.7
	Hispanic	18	7.7
	interracial	16	6.8
	other	8	3.4
Religion	Catholic	40	17.2
	Jewish	88	37.9
	Protestant	70	30.2
	other	34	14.7

Procedures

Convenience sampling was employed as we were anxious to have the results of this study available for inclusion in this volume. Data were collected by students hired for the purpose; they were instructed to solicit as many of their classmates as possible. Because the first few students hired for this purpose were females, the majority of the respondents turned out to be females as well. We do have some data on males and on adolescents whose parents did not divorce until the children were adolescents. However, we do not yet have sufficient data on these groups to report results at this time. Our data collection efforts are proceeding, and subsequent reports will consider other subsamples from the population of children from divorced families.

Instruments

In the interest of making data collection as efficient as possible, the survey instrument administered to the young women in the study was kept as brief as possible. Psychosocial outcomes were assessed by the Youth Self-Report (Achenbach 1991), described in detail in the preceding chapter. The predictors of children's outcomes were assessed by means of a questionnaire developed specifically for this study. It included several background and demographic items and ten items designed to measure the adolescent's perceptions of (1) whether the custodial parent had been or is now depressed; (2) whether the custodial parent has had a problem with substance abuse in the past or currently; (3) whether the respondent's parents have a history of physical abuse or conflict; (4) whether the respondent is satisfied with the amount of time she has to spend with her father; (5) the adequacy of the family's financial situation; (6) the availability of social support; (7) family adaptability; (8) family cohesion; (9) the number of stressful life changes experienced by respondents over their lifetime; and (10) for children whose parents had divorced or been widowed, whether the parent had remarried.

With the exception of the item concerned with remarriage, these survey items were written in such a way as to make them applicable to adolescents from intact as well as divorced families. The results of the study are presented in the paragraphs that follow. They have been organized under three major headings: (1) comparison of the two subsamples of females from divorced families and one sample from intact families with respect to the predictors, (2) comparison of the three samples with respect to the YSR measures of psychosocial adjustment, and (3) the relationships between the predictors and the outcome variables among each of the three groups. The presentation concludes with a comparison of the results obtained in the first and second research studies.

RESULTS

Comparison of Groups on Predictors

Table 14-2 presents the frequency distributions of responses to items assessing the predictor variables for each of the three groups. It includes the results of chi-square tests for the significance of the differences between the groups on these factors.

Table 14-2. Frequency Distributions on Predictors of Adolescent Psychosocial Adjustment, by Group

		Group						
		Parents Divorced during Preschool		Parents Divorced during Latency		Intact Families		
Variable	Value	N	%	N	%	N	%	Chi-square
Parent depression	no	23	60.5	30	73.2	118	80.8	
	yes	15	39.5	11	26.8	28	19.2	7.03*
Parent substance abuse	no	30	78.9	37	90.2	131	89.7	
	yes	8	21.2	4	9.8	15	10.3	3.56
Parent(s) physically abusive	never	12	32.4	25	58.1	95	63.3	
	very little	14	16.2	6	14.0	31	20.7	
	sometimes	6	16.2	9	20.9	17	11.3	
	often	5	13.5	3	7.0	7	4.7	15.92*
Satisfaction with contact with dad	not at all	9	24.3	5	11.9	24	16.0	
	somewhat	15	40.5	21	50.0	71	47.3	
	quite	7	18.9	8	19.0	21	14.0	
	completely	6	16.2	8	19.0	34	22.7	3.74
Family have financial problems?	never	7	18.9	4	9.3	28	18.7	
	sometimes	11	29.7	26	60.5	89	59.3	
	often	13	35.1	5	11.6	26	17.3	
	all the time	6	16.2	8	18.6	7	4.7	22.90***
Number of stressful life changes	none	27	71.1	31	73.8	109	72.2	
	one	10	26.3	11	26.2	39	25.8	
	more	1	2.6	0	0.0	3	2.0	6.69
How flexible are your	not at all	8	24.2	13	31.7	39	26.5	
	somewhat	11	33.3	15	36.6	55	37.4	

* $p < .05$
*** $p < .001$

Table 14-2. (continued)

| | | Group | | | | | | |
| | | Parents Divorced during Preschool | | Parents Divorced during Latency | | Intact Families | | |
Variable	Value	N	%	N	%	N	%	Chi-square
parents?	quite	8	24.2	3	7.3	19	12.9	
(adaptable)	very	6	18.2	10	24.4	34	23.1	4.63
How close	not at all	12	31.6	10	23.3	23	15.2	
are your	somewhat	9	23.7	13	30.2	36	23.8	
family	quite	13	34.2	12	27.9	58	38.4	
members	very	4	10.5	8	18.6	34	22.5	8.47
(cohesion)?								
Have someone	no	11	28.9	6	14.0	20	13.2	
you can confide in?	yes	27	71.1	37	86.0	131	86.8	5.74
Parent	no	12	57.1	10	50.0	—	—	
remarried	yes	9	42.9	10	50.0	—	—	0.92

The table data indicate significant differences among the three groups on three of the ten predictors of adjustment in the study. They differed significantly on the child's perception of whether the parent with whom they spent the most time had been or was now depressed (chi-square = 7.03, df = 1, p < .05). Nearly 40 percent of the respondents in the group whose parents had separated when they were in preschool felt that their custodial parent had shown signs of depression. In contrast, this figure was 26.8 percent among those whose parents had divorced when they were in latency and only 19.2 percent among respondents from intact families.

The groups differed significantly as well with respect to how frequently their parent(s) had been physically abusive (chi-square = 15.92, df = 3, p < .05). With respect to this measure, only 32.4 percent of the young women whose parents had divorced when they were at the preschool stage responded "never" to this question. The corresponding percentage among those whose parents had divorced during their latency stage was 58.1 percent; among the intact family group, 63.3 percent.

Finally, the groups differed significantly on the question concerned with family finances (chi-square = 22.90, df = 22.90, p < .001). On this question the majority (51.3 percent) of the adolescents from families whose parents had divorced during latency indicated they had financial problems either "often" or "all the time." The corresponding percentages were 30.2 percent among those whose parents had divorced when the child was in latency and 22.0 percent among respondents from intact families.

Thus it must be noted that the three groups did differ significantly on several factors that might be thought to influence the adolescents' psychosocial outcomes. Ideally, we would control for these factors by blocking when comparing the three groups on the psychosocial outcome variables. In this study, however, the numbers of cases in the two subsamples from divorced families are too small to permit the use of this statistical control procedure. Therefore we caution the reader that between-group differences in adjustment may result from their status with respect not only to divorce per se, but also to these three predictors. Of course, to the extent that these three populations are reliably different with respect to parental depression, physical abuse, and frequency of financial problems (which they probably are), the issue of control is academic only.

Comparison of Groups on Psychosocial Adjustment Measures

Table 14-3 presents the results of three one-way analyses of variance (ANOVAs) calculated to compare the three groups on the YSR scales

Table 14-3. YSR Poor Social Competence, Internalizing Pathology, and Externalizing Pathology by Group

	Group						
	Parents Divorced during Preschool (n=38)		Parents Divorced during Latency (n=42)		Intact Families (n=149)		
Variable	Mean	SD	Mean	SD	Mean	SD	F
Poor Social Competence	57.21	7.88	56.81	5.55	55.81	6.40	0.92
Internalizing Pathology	65.32	11.29	62.59	8.55	58.07	8.51	11.71***
Externalizing Pathology	60.63	7.89	61.52	10.15	60.21	9.79	0.31

*** $p < .001$

for Poor Social Competence, Internalizing Pathology, and Externalizing Pathology. The table data indicate no significant differences among the groups with respect to the YSR Poor Social Competence Scale or the YSR Externalizing Pathology. The ANOVA for internalizing pathology was significant ($F = 11.71$, $df = 2$ and 226, $p < .001$).

On Internalizing Pathology the greatest pathology was found among respondents whose parents had divorced when they were in preschool (mean = 65.32). The next highest mean was that of the group whose parents had divorced when they were in the latency stage (mean = 62.60). The lowest mean score was that of the adolescents from intact families (mean = 58.07). These findings are consistent with previously reported findings that children from divorced families tend to display poorer adjustment than children from intact families. The findings are also consistent with the observation we made above that female children from divorced families tend to display internalizing pathology, whereas males are more likely to display externalizing behaviors.

Correlates of Psychosocial Adjustment among Adolescents from Divorced and Intact Families

Tables 14-4 through 14-6 present the correlations between the three YSR psychosocial adjustment measures and the ten predictors for each of the three groups included in this study.

Table 14-4. Correlations between YSR Psychosocial Outcome Measures and Predictors of Adjustment among Respondents Whose Parents Separated When They Were in Preschool

Predictor	Poor Social Competence		Correlation with YSR Internalizing Pathology		Externalizing Pathology	
	n	r	n	r	n	r
Parent depression	38	.31*	38	.08	38	.21
Parent substance abuse	38	.22	38	.21	38	.24
Parent(s) physically abusive	37	.48**	37	.30	37	.29

Table 14-4. (continued)

Predictor	Poor Social Competence		Correlation with YSR Internalizing Pathology		Externalizing Pathology	
	n	r	n	r	n	r
Satisfaction with contact with dad	37	.09	37	.17	37	.18
Family have financial problems?	37	.32*	37	.04	37	.17
Number of stressful life changes	38	.34*	38	.30	38	.39*
How flexible are your parents? (adaptability)	33	-.34*	33	-.37*	33	.08
How close are your family members? (cohesion)	38	-.38*	38	-.56**	38	-.26
Have someone you can confide in? (social support)	38	-.32*	38	-.35*	38	-.16
Parent remarried?	21	.08	21	-.28	21	.14

* $p < .05$
** $p < .01$

Table 14-5. Correlations between YSR Psychosocial Outcome Measures and Predictors of Adjustment among Respondents Whose Parents Separated When They Were in the Latency Stage

Predictor	Poor Social Competence		Correlation with YSR Internalizing Pathology		Externalizing Pathology	
	n	r	n	r	n	r
Parent depression	40	.09	40	.40**	40	.05
Parent substance abuse	40	.36*	40	.08	40	.14

Table 14–5. (continued)

	Poor Social Competence		Correlation with YSR Internalizing Pathology		Externalizing Pathology	
Predictor	n	r	n	r	n	r
Parent(s) physically abusive	42	.48**	42	.31*	42	.11
Satisfaction with contact with dad	41	-.09	41	.03	41	.04
Family have financial problems?	39	.15	39	.31*	39	.20
Number of stressful life changes	38	.34*	38	.30	38	.39*
How flexible are your parents? (adaptability)	40	-.34*	40	-.42**	40	-.51**
How close are your family members? (cohesion)	40	-.56**	40	-.39**	40	-.52**
Have someone you can confide in? (social support)	42	-.48**	42	-.39**	42	.08
Parent remarried?	20	.19	20	-.23	20	.06

* $p < .05$
** $p < .01$

Table 14–6. Correlations between YSR Psychosocial Outcome Measures and Predictors of Adjustment among Respondents from Intact Families

	Poor Social Competence		Correlation with YSR Internalizing Pathology		Externalizing Pathology	
Predictor	n	r	n	r	n	r
Parent depression	144	.25**	144	.06	144	.21*

Table 14-6. (continued)

Predictor	Poor Social Competence		Correlation with YSR Internalizing Pathology		Externalizing Pathology	
	n	r	n	r	n	r
Parent substance abuse	144	.21*	144	.14	144	.24**
Parent(s) physically abusive	148	.48***	148	.31***	148	.29***
Satisfaction with contact with dad	148	.10	148	.11	148	.18*
Family have financial problems?	148	.32***	148	.31***	148	.13
Number of stressful life changes	149	.37***	149	.30***	149	.32***
How flexible are your parents? (adaptability)	145	-.29***	145	-.40***	145	.04
How close are your family members? (cohesion)	145	-.24**	145	-.32***	145	-.26***
Have someone you can confide in? (social support)	149	-.26***	149	-.40***	145	-.17*

* $p < .05$
** $p < .01$
*** $p < .001$

The data in Table 14-4 indicate that among the young women whose parents had separated when they were in the preschool years, there is a moderate relationship between the child's perception of the parent as depressed and the YSR Poor Social Competence Scale ($r = .31, p < .05$). Parental substance abuse is not related moderately ($r = .30$ or above) to any of the outcome measures.

Physical abuse on the part of one or both parents was related moderately to both Poor Social Competence ($r = .48$, $p < .01$) and Internalizing Pathology ($r = .30$, $p > .05$). Satisfaction with the amount of time spent with their fathers was not related moderately or above to any of the outcome measures. The adolescent's perception of the frequency of family financial problems was related moderately to scores on Poor Social Competence ($r = .32$, $p < .05$), but not to Internalizing or Externalizing Pathology.

The number of stressful life changes reported by the adolescents in this group was related moderately to all three criterion variables: Poor Social Competence ($r = .34$, $p < .05$), Internalizing Pathology ($r = .30$, $p > .05$), and Externalizing Pathology ($r = .39$, $p < .05$). Adolescents' ratings of family adaptability, family cohesion, and social support were related moderately to scores on both Poor Social Competence and Internalizing Pathology, but not to Externalizing Pathology. These findings are similar to those obtained for the females in Research Study I. The remarriage of the custodial mother was not related moderately or higher to any of the outcome measures in this group.

The data in Table 14–5 indicate that among those young women whose parents had separated during the latency period, reports of maternal depression were related moderately to scores on Internalizing Pathology ($r = .40$, $p < .01$); reports of maternal substance abuse were related moderately to scores on Poor Social Competence ($r = .36$, $p < .05$). Reported frequency of parental physical abuse was related moderately to both Poor Social Competence ($r = .48$, $p < .01$) and Internalizing Pathology ($r = .31$, $p < .05$). As in the case of the young women whose parents separated during the preschool years, satisfaction with the amount of time spent with their fathers was not related to any of the psychosocial outcome variables.

The ratings of the frequency of family financial problems was related moderately to Internalizing Pathology ($r = .31$, $p < .05$). The reported number of stressful life changes was related moderately ($r = .30$ or higher) to all three outcome measures. The same was true of family cohesion and family adaptability. Social support was related moderately to Poor Social Competence ($r = -.48$, $p < .01$) and Internalizing Pathology ($r = -.39$, $p < .01$). Those young women who said that they did have someone they could confide in tended to have lower symptom scores than those who did not. The remarriage of the custodial mother was not related at a moderate or higher level to any of the outcomes.

Among the sample of adolescents from intact families, the relationships tended to be similar in pattern although somewhat less strong in magnitude. Neither parental depression nor parental substance abuse were related at moderate or higher levels to any of the outcomes, although the much larger sample size for this group meant that several correlations of weak magnitude were nevertheless statistically significant.

Parental physical abuse and the frequency of family financial problems were each related moderately to Poor Social Competence and Internalizing Pathology. The reported number of stressful life changes experienced by the adolescent was related moderately to all three outcome measures. Rated family adaptability, family cohesion, and social support were related moderately ($r = .30$ or higher in absolute value) to internalizing pathology, but not to Poor Social Competence or to Externalizing Pathology.

CONCLUSIONS

The value of studying subsamples of children from divorced families representing the combinations of gender, age at the time of the parental separation, custodial arrangement, and current age can be seen by the consistency of the results obtained in the two research studies reported in this volume for corresponding subsamples. A total of thirty correlations were calculated for each subsample in the second research study (ten predictors times three outcome variables). Each can be compared to a correlation for a variable in Research Study I. While the predictors were not measured through identical procedures in the two studies, there is a correspondence between the ten predictor domains in the two studies.

When we make these comparisons for the subsample of young women whose parents separated while they were in their preschool years, we find that (1) ten of the thirty correlations were of moderate or greater magnitude in both studies; (2) fourteen of the thirty were weak in magnitude in both studies; and (3) only six of the thirty correlations were weak in magnitude in one of the studies and moderate or strong in magnitude in the other study. This correspondence indicates that the same factors found to predict psychosocial outcomes for this subsample in the first study tended to be the factors that predicted outcomes for this group in the second study as well. This degree of correspondence is far greater than one would expect by chance, and far greater than the consistency of results typically found when one surveys the literature on the predictors of children's adjustment following divorce.

Referring to the subsample of young women whose parents had divorced while they were in the latency stage, we find a similar pattern. Of the thirty correlations that can be compared in the two studies: (1) fifteen were of moderate or greater magnitude in both studies; (2) twelve were weak in magnitude in both studies; (3) only three were weak in one and moderate or strong in the other. Thus the results of the two studies for respondents whose parents divorced during latency are even more consistent than the results obtained for those whose parents separated during the preschool years.

It remains to be demonstrated in future research whether similarly consistent findings would pertain to other subsamples of children from divorced families. However, the data from these two studies would appear to support our general recommendation to avoid reporting results in which data from different subsamples have been pooled. This practice may constitute a major reason for the inconsistencies found in the literature with respect to the factors predicting the psychosocial adjustment of children from divorced families.

15

SUMMARY AND CONCLUSIONS

BETWEEN- AND WITHIN-GROUP DIFFERENCES IN PSYCHOSOCIAL ADJUSTMENT

The literature review and the results of the research studies reported here clearly indicate that children whose parents divorce tend as a group to manifest poorer psychosocial adjustment than children from intact families. The literature also indicates that these between-group differences tend to persist into adulthood.

However, there is great variability in psychosocial adjustment among children from divorced families, and most of these children fall within the normal ranges on measures of psychosocial adjustment. Several studies have shown that children whose parents divorce generally understand the reasons for the divorce, and they do not tend to think of themselves as having been adversely affected by the event (Kurdek and Siesky 1980, Reinhard 1977, Rosen 1977).

Because of the great variability in adjustment among children and among adult children from divorced families, it makes much more sense to focus research efforts on understanding the factors that predict adjustment among this group rather than dwell on between-group differences between children from divorced and intact families. The following sections summarize what we have learned about these predictors.

CONFLICT BETWEEN PARENTS

An important predictor of children's adjustment is the level of conflict that exists between the parents before, during, and after the divorce. Actually, parental conflict is associated with poor psychosocial adjustment among children from intact as well as divorced families. Indeed, several studies have indicated that the level of parental conflict is a much stronger predictor of adjustment than parental marital status (Hetherington 1979a,b, Long 1986, Mechanic and Hansell 1989, Rutter 1985). The results of the two research studies reported here indicated that actual physical abuse on the part of one or both parents is a particularly important predictor of adjustment.

The long-term adjustment of children from divorced families depends on the conflict displayed by parents around the time of the divorce and whether it remains high in the years after the divorce (Forehand et al. 1988). It has been suggested that one reason why conflict between parents leads to poor adjustment is that conflict tends to inhibit frequent and regular visitation by noncustodial parents (Simons et al. 1994). In addition, to the extent that conflict is stressful, it may impact adversely on parenting behaviors.

For these reasons divorcing spouses owe it to their children to put aside whatever hurt and anger they may feel and to behave in a civil manner toward each other. Clinicians working with the divorcing should always make it a priority to communicate this message. For the same reason, mediated divorces are clearly preferable to litigation.

CUSTODY ARRANGEMENTS

More and more fathers are seeking and gaining custody of their children. Research on custodial fathers has consistently indicated that fathers who do secure custody of their children tend to be confident and competent parents (Gasser and Taylor 1976, Gersick 1979, Hanson 1981, Warshak 1986). In addition, joint custody arrangements are becoming more popular.

The evidence on the relative merits of mother custody versus father custody is mixed. Rosen (1979), comparing children from mother-custody and father-custody families, found no significant differences in adjustment. However, this study did not take into account the match of the sex of the custodial parent and that of the child. Other studies that have considered the sex of parent and child have generally indicated that children tend to be somewhat better adjusted when they are placed with the same-sexed parent (Hetherington et al. 1978,

Santrock and Warshak 1979, Studer 1993). The effect of the sex match of the custodial parent and the child is mediated to a substantial degree by other factors, however, particularly the parenting style of the custodial parent.

Several studies support the widely accepted notion that children from joint custody situations tend to be better adjusted than those from single-parent custody situations (Pojman 1982, Shiller 1986a,b). Several other studies have suggested that parents tend to report high levels of satisfaction with joint physical custody since this arrangement typically gives each parent ample time with the child as well as ample respite time (Maccoby et al. 1988, Steinman et al. 1985). However, it should be noted that divorcing parents who agree to a joint custody arrangement are likely to be on better terms with each other than parents who engage in a battle for custody. Thus, favorable psychosocial outcomes noted among children from joint custody families may also reflect a relative lack of parental conflict.

PSYCHOLOGICAL ADJUSTMENT OF CUSTODIAL PARENT

The psychological adjustment of the custodial parent is an important predictor of children's postdivorce adjustment (Guidubaldi and Perry 1985, Kline et al. 1988, Kurdek and Berg 1983, Wallerstein and Kelly 1980). Kalter and associates (1989) argued that the psychological adjustment of the custodial parent is particularly important because the absence of a second parent in the home eliminates the possibility that he or she can provide a buffer to ameliorate the negative impact of depressed, anxious, or erratic behavior on the part of the first parent. Other investigators have suggested that the psychological adjustment of the custodial parent is important because a well-adjusted parent is more likely than a disturbed parent to display effective parenting behavior (Simons et al. 1994). The research studies reported in this volume indicated that parental depression was related more strongly to the adjustment of girls than boys, and more strongly related to adjustment among children whose parents had separated at an early stage in the life of the child.

Since the event of divorce is by definition a stressful life change, and since divorced persons tend to display more psychopathology than married individuals, it is probably a good idea for divorcing couples to seek out some form of counseling and/or to attend a self-help support group for divorced individuals. Such interventions should be recommended routinely to all divorcing couples, even when there are no obvious signs of emotional or psychological difficulties. It would be most desirable if such services could be provided at no cost or at least very moderate cost, since divorce is typically accompanied by increased financial pressures.

REMARRIAGE OF CUSTODIAL PARENT

Since mother custody has been normative until quite recently, most of the research on remarriage of the custodial parent has been carried out on mothers and stepfathers. Following divorce, the relationship between a custodial mother and her children is often very intense since the mother and her children tend to rely on each other for support and companionship (Keshet 1980). Stepfathers are often viewed as intruders into this relationship, and children tend to be resentful and jealous. This appears to be reflected in a tendency on the part of children to display increased levels of angry, acting-out, externalizing behavior. The literature suggests that these difficulties tend to abate after a few years in the case of male children, but to persist for longer periods among girls.

Negative outcomes following remarriage are by no means inevitable, however. Hetherington (1993) suggested that when the remarriage of a custodial mother occurs before the child reaches adolescence, stepfathers can promote positive outcomes by initially maintaining a relatively low profile. She suggested that they not assume an authoritative role immediately, but rather seek to develop a close relationship with the child while supporting maternal discipline. On the other hand, Hetherington recommended that when the remarriage occurs after the child has reached adolescence, it is better for stepfathers to assume an authoritative parenting role immediately. In the two research studies reported in this book, the remarriage of the custodial parent was not a strong predictor of children's postdivorce adjustment. This may reflect the tendency observed by Visher and Visher (1978, 1983) for stepfathers to deal with potential conflicts by treading very lightly and attempting to meet the needs of all the members of the new family. Nevertheless, appropriate strategies for entering the family constellation may not be instinctively obvious to all stepfathers, so stepfamily counseling, psychoeducational interventions, or stepfamily support groups are probably well advised.

CONTACT WITH NONCUSTODIAL PARENT

Some of the earlier investigations of children's adjustment following divorce endorsed the "father-absence hypothesis," which assumes that the primary negative aspect of divorce is the loss of contact with the noncustodial parent, typically the father (Hetherington et al. 1982, Wallerstein and Kelly 1980, Warshak and Santrock 1983). Paternal support and control are assumed to be crucial for the satisfactory development of children, particularly boys (Kalter et al. 1989).

Several later studies, however, have concluded that many noncustodial fathers rarely visit their children, and that the impact of visitation on children's development is negligible (Thomas and Forehand 1993). Some studies have even concluded that visitation by noncustodial fathers has a negative effect on children's adjustment (Furstenberg et al. 1987, Shook and Jurich 1992).

Based on the two research studies reported here, it appears that these inconsistent findings may well be the result of pooling dissimilar subsamples of children from divorced families. The impact of visitation appears to vary substantially on the basis of custodial arrangement, gender of the child, current age of the child, and age at which the parents separated. In the studies reported here, satisfaction with the frequency and predictability of visitation was unrelated to psychosocial adjustment among most groups, but several moderate to strong negative relationships were observed among girls whose parents divorced after the girls had reached adolescence. In addition, among boys in mother-custody homes whose parents divorced after they reached adolescence, satisfaction with the predictability of paternal visitation was strongly related to externalizing pathology.

It has also been suggested that although the frequency and predictability of visitation may not be among the most important predictors of children's postdivorce adjustment, the quality of the relationship with the noncustodial parent may still be important (Hess and Camera 1979, Koch and Lowery 1984, Simons et al. 1994). Even families where contact between the noncustodial parent and the child is minimal, the child may nevertheless consider this contact very important.

AGE OF CHILD AT TIME OF DIVORCE

Age at the time of the parental separation is an important predictor of children's psychosocial adjustment (Kalter and Rembar 1981). Hodges and Bloom (1984) reviewed the empirical literature on this predictor and concluded that parental separation during the child's preschool years (the oedipal stage) tends to be associated with regression, anxiety, and an inability to develop basic trust. They suggested that children whose parents divorced when the children had reached latency or adolescence were less likely to experience significant adjustment difficulties.

Other studies, however, have suggested that there are qualitative differences in the problems experienced by boys and girls whose parents separated during each of these three different life stages (Kalter and Rembar 1981). This conclusion is consistent with our recommendation to study as separate groups boys and girls whose parents divorced at each of the three different developmental stages.

Finally, it is often assumed erroneously that young adults are not affected adversely by parental divorce. This is most definitely not the case (Farber 1980, Kutner 1988, Swartzman-Schatman and Schinke 1993). A child whose parents separate shortly after he or she goes off to college is often shocked. Such children may feel guilty because they believe that their parents lived unhappily for some time in order to maintain the illusion of a happy family just for them. College student personnel administrators would be well advised to provide counseling or support groups for students who find themselves in this situation.

GENDER

The majority of empirical studies suggest that the adverse impact of parental divorce tends to be greater for boys than for girls (Emery 1982, Guidubaldi et al. 1983, Hodges and Bloom 1984). Other studies support the opposite conclusion (Forehand et al. 1988, Furstenberg and Allison 1985, Santrock and Warshak 1979, Santrock et al. 1982a). Still other studies indicate no significant differences in postdivorce psychosocial adjustment between females and males (Acock and Kiecolt 1989, Kinard and Reinherz 1984).

It seems clear that the effects of divorce tend to be different for boys and girls. Whereas boys tend to manifest highly recognizable aggressive and acting-out behaviors in response to divorce, girls respond with internalizing pathology including anxiety, withdrawal, and depression. This means that the measures chosen to assess psychosocial adjustment are likely to have an influence on the results obtained with respect to gender differences in adjustment. In addition, the source of the data in a given study is likely to affect results. For example, if teachers are employed as the source of behavioral ratings, it is likely that boys will appear less well adjusted than girls simply because teachers are concerned with classroom order, and they notice externalizing behavior.

Another factor mediating the effect of gender is the remarriage of the custodial parent. Depending on how long after the remarriage the study data are collected, the presence of a stepfather may well have a greater negative impact on the psychosocial functioning of girls than it does on boys. These considerations suggest that clinicians working with divorcing families should carefully explore the possibility of less than optimal adjustment among females even if there are no reports of problem behaviors. This would be particularly important when a stepfather has entered the family.

FINANCES AND STRESSFUL LIFE CHANGES

When parents divorce, things change, sometimes dramatically. Family finances are likely to become strained. A custodial mother who formerly stayed at home may return to work or to school or may otherwise increase the amount of time she is away from home. The family may have to move, and the children may have to change schools—all stressful changes that may affect children directly and indirectly through their impact on the adjustment, life satisfaction, and parenting style of the custodial parent. Sandler et al. (1988) have suggested that the number of divorce-related stressful life changes experienced by a child is the most important single predictor of postdivorce adjustment. The results of the two research studies reported in this volume tend to support the importance of such changes. Stressful life changes were related negatively to adjustment measures in many of the subsamples of children of divorce; perceived adequacy of family finances was related to the adjustment measures for several subsamples as well.

SOCIAL SUPPORT

Closely related to the effect of stressful life changes are the effects of stress-buffering social supports. Research clearly indicates that the availability and utilization of social supports is related positively to the postdivorce adjustment of children (Cauce et al. 1982, Drapeau and Bouchard 1993, Farber et al. 1985, Isaacs and Leon 1986). Following parental separation, the number of social supports available to children tends to decrease. Typically, contact with paternal grandparents and other members of the family of the noncustodial father diminishes. In addition, Drapeau and Bouchard (1993) noted that custodial mothers tend to be less supportive and nurturing toward their children than they were prior to the divorce. Children may withdraw to some extent from their peers, further reducing potential sources of support.

Custodial parents also tend to lose sources of support following divorce. Friends tend to divide themselves between the two divorcing spouses. Some friends are so threatened by the prospect of divorce that they sever ties with both separating spouses. The divorcing parties may themselves sever ties with friends, either because they feel embarrassed or because they feel they have somehow failed.

Such loss of social supports is a source of stress (Kressel and Deutsch 1979, McLanahan 1981). The results of the two research studies reported here showed that the availability of social supports was an important predictor of adjustment. Thus it is important for divorcing families to maintain or enhance their social support networks. Clinicians working with divorcing couples should encourage them not to allow themselves to isolate and to take advantage of available supports for emotional support and respite care. Support groups comprising other divorced individuals appear to be particularly important since newly single adults are likely to have more in common with other divorced persons than with married couples. Among children, contact with peers from other divorced families is desirable. In particular, children whose parents have recently separated can benefit from contact with children whose parents divorced some time ago. In this way the children in the rough transition period can see firsthand that divorce is not the end of the world, and that eventually a new equilibrium will be reached. Such contact may be fostered through peer support groups for children of divorce.

FAMILY SYSTEM

Family system characteristics are clearly related to children's postdivorce adjustment. Divorce tends to disrupt family communication and reduce effective parenting behavior (Hetherington et al. 1978). Peer support groups for divorced parents and psychoeducational interventions would appear to be useful in helping divorced parents to avoid being distracted by their own issues surrounding the divorce and to focus their energies on the tasks of parenting. Family counseling may be useful in addressing specific issues that arise with respect to family adaptability and cohesion.

Divorce represents a threat to each of these dimensions. Cohesion is threatened by physical separation, resentment, and acrimony. Parents under stress may respond by becoming rigid and self-involved. This would be expected to reduce the adaptive capacity of the family. The results of the two empirical studies reported in this book showed a number of moderate relationships between family adaptability and cohesion and the outcome measures of psychosocial adjustment.

Family counseling can promote communication and make parents more aware of the impact on children of their individual responses to the immediate stresses of the divorce. Family counseling might also help to promote the development of a civil and cooperative coparenting relationship between the divorced spouses. This in turn would facilitate consistent, authoritative parenting, which has been demonstrated to be related to positive psychosocial outcomes for children.

16

RECOMMENDATIONS FOR CLINICIANS INVOLVED IN THE ASSESSMENT AND TREATMENT OF DIVORCING FAMILIES

THE EXISTING LITERATURE and the results of the investigations reported in the present volume make it possible to provide clinicians with some very specific guidelines to follow when assessing and treating families in the process of divorce. These guidelines pertain to (1) the level and nature of conflict between the parents, (2) the psychological adjustment of the custodial and noncustodial parent and the stepparent(s), (3) the parenting styles and capacities of the custodial and noncustodial parent and the stepparent(s), (4) the stressful life changes associated with the divorce, (5) the supports available to help cope with the stresses of divorce, and (6) the nature of the adjustment difficulties experienced by children. In this chapter recommendations for clinicians are made with respect to each of these areas within the two major headings of assessment and intervention.

ASSESSMENT

Parental Conflict

It is clear that the level of conflict between divorcing spouses is one of the most important predictors of the postdivorce adjustment of children. Therefore, the clinician working with divorcing families must make a careful assessment of the frequency, intensity, and nature of such conflict. This is a difficult and complicated task, because divorcing spouses are not always accurate in their descriptions of the conflict they have experienced for a number of reasons: when one party is extremely bitter about being abandoned or thrown over for another partner, the bitter spouse may downplay his or her feelings of anger and resentment to avoid giving the other party the satisfaction of knowing how devastating the loss has been. On the other hand, the same bitter spouse may exaggerate the extent of the conflict experienced and the resulting bitterness to induce guilt in the partner who initiated the separation, to attempt to alienate the child(ren) from the offending partner, or to bolster one's legal position in disputes over custody and visitation.

Thus the clinician must be specific when inquiring into conflict. The worker must be careful to differentiate between the various forms that conflict can take. How does each spouse feel about the other? If either or both are angry, just how angry are they? Are they angry enough that everything proposed by one party is automatically rejected as unreasonable by the other? Are they angry enough to initiate litigation to resolve disputes rather than engage in mediation? Are they angry enough to act out with verbal or physical aggression?

Where acts of verbal or physical aggression have occurred, it is crucial to determine exactly what has transpired, the frequency of angry exchanges and aggressive episodes, the circumstances under which these behaviors were elicited, and the spouses' perceptions of the likelihood that such episodes will occur again. It goes without saying that each spouse's perceptions of such incidents should be assessed, first with the clinician speaking separately to each and then again with the two spouses together. The separate assessment will avoid one spouse being intimidated by the other and therefore minimizing the report. The joint assessment will provide each spouse with a reality check on their individual perceptions of what has happened.

Specificity in questioning is crucial to avoid the tendency of spouses who have engaged in violent conflict to deny or minimize the seriousness of what has happened. Men and women who have allowed themselves to lose control will likely be embarrassed by their actions. They may tend to distort what they actually did, and their ability to distort their perceptions is likely to be augmented by the anger they were feeling at the time. Thus, the clinician must be prepared to ask, for example, "Exactly what names did you call her?" "Exactly what did you throw at him and how hard?" "Did you have a cut or bruise as a result of this action?"

It is critical to determine whether and how often angry verbal exchanges, insults, and instances of physical aggression occurred in front of or within earshot of the child(ren). It is also extremely important to assess the child's perceptions of the nature, extensiveness, and severity of parental conflict. An angry verbal exchange, which may not be particularly threatening to either spouse, could be terrifying to a child. When divorcing spouses exchange angry insults or make references to each other's past indiscretions or failures, they may simply be ventilating their emotions, but making negative information available to a child can lead to the complete destruction of the child's prior conception of the parent. The observation of actual instances of physical aggression between one's parents can be extremely traumatic to children.

The assessment of parental conflict is also important from the point of view of avoiding the situation in which a child feels compelled to become aligned with one parent (usually the custodial parent) and to reject the other. Wallerstein and Kelly (1980) defined such an alignment as "a divorce-specific relationship that occurs when a parent and one or more children join in a vigorous attack on the other parent" (p. 77). They argued that such alignments are typically fueled by an angry parent who feels betrayed and abandoned, particularly when the spouse has left to be with a new partner. In this situation the angry rejected spouse and the child may develop a shared and mutually reinforcing moral outrage regarding the behavior of the departing parent that may develop into an "organized strategy aimed at harassing the former spouse and sometimes at shaming him or her into returning to the marriage . . . the unspoken agenda was revenge" (Wallerstein and Kelly 1980, p. 78).

Wallerstein and Kelly reported that in their sample most of the children who became so aligned were in the age range from 9 to 12, and that twice as many children aligned with their mothers as with their fathers. These children were assessed clinically as being less well adjusted than children who did not become aligned in this manner. The mothers of these children were described as disturbed, angry women who appeared to be using their child's allegiance in an effort to defend against their own depression.

Gardner (1989) used the term *parent alienation syndrome* to describe "a disturbance in which children are preoccupied with deprecation and criticism of a parent—denigration that is unjustified and/or exaggerated" (p. 266). Such children tend to "blindly accept the allegations of the loved parent against the hated parent" (Ackerman 1995, p. 75). Often the hatred of such children extends to the child's grandparents, aunts, uncles, and any close friends of the hated parent. They may fail to acknowledge greeting cards, refuse presents, or hang up on telephone calls from such individuals. This appears to represent an effort on the part of the child to avoid the cognitive dissonance associated with the fact that other individuals do not necessarily share the child's negative view of the hated parent.

Children drawn into the parental alienation syndrome are likely to express a desire not to visit the hated parent and may refuse to visit altogether. The clinician working with divorcing families must seek to avoid such alignments. The assessment of conflict between the divorcing spouses is critical to this objective because it has been shown that the intensity and longevity of postseparation parental disputes is an important predictor of the emergence of the parental alienation syndrome (Johnston 1993). It is particularly important to assess for any behaviors on the part of one parent that criticize and denigrate the other, whether these behaviors occur in the course of arguments between the two spouses or in other venues.

According to Gardner (1989), such criticism on the part of the loved parent may reach the point where it becomes delusional. He suggests that such mothers may complain so much about the lack of financial support from the father that the children may actually develop a fear of going without food, clothing, and shelter. Such fears will of course have the effect of increasing the child's antipathy toward the noncustodial father. Mothers who conform to this pattern will also exaggerate any minor problems of the father. They may describe a husband who is a social drinker as an alcoholic, or a father who moved out of the marital residence as having "abandoned" the family. Gardner pointed out that when the "brainwashing" of such an angry mother reaches the delusional level, she may actually pretend to have been verbally abused or physically assaulted, when in fact no such abuse occurred. Thus it is patently clear that the clinician must be extremely careful in assessing the level of parental conflict involved in divorcing couples.

Moreover, the clinician should be aware that the means through which the alienation of a parent is effected can be incredibly subtle. When the hated noncustodial father begins to feel that his child is rejecting him, he may redouble his efforts to contact and maintain communication with the child. In this situation the loved custodial mother with whom the child is aligned is likely to interpret these efforts at maintaining contact as "harassment," and may suggest to the child that dad's nightly telephone calls are "disruptive." She may interfere with such phone contacts by saying that the child needs to do homework or see some special television program (Ackerman 1995, p. 76).

Another technique employed by such mothers is to move a great distance away from the father or make it as difficult as possible for the father to reside near his children. According to Ackerman (1995), "[T]hese mothers are much less loving of their children than their actions would indicate, because a loving parent appreciates the importance of a relationship with the noncustodial parent" (p. 76).

The reason for alerting the clinician to the need to assess for the possibility of conflict reflecting the presence of the parental alienation syndrome is that, contrary to what one might expect, the syndrome is rather common. In their low-conflict sample of divorcing families, Wallerstein and Kelly (1980) found that nearly 20 percent of the children aligned with one parent against the other. In high-conflict samples estimates of the proportion of children manifesting parental alienation syndrome has ranged from approximately one-third (Johnston 1993) to nine-tenths (Gardner 1992). The issue of parental alignment and alienation is also related to the next domain discussed in this chapter, the psychological adjustment of the custodial parent.

Psychological Adjustment of Custodial and Noncustodial Parents and Stepparent(s)

Clinicians working with divorcing families must assess the psychological adjustment of all those who may have a role in parenting. This includes the custodial and noncustodial parents and any stepparents. In cases in which a custodial mother relies heavily on her own parents or other relatives for child care, the latter should be assessed as well, and the clinician should become familiar with the family dynamics governing the relationships among parents, children, and other relatives. The literature is clear that the psychological adjustment of the custodial parent is a major predictor of the adjustment of the child (Guidubaldi and Perry 1985, Kline et al. 1988, Kurdek and Berg 1983, Wallerstein and Kelly 1980). There are many reasons for this. One has to do with the possible development of parental alienation syndrome, referred to above. Custodial parents who seek to have their child(ren) align with them in opposition to the noncustodial parent are bitter and angry to the point of becoming delusional, and the children who get caught up in this syndrome have been shown to be less well adjusted than children who are able to avoid such alignment (Wallerstein and Kelly 1980).

Custodial mothers are also frequently depressed and anxious, and may perceive themselves as failures for having allowed their marriages to fail. They may withdraw socially because they feel embarrassed, thus placing great emphasis on their children's companionship. This may result in a tendency to treat the children more like adult friends or confidants than like children. The development of such a relationship between a mother and child may place a great burden on the child to assume responsibility and to act maturely. It may have the effect of taking all the fun out of life for the child. Additionally, if the custodial parent is unduly concerned about possible financial stresses or other significant life changes following a marital separation, the parent's anxiety may be picked up by the child. Kline and his associates (1988) reported significant relationships between the measured anxiety and depression of custodial mothers during the year following the divorce and the psychosocial adjustment of children two years later.

Another way in which the psychological adjustment of a custodial parent can influence a child's adjustment is through the negative effect of psychopathology on one's parenting skills (Bray and Hetherington 1993, Guidubaldi et al. 1986, Heath and Lynch 1988, Hetherington and Clingempeel 1992, Lempers et al. 1989). A custodial parent who becomes chronically disorganized is not likely to provide sufficient structure for a child, and a depressed custodial parent is not likely to provide sufficient stimulation. Simons and colleagues (1994) concluded that single parents tend to make few demands on children and to employ ineffective disciplinary techniques.

Given the many ways in which the psychological adjustment of the custodial parent can affect children's adjustment, it is important for the clinician to assess the adjustment of the custodial parent. One could argue, of course, that parental adjustment is important in intact as well as in divorced families, and that any clinician working with families should assess the adjustment of the parents. This is obviously true, but the issue is probably more crucial for divorced families, for two reasons. First, the divorce is a major stressful event in itself and is likely to be accompanied by other stressful events. Thus a divorcing parent is more likely than a nondivorcing parent to exhibit signs of poor psychological adjustment. Second, when the child has a custodial parent with whom he or she spends most of the time, the impact of any psychopathology displayed by the custodial parent will not be buffered by the presence of the second parent. If the child is receiving most of his or her parenting from a single individual, it is doubly important that this individual be well adjusted.

In divorced families with joint physical custody and in families in which a noncustodial parent is substantially involved in the lives of the children, it is important to assess the level of adjustment of both parents. When a stepparent or other family members are substantially involved in the parenting process, their adjustment should be assessed as well.

Since adults in crisis are not always completely candid about the degree of distress they may be experiencing, clinicians must do much more than simply ask parents how they are feeling or how well they are adjusting to the divorce. A validated scale assessing various dimensions of psychopathology should be administered, such as the SCL-90-R (Derogatis 1983). In addition, measures of subjective well-being and one's sense of personal self-efficacy would be highly useful with parents in divorcing families. The Personal Adjustment Scale of the Adjective Checklist (Gough and Heilbrun 1983) provides subscale scores for both well-being and self-efficacy. Paper and pencil instruments such as these need not take time away from therapy sessions since they can be completed by parents at home.

Substance abuse is rather common among divorcing spouses. Ongoing abuse may have been a factor in precipitating the divorce, or one or both spouses may turn to drugs or alcohol in an effort to cope with the anxiety and depression they experience in connection with the divorce. Clinicians are advised to include in their assessment batteries some brief, objective measure of substance abuse, such as the Michigan Alcohol Screening Test (MAST).

Given the differing perspectives of the parents and the children in divorcing families, it is a good idea to ask each family member individually about the adjustment of the others. Children will likely be aware of any depression or anxiety their mothers or fathers may be experiencing. It is necessary, of course, to keep inquiries in this area easy to understand and specific. One would probably not ask a young boy whether he thought his mother was feeling depressed. Rather, one might ask whether he had seen his mom or dad look sad or cry, whether the house was clean and organized, and whether he was getting to school and his various activities regularly and on time.

Parenting Styles and Capacities of Custodial and Noncustodial Parents and Stepparent(s)

Given the link between parental adjustment and parenting behavior, it makes sense for clinicians to assess the parenting styles and capabilities of all those involved in parenting. Here again, objective measures and reports of family members can be used. The Nurturing Parent (NP) Scale is a convenient twenty-two-item self-report scale based on Berne's (1961, 1966) theory of personal development. The NP scale measures how supportive, nurturing, and growth-sustaining the parent's behaviors are. The Single Parenting Questionnaire (Stolberg and Ullman 1984) measures six dimensions that concern parenting: (1) parental warmth, (2) presence of parent-imposed rules, (3) enthusiasm for parenting, (4) effectiveness of discipline/control procedure, (5) parent's problem-solving skills, and (6) availability of support systems. Again, measures of this nature can be completed by parents at home, then used to direct the clinician toward potentially relevant areas of inquiry during treatment.

An important aspect of parenting to be assessed when there are multiple adults engaged in the parenting process is the extent to which the various adults agree on the rules and regulations that children should follow. Children are likely to seize on inconsistent parenting practices to manipulate adults. For example, a young boy might complain because he is expected to help with the dishes when he is at his father's house, although not at his mom's. Also, if a child is denied some desired item by one parent, he may seek it from the other. The clinician must assess the extent to which the parents and stepparents can agree on general principles of expected behavior and cooperative discussions about what actions should be taken in specific situations.

Stressful Life Events

Stressful life events that typically accompany a divorce include financial pressure arising from the need to support an additional household. Many studies have shown that the loss of income following parental separation is one of the most powerful predictors of children's postdivorce psychosocial adjustment (Bane 1976, Colletta 1979, Desimone-Luis et al. 1979, Espenshade 1979, Hodges et al. 1979, 1984). Interestingly, perceived adequacy of family finances does not appear to be related to the adjustment of children from intact families. Hodges and his associates (1984) found that among intact families there was no relationship between parental perceptions of the adequacy of income and children's measured anxiety or depression. Among divorced families, however, parent perceptions of the adequacy of family income were related negatively to children's anxiety and depression.

The effects of inadequate income on children's adjustment are probably both direct and indirect. A direct effect might arise when children find themselves unable to buy the same types of articles or participate in the same activities as they could prior to the separation. If a child cannot afford the same kind of jacket his peers are wearing, it can be a major blow to his self-esteem. No longer being able to attend a favorite summer camp or having to give up regular weekend ski trips can be similarly distressing to a child. Inadequate income may also have an indirect effect on children's adjustment. A custodial mother may be so distressed by loss of income that she decompensates and becomes an ineffective parent.

Thus it is important for the clinician working with divorcing families to ascertain their financial status, determine the likely impact of loss of income on the family lifestyle, and determine the extent to which parents and children understand the necessity for changes.

Other stressful life changes that often follow upon parental separation include moving, changing schools, diminished time with the custodial parent due to new work obligations, diminished time with the noncustodial parent, loss of supports such as the relatives of the noncustodial parent, and possibly the need to adapt to a stepfamily situation. Sandler and colleagues (1988, 1990) developed the Divorce Events Schedule for Children. This scale is modeled after the Schedule of Recent Experience (SRE) of Holmes and Rahe (1967), but the events were selected as being particularly relevant to children following parental divorce. It is recommended that clinicians administer this instrument routinely to children whose parents are divorcing or have divorced. The scale will not only give an overall estimate of the amount of stress the child has experienced, but will also identify the specific stressful life events experienced, thus allowing the clinician to make inquiries about the meaning to the child of each such event.

Supports Available to Help Families Cope with Stresses Associated with Divorce

The literature on social support makes it clear that the availability and utilization of supports must be assessed when working with divorcing families. There are several reasons for this. First, it is clear from the literature that social supports can have the effect of mitigating some of the stresses associated with divorce. The availability of a relative who can provide babysitting or child care to a custodial mother may give her the freedom to work more hours or simply some "time off" from child-care responsibilities that can be used to socialize or engage in some other form of favored leisure activity. This might promote her psychological adjustment and sense of well-being, which in turn might help her be a better parent. Similarly, the availability of a sibling, relative, or peer in whom a child can confide might prove reassuring. Contact with peers whose parents have also divorced may be particularly helpful. One instrument for assessing social support is the Social Support Rating Scale (SSRS) (U.S. Department of Health, Education, and Welfare 1975). This is a ten-item scale that assesses the respondent's perception of the helpfulness of each of ten different groups of people who might be sources of support. In choosing a measure of support, it is important to keep in mind the distinctions between availability of supports, actual utilization of supports, and perceived helpfulness of these supports. Each domain should be assessed for each parent and child in the family.

Another reason to assess the availability and utilization of supports is the tendency for the number of available supports to decrease following divorce. Children whose parents divorce sometimes undergo a period during which they are somewhat isolated from their peer group (Tietjen 1982, Wyman et al. 1985). This is important, because several studies have indicated a positive relationship between peer support and psychosocial adjustment among children from divorced families (Stolberg and Garrison 1985, Wyman et al. 1985).

Parents who divorce also tend to experience a reduction in the availability of supports following the separation. In most cases divorcing spouses lose contact with their in-laws (Anspach 1976). In some cases the support received from one's own family may decrease following divorce, particularly if they do not approve of the divorce (Kitson et al. 1982). The friends of a divorcing couple tend to choose one spouse or the other (Spanier and Thompson 1984). Friends may withdraw from both of the divorcing spouses because the event of the divorce is threatening to them. The clinician working with divorcing families must determine whether losses of this type have occurred and ascertain their meaning to parents and children.

Nature of Adjustment Difficulties Experienced by Children

In attempting to assess the level of psychosocial adjustment of children from divorcing families, clinicians must keep in mind that the symptoms that emerge are different for boys and for girls. Boys are apt to respond to marital hostility, discord, and disruption by manifesting externalizing pathology—aggression, hostility, and lack of control (O'Leary and Emery 1984). In contrast, girls are likely to respond to divorce with internalizing pathology—anxiety, depression, and overcontrol.

This is an important difference because externalizing pathology is easily recognized and is not tolerated in school. If a boy is disruptive in class, the teacher will recognize that he has a problem because she has a problem with his behavior. She can't do her job if he is acting out. She is likely to write a note to his parents and set in motion the steps that may ultimately get the boy into treatment. Internalizing problems are less frequently recognized and referred. A young girl may be anxious and depressed without disturbing anyone. She may become withdrawn and silent in class. Although she is in as much pain as the acting-out boy, however, she may never get noticed by the teacher, and never referred for treatment.

It is important for the clinician working with divorcing families to assess for all types of pathology, and avoid falling into the trap of giving all of one's attention to the squeaky wheel. According to Kalter and colleagues (1985), research on children's adjustment to divorce had relied too heavily on measures of externalizing behavior problems; they suggested that these studies should also include measures of the types of difficulties experienced by girls, which they identified as depression, anxiety, somatic complaints, poor self-esteem, and poor adjustment in heterosexual relationships. The clinician working with divorcing families would be well advised to assess children in these areas on a routine basis so as not to miss problems with potentially serious effects as time goes on. Here too, the use of standardized self-report measures is recommended. Parents are not particularly reliable sources of data on the adjustment of their children because they have a vested interest in seeing the children as well adjusted, particularly when they are feeling selfish and guilty for disrupting the family constellation by getting divorced. The Youth Self-Report (Achenbach 1991) is recommended for the assessment of children's adjustment because it provides scores for children and adolescents in a number of symptom areas representing both externalizing and internalizing pathology. In addition, the clinician might want to routinely assess the self-concept of each child, using a brief self-report survey like the Rosenberg (1965) Self-Esteem Scale.

INTERVENTIONS

Parental Conflict

If conflict is detected between the separated spouses, the clinician must act in a direct and forceful manner to eliminate it, at least insofar as it affects the child(ren). We tell angry parents who cannot agree that they do not have to like each other, but they owe it to their children to act in a civil and respectful manner toward each other when they interact in the presence of the children. We explain that conflict between parents, whether married or divorced, is probably the single most important predictor of poor outcomes for children. The parents therefore have a moral responsibility to treat each other like human beings and engage in a cooperative coparenting relationship. If they are willing to try to avoid conflict but feel they may have difficulty in controlling their behavior, we immediately initiate behavioral treatment for anger management.

If either parent feels that he or she is unable to comply with the directive against displays of anger, we suggest that there is very little for them to gain by remaining in treatment together. Under these circumstances we seek to work out a fixed, inflexible visitation schedule with a provision for the children to be dropped off and picked up at some neutral location. In this manner the parents literally do not have an opportunity to act out their anger toward each other in front of the children.

When parents continue to display verbal insults or physical aggression, the fixed, inflexible visitation schedule is absolutely essential. High levels of conflict between parents is a reliable predictor of parental alienation syndrome, and the creation of difficulties surrounding visitation is one of the most effective means a custodial parent has to harass a noncustodial parent and make his or her relationship with the child(ren) a source of conflict. In addition, if one or more of the children is aligning with the preferred custodial parent against the hated noncustodial parent, it is much better that the child(ren) have no choice with respect to visitation. In this way their visits to the noncustodial parent cannot be construed by anyone as a "betrayal" of the custodial parent. In essence, fixed and inflexible visitation gets the kids off the hook in the ongoing battle between mom and dad.

When a divorce involves litigation, there is obviously a great potential for conflict to escalate. Attorneys tend to regard "winning" for their clients as their paramount objective. But the steps they must take to win are inevitably going to exacerbate the conflict between the parents. We strongly believe that clinicians should feel an obligation to convince divorcing spouses to submit their conflicts to mediation, a rapidly growing professional specialization. Mediation saves divorcing couples a tremendous amount of money on legal fees at a time when finances are likely to be strained to begin with. Furthermore, mediation is likely to result in a situation in which both parties feel there has been some give and take and the obligations they each take on are reasonable. In contrast, a litigated divorce tends to have a "winner" and a "loser," a situation likely to result in continuing resentment and hostility.

Some professional mediators are attorneys; many others are psychologists. Although the attorneys that engage in mediation tend to be a relatively enlightened group, in the absence of additional training and experience they are not likely to be experts in family processes. For this reason, when the issues requiring resolution extend beyond questions of property and finance to custody, visitation, and the delegation of parental decision-making responsibility, we recommend that the mediator be a psychologist who has had significant experience in the field of family therapy.

Children already exposed to significant conflict between their parents are likely to need treatment. When the conflict has involved physical violence, the children may even manifest the symptoms of post-traumatic stress disorder (PTSD), including night terrors and the tendency to relive violent episodes. Such children are prime candidates for dissociative disorders during the period surrounding the divorce and later in life as well.

If PTSD does not seem to be a problem, the clinician must consider the effect of these angry parental role models on the child's concept of the nature of heterosexual relationships and the appropriateness of using insults, threats, or physical force to obtain one's objectives. Children from divorced families with high levels of conflict need to be exposed to examples of families that "work." This may occur when mom and/or dad remarry, but one cannot depend on this. Age-appropriate reading materials and videos may be employed to give the children of highly conflicted parents another perspective on family relationships.

Obviously, any situation that has involved physical aggression is considered likely to recur; the clinician has an obligation to warn the potential victim(s) and take steps to ensure their safety.

Psychological Adjustment of Custodial and Noncustodial Parents and Stepparent(s)

If any of the adult figures involved in caring for the children of a divorced couple is depressed, anxious, isolated, or involved in substance abuse, the problem(s) must be treated immediately. When depression and anxiety are sufficiently serious, a consultation with a psychiatrist for appropriate medication may well be in order. This can easily be framed as a temporary measure to mitigate the difficult transitional period following the initial separation.

Cognitive behavior therapy is an effective approach to use with parents who have chosen to view the divorce as a catastrophe that signifies the end of the world as they know it. Clinicians need to adopt the challenge model of divorce, and convince their clients that the divorce is a transition with growth-producing potential as well as disruptive effects. Disorganized clients may require life skills training. Isolated clients must be directed toward social activities. Parents Without Partners and similar peer support groups for divorced individuals can be very helpful in overcoming feelings of embarrassment over the failed marriage. Such groups also provide a venue for new social interactions and examples of individuals who have survived divorce. Involvement in Twelve-Step Programs is not only helpful in recovering from substance abuse, but also provides a reason to get out and be active, and an opportunity to meet and socialize with new people.

Individuals contemplating a return to the work force following a protracted absence may well require vocational and educational counseling. Individuals who have stayed at home to care for kids may experience phobic anxiety regarding a return to the work force where they have responsibilities and where they may fail. Such individuals may benefit from systematic desensitization or gradual exposure to vocational experiences with increasingly significant demands.

Parenting Styles and Capacities of Custodial and Noncustodial Parents and Stepparent(s)

Bray and Hetherington (1993) suggested that "authoritative" parenting is associated with good psychosocial adjustment among children. Authoritative parenting is characterized by warmth, support, monitoring, and good communication between parent and child accompanied by firm, consistent control without excessive punitiveness or coerciveness.

In contrast, poor psychosocial adjustment among children has been shown to be associated with "permissive" and "authoritarian" parenting (Maccoby 1992, Maccoby and Martin 1983, Simons et al. 1994). Permissive parenting is characterized by the lack of a clearly established set of behavioral guidelines that children understand. Authoritarian parenting is characterized by strict rules and strict enforcement of the rules, but no explanation of the reasons for the rules and no opportunity for discussion or negotiation between the parent and the child. The authoritarian parent takes the position that the child will "do as I say, because I am your parent." Divorced custodial parents tend to be permissive parents (Simons et al. 1994).

However, parents can be taught why they may be too permissive with children following a divorce, and they can learn to become authoritative parents. When it appears that any of the adults involved in raising a child are not engaging in appropriate authoritative parenting, they should be exposed to parenting skills interventions emphasizing the importance of authoritative parenting and the development of authoritative parenting behaviors.

When divorced parents disagree on the appropriate way to handle a particular parenting issue, the clinician can effect a resolution by adhering to the rule that the more authoritative approach should prevail. Some divorcing couples actually sign a contract with each other in which they appoint an individual, typically the family therapist, to mediate and resolve disagreements between them regarding the appropriate parenting action to take in a particular situation. This arrangement appears to be highly desirable when parents have quite different parenting styles.

Stressful Life Changes Associated with Divorce

The clinician working with a divorcing family should communicate to the family that children's adjustment following divorce is related negatively to the number of stressful life changes. Parents should be encouraged to make as few changes as possible, at least during the first year following parental separation. If the custodial parent and child(ren) can remain in the same home, they should. When children feel that their world is disintegrating in front of them, being able to remain in the same home, the same room, the same bed, is reassuring.

In addition, remaining in the same home typically keeps children in the same school system with the same peer group, which should mitigate the tendency for children of divorce to become isolated. If the parents can afford to do so, they should also strive to continue the extracurricular activities in which the children have been participating. Such activities may be intrinsically rewarding to the child and typically provide still another set of important peer relationships. Sports activities that involve one or more adult coaches provide an additional adult figure to whom the child may turn for support and reassurance.

Furthermore, the clinician should encourage the custodial parent to maintain contact with relatives on the noncustodial parent's side of the family. These relationships are often disrupted by default, without much thought being given to what is happening. If a noncustodial father has only a limited amount of time to spend with his child, he may not wish to spend this time at family functions, during which the child will spend a significant amount of time interacting with other family members. It is extremely important to maintain these relationships, however, not only because they provide valuable social support, but also because they demonstrate that there is a group of people who love the noncustodial parent and hold him or her in high regard. The child's continuing exposure to such a set of individuals will go a long way toward preventing the child from viewing the noncustodial parent negatively and aligning with the custodial parent against the noncustodial parent.

The clinician should strive to communicate to family members that any changes are temporary disruptions to which the family will adapt. Popular books designed to explain divorce to children can be useful in getting family members to understand that the event does not really represent the end of the world.

Supports Available to Help Families Cope with Stresses Associated with Divorce

Clinicians should actively encourage the members of divorcing families to (1) expand rather than constrict their networks of available supports, and (2) take advantage of these support systems. Divorcing spouses need to be shown that the utilization of supports represents good coping behavior. They need to be disabused of thoughts that they should be able to "handle" the situation themselves. They should be encouraged to maintain existing relationships with family and friends. They should also be encouraged to make it clear to all that there is no need to take sides in the divorce or to choose between the two spouses.

Parents and children alike should be encouraged to become involved in peer support groups, which demonstrate that divorce occurs in many families and does not signify something wrong with either the divorcing spouses or their children. Peer support groups provide a forum in which parents and children can share their feelings and anxieties with others who have had similar experiences. Participation in such groups also keeps family members active and may lead to new social relationships. Finally, support groups provide participants with valuable information about how to deal with the many practical problems associated with divorce. Parents may acquire information about a good day care center, a good therapist or tutor, a desirable after-school activity for children, a potential employment opportunity.

Teachers and school guidance counselors represent potentially valuable supports. Clinicians should encourage divorcing spouses to inform school personnel of the divorce so they can be vigilant with respect to any difficulties that may emerge in children. If a young boy is acting out or a young girl appears depressed or anxious in school, prior knowledge of the divorce will help the teacher understand what is going on so he or she can be supportive rather than punitive. Also, teachers can be helpful by monitoring the behavior of other students who might take advantage of the situation to taunt or tease the child of divorcing parents. Depending on the child's age and the class, a teacher may initiate a discussion of divorce and the things that students in the class can do to help a peer whose parents are divorcing.

Nature of Adjustment Difficulties Experienced by Children

Clinicians are urged to be aware of the gender differences in children's responses to parental divorce. The obvious difference noted earlier in this chapter is that boys tend to display anger and aggression and girls experience internalizing pathology, poor self-esteem, and poor adjustment in heterosexual relationships. McDermott (1968) pointed out a less obvious difference between the reactions of boys and girls: boys tend to get their anger out of their systems within a year or two of the divorce. They recover and move on. In contrast, girls initially may appear to handle the divorce well, but they may experience significant difficulties in the long term.

Wallerstein (1985) reported the results of a ten-year follow-up of children of divorce who at the time of the follow-up ranged in age from 12 to 29. She found that among the women in this sample two-thirds expressed a conscious fear of marriage, despite the fact that they did plan to be married. One-third of the females were judged to be seriously conflicted with respect to heterosexual relationships. These women were reluctant to make any commitment, and tended to be involved primarily in short-term relationships.

Thus the clinician working with female children of divorce should actively explore issues of attachment, trust, and sexuality. Conflicts in these areas might not be indicated spontaneously by female children in treatment. In addition, long-term follow-ups on children treated following a parental divorce should be conducted routinely. Peer support groups that comprise other adult children of divorce can help participants to understand that their anxieties and discomfort surrounding heterosexual relationships are predictable results of their family history, and that these difficulties can be overcome.

Along the same line, clinicians are urged to include in family treatment any college-age or older children of divorcing spouses. It is often assumed that older children will understand and accept the divorce. It is also assumed that because a child resides outside the family home he or she should experience few significant divorce-related disruptions, and should therefore adjust to the divorce with relatively little difficulty. This is not the case. Older children whose parents divorce may experience a significant identity crisis when they realize that the parents whom they assumed to be happy were in fact unhappy in their marriage. Adult children may also feel guilt because they believe that their parents remained together unhappily "for the sake of the children." Adult children may also experience loyalty conflicts that manifest themselves in decisions regarding where to spend holidays and vacations. Clinicians should encourage divorcing spouses with older children to explain the divorce, to assure the children that they have no reason to feel guilty, and to indicate that they do not expect the children to have to make a choice between them.

REFERENCES

Abelsohn, D., and Saayman, G. S. (1991). Adolescent adjustment to parental divorce: an investigation from the perspective of basic dimensions of structural family therapy theory. *Family Process* 30:177–191.
Achenbach, T. M. (1966). The classification of children's psychiatric symptoms: a factor analytic study. *Psychological Monographs* 80(7):1–37.
——— (1978). The child behavior profile: I. Boys aged 6–11. *Journal of Consulting and Clinical Psychology* 46:478–488.
——— (1981). Behavioral problems and competencies reported by the parents of normal and disturbed children aged 4 through 16. *Monographs of the Society for Research in Child Development*, Serial No. 188.
——— (1991). *Manual for the Youth Self-Report and Profile*. Burlington, VT: Department of Psychiatry, University of Vermont.
Achenbach, T. M., and Edelbrock, C. (1978). The child behavior profile: II. Boys aged 12–16 and girls aged 6–11 and 12–16. *Journal of Clinical and Consulting Psychology* 47:223–233.
——— (1983). *Manual for the Child Behavior Checklist and Revised Child Behavior Profile*. Burlington, VT: Department of Psychiatry, University of Vermont.
Ackerman, M. J. (1995). *Clinician's Guide to Child Custody Evaluations*. New York: Wiley.
Acock, A. C., and Kiecolt, K. J. (1989). Is it family structure or socioeconomic status? Family structure during adolescence and adult adjustment. *Social Forces* 68(2):553–571.
Ahrons, C. R. (1980). Joint custody arrangements in the postdivorce family. *Journal of Divorce* 6:189–205.
——— (1981). Continuing co-parental relationship between divorced spouses. *American Journal of Orthopsychiatry* 51:415–428.
Ahrons, C. R., and Miller, R. B. (1993). The effect of the postdivorce relationship on paternal involvement: a longitudinal analysis. *American Journal of Orthopsychiatry* 63(3):441–448.

Ahrons, C. R., and Wallisch, L. (1987). Parenting in the binuclear family: relationships between biological and stepparents. In *Remarriage and Stepparenting: Current Research and Theory*, ed. K. Pasley and M. Ihinger-Tallman, pp. 225-256. New York: Guilford.

Allison, P. D., and Furstenberg, F. F. (1989). How marital dissolution affects children: variations by age and sex. *Developmental Psychology* 25(4):540-549.

Amato, P. R. (1987). Family processes in one-parent, stepparent, and intact families: the child's point of view. *Journal of Marriage and the Family* 49:327-337.

——— (1993). Children's adjustment to divorce: theories, hypotheses, and empirical support. *Journal of Marriage and the Family* 55:23-28.

Amato, P. R., and Keith, B. (1991a). Parental divorce and adult well-being: a meta-analysis. *Journal of Marriage and the Family* 53:43-58.

——— (1991b). Parental divorce and the well-being of children: a meta-analysis. *Psychological Bulletin* 110:26-46.

Angell, R. (1936). *The Family Encounters the Depression*. New York: Scribner's.

Anspach, D. (1976). Kinship and divorce. *Journal of Marriage and the Family* 38:323-330.

Astone, N. M., and McLanahan, S. S. (1991). Family structure, parenting practices, and high school completion. *American Sociological Review* 56:309-320.

Atkeson, B. M., Forehand, R., and Rickard, K. M. (1982). The effects of divorce on children. In *Advances in Clinical Psychology*, vol. 4, ed. B. B. Lahey and A. E. Kazadin, pp. 255-281. New York: Plenum.

Bachrach, L. L. (1975). *Marital Status and Mental Disorders: An Analytical Review*. DHEW Publication No. ADM 75-217. Washington, DC: U.S. Government Printing Office.

Baker, R. L., Mednick, B. R., and Hunt, N. A. (1987). Academic and psychological characteristics of low-birthweight adolescents. *Social Biology* 34(1-2), 94-109.

Baker, R. L., Mednick, B. R., and Reznick, C. (1984). Divorce and family instability. In *Influences on Development: A Longitudinal Perspective*, ed. R. L. Baker and B. R. Mednick, pp. 182-204. Boston: Kluwer-Nijhoff.

Bandura, A. (1965). Influences of models' reinforcement contingencies with the acquisition of imitative responses. *Journal of Personality and Social Psychology* 1:589-595.

Bane, M. J. (1976). Marital disruption and the lives of children. *Journal of Social Issues* 32(1):103-117.

Barnes, H., and Olson, D. H. (1982). Parent adolescent communication scale. In *Family Inventories*, ed. D. Olson, H. I. McCubbin, H. Barnes, et al., pp. 22-27. St. Paul, MN: Family Social Science, University of Minnesota.

——— (1985). Parent adolescent communication and the circumplex model. *Child Development* 56:438-447.

Baumrind, D. (1991). Effective parenting during the early adolescent transition. In *Family Transitions*, ed. P. A. Cowan and M. Hetherington, pp. 111-164. Hillsdale, NJ: Erlbaum.

Beavers, W. R. (1976). A theoretical basis for family evaluation. In *No Single Thread: Psychological Health in Family Systems*, ed. J. Lewis, W. Beavers, J. Gossett, and V. Phillips, pp. 299-307. New York: Brunner/Mazel.

——— (1977). *Psychotherapy and Growth: A Family Systems Perspective.* New York: Brunner/Mazel.

——— (1981). A systems model of family for family therapists. *Journal of Marriage and Family Therapy* 7:299–307.

——— (1982). Healthy, midrange, and dysfunctional families. In *Normal Family Processes,* ed. F. Walsh, pp. 112–146. New York: Guilford.

Beavers, W. R., Hampson, R. B., and Hulgus, Y. F. (1985). Commentary: the Beaver systems approach to family assessment. *Family Process* 24:398–405.

Beavers, W. R., and Voeller, M. N. (1983). Family models: comparing and contrasting the Olson Circumplex model with the Beavers systems model. *Family Process* 22:85–98.

Belle, D., ed. (1982). *Stress in Women.* Beverly Hills, CA: Sage.

Bem, S. L. (1974). The measurement of psychological androgyny. *Journal of Consulting and Clinical Psychology* 42(2):155–162.

Berg, B., and Kelly, R. (1979). The measured self-esteem of children from broken, rejected, and accepted families. *Journal of Divorce* 2:363–369.

Berman, W. H. (1985). Continued attachment after legal divorce. *Journal of Family Issues* 6:375–392.

——— (1988). The attachment bond as a unique aspect of divorce. *Journal of Family Issues* 6:333–336.

Berne, E. (1961). *Transactional Analysis in Psychotherapy.* New York: Grove.

——— (1966). *Principles of Group Treatment.* New York: Oxford University Press.

Blau, P. M. (1964). *Exchange and Power in Social Life.* New York: Wiley.

Blazer, D. (1982). Social support and mortality in an elderly community population. *American Journal of Epidemiology* 104:107–123.

Blechman, E. A. (1982). Are children with one parent at psychological risk? A methodological review. *Journal of Marriage and the Family* 44:179–195.

Block, J. H., Block, J., and Gjerde, P. F. (1986). The personality of children prior to divorce: a prospective study. *Child Development* 57:827–840.

Bloom, B. (1985). A factor analysis of self-report measures of family functioning. *Family Process* 24:225–239.

Bloom, B. L., Asher, S. J., and White, S. W. (1978). Marital disruption as a stressor: a review and analysis. *Psychological Bulletin* 85:867–894.

Bohannon, P., and Erikson, R. (1978). Stepping in. *Psychology Today,* December, pp. 53–59.

Bohannon, P., and Yahraes, H. (1979). Stepfathers as parents. In *Families Today: A Research Sampler on Families and Children,* ed. E. Corfamn, pp. 347–362. NIMH Science Monograph. Washington, DC: U.S. Government Printing Office.

Borduin, C. M., and Henggeler, S. W. (1987). Postdivorce mother-son relations of delinquent and well-adjusted adolescents. *Journal of Applied Psychology* 8:273–288.

Borrow, H. (1947). The measurement of academic adjustment. *Journal of the American Association of Collegiate Registrars* 22:274–286.

Bowen, M. (1960). The family as the unit of study and treatment. *American Journal of Orthopsychiatry* 31:40–60.

——— (1978). *Family Therapy in Clinical Practice.* New York: Jason Aronson.

Bozenzweig, H. (1976). The punishment of divorced mothers. *Journal of Sociology and Social Work* 3(3):291-310.

Braiker, H. B., and Kelley, H. H. (1979). Conflict in the development of close relationships. In *Social Exchange in Developing Relationships*, ed. R. I. Burgess and T. L. Huston, pp. 135-168. New York: Academic Press.

Brandwein, R. A., Brown, C. A., and Fox, E. M. (1976). Women and children last: divorced mothers and their families. *Nursing Digest* 10:39-43.

Braver, S. L., Wolchik, S. A., Sandler, I. N., et al. (1993). A longitudinal study of noncustodial parents: parents without children. *Journal of Family Psychology* 7(1):9-23.

Bray, J. (1988). The effects of early remarriage on children's development: preliminary analyses of the development issues in stepfamilies research project. In *The Impact of Divorce, Single-Parenting and Stepparenting on Children*, ed. E. M. Hetherington and J. Arasteh. Hillsdale, NJ: Lawrence Erlbaum.

Bray, J. H., and Hetherington, M. (1993). Families in transition: introduction and overview. *Journal of Family Psychology* 7(1):3-8.

Brown, J. H., Eichenberger, S. A., Portes, P. R., and Christensen, D. N. (1991). Family functioning factors associated with the adjustment of children of divorce. *Journal of Divorce & Remarriage* 17(1/2):81-95.

Buri, J. R., Kirchner, P., and Walsh, J. M. (1987). Family correlates of self-esteem in young American adults. *Journal of Social Psychology* 127(6):583-588.

Burnett, P. C. (1988). *Self-concept and decision-making style in college students*. Unpublished doctoral dissertation, Ohio University, Athens, OH.

Camara, K. A., and Resnick, G. (1988). Interparental conflict and cooperation: factors moderating children's postdivorce adjustment. In *Impact of Divorce, Single-Parenting, and Stepparenting on Children*, ed. E. M. Hetherington and J. D. Arasteh, pp. 169-196. Hillsdale, NJ: Erlbaum.

Campbell, A. (1981). *The Sense of Well-Being in America*. New York: McGraw-Hill.

Carnes, P. J. (1987). *Counseling Sexual Abusers*. Minneapolis: Compcare Publications.

Caspi, A., and Elder, G. H. (1988). Emergent family patterns: the intergenerational construction of problem behavior and relationships. In *Relationships within Relationships: Mutual Influences*, ed. R. A. Hinde and J. Stevenson-Hinde, pp. 218-240. New York: Oxford University Press.

Cauce, A. M., Felner, R. D., and Primavera, J. (1982). Social support in high-risk adolescents: structural components and adaptive impact. *American Journal of Community Psychology* 10(4):417-428.

Chang, P., and Dienard, A. (1982). Single-father caretakers: demographic characteristics and adjustment processes. *American Journal of Orthopsychiatry* 52:236-243.

Cherlin, A. (1978). Remarriage as an incomplete institution. *American Journal of Sociology* 84:634-650.

Cherlin, A., and McCarthy, J. (1985). Remarried couple households: data from the June 1980 current population survey. *Journal of Marriage and the Family* 47(1):23-30.

Chiriboga, D. A., Coho, A., and Stein, J. A., and Roberts, J. (1979). Divorce, stress, and social supports: a study on help-seeking behavior. *Journal of Divorce* 3:121-136.

Christensen, D. H., and Rettig, K. D. (1995). The relationship of remarriage to postdivorce co-parenting. *Journal of Divorce & Remarriage* 24(1/2):73-88.

Clarke, J. (1984). *The family types of schizophrenics, neurotics, and "normals."* Unpublished doctoral dissertation, Department of Family Social Science, University of Minnesota.

Clingempeel, W. G., and Segal, S. (1986). Stepparent-stepchild relationships and the psychological adjustment of children in stepmother and stepfather families. *Child Development* 57:474-484.

Cochrane, M., and Riley, D. (1987). Mother reports of children's social relations, antecedents, concomitants, consequences. *Sex Roles* 17:688-694.

Cochrane, R., and Robertson, A. (1975). Stress in the lives of parasuicides. *Social Psychiatry* 10:161-171.

Coddington, R. D. (1972a). The significance of life events as etiologic factors in the disease of children I: a survey of professional workers. *Journal of Psychosomatic Research* 16:7-18.

——— (1972b). The significance of life events as etiologic factors in the disease of children II: a study of a normal population. *Journal of Psychosomatic Research* 16:205-13.

Cohen, J. (1988). *Statistical Power Analysis for the Behavioral Sciences.* Hillsdale, NJ: Erlbaum.

Colletta, N. D. (1979). The impact of divorce: father absence or poverty? *Journal of Divorce* 3:27-36.

Conger, R. D., Conger, K., Elder, G. H., et al. (1992). A family process model of economic hardship and influences on adjustment of early adolescent boys. *Child Development* 63:526-541.

Coopersmith, S., and Gilbert, R. (1982). *Professional Manual: Behavioral Academic Self-Esteem.* Palo Alto, CA: Consulting Psychologist's Press.

Copeland, A. P. (1984). Child health questionnaire. Unpublished manuscript.

——— (1985). Individual differences in children's reactions to divorce. *Journal of Clinical Child Psychology* 14(1):11-19.

Copeland, A. P., Eisenstein, J. L., and Reiner, E. M. (1984). Relationships between mothers' and children's post-separation adjustment. Paper presented at the meeting of the American Psychological Association, Toronto, August.

Couch, A., and Keniston, K. (1960). Yeasayers & naysayers: agreeing response set as a personality variable. *Journal of Abnormal and Social Psychology* 60(2):151-173.

Crosbie-Burnett, M. (1984). The centrality of the step relationship: a challenge to theory and practice. *Family Relations* 33:459-463.

——— (1988). *Impact of joint versus sole custody, sex of adolescent, and quality of coparental relationship on adjustment of adolescents in remarried families.* Paper presented at the annual meeting of the American Orthopsychiatric Association, San Francisco, CA, August.

Crowne, D. P., and Marlowe, D. (1964). *The Approval Motive.* New York: Wiley.

Darlington, R. B., and Carlson, P. M. (1987). *Behavioral Statistics: Logic & Methods.* New York: Macmillan.

Davis, J. A. (1982). *General Social Surveys, 1972–1982: Cumulative Codebook.* Chicago: National Opinion Research Center.

Davis, J. A., and Smith, T. W. (1986). *General Social Surveys, 1972–1986: Cumulative Codebook.* Chicago: National Opinion Research Center.

Decker, D. J., and Webb, J. T. (1974). Relationships of the social readjustment rating scale to psychiatric patient status, anxiety, and social desirability. *Journal of Psychosomatic Research* 18:125–130.

Demo, D. H., and Savin-Williams, R. C. (1983). Early-adolescent self-esteem as a function of social class: Rosenberg and Pearlin revisited. *American Journal of Sociology* 88:763–774.

Derogatis, L. R. (1983). *SCL-90-R: Administration, Scoring, and Procedures Manual-II.* Towson, MD: Clinical Psychometric Research.

Derogatis, L. R., Lipman, R., Rickels, K., et al. (1974). The Hopkins symptom checklist (HSCL): a self-report symptom inventory. *Behavioral Science* 19:1–12.

Derogatis, L. R., and Spencer, P. (1982). *The Brief Symptom Inventory (BSI).* Baltimore: Johns Hopkins School of Medicine.

Desimone-Luis, J., O'Mahoney, K., and Hunt, D. (1979). Children of separation and divorce: factors influencing adjustment. *Journal of Divorce* 3:37–42.

Dohrenwend, B. S., and Dohrenwend, B. P. (1974). Overview and prospects for research on stressful life events. In *Stressful Life Events,* ed. B. S. Dohrenwend and B. P. Dohrenwend. New York: Wiley.

Dornbusch, S. M., Carlsmith, J. M., Bushwall, S. J., et al. (1985). Single parents, extended households, and the control of adolescents. *Child Development* 56:326–341.

Dozier, B. S., Sollie, D. L., Stack, S. J., and Smith, T. A. (1993). The effects of postdivorce adjustment on coparenting relationships. *Journal of Divorce & Remarriage* 19(3/4):109–123.

Drapeau, S., and Bouchard, C. (1993). Support networks and adjustment among 6 to 11 year olds from maritally disrupted and intact families. *Journal of Divorce & Remarriage* 19(1/2):75–97.

Edwards, E. (1980). *Introduction to Linear Regression Analysis.* New York: Prentice-Hall.

Elder, G. H., and Liker, J. K. (1982). Hard times in women's lives: historical influences across forty years. *American Journal of Sociology* 88:241–269.

Elliot, D. S., Huizinga, D., and Ageton, S. S. (1985). *Explaining Delinquency and Drug Use.* Beverly Hills, CA: Sage.

Elliot, D. S., Huizinga, D., and Millard, S. (1989). *Multiple Problem Youth: Delinquency, Substance Use, and Mental Health Problems.* New York: Springer-Verlag.

Ellis, J. B., and Russell, C. D. (1992). Implications of divorce on reasons for living in older adolescents. *Journal of Divorce & Remarriage* 18(3/4):197–205.

Ellsworth, R. (1979). *CAAP Scale: The Measurement of Child and Adolescent Adjustment.* Roanoke, VA: Institute for Program Evaluation.

Ellwood, M. S., and Stolberg, A. L. (1991). A preliminary investigation of family influences on individual divorce adjustment systems. *Journal of Divorce & Remarriage* 15(1/2):157–174.

Emery, R. E. (1982). Interparental conflict and the children of discord and divorce. *Psychological Bulletin* 92:310–330.

——— (1985). *Comments at the conference on the impact of divorce, single parenting and stepparenting on children.* National Institute of Child Health and Human Development, National Institute of Health, Bethesda, MD, March.

——— (1988). *Marriage, Divorce, and Children's Adjustment.* Beverly Hills: Sage.

Emery, R. E., Hetherington, E. M., and DiLalla, L. F. (1985). Divorce, children, and social policy. In *Child Development Research and Social Policy,* ed. H. W. Stevenson and A. E. Sigal, pp. 189–266. Chicago: University of Chicago Press.

Emery, R. E., and O'Leary, K. D. (1982). Children's perceptions of marital discord and behavioral problems of boys and girls. *Journal of Abnormal Psychology* 10:11–24.

Epstein, N. B., Bishop, D. S., and Levin, S. (1978). The McMaster model of family functioning. *Journal of Marriage and Family Counseling* 4:19–31.

Epstein, N. B., Sigal, J. J., and Rakoff, V. (1962). *Family categories schema.* Unpublished manuscript. Family Research Group of the Department of Psychiatry, Jewish General Hospital, Montreal, Canada, in collaboration with the McGill Human Development Study.

Erikson, E. (1963). *Childhood and Society.* New York: Norton.

Espenshade, T. J. (1979). The economic consequences of divorce. *Journal of Marriage and the Family* 41:615–625.

Eysenck, H. J., and Eysenck, S. B. (1963). *Eysenck Personality Inventory.* San Diego, CA: Educational and Industrial Testing Service.

Farber, S. (1980). *Parental separation and college students' adaptation.* Unpublished doctoral dissertation, Union Graduate School, Cincinnati, OH.

Farber, S. S., Felner, R. D., and Primavera, J. (1985). Parental separation/divorce and adolescents: an examination of factors mediating adaptation. *American Journal of Community Psychology* 13(2):171–185.

Fazio, A. F. (1977). *A concurrent validational study of the NCHS General Well-Being Schedule.* (DHEW Publication No. [HRA] 78-1347.) Hyattsville, MD: National Center for Health Statistics.

Felner, R. D., Stolberg, A., and Cowen, E. L. (1975). Crisis events and school mental health referral patterns in young children. *Journal of Consulting and Clinical Psychology* 43:305–310.

Ferri, E. (1976). *Growing up in a one-parent family: a long-term study on children's development.* Windsor, UK: National Foundation for Educational Research.

Fitts, W. H. (1965). *Tennessee Self-Concept Scale.* Nashville: Counselor Recordings and Tests.

Flynn, T. (1984). Single parenthood. *The Sunday Denver Post,* "Contemporary," March 25, p. 2.

Folkman, S., and Lazarus, R. S. (1980). An analysis of coping in a middle-aged community sample. *Journal of Health and Social Behavior* 21:219–239.

——— (1988). *Manual for the Ways of Coping Questionnaire.* Palo Alto, CA: Consulting Psychologists Press.

Forehand, R., McCombs, A., Long, N., et al. (1988). Early and adolescent adjustment to recent parental divorce: the role of interparental conflict and adolescent sex as mediating variables. *Journal of Consulting and Clinical Psychology* 4:624–627.

Freud, S. (1905). *Three essays on the theory of sexuality.* Standard Edition 7:125-243.
Friedman, E. H. (1991). Bowen's theory and therapy. In *Handbook of Family Therapy,* ed. A. S. Gurman and D. P. Kniskern, pp. 134-170. New York: Brunner/Mazel.
Friedman, E. H., Utada, A., and Morrissey, M. R. (1987). Families of adolescent drug abusers are "rigid": Are these families either "disengaged" or "enmeshed" or both? *Family Process* 26:131-148.
Frith, S., and Narikawa, O. (1972). *Attitudes Toward School.* Los Angeles: Instructional Objectives Exchange.
Fulton, J. A. (1979). Parental reports of children's postdivorce adjustment. *Journal of Social Issues* 35:126-139.
Furstenberg, F. F., and Allison, P. D. (1985). *How marital dissolution affects children: variations by age and sex.* Unpublished manuscript, University of Pennsylvania, Philadelphia.
Furstenberg, F. F., Morgan, S. P., and Allison, P. D. (1987). Paternal participation in children's well-being after marital disruption. *American Sociological Review* 52:695-701.
Furstenberg, F. F., and Nord, C. W. (1985). Parenting apart: patterns of child-rearing after divorce. *Journal of Marriage and the Family* 47:893-904.
Furstenberg, F. F., Nord, C. W., Peterson, J. L., and Zill, N. (1983). The life course of children of divorce: marital disruption and parental contact. *American Sociological Review* 48:656-668.
Gardner, R. A. (1976). *Psychotherapy with Children of Divorce.* New York: Jason Aronson.
—— (1977). Children of divorce—some legal and psychological considerations. *Journal of Clinical Child Psychology* 6:3-6.
—— (1989). *Family Evaluation and Child Custody, Mediation, Arbitration, and Litigation.* Cresskill, NJ: Creative Therapeutics.
—— (1991). Joint custody is not for everyone. In *Joint Custody and Shared Parenting,* ed. J. Folberg, pp. 88-96. New York: Guilford.
—— (1992). *Parental Alienation Syndrome: A Guide for Mental Health and Legal Professionals.* Cresskill, NJ: Creative Therapeutics.
Gasser, R. D., and Taylor, C. M. (1976). Role adjustment of single parent fathers with dependent children. *The Family Coordinator* 25(4):397-401.
Gassner, S., and Murray, E. J. (1969). Dominance and conflict in the interactions between parents of normal and neurotic children. *Journal of Abnormal Psychology* 74(1):33-41.
Gately, D. W., and Schwebel, A. I. (1991). The challenge model of children's adjustment to parental divorce: explaining favorable postdivorce outcomes in children. *Journal of Family Psychology* 5(1):60-81.
Gersick, K. E. (1979). Fathers by choice: divorced men who receive custody of their children. In *Divorce and Separation: Content, Cause and Consequences,* ed. G. Levinger and O. Moles. New York: Basic Books.
Gersten, J. C., Langer, T. S., Eisenberg, J. G., and Orzek, L. (1974). Child behavior and life events. In *Stressful Life Events,* ed. B. S. Dohrenwend and B. P. Dohrenwend, pp. 68-101. New York: Wiley.

Gersten, J. C., Langer, T. S., Eisenberg, J. G., and Simcha-Fagan, S. (1977). An evaluation of the etiologic role of stressful life-change events in psychological disorders. *Journal of Health and Social Behavior* 18:228–244.

Gibbs, J. C., and Widaman, K. F. (1982). *Social Intelligence: Measuring the Development of Sociomoral Reflection.* Englewood Cliffs, NJ: Prentice-Hall.

Glenn, N. D., and Kramer, K. B. (1985). The psychological well-being of adult children of divorce. *Journal of Marriage and the Family* 47(4):905–912.

Glick, P. C. (1989). Remarried families, stepfamilies, and stepchildren: a brief demographic profile. *Family Relations* 38:24–27.

Goode, W. J. (1956). *Women in Divorce.* New York: Free Press.

Gough, H. G., and Heilbrun, A. (1983). *Adjective Checklist Manual.* Palo Alto, CA: Consulting Psychologists Press.

Grant, L. S., Smith, T. A., Sinclair, J. J., and Salts, C. J. (1993). The impact of parental divorce on college adjustment. *Journal of Divorce & Remarriage* 19(1/2):183–193.

Green, R. G. (1989). Choosing family measurement devices for practice and research: SFI and FACES III. *Social Service Review* 63:304–320.

Green, R. G., Harris, R. N., Forte, J. A., and Robinson, M. (1991). Evaluating FACES III and the Circumplex model: 2440 families. *Family Process* 30:55–73.

Green, R. G., Kolevzon, M. S., and Vosler, N. R. (1985). The Beavers-Timberlawn model of family adaptability and cohesion: separate but equal? *Family Process* 24:385–398.

Gregory, I. (1965). Anterospective data following childhood loss of a parent: II. Pathology, performance and potential among college students. *Archives of General Psychiatry* 13:110–120.

Grover, K. J., Paff-Berger, L. A., Russell, C. S., and Schumm, W. R. (1984). The Kansas marital satisfaction scale: a further brief analysis. *Psychological Reports* 54:629–630.

Guidubaldi, J., and Cleminshaw, J. (1983). *Impact of family social support on children's academic and social functioning after divorce.* Paper presented at the American Psychological Association, Toronto, August.

Guidubaldi, J., Cleminshaw, H., Perry, J., and McLaughlin, C. (1983). The impact of parental divorce on children: report of the nationwide NASP study. *School Psychology Review* 12:300–323.

Guidubaldi, J., Cleminshaw, H. K., Perry, J. D., et al. (1986). The role of selected family environment factors in postdivorce adjustment. *Applied Social Psychology Annual* 35:202–237.

Guidubaldi, J., Nastasi, B., Lightel, J., et al. (1984a). *NASP-KSU divorce study: report on grade–sex category differences.* Symposium presented at the Annual Convention of the National Association of School Psychologists, Philadelphia, August.

Guidubaldi, J., and Perry, J. D. (1984). Divorce, socioeconomic status, and children's cognitive-social competence at school entry. *American Journal of Orthopsychiatry* 54:459–468.

——— (1985). Divorce and mental health sequelae for children: a two-year follow-up of a nationwide sample. *Journal of the American Academy of Child Psychiatry* 24:531–537.

Guidubaldi, J., Perry, J. D., and Cleminshaw, H. K. (1984b). The legacy of parental divorce: a nationwide study of family status and selected mediating variables on children's academic and social competencies. In *Advances in Child Psychology, Vol. 7, The Family*, ed. B. Lahey and A. E. Kazdin, pp. 398–439. New York: Plenum.

Hampson, R. B., Beavers, W. R., and Hulgus, Y. F. (1988). Commentary: comparing the Beavers and Circumplex models of family functioning. *Family Process* 27:85–92.

Handley, S. (1985). *The experience of the latency age child in sole and joint custody: a report on a comparative study*. Doctoral dissertation, California School of Marriage and Family Therapy, Encino.

Hanson, S. (1988). Divorced fathers with custody. In *Fatherhood Today: Men's Changing Role in the Family*, ed. P. Bronstein and C. P. Cowan, pp. 171–194. New York: Wiley.

Harter, S. (1982). The perceived competence scale for children. *Child Development* 53:87–97.

Heath, P. A., and Lynch, S. (1988). A reconceptualization of the time since parental separation variable as a predictor of children's outcomes following divorce. *Journal of Divorce* 11(3/4):67–85.

Heisel, J. J., Ream, S., Ratz, R., Rappaport, M., and Coddington, R. D. (1974). The significance of life events as contributing factors in the diseases of children. III: A study of pediatric patients. *Journal of Pediatrics* 83:119–123.

Heller, K., and Swindle, R. W. (1983). Social networks, social support, and coping with stress. In *Preventive Psychology: Theory, Research, and Practice*, ed. R. D. Felner, L. A. Jason, J. N. Moritsugu, and S. S. Farber, pp. 264–280. New York: Pergamon.

Henggeler, S. W., Hanson, C. I., Borduin, C. M., and Haefele, W. F. (1985). *Factor analytically derived dimensions of family interaction*. Unpublished manuscript, Memphis State University, Memphis, TN.

Henggeler, S. W., and Tavormina, J. B. (1980). Social class and race differences in family interaction: pathological, normative, or confounding methodological factors? *Journal of Genetic Psychology* 137:211–222.

Hess, R., and Camara, K. (1979). Postdivorce family relationships as mediating factors in the consequences of divorce for children. *Journal of Social Issues* 35(4):79–92.

Hetherington, E. M. (1972). Effects of father absence on personality development in adolescent daughters. *Developmental Psychology* 7:313–326.

——— (1979a). Divorce: a child's perspective. *American Psychologist* 34:851–854.

——— (1979b). Family interaction and the social, emotional, and cognitive development of children after divorce. In *The Family: Setting Priorities*, ed. T. B. Brazelton and V. C. Vaughn, pp. 71–87. New York: Science and Medicine Publishing.

——— (1989). Coping with family transitions: winners, losers, and survivors. *Child Development* 60:1–14.

——— (1991). Presidential address: families, lies, and videotapes. *Journal of Research on Adolescence* 1(4):323–348.

―――― (1993). An overview of the Virginia longitudinal study of divorce and remarriage with a focus on early adolescence. *Journal of Family Psychology* 7(1):39–56.
Hetherington, E. M., and Clingempeel, W. G. (1992). Coping with marital transitions: a family systems perspective. *Monographs of the Society for Research in Child Development*, Serial No. 227, 57, Nos. 2–3.
Hetherington, E. M., Cox, M., and Cox, R. (1976). Divorced fathers. *Family Coordinator* 25:417–426.
―――― (1978). The aftermath of divorce. In *Mother/Child, Father/Child Relationships*, ed. J. H. Stevens and M. Mathews, pp. 110–155. Washington, DC: National Association for the Education of Young Children.
―――― (1979). Play and social interaction in children following divorce. *Journal of Social Issues* 35:26–49.
―――― (1982). Effects of divorce on parents and children. In *Nontraditional Families: Parenting and Child Development*, ed. M. Lamb, pp. 233–288. Hillsdale, NJ: Erlbaum.
―――― (1985). Long-term effects of divorce and remarriage on the adjustment of children. *Journal of the American Academy of Child Psychiatry* 24:518–530.
Heubeck, B. (1987). *Personal relationship questionnaire.* Unpublished doctoral dissertation, School of Behavioral Sciences, Macquarie University, Sydney.
Hill, J., Holembeck, G., Marlow, L., et al. (1985). Mencheal status and parent–child relations in families of seventh-grade girls. *Journal of Youth and Adolescence* 14:301–316.
Hodges, W. F. (1991). *Intervention for Children of Divorce: Custody, Access, and Psychotherapy,* 2nd ed. New York: Wiley.
Hodges, W. F., and Bloom, B. L. (1984). Parents' report of children's adjustment to marital separation: a longitudinal study. *Journal of Divorce* 8(1):33–50.
Hodges, W. F., Buchsbaum, H. K., and Tierney, C. W. (1983). Parent–child relationships and adjustment in preschool children in divorced and intact families. *Journal of Divorce* 7:43–58.
Hodges, W. F., London, J., and Colwell, J. B. (1990). Stress in parents and late elementary age children in divorced and intact families and child adjustment. *Journal of Divorce & Remarriage* 14(1):63–79.
Hodges, W. F., Tierney, C. W., and Buchsbaum, H. K. (1984). The cumulative effect of stress on preschool children of divorced and intact families. *Journal of Marriage and the Family* 46:611–617.
Hodges, W. F., Wechsler, R. C., and Ballantine, C. (1979). Divorce in the preschool child: cumulative stress. *Journal of Divorce* 3:55–67.
Holdnack, J. A. (1992). The long-term effects of parental divorce on family relationships and the effects on adult children's self concept. *Journal of Divorce & Remarriage* 18:137–155.
Holmes, T., and Rahe, R. (1967). The social readjustment rating scale. *Journal of Psychosomatic Research* 11:213–21.
Howard, T. U., and Johnson, F. C. (1985). An ecological approach to practice with single parent families. *Social Casework: The Journal of Contemporary Social Work* 66:482–489.
Hudson, W. (1982). *The Clinical Management Package.* Chicago: Dorsey.

Irving, H., Benjamin, M., and Tracme, N. (1984). Shared parenting: an empirical analysis utilizing a large Canadian data base. *Family Process* 23:561–569.
Isaacs, M. (1986). The visitation schedule and child adjustment: a three-year study. Unpublished manuscript.
——— (1988). The visitation schedule and child adjustment: a three-year study. *Family Process* 27:251–256.
Isaacs, M. B., and Leon, G. H. (1986). Social networks, divorce, and adjustment: a tale of three generations. *Journal of Divorce* 9(4):1–16.
Isaacs, M. B., Leon, G. H., and Donohue, A. M. (1985). Who are the "normal" children of divorce? *Journal of Divorce* 10:107–119.
Jacobs, J. (1986). Treatment of divorcing fathers: social and psychotherapeutic considerations. *American Journal of Psychiatry* 140:1294–1299.
Jacobson, D. S. (1987). Family type, visiting patterns, and children's behavior in the stepfamily: a linked family system. In *Remarriage and stepparenting*, ed. K. Pasley and M. Ihinger-Tallman, pp. 257–272. New York: Guilford.
Johnson, H. C. (1980). Working with stepfamilies: principles of practice. *Journal of Social Work* 50:304–308.
Johnson, S. M. (1977). *First person singular: living the Good Life Alone.* New York: Harper & Row.
Johnson, S. M., and Lobitz, C. K. (1974). The personal and marital adjustment of parents as related to observed child deviance and parenting behavior. *Journal of Abnormal Child Psychology* 2:193–207.
Johnston, J. R. (1993). Children of divorce who refuse visitation. In *Nonresidential Parenting: New Vistas in Family Living*, ed. C. Depner and J. H. Bray, pp. 109–133. Newbury Park, CA: Sage.
Johnston, J. R., Kline, M., Tschann, J. M., and Campbell, L. E. (1988). Contested custody and visitation: is joint custody and frequent access a solution? Paper presented at the annual meeting of the American Orthopsychiatric Association, San Francisco, CA, March.
Joreskog, K. G., and Sorbom, D. (1981). *LISREL User's Guide.* Chicago: International Educational Services.
Justice, B., and Duncan, D. F. (1976). Life crisis as a precursor to child abuse. *Public Health Reports* 91:110–15.
Justice, B., and Justice, R. (1979). *The Broken Taboo.* New York: Human Sciences Press.
Kafka, J. (1971). Ambiguity for individuation: a critique and reformulation of double-bind theory. *Archives of General Psychiatry* 25:232–239.
Kalter, N. (1977). Children of divorce in an outpatient psychiatric population. *American Journal of Orthopsychiatry* 47:40–51.
——— (1984). Conjoint mother–daughter treatment: a beginning phase of psychotherapy with adolescent daughters of divorce. *American Journal of Orthopsychiatry* 54:490–497.
Kalter, N., Kloner, A., Schreir, S., and Okla, K. (1989). Predictors of children's postdivorce adjustment. *American Journal of Orthopsychiatry* 59(4):605–618.
Kalter, N., and Rembar, J. (1981). The significance of a child's age at the time of parental divorce. *American Journal of Orthopsychiatry* 5(1):85–100.

Kalter, N., Riemer, B., Brickman, A., and Chen, J. W. (1985). Implications of divorce for female development. *Journal of the American Academy of Child Psychiatry* 24:538-544.

Kanner, A. D., Coyne, J. C., Schaefer, C., and Lazarus, R. S. (1981). Comparison of two modes of stress measurement: daily hassles and uplifts vs. major life events. *Journal of Behavioral Medicine* 4:1-39.

Kaslow, F., and Hyatt, R. (1982). Divorce: a potential growth experience for the extended family. *Journal of Divorce* 8:115-127.

Kelly, J. B. (1981). The visiting relationship after divorce: research findings and clinical implications. In *Children of Separation and Divorce: Management and Treatment*, ed. I. R. Stuart and L. D. Abt, pp. 338-361. New York: Van Nostrand Reinhold.

——— (1988a). Longer-term adjustment in children of divorce: converging findings and implications for practice. *Journal of Family Psychology* 2:119-140.

——— (1988b). *Custody agreements and parental interaction at final divorce*. Paper presented at the annual meeting of the American Orthopsychiatry Association, San Francisco.

Kelly, J. B., and Wallerstein, J. S. (1976). The effects of parental divorce: the experiences of the child in early latency. *American Journal of Orthopsychiatry* 46:20-32.

——— (1977). Part-time parent, part-time child: visiting after divorce. *Journal of Child Clinical Psychology* 6:51-54.

Kerr, M. (1981). Family systems theory and therapy. In *Handbook of Family Therapy*, ed. A. S. Gurman and D. P. Kniskern. New York: Brunner/Mazel.

——— (1988). Chronic anxiety and defining a self. *The Atlantic*, September.

Kerr, M., and Bowen, M. (1988). *Family Evaluation*. New York: Norton.

Keshet, J. K. (1980). From separation to stepfamily. *Journal of Family Issues* 1:455-478.

Kinard, E. M., and Reinherz, H. (1984). Marital disruption: effects on behavioral and emotional functioning in children. *Journal of Family Issues* 5:90-115.

Kitson, G. C., Moir, R., and Mason, P. (1982). Family social support in crisis: the special case of divorce. *American Journal of Orthopsychiatry* 52(1):161-165.

Klatskin, E. H. (1972). Developmental factors. In *Children of Separation and Divorce*, ed. I. R. Stuart and L. E. Abt, pp. 42-63. New York: Grossman.

Kliewer, W., and Sandler, I. N. (1993). Social competence and coping among children of divorce. *American Journal of Orthopsychiatry* 63:432-440.

Kline, M., Tschann, J. M., Johnston, J. R., and Wallerstein, J. S. (1988). *A rose by any other name: children's adjustment in joint and sole custody families*. Paper presented at the annual meeting of the American Orthopsychiatry Association, San Francisco, March.

Koch, M., and Lowery, C. (1984). Visitation and the noncustodial father. *Journal of Divorce* 8:47-65.

Kogos, J. L., and Snarey, J. (1995). Parental divorce and the moral development of adolescents. *Journal of Divorce & Remarriage* 23(3/4):177-186.

Kohlberg, L. (1963). Moral development and identification. In *Child Psychology: 62nd Yearbook of the National Society for the Study of Education*, ed. H. W. Stevenson, pp. 277-323. Chicago: University of Chicago Press.

——— (1972). The child as a moral philosopher. *Psychology Today*, September.
——— (1984). *Essays on moral development: Volume II, The Psychology of Moral Development*. New York: Harper & Row.
Kovacs, M. (1982). *The Children's Depression Inventory: a self-rated depression scale for school-aged youngsters*. Unpublished manuscript, University of Pittsburgh, Pittsburgh, PA.
Krauss, S. (1979). The crisis of divorce: growth promoting or pathogenic? *Journal of Divorce* 3(2):107–121.
Kressel, K., and Deutsch, M. (1979). A strategy for studying the differential vulnerability to the psychological consequences of stress. *Journal of Health and Social Behavior* 20:100–108.
Kulka, R. A., and Weingarten, H. (1979). The long-term effects of parental divorce in childhood on adult adjustment. *Journal of Social Issues* 35(4):50–78.
Kunz, J., and Kunz, P. R. (1995). Social support during the process of divorce: it does make a difference. *Journal of Divorce & Remarriage* 24(3/4):111–119.
Kurdek, L. A. (1981). An integrative perspective on children's postdivorce adjustment. *American Psychologist* 36(8):856–866.
Kurdek, L. A., and Berg, B. (1987). Children's beliefs about parental divorce scale: psychometric characteristics and concurrent validity. *Journal of Clinical and Consulting Psychology* 57:712–718.
Kurdek, L. A., Blisk, D., and Siesky, A. E., Jr. (1981). Correlates of children's long-term adjustment to divorce. *Developmental Psychology* 17:565–579.
Kurdek, L. A., and Siesky, A. E. (1978). Divorced single parents' perceptions of child-related problems. *Journal of Divorce & Remarriage* 1:361–370.
——— (1980). Children's perceptions of their parents' divorce. *Journal of Divorce* 3:339–379.
Kurdek, L. A., and Sinclair, R. J. (1988). Adjustment of young adolescents in two-parent nuclear, stepfather, and mother-custody families. *Journal of Consulting and Clinical Psychology* 56(1):91–96.
Kurtzman-Effrom, A. (1980). Children and divorce: help from an elementary school. *Social Casework: The Journal of Contemporary Social Work* 14:305–312.
Kutner, L. (1988). Parents and children: independence and shaken faith. *The New York Times*, December 1.
Leighton, L. A., Stollak, G. E., and Ferguson, L. R. (1971). The personal and marital adjustment of parents as related to observed child deviance and parenting behavior. *Journal of Consulting and Clinical Psychology* 36:252–256.
Lempers, J. D., Clark-Lempers, D., and Simons, R. (1989). Economic hardship, parenting and distress in adolescence. *Child Development* 60:25–39.
Leupnitz, D. A. (1979). Which aspects of divorce affect children. *Family Coordinator* 28:79–85.
——— (1982). *Child custody: a study of families after divorce*. Lexington, MA: Lexington Books.
——— (1986). A comparison of maternal, paternal, and joint custody: understanding the varieties of postdivorce family life. *Journal of Divorce* 9:1–12.
Levinger, G. (1979). A social psychological perspective on marital dissolution. In *Divorce and Separation: Conditions, Causes and Consequences*, ed. G. Levinger and O. C. Moles, pp. 37–60. New York: Basic Books.

Linehan, M., Goodstein, J., Nielson, S., and Chiles, J. (1983). Reasons for staying alive when you're thinking of killing yourself: the reasons for living inventory. *Journal of Consulting and Clinical Psychology* 51:276–286.

Lo, W. H. (1969). Aetiological factors in childhood neurosis. *British Journal of Psychiatry* 115:889–894.

Loeber, R., and LeBlanc, M. (1990). Toward a developmental criminology. In *Crime and Justice: A Review of Research: Where Are We and Where Should We Go?*, ed. M. Tonry and N. Morris, pp. 3–27. New York: Guilford.

Long, B. (1986). Parental discord vs. family structure: effects of divorce on the self-esteem of daughters. *Journal of Youth and Adolescence* 15(1):19–27.

Long, N., Forehand, R., Fauber, R., and Brody, G. H. (1987). Self-perceived and independently observed competence of young adolescents as a function of parental marital conflict and recent divorce. *Journal of Abnormal Child Psychology* 15(1):15–27.

Long, N., Slater, E., Forehand, R., and Fauber, R. (1988). Continued high or reduced interparental conflict following divorce: relation to young adolescent adjustment. *Journal of Consulting and Clinical Psychology* 56(3):467–469.

Longfellow, C. (1979). Divorce in context: its impact on children. In *Divorce and Separation: Context, Causes, and Consequences*, ed. G. Levinger and O. C. Moles, pp. 231–254. New York: Basic Books.

Love, L. R. and Kaswan, J. W. (1974). *Troubled children: their families, school, and their treatments.* New York: Wiley.

Lubin, B., (1967). *Manual for the Depression Adjective Checklists.* San Diego: Educational and Industrial Testing Service.

Maccoby, E. E. (1992). The role of parents in the socialization of children: an historical overview. *Developmental Psychology* 28:1006–1017.

Maccoby, E. E., Buchanan, C. M., Mnookin, R. H., and Dornbush, S. M. (1993). Postdivorce roles of mothers and fathers in the lives of their children. *Journal of Family Psychology* 7(1):24–38.

Maccoby, E. E., and Martin, J. A. (1983). Socialization in the context of the family: parent–child interaction. In *Handbook of Child Psychology*, ed. P. Mussen, pp. 1–101. New York: Wiley.

Maccoby, E. E., Mnookin, R., and Depner, C. (1988). *Postdivorce families: custodial arrangements compared.* Paper presented at the annual meeting of the American Orthopsychiatry Association, San Francisco, March.

MacKinnon, C. E., Stoneman, Z., and Brody, G. H. (1984). The impact of maternal employment and family form on children's sex-role stereotypes and mothers' traditional attitudes. *Journal of Divorce* 8:51–60.

Marsh, H. W., Relich, J. D., and Smith, I. D. (1983). Self-concept: the construct validity of interpretations based on the SDQ. *Journal of Personality and Social Psychology* 45:173–187.

Masheter, C. (1988). *Postdivorce relationships between ex-spouses.* Unpublished doctoral dissertation, University of Connecticut.

Masuda, M., and Holmes, T. H. (1967). Magnitude estimation of social readjustments. *Journal of Psychosomatic Research* 2:219–225.

McDermott, J. (1968). Parental divorce in early childhood. *American Psychiatrist* 15:421–427.

McKenry, P. C., and Price, S. J. (1993). Alternatives for support: life after divorce—a literature review. *Journal of Divorce & Remarriage* 15(3/4):1–19.

McLanahan, S., Wedemeyer, N., and Adelberg, T. (1981). Network structure, social support, and psychological well-being in the single-parent family. *Journal of Marriage and the Family* 43:179–189.

McNair, D., Lorr, M., and Droppleman, L. (1971). *Profile of Mood States*. San Diego: Educational and Industrial Testing Service.

Mechanic, D. (1979). Development of psychological distress among young adults. *Archives of General Psychiatry* 36:1233–1239.

——— (1980). The experience and reporting of common physical complaints. *Journal of Health and Social Behavior* 21:146–155.

Mechanic, D., and Hansell, S. (1989). Divorce, family conflict, and adolescents' well-being. *Health and Social Behavior* 30(1):105–116.

Mednick, B. R., Baker, R., Reznick, C., and Hocevar, D. (1990). Long-term effects of divorce on adolescent academic achievement. *Journal of Divorce* 13(4):69–88.

Menaghan, E. (1983). Marital stress and family transitions: a panel analysis. *Journal of Marriage and the Family* 45(2):371–386.

Miller, I. W., Epstein, N. B., Bishop, D. S., and Keitner, G. I. (1985). The McMaster family assessment device: reliability and validity. *Journal of Marital and Family Therapy* 11:345–356.

Miller, L. C. (1975). *Louisville behavioral check list manual*. Louisville, KY: University of Louisville.

Mirowsky, J., and Ross, C. E. (1986). Social patterns of distress. In *Annual Review of Sociology*, ed. R. H. Turner, 12:23–45.

Mishler, E., and Waxler, N. (1968). *Interaction in Families*. New York: Wiley.

Moos, R. H., and Moos, B. S. (1981). *Family Environment Scale Manual*. Palo Alto, CA: Consulting Psychologists Press.

Mowatt, M. (1972). Group psychotherapy for stepfathers and their wives. *Psychotherapy: Theory, Research and Practice* 9:328–331.

Muransky, J. M., and DeMarie-Dreblow, D. (1995). Differences between high school students from intact and divorced families. *Journal of Divorce & Remarriage* 23(3/4):187–196.

Mutter, A. Z., and Schliefer, N. J. (1966). The role of psychological and social factors in the onset of somatic illness in children. *Psychosomatic Medicine* 28:333–343.

Myers, J. K., Lindenthal, J. J., and Pepper, M. P. (1974). Social class, life events, and psychiatric symptoms. In *Stressful Life Events*, ed. B. S. Dohrenwend and B. P. Dohrenwend, pp. 191–206. New York: Wiley.

Nastasi, B. K. (1988). *Family and child stressors: research findings from a national sample*. Paper presented at the annual meeting of the American Orthopsychiatry Association, San Francisco.

Nelson, M., and Nelson, G. K. (1982). Problems of equity in the reconstructed family: a social exchange analysis. *Family Relations* 31:223–231.

Neubauer, P. (1960). The one-parent child and his oedipal development. *Psychoanalytic Study of the Child* 15:286–309. New York: International Universities Press.

Newcomb, M. D. (1990). Social support and personal characteristics: a developmental and interactional perspective. *Journal of Social and Clinical Psychology* 9:54–68.

Nye, F. I. (1979). Choice, exchange, and the family. In *Contemporary Theories about the Family*, ed. W. Burr, R. Hill, F. I. Nye, and I. Reiss, vol. 2, pp. 1–4. New York: Free Press.
O'Leary, K. D., and Emery, R. E. (1984). Marital discord and child behavior problems. In *Middle Childhood: Development and Dysfunction*, ed. M. D. Levine and R. P. Satz, pp. 345–364. Baltimore: University Park Press.
Olson, D. H. (1979). *New cutting points for levels of cohesion and adaptability: 1979*. St. Paul, MN: University of Minnesota.
——— (1980). *Parent-Adolescent Communication Scale*. St. Paul, MN: Family Social Science, University of Minnesota.
——— (1986). Circumplex model VII: validation studies and FACES III. *Family Process* 25:337–351.
——— (1989). Circumplex model of family systems VIII: validation studies and FACES III. *Family Process* 22:85–97.
——— (1991). Commentary: three-dimensional (3-D) Circumplex model and revised scoring of FACES-III. *Family Process* 30:74–79.
Olson, D. H., Bell, R., and Portner, J. (1978a). *FACES Manual and Item Booklet*. Minneapolis: Department of Family Social Science, University of Minnesota.
Olson, D. H., and Killorin, E. (1984). *Clinical Rating Scale for the Circumplex Model*. Department of Family Social Science, University of Minnesota.
Olson, D. H., and Lavee, Y. (1989). Family systems and family stress: a family life cycle perspective. In *Family Systems and Life Span Development*, ed. K. Kreppner and R. M. Lerner, pp. 114–138. Hillsdale, NJ: Erlbaum.
Olson, D. H., McCubbin, H., Barnes, H., et al. (1983a). *Families: What makes them work?* Beverly Hills, CA: Sage.
Olson, D. H., Portner, J., and Bell, R. (1982). *FACES II: Family Adaptability and Cohesion Evaluation Scales*. Department of Family Social Science, University of Minnesota.
Olson, D. H., Portner, J., and Lavee, Y. (1985). *FACES III: Family Adaptability and Cohesion Evaluation Scales*. St. Paul: University of Minnesota.
Olson, D. H., Russell, C., and Sprenkle, D. (1979a). Circumplex model of marital and family systems: II. Empirical studies and clinical intervention. In *Advances in Family Intervention, Assessment, and Theory*, ed. J. P. Vincent, vol. 1, pp. 218–243. Greenwich, CT: JAI Press.
——— (1983b). Circumplex model of marital and family systems: VI. Theoretical update. *Family Process* 22:69–84.
Olson, D. H., Sprenkle, D. H., and Russell, C. S. (1979b). Circumplex model of marital and family systems: I. Cohesion and adaptability dimensions, family types, and clinical applications. *Family Process* 18(1):3–28.
Olson, D. H., and Tiesel, J. (1991). *FACES II: Linear Scoring and Interpretation*. Minneapolis: Department of Family Social Science, University of Minnesota.
Oltmanns, T. F., Broderick, J. E., and O'Leary, K. D. (1977). Marital adjustment and the efficacy of behavior therapy with children. *Journal of Consulting and Clinical Psychology* 45(5):724–729.
Orthner, D., and Lewis, K. (1979). Single-father competence in childrearing. *Family Law Quarterly* 13:27–47.

Parsons, T., and Bales, R. F. (1965). *Family, Socialization and Interaction Process*. New York: Free Press.

Patterson, G. R., Reid, J. B., and Dishion, T. J. (1992). *Antisocial Boys*. Eugene, OR: Castalia.

Paykel, E. S. (1974). Life stress and psychiatric disorder. In *Stressful Life Events*, ed. B. S. Dohrenwend and B. P. Dohrenwend, pp. 135–150. New York: Wiley.

Pedro-Carrol, J. L., and Cowen, E. L. (1985). The children of divorce intervention program: an investigation of the efficacy of a school-based prevention program. *Journal of Clinical and Consulting Psychology* 53:603–611.

Peterson, A. C., and Hamburg, B. A. (1986). Adolescence: a developmental approach to problems and psychopathology. *Behavior Therapy* 17:480–499.

Pett, M. G. (1982). Correlates of children's social adjustment following divorce. *Journal of Divorce* 5(4):25–39.

Piers, E., and Harris, D. (1969). *The Piers-Harris Children's Self-Concept Scale*. Los Angeles: Western Psychological Services.

Pojman, E. (1982). *Emotional adjustment of boys in sole custody and joint custody compared with adjustment of boys in happy and unhappy marriages*. Unpublished doctoral dissertation, California Graduate Institute, Los Angeles.

Porter, B., and O'Leary, K. D. (1980). Marital discord and childhood behavior problems. *Journal of Abnormal Child Psychology* 8(3):287–295.

Portes, P. R., Haas, R. C., and Brown, J. (1991). Identifying family factors that predict children's adjustment to divorce. *Journal of Divorce* 15:87–103.

Program for Prevention Research (1991). *The Children's Coping Checklist*. Unpublished manuscript, Department of Psychology, Arizona State University, Tempe.

Propst, L. R., Pardington, A., Ostrom, R., and Watkins, P. (1986). Predictors of coping in divorced single mothers. *Journal of Divorce* 9(3):33–53.

Quay, H. C., and Peterson, D. R. (1975). *Manual for the behavior problem checklist*. Unpublished manuscript, University of Miami, Coral Gables, FL.

——— (1983a). *Revised Behavior Problem Checklist*. Unpublished manuscript, University of Miami.

——— (1983b). *Manual for the behavior problem checklist*. Unpublished manuscript, University of Miami.

Radloff, L. S. (1977). The CESD scale: a self-report depression scale for research in the general population. *Applied Psychological Measurement* 1:385–401.

Radloff, L. S., and Rae, D. S. (1979). Susceptibility and precipitating factors in depression: sex differences and similarities. *Journal of Abnormal Psychology* 88:174–181.

Raschke, H. J. (1977). The role of social participation in postseparation and postdivorce adjustment. *Journal of Divorce* 2:129–140.

Reinhard, D. W. (1977). The reaction of adolescent boys and girls to the divorce of their parents. *Journal of Clinical Child Psychology* 6:21–23.

Riley, D., and Cochrane, M. (1987). Children's relationships with non parental adults: sex-specific connections to early school success. *Sex Roles* 17:637–656.

Robinson, B. E. (1984). The contemporary American stepfather. *Family Relations* 33:381–388.

Roderick, J., Henggeler, S., and Hanson, J. C. (1986). An evaluation of the family adaptability and cohesion evaluation scales (FACES) and the Circumplex model. *Journal of Abnormal Child Psychology* 14:77–87.

Rohrlich, J. A., Ranier, R., Berg-Cross, L., and Berg-Cross, G. (1977). The effects of divorce: a research review with a developmental perspective. *Journal of Clinical Child Psychology* 6:15-20.

Rosen, R. (1977). Children of divorce: what they feel about access and other aspects of the divorce experience. *Journal of Clinical Child Psychology* 6(2):24-27.

——— (1979). Some crucial issues concerning children of divorce. *Journal of Divorce* 3(1):19-25.

Rosenberg, F. R., and Pearlin, L. I. (1978). Social class and self-esteem among children and adults. *American Journal of Sociology* 84:53-77.

Rosenberg, M. (1965). *Society and the Adolescent Self-Image*. Princeton, NJ: Princeton University Press.

——— (1979). *Conceiving the self*. New York: Basic Books.

Rosenthal, D. A., Gurney, R. M., and Moore, S. M. (1981). From trust to intimacy: a new inventory for examining Erikson's stages of psychosocial development. *Journal of Youth and Adolescence* 10:525-537.

Runyon, N., and Jackson, P. L. (1988). Divorce: its impact on children. *Perspective in Psychiatric Care* 3(4):101-105.

Russell, C. S. (1979). Circumplex model of marital and family systems III: Empirical evaluation with families. *Family Process* 18:29-45.

Rutter, M. (1970). Sex differences in response to family stress. In *The Child in His Family*, ed. E. J. Anthony and C. Koupernick. New York: Wiley.

——— (1985). Resilience in the face of adversity: protective factors and resistance to psychiatric disorder. *British Journal of Psychiatry* 147:598-611.

Sabatelli, R. M. (1984). *Marital Comparison Level Index*. Storrs, CT: University of Connecticut.

Sandler, I. N., and Block, T. B. (1979). Life stress and maladaptation of children. *American Journal of Community Psychology* 7:425-440.

Sandler, I., Wolchik, S. A., and Braver, S. L. (1984). Social support and children of divorce. In *Social Support: Theory, Research, and Application*, ed. I. G. Sarason and D. R. Sarason, pp. 67-82. The Hague, Netherlands: Maritnus Nijhoff.

——— (1988). The stressors of children's postdivorce environments. In *Children of Divorce: Empirical Perspectives on Adjustment*, ed. S. A. Wolchik and P. Karoly, pp. 111-143. New York: Gardner.

Sandler, I., Wolchik, S. A., Braver, S. L., and Fogas, B. (1986). Significant events of children of divorce: toward the assessment of a risky situation. In *Crisis Intervention with Children and Families*, ed. S. M. Auerbach and A. Stolberg, pp. 65-83. New York: Hemisphere.

——— (1990). *Stability and quality of life events and psychological symptomatology in children of divorce*. Unpublished manuscript.

Santrock, J. W. (1972). Relation of type and onset of father absence to cognitive development. *Child Development* 43:455-469.

——— (1975). Father absence, perceived maternal behavior and moral development in boys. *Child Development* 46:753-757.

Santrock, J. W., and Warshak, R. A. (1979). Father custody and social development in boys and girls. *Journal of Social Issues* 35(4):112-135.

Santrock, J. W., Warshak, R. A., and Elliott, G. L. (1982a). Social development and parent–child interaction in father-custody and stepmother families. In *Nontraditional Families*, ed. M. E. Lamb, pp. 289-314. Hillsdale, NJ: Erlbaum.

Santrock, J. W., Warshak, R. A., Lindbergh, C., and Meadows, L. (1982b). Children's and parents' observed social behavior in stepfather families. *Child Development* 53:472–480.

Sarason, I., Johnson, J., and Siegel, J. (1978). Assessing the impact of life changes: development of the life experiences survey. *Journal of Consulting and Clinical Psychology* 46:932–946.

Sarason, I. G., Levine, H. M., Basham, R. B., and Sarason, B. R. (1983). Assessing social support: the Social Support Questionnaire. *Journal of Personality and Social Psychology* 44(1):127–139.

Sarason, I. G., Sarason, B. R., Shearin, E. N., and Pierce, G. R. (1987). A brief measure of social support: practical and theoretical implications. *Journal of Social and Personal Relationships* 4:497–510.

Satir, V. (1964). *Conjoint family therapy: a guide to theory and technique.* Palo Alto, CA: Science and Behavior Books.

Schaefer, H. R., Coyne, J. C., and Lazarus, R. S. (1981). The health-related functions of social support. *Journal of Behavioral Medicine* 4(4):381–406.

Schectman, K. L., Bergen, B., Schumm, W. R., and Burgaighis, M. A. (1985). Characteristics of the Kansas marital satisfaction scale among female participants in community childbirth classes. *Psychological Reports* 56:537–538.

Schumm, W. R., Nichols, C. W., Schectman, K. L., and Grigsby, C. C. (1983). Characteristics of responses to the Kansas marital satisfaction scale in a sample of 84 married mothers. *Psychological Reports* 53:567–572.

Schumm, W. R., Scanlon, E. D., Crow, C. I., et al. (1983). Characteristics of the Kansas marital satisfaction scale on a sample of 79 married couples. *Psychological Reports* 53:583–588.

Shaver, P., and Hazan, C. (1985). *Romantic love conceptualized as an attachment process.* Paper presented at the 93rd Annual Convention of the American Psychological Association, Los Angeles, August.

Shiller, V. (1986a). Joint versus maternal custody for families with latency age boys: parent characteristics and child adjustment. *American Journal of Orthopsychiatry* 56:486–489.

——— (1986b). Loyalty conflicts and family relationships in latency age boys: a comparison of joint and maternal custody. *Journal of Divorce* 9:17–38.

Shook, N. J., and Jurich, J. (1992). Correlates of self-esteem among college offspring from divorced families: a study of gender-based differences. *Journal of Divorce & Remarriage* 18(3/4):151–176.

Simons, R. L., Lorenz, F. O., Wu, C., and Conger, R. D. (1993). Support from spouse as mediator and moderator of the impact of economic strain upon parenting. *Developmental Psychology* 29:368–381.

Simons, R. L., Whitbeck, L. B., Beamon, J., and Conger, R. D. (1994). The impact of mother's parenting, involvement by nonresidential fathers, and parental conflict on the adjustment of adolescent children. *Journal of Marriage and the Family* 56:356–374.

Skitka, L. J., and Frazier, M. (1995). Ameliorating the effects of parental divorce: Do small group interventions work? *Journal of Divorce & Remarriage* 24(3/4):159–179.

Skopin, A. R., Newman, B. M., and McKenry, P. C. (1993). Influences on the quality of stepfather–adolescent relationships: views of both family members. *Journal of Divorce* 19(3/4):181–197.

Slater, E. J., Stewart, K., and Linn, M. (1983). The effects of family disruption on adolescent males and females. *Adolescence* 18:933.

Smith, T. A. (1992). Family cohesion in remarried families. *Journal of Divorce & Remarriage* 17(1/2):49–66.

Solomon, C. R. (1995). The importance of mother–child relations in studying stepfamilies. *Journal of Divorce & Remarriage* 24(1/2):88–98.

Spanier, G. B., and Castro, R. F. (1979). Adjustment to separation and divorce: a qualitative analysis. In *Divorce and Separation*, ed. G. Levinger and O. Moles, pp. 168–183. New York: Basic Books.

Spanier, G. B., and Glick, P. C. (1981). Marital instability in the United States: some correlates and recent changes. *Family Relations* 30:329–338.

Spanier, G. B., and Thompson, L. (1984). *Parting: The Aftermath of Separation and Divorce*, Newbury Park, CA: Sage.

Spence, J. T., Helmreich, R. L., and Holahan, C. K. (1979). Negative and positive components of psychological masculinity and femininity and their relationships to self-reports of neurotic and acting out behaviors. *Journal of Personality and Social Psychology* 37(10):1673–1682.

Spielberger, C. D. (1973). *STAIC Preliminary Manual*. Palo Alto, CA: Consulting Psychologists Press.

Spielberger, C. D., Gorsuch, R., and Lushene, R. (1970). *STAI Manual for the State-Trait Anxiety Inventory*. Palo Alto, CA: Consulting Psychologists Press.

Steinberg, L., Mounts, N. S., Lamborn, S. D., and Dornbusch, S. M. (1991). Authoritative parenting and adolescent adjustment across varied ecological niches. *Journal of Research on Adolescence* 1:19–36.

Steinman, S. (1981). The experiences of children in a joint custody arrangement: a report of a study. *American Journal of Orthopsychiatry* 51:3.

Steinman, S., Zemmelman, S., and Knoblauch, T. (1985). A study of parents who sought joint custody following divorce: who reaches agreement and sustains joint custody and who returns to court. *Journal of the American Academy of Child Psychiatry* 24:554–562.

Stevenson, M. R., and Black, K. N. (1988). Parental absence and sex-role development: a meta-analysis. *Child Development* 59:795–814.

Stolberg, A. L. (1980). *Environmental Change and Psychopathology in Children of Divorce*. Paper presented at the meeting of the Southeastern Conference of Human Development, Alexandria, VA, April.

Stolberg, A. L., and Anker, J. M. (1983). Cognitive and behavioral changes in children resulting from parental divorce and consequent environmental changes. *Journal of Divorce* 7:23–41.

Stolberg, A. L., and Busch, J. (1985). A path analysis of factors predicting children's divorce adjustment. *Journal of Clinical Psychology* 14(1):49–54.

Stolberg, A. L., Camplair, C., Currier, K., and Wells, M. J. (1987). Individual, familial, and environmental determinants of children's postdivorce adjustment and maladjustment. *Journal of Divorce* 11(1):51–70.

Stolberg, A. L., and Garrison, K. M. (1985). Evaluating a primary prevention program for children of divorce. *American Journal of Community Psychology* 13:111-124.

Stolberg, A. L., and Ullman, A. (1984). Assessing dimensions of single parenting: the single parenting questionnaire. *Journal of Divorce* 8(2):31-45.

Strahan, R., and Gerbasi, K. C. (1972). Short, homogeneous versions of the Marlowe-Crowne social desirability scale. *Journal of Clinical Psychology* 28:191-193.

Studer, J. (1993). A comparison of the self-concepts of adolescents from intact, maternal custodial, and paternal custodial families. *Journal of Divorce & Remarriage* 19(1/2):219-227.

Swartzman-Schatman, B., and Schinke, S. P. (1993). The effect of mid-life divorce on late adolescent and young adult children. *Journal of Divorce & Remarriage* 19(1/2):209-218.

Szott, M. A. (1990). *Identification of factors affecting children's divorce adjustment with custodial fathers*. Unpublished doctoral dissertation, University of Chicago. Dissertation Abstracts International, 51, 1174A.

Tayler, L., Parker, G., and Roy, K. (1995). Parental divorce and its effects on the quality of intimate relationships in adulthood. *Journal of Divorce & Remarriage* 24(3/4):181-202.

Tepp, A. (1983). Divorced fathers: predictors of continued paternal involvement. *American Journal of Psychiatry* 140:1465-1469.

Thibaut, J. W., and Kelly, H. (1959). *The Social Psychology of Groups*. New York: Wiley.

Thomas, A. M., and Forehand, R. (1993). The role of paternal variables in divorced and married families: predictability of adolescent adjustment. *American Journal of Orthopsychiatry* 63(1):126-135.

Thomas, S. P. (1982). After divorce: personality factors related to the process of adjustment. *Journal of Divorce* 5(3):19-36.

Thomas, V. K., and Cierpka, M. (1989). *FACES III and FAM III: A comparison of family assessment instruments*. Presentation at the 1989 National Council on Family Relations Annual Conference, New Orleans, LA.

Tietjen, A. M. (1982). Conceptual, methodological, and theoretical problems in studying social support as a buffer against life stress. *International Journal of Behavioral Development* 5:111-130.

Toomin, M. (1974). The child of divorce. In *Therapeutic Needs of the Family: Problems, Descriptions, and Therapeutic Approaches*, ed. H. Hardy and J. Cull. Springfield, IL: Charles C Thomas.

Tuckman, J., and Regan, R. A. (1966). Intactness of the home and behavioral problems in children. *Journal of Child Psychology and Psychiatry* 7:225-233.

Ulenhuth, E. H., and Paykel, E. S. (1973). Symptom intensity and life events. *Archives of General Psychiatry* 25:473-477.

U.S. Bureau of the Census (1984). *Census of Population and Housing, 1980 (Summary Tape File 3a)*. Washington, DC: U.S. Government Printing Office.

U.S. Department of Health, Education, and Welfare (1975). *National Longitudinal Study of the High School Class of 1972: Student Questionnaire and Test Results by Sex, High School Program, Ethnic Category, and Father's Education*. Washington, DC: U.S. Government Printing Office.

U.S. Federal Register (1985). Annual Revision of the Poverty Income Guidelines 50:9517–9518.

Veevers, J. E. (1991). Traumas versus strengths: a paradigm of positive versus negative divorce outcomes. Journal of Divorce 15(1):99–126.

Velicer, W. R., Govia, J. M., Cherico, N. P., and Corriveau, D. P. (1985). Item format and the structure of the Buss-Durkee hostility inventory. Aggressive Behavior 11:65–82.

Villwock, D. (1987). Closeness in father–offspring relationships: Do differences linked to parental marital status persist in a multivariate approach? Unpublished doctoral dissertation, Purdue University, West Lafayette, IN.

Visher, E., and Visher, J. (1978). Common problems of stepparents and their spouses. American Journal of Orthopsychiatry 48:252–262.

——— (1983). Step-parenting: blending families. In Stress and the Family (Vol. I): Coping with Normative Transitions, ed. H. I. McCubbin and C. R. Figley, pp. 132–158. New York: Brunner/Mazel.

Walker, L. S., McLaughlin, F. J., and Greene, J. W. (1988). Functional illness and family functioning: a comparison of healthy and somaticizing adolescents. Family Process 27:317–325.

Wallerstein, J. S. (1977). Responses of the preschool child to divorce: those who cope. In Child Psychiatry Treatment and Research, ed. M. R. McMillan and S. Henao. New York: Brunner/Mazel.

——— (1984). Children of divorce: preliminary report of a 10-year follow-up study of young children. American Journal of Orthopsychiatry 54:444–458.

——— (1985). Children of divorce: preliminary report of a ten-year follow-up of older children and adolescents. Journal of the American Academy of Child Psychiatry 24:545–553.

——— (1988). Children after divorce: wounds that don't heal. Perspectives in Psychiatric Care 23(3,4):107–113.

——— (1989). Men, Women, and Children a Decade after Divorce. New York: Tickner & Fields.

Wallerstein, J. S., and Corbin, S. B. (1989). Daughters of divorce: report of a ten-year follow-up. American Journal of Orthopsychiatry 59:593–604.

Wallerstein, J., and Kelly, J. B. (1974). The effects of parental divorce: the adolescent experience. In The Child and his Family: Children at Psychiatric Risk, ed. E. A. Risk and C. Koupernick. New York: Wiley.

——— (1975). The effects of parental divorce: experiences of the preschool child. American Academy of Child Psychiatry 14:600–616.

——— (1976). The effects of parental divorce: experiences of the child in later latency. American Journal of Orthopsychiatry 46:256–269.

——— (1980). Surviving the Breakup: How Children and Parents Cope with Divorce. New York: Basic Books.

Warshak, R. A. (1986). Father custody and child development: a review and analysis of psychological research. Behavioral Science and the Law 4:185–202.

Warshak, R. A., and Santrock, J. W. (1983). The impact of divorce in father-custody and mother-custody homes: the child's perspective. In Children and Divorce, ed. L. A. Kurdek, pp. 90–104. San Francisco: Jossey-Bass.

Weinraub, M., and Wolf, B. M. (1983). Effects of stress and social supports on mother-child interactions in single- and two-parent families. *Child Development* 54:1297-1311.

Weinstein, S. R., Noam, G. G., Grimes, K., et al. (1990). Convergence of DSM-III diagnoses and self-reported symptoms in child and adolescent inpatients. *Journal of the American Academy of Child and Adolescent Psychiatry* 29:627-634.

Weiss, R. S. (1975). *Marital Separation.* New York: Basic Books.

——— (1976). The emotional impact of marital separation. *Journal of Social Issues* 32:135-145.

——— (1979a). *Going It Alone.* New York: Basic Books.

——— (1979b). Growing up a little faster: the experience of growing up in a single-parent household. *Journal of Social Issues* 35(4):97-111.

Weissman, M. M., and Bothwell, S. (1976). Assessment of social adjustment by patient self-report. *Archives of General Psychiatry* 33:1111-1115.

Weissman, M. M., Prushoff, B. A., Thompson, W. D., et al. (1976). *Social adjustment by self-report in a community sample and in psychiatric outpatients.* Unpublished manuscript, Yale University, New Haven, CT.

Werner, E. E. and Smith, R. S. (1982). *Vulnerable but Invincible: A Longitudinal Study of Resilient Children and Youth.* New York: McGraw-Hill.

West, S. G., Ramirez, R. R., Brown, C., et al. (1987). *Divorce education and support groups: two evaluations with inner city children. Preventive interventions for children of divorce.* Symposium conducted at the meeting of the American Psychological Association, August.

Whitehead, L. (1979). Sex differences in children's responses to family stress: a reevaluation. *Journal of Child Psychology and Psychiatry* 20:247-254.

Wolchik, S. A., Ramirez, R., Sandler, I. N., et al. (1993). Inner-city, poor children of divorce: negative divorce-related events, problematic beliefs and adjustment problems. *Journal of Divorce and Remarriage* 19(1/2):1-19.

Wolchik, S. A., Sandler, N. I., and Braver, L. S. (1989). Children's social network: measurement issue. In *Children's Social Network and Social Support,* ed. D. Bell, pp. 152-171. New York: Wiley.

Wolin, S. J., and Wolin, S. (1993). *The resilient self: how survivors of troubled families rise above adversity.* New York: Villard.

Woody, J. D., Colley, P. E., Schlegelmilch, J., et al. (1984). Child adjustment to parental stress following divorce. *Social Casework: The Journal of Contemporary Social Work,* September, pp. 405-412.

Wyman, P. A., Cowen, L. E., Hightower, A. D., and Pedro-Carol, J. L. (1985). Perceived competence, self-esteem, anxiety in latency-aged children of divorce. *Journal of Clinical Child Psychology* 14:20-26.

Zaslow, M. J. (1988). Sex differences in children's response to parental divorce: research methodology and postdivorce family forms. *American Journal of Orthopsychiatry* 58(3):355-378.

——— (1989). Sex differences in children's response to parental divorce: samples, variables, ages, and sources. *American Journal of Orthopsychiatry* 59(1):118-141.

Zill, N. (1988). Behavior, achievement, and health problems among children in stepfamilies. In *Impact of Divorce, Single Parenting, and Stepparenting on Children,* ed. E. M. Hetherington and J. D. Arasteh, pp. 324-368. Hillsdale, NJ: Erlbaum.

Zill, N., Morrison, D. R., and Coiro, M. J. (1993). Long-term effects of parental divorce on parent–child relationships, adjustment, and achievement in young adulthood. *Journal of Family Psychology* 7(1):91–103.

Zuckerman, M., and Lubin, B. (1965). *Multiple Affect Adjective Checklist.* San Diego: Edits Publishers.

INDEX

Abelson, D., 5, 7, 17, 243, 244, 245, 246
Absent father hypothesis, noncustodial parent, 91–93
Abuse. *See* Physical abuse
Achenbach, T. M., 6, 17, 54, 57, 63, 183, 198, 215, 241, 244, 273, 274, 321, 351
Ackerman, M. J., 343, 345
Acock, A. C., 27, 73, 74, 75, 80, 145, 155, 156, 180, 182, 183, 185, 259, 337
Adolescents
 child's age level, 115–117
 Research Study I results (original analysis), 284–285, 290–292
 Research Study II results, 325–330
Adult child, child's age level, 142–144
Age level, of child, 108–144. *See also* Child's age level
Ahrons, C. R., 35, 50, 85
Allison, P. D., 108, 121, 126, 127, 128, 129, 130, 131, 132, 145, 152, 153, 165, 177, 257, 337
Amato, P. R., 9, 14, 77, 78, 79, 80, 81, 82, 84, 92, 101
Angell, R., 229
Anker, J. M., 202
Anspach, D., 202, 203, 350
Assessment, clinician recommendations, 341–351. *See also* Clinician recommendations

Astone, N. M., 65
Atkeson, B. M., 23, 34
Bachrach, L. L., 182
Baker, R. L., 27, 146
Bales, R. F., 42
Bandura, A., 42
Bane, M. J., 181, 260, 348
Barnes, H., 232, 233, 234, 235, 236, 237
Baumrind, D., 69
Beavers, W. R., 220, 223, 224, 228, 229, 230, 231, 232, 263
Belle, D., 218
Bem, S. L., 14, 41
Berg, B., 27, 52, 145, 154, 199, 259, 334, 345
Berman, W. H., 37
Berne, E., 63, 348
Black, K. N., 14
Blau, P. M., 94
Blazer, D., 276
Blechman, E. A., 185
Block, J. H., 23
Block, T. B., 186, 187, 260, 276
Bloom, B. L., 108, 110, 111, 112, 116, 138, 139, 141, 145, 147, 148, 178, 180, 240, 337
Bohannon, P., 14, 89
Borduin, C. M., 108, 121, 122, 123, 124, 125, 126

Borrow, H., 119
Bothwell, S., 54
Bouchard, C., 200, 201, 203, 262, 339
Bowen, M., 16, 17, 229
Bozenzweig, H., 182
Braiker, H. B., 12
Brandwein, R. A., 182, 205
Braver, S. L., 94, 95, 96, 97, 287
Bray, J. H., 17, 64, 72, 346, 354
Brown, J. H., 246, 247, 248
Burnett, P. C., 75
Busch, J., 56, 260

Camara, K. A., 6, 17, 93, 98, 102, 201, 336
Campbell, A., 185
Carlson, P. M., 133
Carnes, P. J., 222
Caspi, A., 36
Castro, R. F., 200, 203, 204
Cauce, A. M., 200, 207, 208, 209, 210, 211, 212, 262, 339
Challenge model, of divorce, psychosocial adjustment of children to, 10–13, 17
Chang, P., 43
Cherlin, A., 70
Children
  gender differences, 145–177. *See also* Gender differences
  psychosocial adjustment of
    custodial parent adjustment and, 64–69
    to divorce, 1–20. *See also* Divorce
    parental conflict and, 21–23. *See also* Parental conflict
    to remarriage of custodial mother, 86–89
    relationship with noncustodial parent, 102–107
    predictive model, 256–257
    social support
      decrements, 201–203
      psychological adjustment, 206–213
Child's age level, 108–144
  adolescents, 115–117
  adult child, 142–144
  child adjustment and, short- and long-term effects, 109–110

conclusions, 337
gender differences and, 134–142
latency-aged children, 112–115
outcomes, 117–134
  early ages, 117–121
  later ages, 121–134
overview, 108–109
predictive model, 257–259
preschool children, 110–112
Chiriboga, D. A., 200
Christensen, D. H., 85, 86
Cierpka, M., 224
Clarke, J., 222
Cleminshaw, H. K., 201
Clingempeel, W. G., 65, 98, 255, 256, 346
Clinician recommendations, 341–358
  assessment, 341–351
    child's adjustment difficulties, 350–351
    parental conflict, 341–345
    parenting styles, 347–348
    parent psychosocial adjustment, 345–347
    social supports, 349–350
    stress, 348–349
  interventions, 352–358
    child's adjustment difficulties, 357–358
    parental conflict, 352–353
    parental psychosocial adjustment, 354
    parenting behavior, 354–355
    social support, 356–357
    stress, 355–356
Cochrane, M., 202, 203
Cochrane, R., 186
Coddington, R. D., 186, 187
Cohen, J., 151, 271
Colletta, N. D., 181, 348
Conflict
  defined, xiii–xiv
  parental, 21–30. *See also* Parental conflict
  parental conflict mediation, noncustodial parent, 94–98
Conger, R. D., 36
Coopersmith, S., 8

Copeland, A. P., 56, 57, 58
Corbin, S. B., 181, 261
Cowen, E. L., 202
Critical stage theory, child's age level, child adjustment and, 109
Crosbie-Burnett, M., 16, 17, 72, 76
Crowne, D. P., 276
Cumulative effect hypothesis, child's age level, child adjustment and, 109
Custodial arrangements, 40–51
　conclusions about, 333–334
　custodial fathers, research on, 42–43
　gender differences, literature review (Zaslow), 169–171
　historical perspective, 40–42
　joint custody, 49–51
　mother-custody/father-custody comparisons, 43–49
　predictive model, 253–254
Custodial parent. See also Father-custody; Mother-custody; Noncustodial parent
　psychosocial adjustment of, 52–69
　　clinician recommendations, 345–347
　　conclusions about, 334–335
　　fathers, 62–64
　　mothers, 53–59
　　mothers and fathers, 59–62
　　overview, 52–53
　　parenting behavior and child adjustment, 64–69
　　predictive model, 254–255
　　Research Study I results (original analysis), 282–284
　remarriage of, 70–90. See also Remarriage
　　conclusions, 335–336
　　predictive model, 255–256
　　Research Study I results (separately analyzed), 309–311
　substance abuse by, Research Study I results (separately analyzed), 296–298

Darlington, R. B., 133
Davis, J. A., 73, 149
Decker, D. J., 186

DeMarie-Dreblow, D., 1, 12
Demo, D. H., 180, 260
Depression, of mother-custody, Research Study I results (separately analyzed), 294–296
Derogatis, L. R., 54, 67, 215, 240, 241, 347
Desimone-Luis, J., 73, 181, 348
Deutsch, M., 205, 339
Dienard, A., 43
Disaster theory, of divorce, 2–10
Dishion, T. J., 36
Divorce
　age level of child at, 108–144. See also Child's age level
　child's gender differences, 145–177. See also Gender differences
　psychosocial adjustment of children to, 1–20
　　as challenge, 10–13
　　disaster theory, 2–10
　　overview, 1–2
　　positive outcomes, 14–15
　　postdivorce adjustment correlates, 15–20
　remarriage and, 70–90. See also Remarriage
Dohrenwend, B. P., 187
Dohrenwend, B. S., 187
Dornbusch, S. M., 80
Dozier, B. S., 23, 37, 38, 39
Drapeau, S., 200, 201, 203, 262, 339
Duncan, D. F., 186

Economic distress model, described, 179–185
Edelbrock, C., 6, 17, 54, 57, 63, 183, 198, 215, 244
Edwards, E., 271
Elder, G. H., 27, 36, 73, 180
Elliot, D. S., 66
Ellis, J. B., 108, 117, 118, 121, 257
Ellsworth, R., 59
Ellwood, M. S., 240, 241, 242, 243
Emery, R. E., 2, 12, 15, 16, 22, 23, 34, 108, 121, 126, 145, 147, 164, 165, 171, 172, 173, 248, 259, 337, 351
Erikson, E. H., 113

Erikson, R., 14
Espenshade, T. J., 181, 260, 348
Eysenck, H. J., 122
Eysenck, S. B., 122

Family systems, 219–249
  conclusions about, 339–340
  overview, 219–220
  predictive model, 262–264
  psychosocial adjustment and, 232–249
  remarriage and, 77–86
  Research Study I results (original analysis), 286–287
  Research Study I results (separately analyzed), 314–317
  theories, 220–232
Farber, S. S., 109, 142, 191, 200, 211, 212, 213, 240, 262, 337, 339
Father-absence hypothesis, noncustodial parent, 91–93
Father-custody. *See also* Custodial parent; Mother-custody; Non-custodial parent
  mother-custody compared, 43–49
  psychosocial adjustment of father, 62–64
  psychosocial adjustment of mother and father, 53–59
  research on, 42–43
Fazio, A. F., 60
Felner, R. D., 114
Ferri, E., 23
Fitts, W. H., 212
Flynn, T., 179
Folkman, S., 58, 213
Forehand, R., 23, 26, 27, 29, 36, 98, 102, 145, 154, 155, 257, 333, 336, 337
Frazier, M., 1, 8
Freud, S., 42
Friedman, E. H., 16, 228
Frith, S., 207
Furstenberg, F. F., 65, 108, 121, 126, 127, 128, 129, 130, 131, 132, 145, 152, 153, 165, 177, 257, 259, 336, 337

Gardner, R. A., 50, 108, 109, 110, 343, 344, 345
Garrison, K. M., 202, 350

Gasser, R. D., 42, 62, 333
Gassner, S., 21
Gately, D. W., 1, 12, 13, 14, 18
Gender differences, 145–177
  child's age level and, 134–142
  conclusions about, 337–338
  literature review (Zaslow), 166–177
    adjustment reaction timing, 175–176
    criteria selection, 173–175
    custody and remarriage, 169–171
    data sources, 176–177
    methodological rigor, 167–169
    population samples, 171–172
  no effect, 154–156
  overview, 145–146
  predictive model, 259–260
  qualitative differences, 157–166
  Research Study I results (original analysis), 285
  worse for boys, 146–148
  worse for girls, 148–154
Gerbasi, K. C., 277
Gersick, K. E., 42, 62, 333
Gersten, J. C., 186
Gibbs, J. C., 14
Gilbert, R., 8
Glenn, N. D., 148, 149, 150, 151
Glick, P. C., 70
Goode, W. J., 204
Gough, H. G., 62, 347
Grant, L. S., 108, 117, 119, 120, 257
Green, R. G., 220, 222, 223, 224, 225, 226, 227, 228
Gregory, I., 145
Guidubaldi, J., 1, 5, 17, 18, 52, 53, 65, 93, 94, 145, 165, 167, 201, 248, 255, 259, 334, 337, 345, 346

Hampson, R. B., 223
Handley, S., 49
Hansell, S., 22, 23, 29, 30, 31, 252, 333
Hanson, S., 41, 42, 333
Harris, D., 63
Harter, S., 27, 33, 57
Hazan, C., 12
Heath, P. A., 65, 255, 346
Heilbrun, A., 62, 347

Heisel, J. J., 186
Heller, K., 211
Henggeler, S. W., 108, 121, 122, 123, 124, 125, 126
Hess, R., 17, 93, 98, 102, 201, 336
Hetherington, E. M., 1, 5, 6, 14, 17, 18, 22, 27, 35, 45, 61, 64, 65, 69, 70, 71, 72, 76, 84, 86, 87, 88, 91, 92, 93, 108, 117, 119, 141, 145, 146, 147, 161, 162, 163, 164, 165, 169, 170, 174, 175, 179, 180, 201, 202, 203, 218, 219, 255, 256, 259, 333, 335, 336, 339, 346, 354
Heubeck, B., 12
Hill, J., 84
Hodges, W. F., 108, 110, 111, 112, 116, 138, 139, 141, 145, 147, 148, 167, 179, 181, 189, 190, 260, 261, 337, 348
Holdnack, J. A., 237, 238, 239
Holmbeck, G., 84
Holmes, T. H., 178, 185, 186, 349
Howard, T. U., 1, 2
Hudson, W., 225
Hyatt, R., 18

Interventions, clinician recommendations, 352–358. *See also* Clinician recommendations
Irving, H., 50
Isaacs, M. B., 1, 5, 6, 7, 8, 35, 200, 202, 203, 213, 214, 216, 217, 262, 339

Jackson, P. L., 108, 110, 111, 112, 113, 114, 115, 116
Jacobs, J., 92
Jacobson, D. S., 98, 256
Johnson, F. C., 1, 2
Johnson, H. C., 70
Johnson, S. M., 22, 204
Johnston, J. R., 16, 344
Joint custody, research on, 49–51
Joreskog, K. G., 128
Jurich, J., 93, 98, 99, 146, 160, 161, 180, 257, 260, 336
Justice, B., 186

Kafka, J., 229
Kalter, N., 53, 54, 55, 56, 57, 93, 108, 109, 114, 116, 134, 136, 137, 138, 142, 146, 148, 157, 158, 159, 160, 161, 171, 172, 173, 174, 183, 184, 193, 194, 201, 254, 256, 259, 334, 336, 337, 351
Kaslow, F., 18
Kaswan, J. W., 21
Keith, B., 9
Kelley, H. H., 12, 94
Kelly, J. B., 1, 2, 3, 4, 17, 18, 22, 35, 49, 52, 53, 89, 91, 92, 93, 98, 109, 110, 112, 113, 115, 116, 141, 154, 169, 188, 192, 201, 219, 248, 256, 334, 336, 343, 345
Kelly, R., 27
Kerr, M., 2, 16
Keshet, J. K., 71, 335
Kiecolt, K. J., 27, 73, 74, 75, 80, 145, 155, 156, 180, 182, 183, 185, 259, 337
Killorin, E., 222
Kinard, E. M., 145, 259, 337
Kitson, G. C., 203, 350
Klatskin, E. H., 112
Kliewer, W., 18
Kline, M., 49, 52, 334, 345
Koch, M., 35, 102, 336
Kogos, J. L., 1, 14, 15
Kohlberg, L., 14, 113
Kovacs, M., 8, 54, 183
Kramer, K. B., 148, 149, 150, 151
Krauss, S., 10
Kressel, K., 205, 339
Kulka, R. A., 117, 119, 145, 146, 174
Kunz, J., 205, 206, 217
Kunz, P. R., 205, 206, 217
Kurdek, L. A., 1, 10, 11, 12, 14, 18, 52, 98, 145, 154, 167, 199, 200, 256, 259, 332, 334, 345
Kurtzman-Effron, A., 202
Kutner, L., 109, 142, 337

Latency-aged children, child's age level, 112–115
Lavee, Y., 222, 224
Lazarus, R. S., 58, 213
LeBlanc, M., 68
Lempers, J. D., 65, 346
Leon, G. H., 200, 202, 203, 213, 214, 216, 217, 262, 339

Leupnitz, D. A., 23, 49, 98, 257
Levinger, G., 94
Lewis, K., 43
Liker, J. K., 27, 73, 180
Linehan, M., 118
Lo, W. H., 22
Lobitz, C. K., 22
Loeber, R., 68
Long, N., 22, 23, 24, 25, 26, 30, 32, 34, 251, 252, 333
Longfellow, C., 110
Lorenz, F. O., 36
Love, L. R., 21
Lowery, C., 35, 102, 336
Lubin, B., 58, 191, 212, 213
Lynch, S., 65, 255, 346

Maccoby, E. E., 36, 49, 50, 67, 100, 101, 254, 334, 355
MacKinnon, C. E., 14
Marlow, L., 84
Marlowe, D., 276
Marsh, H. W., 12, 47
Martin, J. A., 36, 67, 254, 355
Masheter, C., 37
Masuda, M., 186
McCarthy, J., 70
McDermott, J., 110, 148, 173, 357
McKenry, P. C., 202, 204, 205
McLanahan, S. S., 65, 182, 205, 339
McNair, D., 57
Mechanic, D., 22, 23, 29, 30, 31, 252, 333
Mednick, B. R., 184, 185, 194, 195, 196, 197, 260
Menaghan, E., 178
Miller, I. W., 223
Miller, L. C., 187
Miller, R. B., 35
Mirowsky, J., 185
Mishler, E., 229
Moos, B. S., 12, 18, 242, 263
Moos, R. H., 12, 18, 242, 263
Mother-custody. *See also* Custodial parent; Father-custody; Non-custodial parent
  father-custody compared, 43-49
  psychosocial adjustment of mother, 53-59
  psychosocial adjustment of mother and father, 53-59
  remarriage, 73-77
    child's adjustment to, 86-89
  Research Study I results (separately analyzed), depression, 294-296
Mowatt, M., 89
Multiple life stresses model, described, 185-199
Muransky, J. M., 1, 12
Murray, E. J., 21

Narikawa, O., 207
Nastasi, B. K., 92
Negative outcome prediction, parental conflict, 35-39
Nelson, G. K., 71
Nelson, M., 71
Neubauer, P., 110, 111
Newcomb, M. D., 276
Noncustodial parent, 91-107. *See also* Custodial parent; Father-custody; Mother-custody
  child's relationship with, 102-107
  clinician recommendations, 345-347
  predictive model, 256-257
  Research Study I results (original analysis), 284-285
  contact with
    conclusions about, 336
    negative outcome prediction, 35-36
    Research Study I results (separately analyzed), 304-307
  father-absence hypothesis, 91-93
  parental conflict mediation, 94-98
  visitation by, impacts of, 98-102
Nord, C. W., 65
Nye, F. I., 94

O'Leary, K. D., 12, 21, 171, 172, 173, 351
Olson, D. H., 83, 89, 220, 221, 222, 223, 224, 225, 228, 229, 230, 231, 232, 233, 234, 235, 236, 237, 244, 263, 274, 275
Oltmanns, T. F., 22
Orthner, D., 43

Parental conflict, 21-30
  among divorced couples, 23-34

child adjustment and, 21–23
clinician recommendations, assessment, 341–345
conclusions about, 332–333
interventions, clinician recommendations, 352–353
negative outcome prediction, 35–39
predictive model, 251–253
Parenting behavior
  clinician recommendations, 347–348
  interventions, 354–355
  parental conflict, negative outcome prediction, 36–39
  psychosocial adjustment of custodial parent and children, 64–69
  Research Study I results (separately analyzed), 298–302
Parsons, T., 42
Patterson, G. R., 36
Paykel, E. S., 186
Pedro-Carrol, J. L., 202
Perlin, L. I., 180, 260
Perry, J. D., 1, 5, 17, 18, 52, 53, 93, 94, 248, 334, 345
Peterson, D. R., 24, 27, 33, 36, 121
Pett, M. G., 53, 59, 60, 61, 202
Physical abuse, parental, Research Study I results (separately analyzed), 302–304
Piers, E., 63
Pojman, E., 50, 334
Porter, B., 21
Postdivorce adjustment correlates, psychosocial adjustment of children to, 15–20
Predictive model, 250–268
  child's age level, 257–259
  comprehensive, 264–265
  custodial arrangements, 253–254
  custodial parent
    psychosocial adjustment of, 254–255
    remarriage of, 255–256
  elaboration needs, 268
  family system, 262–264
  future studies, 267–268
  gender differences, 259–260

  noncustodial parent, child's relationship with, 256–257
  overview, 250
  parental conflict, 251–253
  research methodological recommendations, 265–266
  social support, 262
  stress, 260–262
Predictors, development of, xiii–xiv
Preschool children, child's age level, 110–112
Price, S. J., 202, 204, 205
Propst, L. R., 58, 213

Quay, H. C., 24, 27, 33, 36, 121

Radloff, L. S., 30, 182
Rae, D. S., 182
Rahe, R., 178, 185, 349
Raschke, H. J., 200
Recency theory, child's age level, child adjustment and, 109
Regan, R. A., 172
Reid, J. B., 36
Reinhard, D. W., 10, 167, 332
Reinherz, H., 145, 259, 337
Remarriage, 70–90
  child adjustment to custodial mother's remarriage, 86–89
  custodial mother, 73–77
  custodial parent
    conclusions, 335–336
    predictive model, 255–256
    Research Study I results (separately analyzed), 309–311
  family system functioning and, 77–86
  gender differences, literature review (Zaslow), 169–171
  overview, 70–73
  Research Study I results (original analysis), 286
Rembar, J., 108, 109, 134, 136, 137, 138, 142, 146, 157, 158, 159, 160, 161, 337
Research Study I, 269–318
  methods, 270–277
    instruments, 272–277
    procedure, 271–272

subjects, 270–271
overview, 269–270
results (original analysis), 277–292
  predictors, 282–289
  psychosocial adjustments, 290–292
  sample description, 278–282
results (separately analyzed), 293–318
  conclusions, 317–318
  depression of custodial mother, 294–296
  family systems, 314–317
  financial factors, 307–309
  generally, 293–294
  noncustodial parent contacts, 304–307
  parental anger, 298–300
  parental insults, 300–302
  parental physical abuse, 302–304
  remarriage, 309–311
  social support, 313–314
  stress, 311–312
  substance abuse of custodial parent, 296–298
Research Study II, 319–331
  conclusions, 330–331
  methods, 319–321
    instruments, 321
    procedure, 320–321
    subjects, 319–320
  results, 322–330
    predictors, 322–324
    psychosocial adjustment measures, 324–330
Resnick, G., 6
Rettig, K. D., 85, 86
Riley, D., 202, 203
Robertson, A., 186
Robinson, B. E., 71
Roderick, J., 222
Rohrlich, J. A., 110
Rosen, R., 10, 43, 145, 167, 219, 332, 333
Rosenberg, F. R., 180, 260
Rosenberg, M., 30, 54, 99, 351
Rosenthal, D. A., 12
Ross, C. E., 185
Runyon, N., 108, 110, 111, 112, 113, 114, 115, 116
Russell, C. D., 108, 117, 118, 121, 257
Russell, C. S., 220
Rutter, M., 22, 178, 217, 218, 333

Saayman, G. S., 5, 7, 17, 243, 244, 245, 246
Sabatelli, R. M., 88
Sandler, I., 186, 187, 190, 198, 199, 240, 241, 260, 276, 338, 349
Sandler, I. N., 18
Santrock, J. W., 6, 14, 40, 41, 44, 45, 46, 47, 48, 53, 59, 92, 112, 145, 148, 169, 170, 171, 174, 254, 259, 334, 336, 337
Sarason, I., 193, 241, 275
Satir, V., 21
Savin-Williams, R. C., 180, 260
Schaefer, H. R., 217
Schinke, S. P., 109, 143, 337
Schumm, W. R., 225
Schwebel, A. I., 1, 12, 13, 14, 18
Segal, S., 98, 256
Shaver, P., 12
Shiller, V., 50, 334
Shook, N. J., 93, 98, 99, 146, 160, 161, 180, 257, 260, 336
Siesky, A. E., 1, 10, 11, 14, 145, 167, 259, 332
Simons, R. L., 19, 23, 35, 36, 37, 65, 66, 67, 68, 69, 102, 103, 104, 106, 255, 257, 333, 334, 336, 355
Sinclair, R. J., 1, 12, 18
Skitka, L. J., 1, 8
Skopin, A. R., 70, 88, 89
Slater, E. J., 14
Sleeper effects, divorce, disaster theory, 4
Smith, R. S., 188, 260
Smith, T. A., 72, 83, 84
Smith, T. W., 73
Snarey, J., 1, 14, 15
Social support, 200–218
  clinician recommendations
    assessment, 349–350
    interventions, 356–357
  conclusions about, 338–339
  decrements, 201–206
    among children, 201–203
    among parents, 203–206

overview, 200–201
predictive model, 262
psychological adjustment, 206–218
  among children, 206–213
  among parents, 213–218
  Research Study I results (separately analyzed), 313–314
Solomon, C. R., 72
Sorbom, D., 128
Spanier, G. B., 70, 200, 203, 204, 350
Spence, J. T., 41
Spencer, P., 54
Spielberger, C. D., 54, 58, 183, 191, 211, 213
Steinman, S., 50, 334
Stevenson, M. R., 14
Stolberg, A. L., 56, 188, 189, 199, 202, 240, 241, 242, 243, 260, 348, 350
Strahan, R., 277
Stress, 178–199
  clinician recommendations
    assessment, 348–349
    interventions, 355–356
  economic distress model, 179–185
  multiple life stresses model, 185–199
  overview, 178–179
  parental conflict, negative outcome prediction, 35
  predictive model, 260–262
  Research Study I results (original analysis), 285–286
  Research Study I results (separately analyzed), 311–312
  social support and, 200–218. See also Social support
Studer, J., 47, 48, 49, 72, 75, 76, 334
Substance abuse, of custodial parent, Research Study I results (separately analyzed), 296–298
Swartzman-Schatman, B., 109, 143, 337
Swindle, R. W., 211
Szott, M. A., 40, 41, 53, 62, 63, 64, 255

Tavormina, J. B., 122
Tayler, L., 1, 12
Taylor, C. M., 42, 62, 333
Tepp, A., 35

Thibaut, J. W., 94
Thomas, A. M., 36, 98, 102, 257, 336
Thomas, S. P., 19
Thomas, V. K., 224
Thompson, L., 204, 350
Tiesel, J., 275
Tietjen, A. M., 202, 350
Toomin, M., 110
Tuckman, J., 172

Ulenhuth, E. H., 186
Ullman, A., 240, 348

Veevers, J. E., 1, 2
Velicer, W. R., 66
Villwock, D., 99
Visher, E., 71, 335
Visher, J., 71, 335
Visitation, by noncustodial parent, impacts of, 98–102
Voeller, M. N., 220, 228, 229, 230, 231, 232, 263

Walker, L. S., 222, 275
Wallerstein, J. S., 1, 2, 3, 4, 17, 18, 52, 89, 92, 93, 109, 110, 112, 113, 115, 116, 117, 119, 141, 154, 169, 181, 188, 192, 201, 219, 248, 256, 261, 334, 336, 343, 345, 357
Wallisch, L., 85
Warshak, R. A., 6, 14, 40, 41, 43, 44, 45, 46, 47, 48, 53, 59, 92, 93, 145, 148, 169, 170, 174, 254, 333, 334, 336, 337
Waxler, N., 229
Webb, J. T., 186
Weingarten, H., 117, 119, 145, 146, 174
Weinraub, M., 218
Weiss, R. S., 1, 2, 37, 219, 220
Weissman, M. M., 54, 60
Werner, E. E., 188, 260
West, S. G., 197
Whitehead, L., 176
Widaman, K. F., 14
Wolchik, S. A., 197, 198, 199, 201, 241
Wolf, B. M., 218
Wolin, S., 1, 13, 17
Wolin, S. J., 1, 13, 17

Woody, J. D., 188, 191, 192, 212, 213
Wu, C., 36
Wyman, P. A., 202, 350

Yahraes, H., 89

Zaslow, M. J., 146, 164, 166–177
Zill, N., 108, 121, 132, 133, 134, 164, 165, 166, 257, 287
Zuckerman, M., 191, 212

ABOUT THE AUTHORS

James A. Twaite, Ph.D., Ed.D., is a consulting and clinical psychologist specializing in the design and analysis of psychological research on clinically relevant topics. A Phi Beta Kappa graduate of Tufts University, he holds a doctorate in econometrics from the Fletcher School of Law and Diplomacy (Tufts/Harvard) and a doctorate in psychology from Teachers College, Columbia University. His academic honors include a Woodrow Wilson Dissertation Fellowship and election to the Columbia University chapter of Sigma Xi, the scientific research society. Dr. Twaite, widely published, is the author of recent articles in the *Journal of Psychiatry and Law*, *Social Work*, and the *American Journal of Orthopsychiatry*, as well as the books *Introductory Statistics* and *The Black Elderly: Satisfaction and Quality of Later Life*.

Daniel Silitsky, Ph.D., holds degrees from Queens College and Long Island University, as well as a doctorate in marriage and family therapy from Seton Hall University. He was an instructor at Seton Hall in the Professional Psychology and Family Therapy department. Former Director of Family Counseling for the New York City Board of Education, he is presently Director of Pupil Personnel Services at a New York City high school. He also serves as trainer in crisis intervention and parent involvement with at-risk teens for the New York City Board of Education. Dr. Silitsky maintains a private practice in East Brunswick, New Jersey.

Anya K. Luchow, Ph.D., is a psychologist and mediator in private practice. She specializes in relationships, families, and children with special needs. She received her B.A. from Barnard College and her doctorate in psychology from Teachers College, Columbia University. She was an instructor and later served as Freshman Dean at Barnard. Dr. Luchow teaches parenting classes and facilitates parenting groups. She also lectures extensively on parenting children with physical disabilities, pervasive developmental disorder, ADD/ADHD, children of divorce, and adopted children. The author of several articles in the *Journal of Psychiatry and Law*, she currently co-writes, with her daughter, a monthly column on parenting special-needs children for *In Motion* magazine.